Environmental Constitutionalism in the Anthropocene

This book examines the relationship between man and nature through different cultural approaches to encourage new environmental legislation as a means of fostering acceptance at a local level.

In 2019, the International Union of Geological Sciences (IUGS) recognised that we have entered a new era, the Anthropocene, specifically characterised by the impact of one species, mankind, on environmental change. The Anthropocene is penetrating the discourse of both hard sciences and humanities and social sciences, by posing new epistemological as well as practical challenges to many disciplines. Legal sciences have so far been at the margins of this intellectual renewal, with few contributions on the central role that the notion of Anthropocene could play in forging a more effective and just environmental law. By applying a multidisciplinary approach and adopting a Law as Culture paradigm to the study of law, this book explores new paths of investigation and possible solutions to be applied. New perspectives for the constitutional framing of environmental policies, rights, and alternative methods for bottom-up participatory law-making and conflict resolution are investigated, showing that environmental justice is not just an option, but an objective within reach.

The book will be essential reading for students, academics, and policymakers in the areas of law, environmental studies, and anthropology.

Domenico Amirante is Full Professor of Italian and Comparative Public Law, Director of the Ph.D. Program in Comparative Law and Processes of Integration; Director of the Triennial Course in Political Science, Faculty of Political Science, University of Campania Luigi Vanvitelli. He was Director of the Ph.D. Program on Italian and Comparative Public and Environmental Law, University of Naples II from 2001 to 2010. He has been appointed as expert member within the project for the Global Pact for the Environment. He has also been appointed by the Italian Ministry of the Environment as expert member of the Commission for Environmental Amendments to the Italian Constitution.

Silvia Bagni is Associate Professor of Comparative Public Law, Faculty of Political and Social Sciences, University of Bologna. She has a Ph.D. in Constitutional Law from the University of Bologna and MA in Bioethics from the UPRA, Rome. She is an expert for the Harmony with Nature Program, Panel 1, Earth-centered Law, United Nations and a member of the Alma Mater Research Institute on Global Challenges and Climate Change.

Juris Diversitas
Series Editor:
Ignazio Castellucci; *University of Teramo, Italy*

Rooted in comparative law, the *Juris Diversitas* series focuses on the interdisciplinary study of legal and normative mixtures and movements. Our interest is in comparison broadly conceived, extending beyond law narrowly understood to related fields. Titles might be geographical or temporal comparisons. They could focus on theory and methodology, substantive law, or legal cultures. They could investigate official or unofficial 'legalities', past and present and around the world. And, to effectively cross spatial, temporal, and normative boundaries, inter- and multi-disciplinary research is particularly welcome.

Other titles in this series:

Stateless Law
Evolving Boundaries of a Discipline
Edited by Helge Dedek and Shauna Van Praagh

The Diffusion of Law
The Movement of Laws and Norms Around the World
Edited by Sue Farran, James Gallen, Jennifer Hendry and Christa Rautenbach

Indigenous Rights in Scandinavia
Autonomous Sami Law
Edited by Christina Allard and Susann Funderud Skogvang

Law Between Buildings
Emergent Global Perspectives in Urban Law
Edited by Nisha Mistry and Nestor M. Davidson

Law in the Time of Oxymora
A Synesthesia of Language, Logic and Law
Rostam J. Neuwirth

Normative Pluralism and Human Rights
Social Normativities in Conflict
Edited by Kyriaki Topidi

Global Perspectives in Urban Law
The Legal Power of Cities
Edited by Nestor M. Davidson and Geeta Tewari

Law and the New Urban Agenda
Edited by Nestor M. Davidson and Geeta Tewari

Law and Food
Regulatory Recipes of Culinary Issues
Edited by Salvatore Mancuso

Law and the Language of Food
Metaphors of Recipes and Rules
Edited by Salvatore Mancuso

Environmental Constitutionalism in the Anthropocene
Values, Principles and Actions
Edited by Domenico Amirante and Silvia Bagni

For more information about this series, please visit: www.routledge.com/Juris-Diversitas/book-series/JURISDIV

Environmental Constitutionalism in the Anthropocene

Values, Principles and Actions

Edited by Domenico Amirante and Silvia Bagni

Routledge
Taylor & Francis Group
LONDON AND NEW YORK

First published 2022
by Routledge
4 Park Square, Milton Park, Abingdon, Oxon OX14 4RN

and by Routledge
605 Third Avenue, New York, NY 10158

Routledge is an imprint of the Taylor & Francis Group, an informa business

British Library Cataloguing-in-Publication Data
A catalogue record for this book is available from the British Library

Library of Congress Cataloging-in-Publication Data
Names: Amirante, Domenico, editor. | Bagni, Silvia, editor.
Title: Environmental constitutionalism in the anthropocene : values, principles and actions / edited by Domenico Amirante & Silvia Bagni.
Description: Abingdon, Oxon ; New York, NY : Routledge, 2022. | Series: Juris diversitas | Includes bibliographical references and index.
Identifiers: LCCN 2021050931 | ISBN 9781032007175 (hardback) | ISBN 9781032007236 (paperback) | ISBN 9781003175308 (ebook)
Subjects: LCSH: Environmental law, International. | Constitutional law—Environmental aspects. | Geology, Stratigraphic—Anthropocene.
Classification: LCC K3585 .E5766 2022 | DDC 344.04/6—dc23/eng/20220131
LC record available at https://lccn.loc.gov/2021050931

ISBN: 978-1-032-00717-5 (hbk)
ISBN: 978-1-032-00723-6 (pbk)
ISBN: 978-1-003-17530-8 (ebk)

DOI: 10.4324/9781003175308

Typeset in Galliard
by Apex CoVantage, LLC

Contents

Contributors

Domenico Amirante (ORCID: 0000-0002-4553-8133) is Full Professor of Italian and Comparative Public Law, Director of the Ph.D. Program in Comparative Law and Processes of Integration; Director of the Triennial Course in Political Science, Faculty of Political Science, University of Campania Luigi Vanvitelli. He was Director of the Ph.D. Program on Italian and Comparative Public and Environmental Law, University of Naples II from 2001 to 2010. He has been appointed as expert member within the project for the Global Pact for the Environment. He has also been appointed by the Italian Ministry of the Environment as expert member of the Commission for Environmental Amendments to the Italian Constitution.

Ramiro Ávila Santamaría holds a Ph.D. in Legal Sociology from the University of the Basque Country (UPV), a MA in Legal Sociology from the International Institute of Legal Sociology of Oñati-UPV, and a MA in Law from Columbia University in New York City; he is a lawyer and has a degree in Legal Sciences from the Pontifical Catholic University of Ecuador (PUCE). He currently is judge of the Constitutional Court of Ecuador and also works as a plant teacher of the Law Area of the Universidad Andina Simón Bolívar-Sede Ecuador. As author and editor, he has published, among others: *El neoconstitucionalismo andino* (Quito 2016), *La (in) justicia penal en la democracia constitucional de derechos* (Quito, 2013), *Neoconstitucionalismo transformador* (Quito 2011) and *Derechos y garantías: Critical essays* (Quito, 2010).

Silvia Bagni (ORCID: 0000-0003-3560-0914) is Associate Professor of Comparative Public Law, Faculty of Political and Social Sciences, University of Bologna. She has a Ph.D. in Constitutional Law from the University of Bologna and a MA in Bioethics, from the UPRA, Rome. She is an expert for the Harmony with Nature Program, Panel 1, Earth-centered Law, United Nations and a member of the Alma Mater Research Institute on Global Challenges and Climate Change.

Philippe Billet (ORCID: 0000-0001-9346-5832) is Ph.D. in Environmental Law, Professor of Public Law at the University Jean Moulin – Lyon 3, and Director of the Institute of Environmental Law (CNRS, UMR 5600,

EVS-IDE – University of Lyon). He is Honorary President of the French Society for Environmental Law, and he has been studying for more than 30 years the environmental issues from a legal perspective. He is also expert for the Committee for the Green Economy, a member of the National Council for the Protection of Nature and of the Polar Environment Committee. Among his latest publications: *Les grands arrêts du droit de l'environnement* [Landmark Judicial Decisions on Environmental Law] (Paris: Dalloz, 2017; with E. Naim-Gesbert, eds).

Enrico Buono (ORCID: 0000-0001-5101-6529) holds Master's degrees in both Law and Political Science from the University of Naples Federico II, is a Ph.D. candidate in *Diritto Comparato e Processi di Integrazione* at the Department of Political Science, Jean Monnet, University of Campania Luigi Vanvitelli, and has been *Investigador Visitante* at the Facultad de Derecho y Ciencias Políticas in Universidad Católica Boliviana San Pablo.

Maria Sarah Bussi is a lawyer and Ph.D. candidate in *Diritto Comparato e Processi di Integrazione* at the University of Campania Luigi Vanvitelli, Italy. Her current research topic focuses on judicial activism in Indian and Brazilian legal systems. Comparative public law, environmental law, and media law are her main areas of interest and study.

Luigi Colella (ORCID: 0000-0002-6206-7062) is a lawyer, Post-doctoral Researcher in Comparative Public Law, and Lecturer at the Department of Political Science at the University of Campania Luigi Vanvitelli. His research fields include European and comparative environmental policies and legal framework. Among his latest publications: *Il diritto dell'energia nucleare in Italia e in Francia Profili comparati della governance dei rifiuti radioattivi tra ambiente, democrazia e partecipazione* (Rome: Aracne, 2017).

Zainab Lokhandwala (ORCID: 0000-0002-2506-3425) is currently pursuing her Ph.D. from SOAS University of London. Her Ph.D. thesis is titled "Indian Farmers and Rights over Bio-Genetic Resources: Towards Greater Food Sovereignty." She is also a teaching fellow at the Centre for International Studies and Diplomacy, SOAS. Zainab completed her LLM in Environmental Law at SOAS in 2018. She is an advocate registered at the Calcutta High Court (India) and has worked as a researcher at the National University of Juridical Science (NUJS) and National Law University Delhi. Zainab graduated from ILS Law College (India) in 2014.

Elizabeth Macpherson (ORCID: 0000-0003-1021-9930) is an Associate Professor in Environmental and Natural Resources Law at the University of Canterbury. Her research interests are in comparative environmental and natural resources law, human rights, and Indigenous rights in Australasia and Latin America. She has published widely on these topics, including the book *Indigenous Water Rights in Law and Regulation: Lessons from Comparative Experience* (2019, Cambridge University Press). She currently co-leads two major externally funded research projects: the Sustainable Seas National Science Challenge project funded by the New Zealand Government on *Law and Policy for Ecosystem-Based Marine Management*; and the Norwegian Research Council–funded project *Riverine Rights: Exploring the Currents and Consequences of Legal Rights for Rivers.*

Werner Menski (ORCID: 0000-0002-2058-2074), MA, Ph.D., is Professor Emeritus of South Asian Laws in the School of Law at SOAS, University of London. He is specialised in both Hindu and Muslim Law and has also published widely on comparative research on legal systems in Asia and Africa. He obtained an interdisciplinary MA from the University of Kiel in Germany in 1977 and then taught South Asian Studies at Bochum University in 1977–1980 before moving to London, where he obtained his Ph.D. in Hindu Law in 1984. At SOAS, since 1981 and until 2014, he has taught courses on South Asian laws, comparative legal theory, ethnic minorities and the law, and family law, and has been Professor of South Asian Laws since 2004. He has published almost 300 articles since 1980, and his major books are *Muslim Family Law* (1998, with David Pearl); *Modern Indian Family Law* (2001); *Hindu Law: Beyond Tradition and Modernity* (2003); *Comparative Law in a Global Context: The Legal Systems of Asia and Africa* (2006). He has been the editor of *South Asia Research* (SAGE) since 2004 and is a member of numerous editorial advisory boards. He has been Visiting Professor at several South Asian universities and also maintains close links with universities in Japan and continental Europe.

Rajnish Saryal (ORCID: 0000-0002-4826-0456) is Assistant Professor of Political Science at Panjab University Regional Centre, Ludhiana, India and also teaches at Institute of Social Science Research and Education, Panjab University, Chandigarh, India. He holds an MA in Political Science and M.Phil., Ph.D. in Environmental Issues and Indian Foreign Policy from the Faculty of Arts, Panjab University, Chandigarh, India. His area of research interests are climate change and religion, climate change politics and IR theories, and sustainable development. His recent publication on climate change is Saryal, Rajnish (2018), "Climate Change Policy of India Modifying the Environment," South Asia Research, 38(1), pp. 1–19.

Luis Armando Tolosa Villabona is a lawyer and philosopher, and a specialist in different legal areas. He is a Magister and Doctor in Law with a laureate thesis *summa cum laude*, and a university professor. He is currently a Colombian Court Supreme Justice, serving in the Civil Chamber. He has been a speaker in different national and international scenarios. He has published, among others: "Current problems of cassation and challenges in the social rule of law," "Cassation, guardianship, de facto channels and fundamental rights," "Theory and Technique of Cassation," and "Charta, our land." He is reporting judge of more than 8,000 decisions in Colombia, among them the *habeas corpus* that granted the right to freedom to the spectacled bear, *Chucho*, as a subject of rights, and the judgment that ordered the protection of the Amazon, as a subject of rights, commanding concrete actions to combat climate change.

Kyriaki Topidi (ORCID: 0000-0003-2330-662X) is Head of the cluster "Culture & Diversity" at the European Centre for Minority Issues (ECMI), Flensburg, Germany. She holds a Degree in Law from the Robert Schuman Faculty of Law in Strasbourg, an MA in International Studies from the University of Birmingham, and a Ph.D. in European Studies from Queen's University Belfast. She was a Senior Lecturer at the Faculty of Law of the University of Luzern in Switzerland. She has also worked as Managing Director of the Centre for Comparative Constitutional Law and Religion at the same institution.

Pasquale Viola (ORCID: 0000-0002-9725-284X) holds a Ph.D. in Comparative Law and Processes of Integration. His research fields regard climate change policies and legislation, environmental law, comparative constitutional law, and legal theory. He currently collaborates on research projects at the Charles University and at the University of Bologna. He has been Visiting Researcher in Asian and European Academic Institutions, and has been invited as lecturer and speaker at several international fora.

Acknowledgments

A collective book is often the result of diverse sensibilities, different styles, sometimes divergent approaches and ideas. On the contrary, in the case of our book, the trajectory illustrates a progressive convergence of plural experiences and points of view around a common theme: the interconnections between man and environment (*rectius*, between man and nature). As Professor Menski will recall at the end of our volume, we started from a typical academic discussion on legal pluralism and socio-legal comparative law, to develop an intense exchange focused more specifically on practice-related and action-oriented concerns to frame and reinforce environmental protection. This evolution took several years and progressed through many common activities over the last decade, such as symposia, seminars, doctoral courses, and, especially, intensive doctoral training in summer and winter schools.

For this reason, framing an acknowledgment of gratitude for all the people that have supported the publication of this book is even harder than coordinating the editing processes and contributing to the contents. As first, it goes without saying that the inspiring intellectual environment of Juris Diversitas – through the brilliant guide of its President Olivier Moreteau and both Vice Presidents Salvatore Mancuso and Ignazio Castellucci – has been the underneath force that influenced our work from the "idea" to the last proofread. In this "rite of passage from the idea to the paper," the help of Ignazio Castellucci as Series Editor and the aid of the Routledge staff have been crucial in every single step. Referees have been patient and extremely precise in providing suggestions and remarks, while many other colleagues have been really generous in sharing their knowledge with us in different venues. Amongst the conferences and other events that gave us the opportunity to collect fruitful feedbacks, we would mention the Summer School on "Legal Pluralism & Human Rights" and the events coordinated by Kyriaki Topidi in Luzern and Lausanne, and the Summer Schools Series "Comparative Law in the Global Age: Theoretical and Practical Challenges" of the Doctoral Programme on Comparative Law and Processes of Integration of the University of Campania *Luigi Vanvitelli*, co-organised with Ranbir Singh, Mahendra Pal Singh, and Paramjit Jaswal, which strengthened the cooperation with our Indian partners from the National Law University Delhi and the Rajiv Gandhi National

University of Law (Patiala). For this intellectual journey, we all are grateful to Werner Menski, the driving force and the bright soul of our events.

This book was conceived as an interdisciplinary path, merging diverse cultural influences and academic backgrounds, with the aim of going beyond a formalistic approach to environmental law, and suggesting a more holistic understanding of the Anthropocene. There is a whole body of immaterial subjects and forces that this book has endeavoured to reveal. Thus, we would like to express our deep gratitude to the Earth-system, to Nature, and to all those entities that influence our life – and our understanding of it – over the millennia.

Introduction

Domenico Amirante and Silvia Bagni

Anthropocene and the Law: Exploring New Paths

Climate change and the rapid exhaustion of the Earth's biocapacity are today unavoidable and urgent issues on the global agenda. Since the beginning of the new millennium, we have been "welcomed to the Anthropocene" by the Nobel Laureate Paul Crutzen, followed by many other scientists from various disciplines. In 2019, the International Union of Geological Sciences (IUGS) recognised the Anthropocene, specifically as a new era characterised by the impact of one species, mankind, on environmental change. The concept of Anthropocene thus emphasises the shift in the relations between man and the environment. While in past ages human beings have lived sustainably, in harmony with Nature, respecting the limits of planetary boundaries and ecological rules, today social, economic, and political institutions are struggling to effectively reduce or stop an exploitation trajectory of natural resources that is going well beyond the regeneration capacity of local and global ecosystems.

The Anthropocene thesis is entering the discourse of both hard sciences and humanities/social sciences addressing new epistemological as well as practical challenges to history, literature, art history, anthropology, geography, to quote only a few. Legal sciences have so far been at the margins of this intellectual renewal, with limited contributions on the role that the notion of Anthropocene could play in forging a more effective and just environmental law. In fact, the sophisticated environmental set of rules consolidated at the international and national level since the 1970s has not been able to keep the balance between economic development and growth priorities, on the one hand, and the need to preserve the environment, on the other. In order to remedy such failures, the legal framework in which international organisations, states, corporations, and individuals operate should be redesigned so as to offer new political and legal tools. By applying a multidisciplinary approach and adopting a "Law as Culture" paradigm, this book explores new paths of investigation and possible solutions to be applied, under the garb of Anthropocene. New perspectives for the constitutional framing of environmental policies, rights, and alternative methods for bottom-up participatory law-making and conflict resolution will be investigated,

DOI: 10.4324/9781003175308-1

showing that environmental justice is not just a theoretical or academic option, but an important objective within reach.

International organisations like the UN and most national governments are fully aware of these assumptions and are trying to tackle the survival issues that have been generated so far. The European Union, with its newly elected EU Commission (2019), has launched one of the most ambitious environmental programmes ever presented: a Green Deal, aiming at the full decarbonisation of Europe by 2050 as its main result. On the other hand, the UN started a process of reframing the Sustainable Development Goals, to align them with the higher environmental objectives pointed out by the main scientific reports on the state of the planet. Scientific dissemination has multiplied books, reviews, and other editorial products dedicated to climate change and the environment. The present book is a collective effort aimed at filling a gap in the literature, related to the lack of consideration of the specific impact of the Anthropocene on law both in terms of legal reasoning and of the new perspectives for international and especially constitutional law. Together, many of the authors of the book have participated in extended discussions in a series of international seminars and doctoral training seminars since the beginning of the 2010s (in different locations of Europe and India). As underlined by Professor Werner Menski (who gifted us a fascinating afterword to the book), we realised over the years how this particular international academic co-operation has turned from an 'academic' pursuit of legal pluralism and socio-legal comparative law towards a comparative constitutional law approach, focused more specifically on practice-related, action-oriented concerns to strengthen environmental protection.

Our methodological premise was not to focus mainly on the analysis of the causes of the environmental crisis, which are before the eyes of all and are fully acknowledged even by the "politically correct" international organisations of the United Nations. We adhere to and support the extensive proofs that scientists have been producing since a long time on the matter, but we also think that conscious people, from politicians to young activists, to university students, should be interested in the constructive part of the story: re-shaping the role of law (and somehow the "rule of law") in environmental matters and finding coherent frameworks and concrete solutions. As lawyers, we must recognise that a panoply of environmental policies and legislations was produced over the past decades. Nevertheless, the strategies for reduction of and adaptation to climate change in the Anthropocene require a radical renewal of the instruments for political action and of the related legal instruments, not only on an international scale, but most significantly at the state and local community levels. In this context, constitutional law is called upon to play a pivotal role, incorporating innovations from the international context and articulating an effective and clear framework for political and administrative authorities (national and local) as well as for civil society. A meaningful reflection on the new relationship between constitutional law and the environment is necessary to bridge the existing gap between international environmental principles and the everyday (often random) legislative and administrative practices in many states and local institutions.

From a general perspective, the main issue is not the quantity or even the quality of legislation, but the cultural framework and paradigms lying behind it. This represents the innovative element of this book that we want to offer to our readers. To make policies and legislations more effective, it is necessary to face a change in the way we learn, interpret, and apply environmental law, and possibly law in general. In this perspective, we should be inspired by approaches like the "ecology of law" paradigm proposed by Capra and Mattei (2015), based on a paradigm shift from a mechanistic to a holistic and ecological worldview ("from seeing the world as a machine to understanding it as a network"), or like the planetary boundaries framework, theorised by Steffen and others (2015). For lawyers, this implies renunciation to consider law as a sort of "secret mystery," understandable only by a specialised clergy, and to have a more co-operative mindset towards other sciences. So, this book is innovative among the scientific legal literature on environmental law because it adopts a multidisciplinary approach and applies a *Law as Culture* epistemology to the study of these issues.

In the wave of the cultural studies that flourished between the 1950s and 1960s, Law as Culture is a legal approach based on pioneering anthropological, social, and philosophical studies, such as those of C. Geertz, P. Kahn, and P. Bourdieu (which we may consider as classics nowadays). The intersection of those disciplines with the field of law has been particularly debated among legal comparatists, eventually agreeing that law cannot be studied and understood isolated from the cultural context in which it is produced, observed, and applied. Extra-legal factors are intrinsically related to the nature of norms and the legal professions, so legal anthropology and sociology become crucial epistemological instruments for the lawyer. For this reason, the first part of the book is dedicated to the analysis of the relationship between man and Nature from different cultural cosmovisions, both religious and not (Christianity, Islam, Hinduism, Buddhism, Ubuntu, *Sumak kawsay–Buen vivir*). This part of the book will give to the reader some epistemological clues to understand the context in which environmental law in the Anthropocene will have to operate, and to envision the most appropriate means of adapting each legal system to local cultures, in order to avoid rejection crisis. It will also offer precious tools for comparison: being able to have a synchronic picture of the relationship between man and Nature in the various chthonic traditions (Glenn, 2014), which makes evident the many analogies underlying the modern style of life that globalisation has imposed, may suggest useful hints for rediscovering our ecological traditions or for revealing new models to experience.

Another methodological choice for our book was "investing in comparative law," an approach rarely used in environmental law (for some exceptions see Robinson, 1997, and Viñuales, 2019). Of course, in legal environmental studies, framed since the beginning by an international law methodology (with its unifying monistic approach) there are studies on national experiences, traceable in specialised reviews or collective books, but they are often in the form of descriptive "country reports," whether by national or foreign authors, thus lacking comparative law vision and methodology. We think that comparative law gives an "added value" to environmental legal studies through the use of its typical heuristic instruments, such as taxonomies, wide-ranging historical analyses, the study of the legal formants and of the legal traditions, and, more recently, mature reflections on the mixed and hybrid character of many legal instruments (Menski, 2009).

The editors and many of the authors of this book felt the urge for a discussion and a systematisation of the recent developments in environmental constitutionalism (see Boyd, 2012, May and Daly, 2014, Kotzé, 2015, and Manzano, 2020), by integrating them in the "great constitutional debates," namely in the wider framework of the relations between the state, the constitution, the social communities (including minorities/indigenous people), and the diverse conception of the person/individual. In this specific area, comparative law offers the essential methodological toolbox both to assess the innovations and the challenges related to the development of environmental constitutionalism, and to open up a dialogue among the "constitutional cultures" that support its recent affirmation, as the first part of the book demonstrates. Then, in the second and third part of the book we apply this interdisciplinary approach to explore the normative implications of the interaction between ecology and the law. Authors concentrate on the constitutional and international legal framework, focusing on the description of the main features of a "glocal ecological system of law," whose values and principles are directed to preserving or re-building harmony between all the components of the Earth ecosystem. Other chapters explore the debate on the recognition of nature and "natural beings" and the perspective of the "non-human persons" (animals, rivers, forests, and marine ecosystems) as legal subjects, both in general theory of law and in relation to specific cases in various legal cultures. We examine multiple examples and cases from legal systems that have already experienced alternative ways of implementing environmental values (i.e. the recognition of Nature rights and of legal personality of natural elements in Australia, New Zealand, Colombia, and India) and, more recently, climate justice (see the recent judicial decisions on climate justice such as Urgenda, Juliana, the CAN Europe case, the Irish case).

Values

The first part of the book is dedicated to environmental values through an interdisciplinary collection of contributions. It starts with a chapter on "Integral Ecology and Environmental Law in the Anthropocene: The Perspective of the Catholic Church," where Luigi Colella delves into the relationship between religion and the environment, starting from Catholicism. The author gives counterarguments against the widespread historical reading that the Christian vision of man as *dominus* over Nature is the cultural origin of the current ecological crisis. The main focus of the chapter is on the encyclical *Laudato Sì*, where Pope Francis has drawn the path for an integral ecological conversion of all humanity. Besides, the author underlines also how the social doctrine of the Catholic Church has always pointed out the necessity of connecting rights to duties of solidarity and environmental sustainability.

Rajnish Saryal, in his contribution on "Ecological Crisis: The Self, the State and the Hindu Ethics," proposes Hindu religion as a possible source for ethical and moral values, able to address environmental issues in India and worldwide. Saryal underlines the need for a new ethics to tackle environmental issues but advises that for many critics this means revitalising religions and so it is perceived as anachronistic. On the contrary, following the recent literature, the author shares the idea that Asian religions offer alternatives to the individualistic ethics that has backed today's environmental crisis. He concentrates on the concept of Dharma that "establishes the interconnectedness and interdependence between man and nature through the system of rights and obligations." The idea of interconnectedness of all beings is at the core of Hinduism, in all stages of its historical development, as it emerges from the analysis of many religious texts. The same perspective can be appreciated also in Andean *sumak kawsay* or in African *Ubuntu*, as will emerge in the following chapters of this book.

Kyriaki Topidi, in her chapter on "Ubuntu as a Normative Value in the New Environmental World Order," explores African cosmology and its relationship with environmental issues. The author enlists the so-called "five values of *ubuntu*" (survival, compassion, spirit of solidarity, respect, and dignity), which have been somehow incorporated in the South African constitutional framework. She also takes into consideration the critique about the notion of *ubuntu*, mainly regarding its vagueness and its supposed incompatibility with human rights, due to its communitarian rationale. As in other chapters dealing with indigenous cultures, Topidi underlines that the revival of these philosophies or cosmovision supports the case of a new legal paradigm in environmental law, based on interconnectedness among humans and Nature, but it is also to be considered a reaction to neo-colonialism in a broader sense, involving also minority and peoples' rights. *Ubuntu*'s primary source of normativity is the relationship with and between people, and not the individual. In environmental governance, this relational dimension would foster a different hierarchy of values and interests that government and society should protect, for the survival of the whole human society.

Ramiro Ávila Santamaría, in his chapter "Rights of Nature vs. Human Rights? An Urgent Shift of Paradigms," analyses the innovative potential of the Andean neo-constitutionalism, symbolised by the 2008 Ecuadorian Constituent Process. He considers the "ecological pact" contained in this constitution as a new utopia that can help tackling the current environmental crisis. According to Ávila, the actual situation is the result of centuries of western cultural domination, started with the violent conquest of America, and characterised by three basic pillars: rationalism, colonialism, and capitalism. *Sumak kawsay*, the Quechua indigenous worldview, represents a different way to conceive the plenitude of living, based on decoloniality and a non-capitalist system, and could be used as a model for the construction of a different legal relationship between humans and Nature.

In the following chapter, on "Environmental Ethics in Islam," Zainab Lokhandwala guides us into the insights of Islamic environmental values. In fact, Islamic sources of law reveal a richness of ecological and eco-juridical principles. Due to the complexity of Islamic law, and of its manifold cultural and geographical declinations, the author prefers to use the expression "Islamic environmental ethics" to refer of the sets of values that address the protection of Nature. Five main principles are identified (*tawheed*, *ubudiyat*, *amanat*, conservation, *meezan*), from which it appears that even if humans have a privileged position with respect to Nature, they are also bound to respect and protect her, as a creation of the Almighty. Lokhandwala then tries to explain how these principles can be applied in Muslim countries to reframe environmental laws and policies, with some relevant examples such as the 2015 Islamic Declaration on Climate Change.

Enrico Buono, in his chapter on "The Noble Eightfold Path in the Anthropocene: Buddhist Perspectives on Environmental Constitutionalism," completes the analysis on the contribution of religious and philosophical values to solve environmental problems, addressing Buddhism. After attempting to define what Buddhist law is, and which are its main sources, the author focuses on its environmental interpretation, through the principles of interdependency and karma. These two principles, especially the second one, related to personal responsibility, are the core elements of each religious and philosophical tradition analysed in this first section and of the ecosystemic approach that scientists indicate at the basis of Ecology. The chapter ends with an assessment on the constitutional systems of some of the countries falling into what Buono proposes as a new category of "Buddhist Environmental Constitutionalism."

Principles and Rules

The second part of our book focuses on principles and rules. Authors walk through "multi-level environmental law and governance," as Domenico Amirante points out in his chapter, preferring this expression to more catchy terms such as transnational, environmental law or global environmental constitutionalism, because the expression is able to better describe the interdependent relationship between each layer of the legal system.

With Pasquale Viola and Domenico Amirante, we delve into the constitutional dimension of environmental protection. In his chapter, "From the Principles of International Environmental Law to Environmental Constitutionalism: Competitive or Cooperative Influences?", Viola analyses historically the significant changes through which both international and constitutional laws have gone in their attitude towards the environment. First, he offers a detailed account on the international legal framework that since the 1970s has created a detailed set of principles and rules related to the environmental domain. Then, the author turns his attention to the new waves of constitutionalism (transformative, global, and *nuevo constitucionalismo latinoamericano*), searching for the role the protection of the environment plays in each of these categories. Recalling the taxonomy proposed by Amirante in this book, he explains with the metaphor of "the good, the bad, and the ugly" the different attitudes of scholars towards environmental constitutionalism.

Domenico Amirante, in the chapter "Environmental Constitutionalism through the Lens of Comparative Law: New Perspectives for the Anthropocene," blames the insufficient attention reserved by legal scholars, both constitutionalists and comparatists, to this central social and legal phenomenon. He proposes a new theoretical framework to define environmental constitutionalism, a taxonomy of constitutions based on the attention they reserve (or do not reserve) to the protection of the environment ("Environmental Constitutions"; "Revised Environmental Constitutions"; and "Silent Environmental Constitutions"). The synchronic and textual comparison is accompanied by a historical one, pinpointing three phases of development of environmental constitutional law. Finally, the common core of the "adult phase" of environmental constitutionalism is identified in the relationship between each specific environmental constitutional system and the cultural, philosophical, and religious context in which it is grown, inviting scholars to an interdisciplinary approach to the matter that inevitably must involve legal pluralism.

Elizabeth Macpherson, in her chapter on "Ecosystem Rights and the Anthropocene in Australia and Aotearoa New Zealand," analyses ecosystem rights in the region, asking herself if it is possible to speak of an original Australasian model of transnational environmental constitutionalism. She underlines that although the various judicial cases raised in this region have been considered flagships of the Nature's rights movement, they have to be seen as typical indigenous rights cases, where indigenous people have been recognised as having some forms of ownership and control over traditional land and resources, after centuries of exploitation and discriminations. Macpherson concludes her chapter by stating that the most significant contribution offered by the quoted cases lies in their "relational" function, proposing new management's methods that involve the recognition of legal pluralism (in these cases, Māori customary law). The indirect consequence of this interactive decision-making process is the recognition of the intrinsic value of the harmonic relationship between Man and Nature, descending from the traditional indigenous cosmovision.

This part ends with the chapter "The Animal as a Concern for a Renewed Analysis of the Legal Link between Human and the Environment" by Philippe Billet, expressing a critical but constructive opinion about the legal qualification of animals. Starting from an account on the classical *summa divisio* between "subjects" and "things" in the Western legal tradition, Billet demonstrates its inadequacy to tackle the questions of the legal status of natural elements on the whole, illustrating how, in recent years, legislators have broadened the scope of legal personhood to incorporate natural elements such as rivers, mountains, glaciers. Similarly, animals have been recognised as having certain rights. The author reflects on the reasons to differentiate animals from other inanimate things (being sensitive, the animal becomes a non-human person), concluding that even if this new perspective is fascinating, it tends paradoxically to offer an anthropocentric solution to a non-anthropocentric problem.

Actions and Enforcement

The last part of the book treats the problems of the enforcement of environmental law, considering courts as main actors in the battle for the protection of the environment, as the more urgent global challenge for humanity.

Maria Sarah Bussi, in her chapter "Courting the Environment: Public Interest Actions in the Global South," focuses on public interest litigation as a remedy suitable to tackle environmental problems, offering a solution to one of the biggest hurdles in environmental justice that is standing. After describing the origin of public interest litigation in the United States, the author analyses its propagation in the rest of the world, especially in countries of the Global South, that have substantially enlarged the scope of this action and transformed it in an instrument of social justice. Drawing a comparison between the Indian Public Interest Litigation and the Brazilian *Ação popular* and *Ação civil pública*, Bussi underlines how in both countries the considerable development of a corpus of judicial principles of environmental law is rooted not only in their respective legal systems but also in their traditional and religious cultures.

Silvia Bagni, in her chapter "The Enforcement of New Environmental Rights through the Courts: Problems and Possible Solutions," advocates for an ecosystemic shift of the environmental legal paradigm. She takes into consideration some new trends in constitutional environmental law: the recognition of Nature as a subject of rights and the claim of a (human or constitutional) right to a stable climate, capable of ensuring our survival on the planet. The analysis of the relevant case-law is focused upon cases often originated by young people representing the future generations, or by indigenous people affected by the overexploitation of their historical lands. In her conclusions, she underlines the divergent cultural approach to environmental issues by countries from the Global North and from the Global South, a finding that confirms various assumptions made in the previous chapters of this book.

Luis Armando Tolosa Villabona, in his chapter "Vanguardism and Environmental Justice Developments in Colombia," describes the role that the Colombian judiciary is playing in re-shaping environmental law, following principles and values enshrined in the pre-Columbian history of the many indigenous peoples of South America. Judges are skilfully applying the 1991 "environmental" Constitution, fostering an intercultural interpretation that the author defines as "an ecocentric-anthropic conception." On a number of occasions, this jurisprudence led the apex Courts of the Nation to recognise the legal status of "holders of rights" to natural elements such as rivers or the Amazon itself. In the conclusions, the author strongly encourages everyone to do his part in the battle for the protection of our planet, legitimising judicial activism in environmental matters.

An Open-Ended Conclusion

This collective book does not propose a conclusion. Its primary ambition is to open a debate on environmental constitutionalism under the garb of the

Anthropocene involving not only the specialists of environmental law, but also constitutional and comparative lawyers, and possibly a large public. The same ambition drove us to involve authors from different parts of the world and various legal systems and cultural traditions. We intend to lay down a bridge over the troubled waters of the Anthropocene to facilitate a dialogue across legal cultures, legal traditions, and different *Weltanschauungen* concerning the relation between Man and Nature. But we feel, at the same time, the urge for action: while working globally for finding a "middle ground," a shareable framework for environmental constitutionalism, we must act locally to tackle the challenges of everyday threatening the survival of life on Earth.

This is the message of the inspiring afterword to the book, offered to the readers by Werner Menski and titled "Final Rallying Call on the Brutal Realities of the Anthropocene and the Necessity of Cosmoprudence to Minimise Human Suffering." The counter-narrative proposed alongside the entire book stimulates in the author both a sense of urgency towards the challenges that environmental degradation poses to humanity, and an opportunity to propose a new method to tackle those problems "through holistic, law-related strategies of affirmative action," which he calls "Cosmoprudence," drawing from the Indian constitutional concept of "complete justice." Recalling Upendra Baxi's seminal work (2014), Menski suggests that, in the current context of environmental emergencies, this approach could substitute Baxi's "Demosprudence" and lead to the fulfilment of "complete justice" for all the victims of unjust development.

Without pretending to indicate an ultimate solution or assuming to have found the "holy grail" for environmental protection, we can conclude this short introduction by recalling some guiding ideas of our book.

On values: The anthropocentric and mechanistic worldview that has colonised the world since the European Renaissance is now facing its self-produced ecological disaster. At the same time, the mainstream dogma is now challenged by different competing cultures striving to emerge from the oblivion to which they had been forced, as cultural diversity is now been presented as a resource to save the Earth System.

On principles: Constitutional law has been built on liberalism, but in the 20th century has also been influenced by socialism and nourished with human rights theories. Would there be a chance for constitutional law to be contaminated with indigenous cosmovision and ecosystemic laws forging new constitutional principles?

On effectiveness: The current rights-centred model of law must be submitted to a revision and rebalancing in the light of the emerging ecological values and principles: fundamental legal concepts such as substantive rights and procedures for conflict resolutions appear ineffective if considering new legal subjects or new legal values to be protected. Even the role of judges could be affected by the cultural shift imposed by the Anthropocene, where intercultural management of natural resources should be encouraged, and disputes solved searching the active cooperation by all the parties involved.

The two keywords we all have recurrently evoked throughout the whole book are *interdependence* and *responsibility*. From Australasia to South Africa, from South America to India, from France to Italy, Germany and Greece, all authors agree on the relational dimension between humans, non-humans, and the environment and suggest that this specific perspective should be further questioned in order to understand its normative implications and how it could be translated into the realm of law and policies.

Bibliography

Baxi U., 'Demosprudence Versus Jurisprudence: The Indian Judicial Experience in the Context of Comparative Constitutional Studies' (2014) 14 *Macquarie Law Journal* 3–23.

Boyd D.R., *The Environmental Rights Revolution: A Study on of Constitutions, Human Rights and Environment* (University of British Columbia Press 2012).

Capra F. and Mattei U., *The Ecology of Law: Toward a Legal System in Tune with Nature and Community* (Berrett-Koehler 2015).

Glenn H.P., *Legal Traditions of the World: Sustainable Diversity in Law* (5th edn, OUP 2014).

Jaria-Manzano J., *La Constitución del Antropoceno* (Tirant lo Blanch 2020).

Kotzé L.J., *Global Environmental Constitutionalism in the Anthropocene* (Hart Publishing 2016).

May J.R. and Daly E., *Global Environmental Constitutionalism* (CUP 2014).

Menski W., *Comparative Law in a Global Context: The Legal Systems of Asia and Africa* (CUP 2009).

Robinson N.A., 'Comparative Environmental Law: Evaluating How Legal Systems Address "Sustainable Development"' (1997) 27 *Environmental Policy and Earlier Law* 338.

Viñuales J.E., 'Comparative Environmental Law: Structuring a Field' in Emma Lees and Jorge E. Viñuales (eds), *The Oxford Handbook of Comparative Environmental Law* (OUP 2019).

Part I

Values

1 Integral Ecology and Environmental Law in the Anthropocene

The Perspective of the Catholic Church

Luigi Colella

1. Environment, Religion and the Law: The Three Pillars of the Ecological Transition

Over the last years, the relationship between the environment, law and religion acquired great significance, especially with relation to the ecological transition. Today, it is generally accepted that the issue of environmental protection cannot be considered only from a technical-scientific or economic perspective: it involves societies, law and religion, affecting constituent processes and legislative reforms and influencing communities.[1] Both natural sciences and humanities agree that the present ecological crisis mainly arises from a substantial neglect of the relationship between man and nature. We lost sight of the "wisdom of the Earth" (or Ecosophy), that wisdom that we must recognize and own if we want to "save ourselves".[2]

The relationship between religion and the environment represents a foundation for the law of many communities; it has influenced a great number of legal traditions and has also conditioned, in recent years, most secular Western systems.[3] Monotheistic religions have instilled their values in the elaboration of extremely modern juridical rules, building an articulated ecological model centered on the primacy of the rights of human beings.[4] Through their activity in the public sphere, religions have experienced the "ecological vocation" of cults, fueling an international debate on the protection of human rights, and contributing to the development of global environmental right in a cosmopolitan[5] and multicultural state.[6]

1 Susanna Mancini (ed), *Constitutions and Religion* (Elgar 2020).
2 Raimon Panikkar, *Ecosofia. La saggezza della terra* (Jaca book 2015).
3 H. Patrick Glenn, *Legal Traditions of the World: Sustainable Diversity in Law* (OUP 2014).
4 Maria Rosaria Piccinni, *La tutela dell'ambiente nel diritto delle religioni* (Aracne 2015).
5 H. Patrick Glenn, *The Cosmopolitan State* (OUP 2013).
6 Domenico Amirante, *Lo Stato multiculturale. Contributo alla teoria dello Stato dalla prospettiva dell'Unione Indiana* (BUP 2015).

DOI: 10.4324/9781003175308-3

Today the relationship between *religion* and *the environment*[7] is recognized in all religions of the world, resulting in environmental protection as a collective projection of religious freedom. In the Abrahamic religions (Jewish, Christian and Muslim) that seek the essence of faith in a written document (Torah, New Testament and Koran), the concept of "nature" is superimposed on "creation".[8] In the biblical theological tradition,[9] men are assigned a privileged place and, as "made in the image of God", they are ontologically different from all other living beings. In Eastern religions – which have always been considered more intimist – the relationship between the environment and religion has a unique peculiarity: *Buddhism* and *Hinduism*, but also other minor religions such as *Sikhism* and *Jainism*,[10] conceive the relationship between religion and environment as more "natural" because they consider man as a part of nature, and recognize a tendential similarity between human rights and the rights of nature itself.

Recently, in a comparative perspective, an outstanding contribution to the global ecological revolution came from the Catholic Church, particularly from Pope Francis' extraordinary Encyclical *Laudato Si'*.[11] In this document, the Head of the Catholic Church, also inspired by the dialogues with the 'green' Patriarch Bartholomew I (Head of the Orthodox Church), started a new process aimed at building an *integral ecological dimension* of human conduct, implying the awareness that all living beings, believers and non-believers, must contribute to the 'custody' of the *Common Home*, following the example of the first environmentalist in Western history, St. Francis of Assisi.[12] In his Encyclical on the environment, the Pope, recalling the Canticle of St. Francis, recognizes that the excess of anthropocentrism led to the breaking of the "sacred" balance between human beings and the environment. Thanks to the thrust of the Encyclical on the "common home", a process of "religious greening" has started, contributing to shift the focus on safeguarding creation, now also understood as an international responsibility by the United Nations. In this context, the *environment* must be conceived, above all, as a *natural and ecological balance*, a sort of "Common

7 Willis Jenkins and Christopher Key Chapple, 'Religion and Environment' [2011] 36 *Annual Review of Environment and Resources* 441.

8 Siguard Bergmann, 'New Developments in the Field' in Willis Jenkins, Mary Evelyn Tucker, Jhon Grim (eds), *Routledge Handbook of Religion and Ecology* (Routledge 2017) 13. See also Ernst Conradie, *Christianity and Ecological Theology: Resources for Further Research* (SUN Press 2006).

9 David E. Cooper and Joy A. Palmer (eds), *Spirit of the Environment. Religion, Value and Enviroznmental Concern* (Routledge 1998).

10 On the Jainism philosophy see Aidan Rankin, *Jainism and Environmental Philosophy. Karma and the Web of Life* (Routledge 2018).

11 Pope Francis, *Encyclical Letter Laudato Si' of the Holy Father Francis on Care for Our Common Home* (2015), http://w2.vatican.va/conte nt/francesco/en/encyclicals/documents/papa-francesco_20150 524_enciclica-laudato-si.html.

12 Jan J. Boersema, 'Why is Francis of Assisi the Patron Saint of Ecologists?'[2020] 14 *Science & Christian Belief* 51.

Home" in which all living beings must coexist in harmony and peace, each participating in the project of Creation in its own way.

At the same time, *religion*, also understood as a spiritual *balance* for the human soul, recalls, in one of its many meanings, the term *re-ligare*, which means "restoring" broken relationships. The concept of religion as a quest for balance helps in overcoming selfish individualistic positions and conceiving the community as a prerequisite for salvation. Law, understood as justice and conciliation of conflicting interests, becomes a suitable instrument to maintain social cohesion, though the ideas of coherence, harmony and continuity between God and his creatures. Thus, law must maintain the balance (*aequitas*) and guarantee justice (*virtus*). After all, *environment, religion and law* are all in balance, and represent the three pillars of the new global ecological transition, from which we must start to overcome the catastrophe and rediscover the "universal equilibrium", the beginning and end of life on Earth. In this context, the "ecological vocation" of Catholic religion, to which this work is dedicated, has contributed, and can still contribute, to the affirmation of a *holistic* vision of environmental law,[13] progressively implying the international recognition of new ecological rights and duties, such as, for example, the "right to climate" as a common good, the right to water of all peoples, the duty to reduce the ecological debt and to preserve natural and cultural biodiversity, the right and duty to protect future generations, the right and duty to world peace, to solidarity between nations and cultures, and finally the dialogue between peoples and religions in the spirit of universal brotherhood and social friendship.

2. The Ecological Vocation of the Catholic Church

In a classical historical reading, the anthropological vision of the environment, according to which men dominate nature, has been considered as the basis of the current global ecological crisis. According to Lynn White, when communities were animist and polytheistic, they observed the surrounding nature with wonder and respect, associating gods with springs, woods and crops, to gain their favor and thank them for the gifts they provided through natural cycles.[14] The advent of the Jewish and then Christian religion affirmed the existence of a single God who created the world, who attributes a position of *dominus* over nature to men. For Toynbee,[15] the Book of Genesis is referred to as an unlimited license granted by God to men. This interpretation is not reflected in the Bible, nor in the later Christian writings, as one can see even from a superficial reading of the Psalms or the Gospels. The Catholic Church – after the Second Vatican Council – reacted to the criticism based on the vision of men as absolute rulers of the

13 Louis J. Kotzé, *Global Environmental Constitutionalism in the Anthropocene* (Hart Publishing 2019).

14 Lynn J. White, 'The Historical Roots of Our Ecologic Crisis' [1967] 155 *Science* 1203.

15 Arnold. J. Toinbee, 'The Genesis of Pollution' [1973] 15 *Horizon* 4.

planet, affirming a new ecological interpretation of the biblical texts. The latter no longer describes man as *dominus* of Creation, but as authentic *collaborator* and guardian of the "garden of God".

In the first half of the 1960s, two globally significant cultural and political processes developed at the same time: a profound renewal of the Catholic Church and the progressive emergence of environmental problems at a global level. The works of the Second Vatican Council, starting from October 1962, marked a significant turn of the Catholic Church towards the new themes of economics, culture and politics. While the atomic bomb was threatening the future of humanity, the gap between the rich and poor was accentuated, and, in rich countries, consumerism triumphed, spreading a new morality based on big businesses, with the risk of destroying the barriers of democracy and law. The Catholic silence on environmental issues broke in an authoritative way at the end of 1970, when various events contributed to making the ecological crisis one of the most visible and debated global problems. A stimulating article by Bartolomeo Sorge[16] on the Christian critique of technology, published in July 1970,[17] represents an historical turning point: for the first time, the Catholic Church directed attention to the ecological crisis. Sorge was most certainly inspired by the speech delivered by Paul VI to the F.A.O. Assembly on 16th November 1970, which, for the first time, contained an official reference to environmental issues. In this speech it was established that

> the concrete implementation of these technical possibilities at an accelerated pace does not occur without damaging repercussions on the balance of our natural environment. The gradual worsening of the so called "ecosystem" risks leading to a true ecological catastrophe due to industrial civilisation. We can already see that the air we breathe is stale, the water we drink is polluted, and that the beaches, lakes, even the oceans are contaminated. This makes us fear a true "biological death" in the near future, if vigorous measures are not courageously decided and strictly applied, without delay.[18]

Since the Eighties, the themes of the relationship between man and the environment, of the protection of Creation and of a balanced use of natural resources, represent topical issues for the Catholic Church. However, on a pastoral level, these themes received a systematic and authentic treatment only with John Paul II and even more with Benedict XXV. Particularly in 1990, on the *World Day of Peace*, in the message entitled "Peace with God the Creator; Peace with all Creation", Pope John Paul II urged the Christian community to start

16 Sociologist, leading intellectual of the Jesuits, future consultant to Paul VI in the field of the social doctrine of the Church and since 1973 director of the review "La Civiltà Cattolica".

17 Bartolomeo Sorge, 'La crisi ecologica. Un problema di scienza e di cultura' [1970] 4 *La civiltà cattolica* 417.

18 Message of Paolo VI.

a dialogue on environmental problems. At the second UN Conference on the environment held at Rio de Janeiro in 1992, the concept of *sustainable development*, as a legal principle, was given a legal value, and considered as the key to modern environmental policies. The Catholic Church, directly participating to this epochal summit, expressly recalled the duty of ethics against selfishness, reaffirming the need for a more equitable distribution of the resources available on Earth.

In this perspective, the civil commitment of the universal Church towards a renewed conception of development at a global level was declared. It was affirmed as an opportunity to remove the inequalities between peoples (from the North and the South of the World) and between present and future generations, while respecting Christian values. Therefore, even at that time, the Catholic Church believed that all environmental programs should revolve around the concept of *human dignity* and the freedom of everyone. For the Holy See it was, in fact, necessary to emphasize a new personal dimension of the notion of environment, identifying "the human person, its dignity" and its "integral development" as the origin and ultimate goal of environmental policies. John Paul II directed men to cultivate and guard the garden of the world, since human beings have a specific responsibility towards the living environment, in relation not only to the present generations, but also to the future ones. His great intuition consisted in having been able to provide a clear and fully working definition of the environment, understood as a "home" and at the same time as a "resource" for men. Benedict XVI himself addressed the ecological issue in a global perspective by inviting the international community, on the 20th anniversary of the Rio Conference on *Environment and Development* celebrated in 2012, to recover a new "human ecology". These are all topics recalled in a more systematic key by Benedict XVI himself in his Encyclical *Caritas in Veritate.*[19] In 2015, the Encyclical *Laudato Si'* by Pope Francis announces the intention to rediscover a new *human ecology*, unquestionably understood as the reconquering of a solidal sensitivity and a renewed ethical-cultural perspective, very different from those that have dominated the world in recent centuries. If men and women had a position of primacy in the Creation, the biblical text also shows the links between human beings and material world. The Book of Genesis, in fact, says: "The Lord God took the man and put him in the Garden of Eden to work it and take care of it" (2.15). The two Hebrew verbs "to cultivate" and "to guard" indicate that *homo faber*, the working man, transforms and protects nature in a relationship of alliance. They also have the meaning of "serving" and "observing", the same terms used to indicate the commitment to the alliance with God. Therefore, in contact with nature, human beings find their right dimension: they rediscover themselves as creatures, but at the same time the only ones "capable of knowing God" because they are interiorly open to infinity.

19 Benedetto XVI, *Caritas in Veritatem* (CiV 2009).

3. The Encyclical *Laudato Si'* and the Rule of Law: A "Magna Carta" for Ecological Rights and Duties

On 24 May 2015 (day of the Pentecost), Pope Francis delivered to the world a revolutionary message for the future of humanity. Today, after five years, when the environment represents the core of the international policies of every state on Earth, this enlightening work is still a reference, a *Universal Declaration for Creation* with a strong political, economic and spiritual meaning.[20] In May 2017, the visit to the Vatican of the former American President Donald Trump (a famous climate change denier) will be remembered because it highlighted the strong ecological message that Pope Francis intended to give to the richest of the world. On that occasion, the Pope intended to symbolically stir up the world's most powerful people, delivering to the President of the United States a copy of the Encyclical *Laudato Si'* as a "gift" for his visit to Rome. The epochal message of this Encyclical marked the beginning of an ecological revolution initiated by the Catholic Church and inspired a new integral ecology, which is inevitably destined to produce effects not only on the religious sphere, but also on the political and the legal ones.

Starting from these considerations, Pope Francis's apostolic message recalls the greatness and beauty of the Creation, as a work of God for men according to which

> human existence is based on three closely connected fundamental relationships: the relationship with God, the one with others and the one with the earth. Today these three vital relationships are broken, not only outside, but also inside us. This break is a sin.[21]

The Pope, starting precisely from the Canticle of St. Francis (considered as the greatest example of integral ecology, lived with joy) intends to awaken the consciences of all people, from believers to non-believers, from politicians to institutions, economists, entrepreneurs. According to Pope Francis, humanity still has the ability to cooperate to build our common home and he states that not everything is lost. For this reason, he invites everyone to recognize the richness that religions can offer to integral ecology and to the full development of the human race.

In this context, the Encyclical insists on the concept of "integral ecology", which clearly includes the human and social dimensions, inseparably linked with

20 Luigi Colella, 'Ambiente, religione e diritto al "tempo del Creato": *prime note comparative tra i fondamenti ecologici della chiesa cattolica e del sikhismo indiano*' [2019] 4 *AmbienteDiritto.it* 13.

21 Antonio Spadaro, "Laudato Si". Guida alla lettura dell'enciclica di papa Francesco' [2015] *La Civiltà cattolica* 3961 III 3.

the environmental issue. A careful reading of the Encyclical incites to strive for a conciliation of the notions of *sustainable development* and *integral ecology*.[22] Healthy, balanced and promoted development in harmony with nature (capable of safeguarding the rational use of resources while respecting the rights of future generations) is undoubtedly a concept not that far from integral ecology. In fact, the *Laudato Si'* discourse and the *Sustainable Development Goals* (SDGs), adopted in New York in September 2015, share some common universal ambitions.[23] Both documents analyze the links between climate and development, both formulate collective responses to global ecological challenges, both are addressed to all states, all human communities and all individuals. Thus, if the *17 objectives* of the SDGs are conceived as inseparable, at the same time, according to Pope Francis the environmental and social crisis go hand in hand, and therefore the ecological transition requires an "integral approach" to fight poverty, to give back dignity to men and to preserve nature.[24] The reconstruction of a good relationship between men and nature, between people and the environment, according to the original design of the Creator, *is based on some "cardinal points" of integral ecology: the* ecological debt, *the* right to the climate, *the* right to water and the protection of *biodiversity*. In order to save the planet, first of all, it is necessary to relieve the *ecological debt* that has been produced in recent decades to the detriment of the poorest people in the world, and to bridge the gap between the North and the South of the world. In the face of climate change, the Pope recalls that against climate change the responsibilities are differentiated, and those of the rich and developed countries are largely superior. In an integral ecology framework, emphasis must also be placed on the *issue of water* as a right for everyone and as a common good. Finally, the *protection of biodiversity* is undoubtedly linked to the protection of Creation; the Pope, in the Encyclical *Laudato Si'*, but also in his latest speeches on the environment, reminds Catholics and non-Catholics that, every year, thousands of natural species disappear, that they will be lost forever and that our children will not be able to see them.

In a period of great emergency, linked to the management of the COVID-19 pandemic, the reflections on theological, philosophical and legal issues share the same concern: recovering the deeper meaning of human existence, namely, of the relationship between human beings and the environment.

22 Jaime Tatay-Nieto, 'Sustainability, the Pontifical Academy of Sciences, and the Catholic Church's Ecological Turn' [2020] 11 *Religions* 488.

23 Jaime Tatay-Nieto, 'L'Agenda 2030 per lo sviluppo sostenibile e le religioni' [2021] 1 *La Civiltà Cattolica* 105. See also Jaime Tatay-Nieto, 'Creer en la sostenibilidad. Las religiones ante el reto medioambiental' [2019] 172 *Cristianisme i Justícia* 105–117.

24 Pasquale Ferrara, 'Sustainable International Relations. Pope Francis' Encyclical Laudato Si' and the Planetary Implications of "Integral Ecology"' [2019] 10 *Religions* 466; Eoin O'Neill, 'The Pope and the Environment: Towards an Integral Ecology?' [2016] 25 *Environmental Politics* 749.

4. Sustainable Development and Biodiversity: The Philosophy of the Catholic Church

Population growth and scientific progress are common features of the Anthropocene. With the aim of providing an account on the interrelation between humankind and the earth, Pope Francis describes the *rapidación* as the process of acceleration that fosters environmental degradation caused by anthropocentrism. The Encyclical *Laudato Si'* recalls the aforementioned account from different perspectives: i) the intimate fragility of our planet; ii) the confidence in a global connection that includes everything; iii) the critique to the new technocratic paradigm;[25] iv) the call to pursue different ways of economic and technological understanding; v) the intrinsic value of each creature; vi) the human sense of ecology; vii) the need for sincere and honest debates; viii) the commitment of international and local politics; ix) the throw-away culture and the proposal of a new lifestyle.

The relevance of this Encyclical is also connected to the international community's interest in ensuring the right to life[26] and the right of access to water as the first source of life,[27] and as a common good. From this perspective, Pope Francis highlights that access to safe and drinkable water is a fundamental resource of Creation[28] for religions, an essential, fundamental and universal human right, because it determines the survival of people and therefore it is a condition for the exercise of other human rights. To this end, depriving the poor of access to water is like denying the right to life rooted in their inalienable dignity.

Considering that the Universal Declaration of Human Rights of 1948 provides no references to the right to water, we could still implicitly find hints in article 25: "everyone has the right to a standard of living sufficient to guarantee health and his/her well-being and that of his/her family, with particular regard to food, clothing, housing, medical care and necessary social services." In 2010, thanks to the call of a number of Latin American countries, the UN General Assembly and the Human Rights Council approved two important Resolutions,[29] assigning the status of a human, universal, autonomous and specific right to the access to water and sanitation. The availability and sustainable management of water and sanitation facilities for everyone represents the sixth goal of the UN Agenda 2030 for Sustainable Development. In spite of the lack of any direct mention to the human right to water, the target is to ensure universal access to drinking water

25 Robert McKim, 'Opposing the "technocratic paradigm" and "appreciating the small things"' in Robert McKim (ed) *Laudato Si' and the Environment: Pope Francis' Green Encyclical* (Routledge 2020).

26 Vandana Shiva, *Water Wars: Privatisation, Pollution and Profit* (North Atlantic Books 2016).

27 See Dicastery for promoting integral human development, *Aqua Fons Vitae. Orientations on Water: Simbol of the Cry of thr Poor and the Cry of the Earth* (Vatican City 2020), www.humandevelopment.va/content/dam/sviluppoumano/documenti/Aqua%20fons%20vitae%20_%2003%202020.pdf.

28 S. Bergmann, *Weather, Religion and Climate Change* (Routledge 2021).

29 See the Resolution of the United Nations Assembly 64/92 of 28 July 2010.

and sanitation through affordable prices, as well as efficient and sustainable management. However, legal aspects regarding the right to water are still fostering scholarly debates and different jurisprudences, in order to define whether it is a fundamental right. In this regard, the Catholic Church implemented the idea of a right to water as common good, universal natural right and new social right of constitutional relevance.

Another leading theme of Pope Francis' ecological revolution concerns the good management of waste and the implementation of circular economy. According to the Catholic Church, information on environmental sustainability is necessary, raising awareness on the spread of the throw-away culture, the overcoming of the linear economy, the reduction of waste production and the importance of recycling. Such an approach is quite similar to the EU efforts in policies and legislations for the implementation of plastic-free strategies, the prevention and the reduction of waste at the source. In reference to this new approach, three main processes play a pivotal role: i) the transition from linear economy to circular economy, ii) the recognition of environmental law as a fundamental human right, iii) the beginning of a new lifestyle inspired by integral ecology. Through the aforementioned three processes or "steps", circular economy (considered as a lifestyle) should deny the "sick economy" model and its effects (unequal economic growth that disregards fundamental human values), fostering the integral protection of the environment.

Along with the protection of the environment, issues related to biodiversity represent a commitment of the international community and a priority for states. In several occasions, the Catholic Church has emphasized the need to protect biodiversity. Pope Francis specifically reflects on "those lungs of the planet rich in biodiversity", such as the Amazon, the Congo River basin, the other great water basins and glaciers. In reference to the proposals for the internationalization of the Amazon, in 2015 Pope Francis warned the international community through blaming the economic interests of multinational corporations. Furthermore, in 2019, Pope Francis' Apostolic Exhortation *Querida Amazonia* highlighted the relationship between humankind, nature, local cultures and the globalized world. This call represents a sort of "invitation" for the international community to take care of territories that are fundamentals for the whole planet. The Pope's vision helps us to reflect on how Amazonia must be considered a common good in legal terms, i.e. a good of and for everyone.

In spite of legalistic and formalistic approaches to the aforementioned issues, some Courts started a new "green" process, as in the case of the Colombian Supreme Court, which recognized Colombian Amazonia as bearer of rights, while outlining the state obligation to protect, maintain and restore it,[30] following the principles of precaution, intergenerational equity and solidarity, in order to protect the ecosystem surrounding Colombian Amazonia. As the United Nations Declaration on Indigenous Peoples of 2007 recalls, the aboriginal peoples teach

30 See the judgment of the Colombian Supreme Court STC 4360–2018.

us that we cannot take care of the earth if we do not love and respect it, as a form of wisdom of "good living" in "harmony with the earth". In this perspective, Pope Francis' Encyclical *Fratelli Tutti* imagines an "open world" without borders, in which dialogue, multiculturalism, solidarity, the social function of property, the "principle of the common destination of goods", human brotherhood and social friendship prevail.

5. Integral Ecology and Climate Change

Today, a broad scientific consensus has formed around the alarming effects of climate change, represented by increasing sea level rise, extreme weather conditions and the spread of zoonotic diseases (including the recent COVID-19 pandemic).

Since 2015, the religions of the world – with Catholicism and Islam in the lead[31] – have turned their attention to climate change, recognized as a central topic for ecological conversion.[32] Ecological conversion must be understood in an integral way, as a transformation of the relationships we have with our sisters and brothers, with other living beings, with creation in its very rich variety, with the Creator who is the origin of all life. In this context, the Catholic Church has significantly contributed to global environmental awareness. The Encyclical *On Care for Our Common Home* openly addresses climate change, considered as a global concern with massive environmental, socioeconomic and political implications. In light of the 2015 Paris Agreement, the Catholic Church has underlined the relevance of the relationship between religion and the environment, treating the latter as 'a common good, belonging to everyone, and for everyone.' Despite these encouraging signs, the results of the *United Nations Climate Change Conference* (COP25) – held in December 2019 in Madrid – confirmed that the international community has a long way to go to reach carbon neutrality. Due to the intransigence of some countries, in fact, a consensus on Article 6 of the Paris Agreement, which covers the regulation of carbon markets, has not yet been reached; this most divisive issue is also considered at the last summit in Scotland in 2021.

In the year 2019, the Encyclical *Laudato Si'* helped recognize the environment as an asset with constitutional relevance, to be protected by the international community. The European Parliament Resolution of 14 March 2019 on climate change has set ambitious targets for emission reduction, to be met by 2030 in order to reach zero emissions by 2050. Following this Resolution, the European

31 *Islamic Declaration on Global Climate Change* (2015), https://cambridgecentralmosque.org/wp-content/uploads/2020/03/writings-climate-declaration-mwb.pdf. The declaration is based on an environmental framework derived from Islamic principles and faith-based climate activism: see Antar Solhy Abdellah, 'The Islamic Declaration on Global climate change; An Ideological Discourse Analysis' [2020] 2 *Middle Eastern Journal of Research in Education and Social Sciences* 77.

32 Philip Jenkins, *Climate, Catastrophe, and Faith. How Changes in Climate Drive Religious Upheaval* (Oxford University Press 2021).

Commission presented on 11 December 2019 the *Green New Deal*, a strategy in which the European Union assumes the role of global leader, introducing more sustainable economic practices.

From a comparative perspective, the "constitutionalization" of the fight against climate change arouses great interest. By way of example, we can recall the new Cuban Constitution (2019) which – in addition to the promotion of sustainable development (Article 13) – aims at the "protection and conservation of the environment . . . responding to climate change" (Article 16). Similar experiences are represented by the Constitution of the Dominican Republic (2015), which provides for a territorial organization plan that ensures "the efficient and sustainable use of the nation's natural resources, in accordance with the need to adapt to climate change" (Article 194), and the Constitution of Ivory Coast (2016) which, in its *Preamble*, expresses the commitment of its people to contribute "to climate protection and to maintaining a healthy environment for future generations". Most recently, the public debate in France has revolved around the "constitutionalization" of the *acquis* under the 2015 Paris Agreement. The French reform proposal aims to modify Article 1 of the Constitution, qualifying France as an "Ecological" Republic that has three duties (ensuring "the economic and fair use of natural resources", guaranteeing "the conservation of biological diversity" and fighting "climate change within the framework of planetary boundaries"), informed by the paradigm of intergenerational solidarity. This proposal has not been approved but it is important because it stems from the contributions of the *Convention Citoyenne pour le Climat*, a model of public participation and unprecedented direct democracy, in which French citizens have been active agents of environmental legislative processes.

Another aspect of interest is *climate change litigation*: the possibility of providing humanitarian protection for environmental reasons, by according protection to environmental refugees, has been brought to the judges' attention. Nowadays, "environmental refugees" – also known as "eco refugees" or "climate refugees" – are deemed to represent a large portion of asylum seekers around the world. As assessed by the United Nations in the *Global Compact on refugees*, migratory movements are affected by different factors, climate change being one of them. In this regard, Italian judges – in relation to an asylum seeker from Niger – have established that violations to the "ineliminable core value of personal dignity", do not only cover situations of armed conflict, but also any circumstance that might threaten fundamental rights to life, which also include environmental disasters, unsustainable exploitation of natural resources and other consequences of climate change.[33]

In the *Urgenda case*,[34] climate neutrality obligations were enforced by a European state for the first time. The Dutch Supreme Court established the obligation

33 See the judgment of the Italian Supreme Court of Cassation 5022–2021.

34 On 20 December 2019, the Dutch Supreme Court, the highest court in the Netherlands, upheld the previous decisions in the Urgenda Climate Case, stating that the Dutch

for the State to emit 25% less greenhouse gases in 2020 than in 1990 (in accordance with Articles 2 and 8 of the European Convention on Human Rights). It should furthermore be noted that the Administrative Court of Paris – at the beginning of 2021 – condemned France for failing to take the necessary steps to address the climate emergency, treating the results as an "environmental damage" (Article 1246 of the French civil code).

One last point concerns the active participation of citizens and NGOs (environmental and humanitarian) for the improved understanding of environmental issues. Catholic movements are promoting an ethical culture of environmental awareness. A clear example of this is represented by the *Global Catholic Climate Movement* (GCCM), born at the center of two transformative events that would shape the attitude of the Catholic Church towards ecological crises: the publication of the Encyclical *Laudato Si'* and the Paris Agreement.

6. Beyond *Anthropocene*: Environmental Constitutionalism and the *New Alliance* Between Humanity and the Environment

It has been argued that a deep ethical crisis lies at the root of the ecological crisis faced by the planet today, due to the prevailing paradigms of anthropocentrism, which have subverted the relationship between humanity and nature.[35] According to some authors, a roadmap out of this ecological crisis can be found in the reconstruction of the symbiotic relations between man and the environment (*Symbiocene*).[36] Other authors point out the importance of overcoming the *Anthropocene* – characterized by human domination over nature – and head into a new geological age, the *Ecocene*,[37] based on ecosystemic egalitarianism and the care for every living species.

In our opinion, religions can play a fundamental role in tackling climate change. Religions can guide the process of rebuilding the broken relations between men and nature towards an ecological conversion. According to the Encyclical on *Care for Our Common Home*, an ecological transition should be achieved through this integral conversion, which implies that the relationships between men and God, between men and creation, and between men themselves should be restored.

---

government has obligations to urgently and significantly reduce emissions: see *State of the Netherlands v. Urgenda Foundation, De Staat Der Nederlanden v. Stichting Urgenda*, www.urgenda.nl/wp-content/uploads/ENG-Dutch-Supreme-Court-Urgenda-v-Netherlands-20-12-2019.pdf.

35 Joshtrom Kureethadam, *The Ten Green Commandments of Laudato Si'* (Liturgical Press 2019).

36 Rod Gilbert, *Environmental Humanities and Theologies. Ecoculture, Literature and the Bible* (Routledge 2018).

37 Santa De Siena, *Ecocene. Per un postumano tecnopolitico o ecopolitico?* (Orthotes Editrice 2019).

Integral ecology introduces a new paradigm in which men are no longer *masters*, but *guardians* of the environment.

The Catholic Church identifies the guiding principles of integral ecology with a global environmental legal framework inspired by *green humanism*.[38] In the Encyclical *Laudato Si'*, the Catholic Church has, in fact, underlined the role played by law to drive local, state and international actors towards a global ecological revolution. Law should be an "effective moderator", enacting the "rules of conduct" and promoting the common good. However, the establishment of new rights is not enough to minimize environmental damages: according to the Encyclical *Laudato Si'*, a new ecological citizenship requires both rights and duties. In fact, the duties define the space of rights, advocating their protection as a commitment. This reflection finds an echo in the current debate over the two dimensions of environmental constitutionalism, with positions ranging from the protection of environmental rights as *human rights* to the enforcement of *environmental duties* by the most recent constitutions of the *nuevo constitucionalismo* in Latin America, such as those of Ecuador and Bolivia.[39]

These deontic implications were already anticipated by Catholic legal scholars like Giorgio La Pira[40] – a forerunner of integral ecology – according to whom the full development of the individual requires not only the recognition of *individual freedoms*, but also of *social rights*, such as the right to a healthy environment. From a Catholic standpoint, rights must be complemented by "mandatory duties of political, economic and social solidarity", as an expression of intergenerational solidarity and environmental sustainability (Article 2 of the Italian Constitution).

The social doctrine of the Catholic Church is based on four pillars: *personality*,[41] *solidarity*, *subsidiarity*[42] and – what is most interesting to us – *sustainability*. Contemporary constitutional law is translating these values into *environmental management principles*[43] such as the principles of *prevention*, *precaution* and *non-regression*, which are also starting to be recognized at the international level, as

38 Jaques Maritain, *The Person and the Common Good* (University of Notre Dame Press 1966).

39 Serena Baldin, *Il* buen vivir *nel costituzionalismo andino. Profili comparativi* (Giappichelli 2019); see also Silvia Bagni (ed), *Dallo Stato del bienestar allo Stato del buen vivir. Innovazione e tradizione nel costituzionalismo latino-americano* (Filodiritto 2013).

40 Giorgio La Pira is a Catholic legal scholar and a member of the Italian Constituent Assembly. On Giorgio la Pira's contribution to environmental protection see Grazia Dormiente, *Giorgio La Pira. Ambientalista dei Si* (Libreria Editrice Vaticana 2011). On the Catholic thought of Giorgio La Pira in the Italian Constituent Assembly, see Paolo Maddalena, 'Postfazione' in Giulio Alfano (ed) *Giorgio La Pira. Un domenicano alla Costituente* (Solfanelli 2016) 148. See also Nino Giordano, *Giorgio La Pira e la Costituzione. Relazioni e interventi nell'Assemblea Costituente* (Libreria editrice Vaticana 2016).

41 Giogio La Pira, *Il valore della persona umana* (Edizioni Polistampa 2009).

42 Vincenzo Pepe, 'Il principio di sussidiarietà e la chiesa cattolica' in Vincenzo Pepe and Luigi Colella (eds) *Saggi di diritto pubblico italiano e comparato* (Edizioni Palazzo Vargas 2019) 84.

43 Domenico Amirante, *Diritto ambientale italiano e comparato. Principi* (Jovene 2003).

in the draft of the *Global Pact of Environment*.[44] From an ethical point of view, universal ecological transition depends on the principle of ecological responsibility, which binds together environmental protection and human dignity. This implies the environmental education of younger generations since the spread of a "culture of care for our common home" represents a crucial challenge towards the recovery of the environment. This paradigm shift requires considering different ways of living built upon "a healthy pressure on those who hold political, economic and social power". Institutional structures should promote "good practices" and not only discourage "bad practices", in order to facilitate collective initiatives inspired by the aforementioned notion of common good.[45] It should be noted that in recent years the Vatican State – inspired by the principles of the Encyclical *Laudato Si'* – has implemented a series of "green" practices and environmental policies to ensure the ecological transition (e.g.: zero pesticides, water supply without waste, organic waste transformed into compost, no single-use plastics, LED lights, solar panels and photovoltaic systems for the production of electricity): it could arguably be defined the *greenest State in the world*.

The engagement of the Catholic Church has paved the way to the ecological commitment of politicians and scientists to the ecological transition[46] according to a new humanism.[47] Joe Biden, Ursula von der Leyen and Mario Draghi are some of the new world leaders who have recognized the urgency of *ecological transition* as a priority in their governmental agendas. Italian Prime Minister Mario Draghi has recently stated that "natural tragedies are the earth's response to our mistreatment." In other words, a new approach to integral ecology – at once on the social and economic plan – can no longer be postponed.

Religions in the Anthropocene can play a pivotal role in the "greening" of global environmental law: in this historical moment, a renewed Environmental Constitutionalism can act as a guideline for the ecological transition. This paradigm shift will require a "new alliance between human beings and the environment",[48] a new way of life inspired by a spirit of renewed universal fraternity.[49]

44 On the Global Pact proposal, see Domenico Amirante, 'The Global Pact for the Environment: A General Instrument to Face Climate Change' (2019) 10 *Jindal Global Law Review*, 61–72.

45 See Tavolo interdicasteriale della Santa Sede sull'ecologia integrale, *In cammino per la cura della Casa Comune. A cinque anni dalla Laudato si'* (Libreria Editrice Vaticana 2020).

46 Gael Giraud, *Transizione ecologica. La finanza a servizio della nuova frontiera dell'economia* (Emi 2015).

47 *Laura Westra, Ecological Integrity and Global Governance Science, Ethics and the Law* (Routledge 2018).

48 See Papa Francesco, *Messaggio per High Level Virtual Climate Ambition* (2020), www.vaticannews.va/it/papa/news/2020-12/papa-francesco-virtual-climate-ambition-summit-accordi-parigi.html.

49 Paul Ricoeur, *Sé come un altro* (Jaca Book 2011). On the proximity principle in a comparative perspective see Vincenzo Pepe, *La prossimità nella comparazione giuridica* (Edizioni Scientifiche Italiane 2015). Papa Francesco, *Documento sulla Fratellanza umana per la pace mondiale e la convivenza comune*, www.vatican.va/content/francesco/it/travels/2019/outside/documents/papa-francesco_20190204_documento-fratellanza-umana.html.

Bibliography

Abdellah A.S., 'The Islamic Declaration on Global Climate Change; An Ideological Discourse Analysis' (2020) 1 *Middle Eastern Journal of Research in Education and Social Sciences* 77.

Amirante D., *Diritto ambientale italiano e comparato. Princìpi* (Jovene 2003).

Amirante D., *Lo Stato multiculturale. Contributo alla teoria dello Stato dalla prospettiva dell'Unione Indiana* (Bangladesh University of Professionals 2015).

Amirante D., 'The Global Pact for the Environment: A General Instrument to Face Climate Change' (2019) 10 *Jindal Global Law Review* 61–72.

Bagni S. (ed), *Dallo Stato del bienestar allo Stato del buen vivir. Innovazione e tradizione nel costituzionalismo latino-americano* (Filodiritto 2013).

Baldin S., *Il buen vivir nel costituzionalismo andino. Profili comparativi* (Giappichelli 2019).

Benedetto XVI, *Caritas in Veritatem* (CiV 2009).

Bergmann S., 'New Developments in the Field' in Willis Jenkins, Mary Evelyn Tucker and Jhon Grim (eds), *Routledge Handbook of Religion and Ecology* (Routledge 2017).

Bergmann S., *Weather, Religion and Climate Change* (Routledge 2021).

Boersema J.J., 'Why is Francis of Assisi the Patron Saint of Ecologists?' [2020] *Science & Christian Belief* 51.

Colella L., 'Ambiente, religione e diritto al "tempo del Creato": *prime note comparative tra i fondamenti ecologici della chiesa cattolica e del sikhismo indiano'* (2019) 4 *AmbienteDiritto.it* 13.

Conradie E., *Christianity and Ecological Theology: Resources for Further Research* (SUN Press 2006).

Cooper D.E. and Palmer J.A. (eds), *Spirit of the Environment. Religion, Value and Environmental Concern* (Routledge 1998).

De Siena S., *Ecocene. Per un postumano tecnopolitico o ecopolitico?* (Orthotes Editrice 2019).

Dicastery for promoting integral human development, *Aqua fons vitae. Orientations on Water: Symbol of the Cry of the Poor and the Cry of the Earth* (Vatican City 2020), www.humandevelopment.va/content/dam/sviluppoumano/documenti/Aqua%20fons%20vitae%20_%2003%202020.pdf.

Dormiente G., *Giorgio La Pira. Ambientalista dei Si* (Libreria Editrice Vaticana 2011).

Ferrajoli L., *L'acqua come bene comune e il diritto all'acqua come diritto fondamentale, Relazione al Convegno internazionale sul diritto all'acqua* (Gorizia 2003).

Ferrara P., 'Sustainable International Relations. Pope Francis' Encyclical Laudato Si' and the Planetary Implications of "Integral Ecology"' [2019] *Religions* 466.

Gilbert R., *Environmental Humanities and Theologies. Ecoculture, Literature and the Bible* (Routledge 2018).

Giordano N., *Giorgio La Pira e la Costituzione. Relazioni e interventi nell'Assemblea Costituente* (Libreria editrice Vaticana 2016).

Giraud G., *Transizione ecologica. La finanza a servizio della nuova frontiera dell'economia* (Emi 2015).

Glenn H.P., *The Cosmopolitan State* (OUP 2013).

Glenn H.P., *Legal Traditions of the World: Sustainable diversity in law* (OUP 2014).

Islamic Declaration on Global Climate Change (2015), https://cambridgecentralmosque.org/wp-content/uploads/2020/03/writings-climate-declaration-mwb.pdf.

Jenkins W. and Chapple C.K., 'Religion and Environment' [2011] *Annual Review of Environment and Resources* 441.
Kotzé L.J., *Global Environmental Constitutionalism in the Anthropocene* (Hart Publishing 2019).
Kureethadam J., *The Ten Green Commandments of Laudato Si'* (Liturgical Press 2019).
La Pira G., *Il valore della persona umana* (Edizioni Polistampa 2009).
Maddalena P., 'Postfazione' in Giulio Alfano (ed), *Giorgio La Pira. Un domenicano alla Costituente* (Solfanelli 2016).
Mancini S. (ed), *Constitutions and Religion* (Elgar 2020).
Maritain J., *The Person and the Common Good* (University of Notre Dame Press 1966).
McKim R., 'Opposing the "Technocratic Paradigm" and "Appreciating the Small Things"' in R. McKim (ed), *Laudato Si' and the Environment: Pope Francis' Green Encyclical* (Routledge 2020).
State of the Netherlands v. Urgenda Foundation, *De Staat Der Nederlanden v. Stichting Urgenda*, www.urgenda.nl/wp-content/uploads/ENG-Dutch-Supreme-Court-Urgenda-v-Netherlands-20-12-2019.pdf.
O'Neill E., 'The Pope and the Environment: Towards an Integral Ecology?' (2016) 25 *Environmental Politics* 749.
Panikkar R., *Ecosofia. La saggezza della terra* (Jaca Book 2015).
Papa Francesco, *Messaggio per High Level Virtual Climate Ambition* (2020), www.vaticannews.va/it/papa/news/2020-12/papa-francesco-virtual-climate-ambition-summit-accordi-parigi.html.
Pepe V., *La prossimità nella comparazione giuridica* (Edizioni Scientifiche Italiane 2015).
Pepe V., 'Il principio di sussidiarietà e la chiesa cattolica' in V. Pepe and L. Colella (eds), *Saggi di diritto pubblico italiano e comparato* (Edizioni Palazzo Vargas 2019).
Piccinni M.R., *La tutela dell'ambiente nel diritto delle religioni* (Aracne 2015).
Rankin A., *Jainism and Environmental Philosophy. Karma and the Web of Life* (Routledge 2018).
Ricoeur P., *Sé come un altro* (Jaca Book 2011).
Shiva V., *Water Wars: Privatisation, Pollution and Profit* (North Atlantic Books 2016).
Sorge B., 'La crisi ecologica. Un problema di scienza e di cultura' (1970) 4 *La civiltà cattolica* 417.
Spadaro A., '"*Laudato Si'". Guida alla lettura dell'enciclica di papa Francesco*' [2015] *La Civiltà cattolica* 3961, III 3.
Tatay-Nieto J., 'Creer en la sostenibilidad. Las religiones ante el reto medioambiental' [2019] *Cristianisme i Justícia*.
Tatay-Nieto J., 'Sustainability, the Pontifical Academy of Sciences, and the Catholic Church's Ecological Turn' (2020) 11 *Religions* 488.
Tatay-Nieto J., 'L'Agenda 2030 per lo sviluppo sostenibile e le religioni' (2021) 1 *La Civiltà Cattolica* 105.
Tavolo interdicasteriale della Santa Sede sull'ecologia integrale, *In cammino per la cura della Casa Comune. A cinque anni dalla Laudato si'* (Libreria Editrice Vaticana 2020).
Toinbee A.J., 'The Genesis of Pollution' (1973) 15 *Horizon* 4.
United Nations, *The Global Compact on Refugees* (UN 2018), www.unhcr.org/ph/the-global-compact-on-refugees.
Westra L., *Ecological Integrity and Global Governance Science, Ethics and the Law* (Routledge 2018).
White L.J., 'The Historical Roots of Our Ecologie Crisis' (1967) 155 *Science* 1203.

2 Ecological Crisis

The Self, State and the Hindu Ethics

Rajnish Saryal

1. Introduction

The concerns for, deteriorating condition of the environment and preservation of flora and fauna has led to the growth of scholarship that advocates the study and analysis of environmental issues by using the categories of morality, ethics and religion in the recent time. The issue of the environment-religion connection was highlighted by Lynn White Jr., who argued that the historical roots of ecological crisis lie in Christianity and Western culture. He argued, "What people think about their ecology depends on what they think about themselves in relation to things around them. Human ecology is deeply conditioned by beliefs about our nature and destiny – that is, by religion".[1] The arguments forwarded by White Jr. in his article paved the way for the growth of a discourse on relationship between religion and environment. The famous encyclical letter "Laudato Si' " (2015) of Pope Francis on care for our common home brought the environmental issues further within the fold of religion. Almost all the major religions of the world have their respective declarations to address one of the greatest ecological challenges of humanity today – climate change.[2] In this chapter, I am analysing the Hindu religion as a possible source of ethical and moral values for the individual as well as the state to address environmental issues in India as well as worldwide.

2. Defining Hinduism

The majority of India's population belongs to the Hindu religion.[3] But what is Hindu religion? This question requires a little deep attention since Hinduism as

1 Lynn White Jr., 'Historical Roots of Ecological Crisis' (1967) 155(3767) *Science* 1203–1207, 1205.

2 Parliament of World Religions, 'Declaration on Climate Change of the 2015Parlimant of the World's Religion' (2015), https://parliamentofreligions.org/civicrm/petition/sign?sid=4&reset=1.

3 Census Commissioner of India (2011), Ministry of Home Affairs, Government of India https://censusindia.gov.in/2011census/C-01.html.

DOI: 10.4324/9781003175308-4

a religion cannot be defined on the same parameters of Christianity and Islam. Hawley argues, "Hindus had a concept of India as sacred space and they had histories and epics that established their complex common ancestry, but they never developed a concept of themselves as a society unified by religion".[4] It is difficult, in fact impossible, to designate any single religious text or ritual as common to all the groups of people called Hindu. Moreover, the entrenched Hindu belief of reincarnation is absent even in the Vedas and rejected later by *Charvakas*, *Kapalikas* and modern-time reformers like M.N. Roy.[5] Monier Williams uses the analogy of a Banyan tree to describe Hindu religion. A "single stem [of Banyan tree] sends out numerous branches destined to send roots to the ground and become trees themselves, till the parent stock is lost in a dense forest of its own offshoots".[6] This analogy also highlights the Hindu religious idea of interconnectedness of all beings, which is perhaps common to all the diverse strands of Hinduism.

The term "Hindu" has a comparatively recent origin and it was first used by the outsider Mohammedan aggressors to designate the native people who did not convert to Islam. Hindus were, as also shown further later, the people on the other side of the river Sindhu. Later, the British census in India made Hindu an official category of religion.[7] Romila Thaper traces the origin of the term Hindu in the inscriptions of the Achaemenid empire which refers to the geographical region of the "Indus or Sindhu as Hi(n)dush". A more common usage of the term Hindu is found in later Arabic texts that refer to the people of Indian subcontinent and people who lived across the Indus River.[8] In fact, Hinduism at best can be defined as the religion of a community of communities which subscribes to varied rituals and actions rather believes in a unified faith, as is the case with Christianity and Islam. Romila Thapar argues that contrary to the presumption, the notion of Hindu community is not very old. "Even in the normative texts of *Brahmanism*, the *Dharmaśāstras*, it is conceded that there were a variety of communities, determined by location, occupation and caste, none of which were necessarily bound together by a common religious identity".[9]

The contemporary articulation of Hinduism as a unified religion mostly by orientalist scholars has been subjected to fierce debate in the recent literature.[10]

4 John Stratton Hawley, 'Naming Hinduism' (1991) 15(3) *The Wilson Quarterly* 20–34, 24.
5 Prasenjit Duara, 'The New Politics of Hinduism' (1976) 15(3) *The Wilson Quarterly* 42–50, 43.
6 Hawley (n 4) 22.
7 Max Weber, *The Religion of India: The Sociology of Hinduism and Buddhism* (Hans H. Gerth and Don Martindale trs, The Free Press 1958) 4.
8 Romila, Thapar, 'Imagined Religious Communities? Ancient History and the Modern Search for a Hindu Identity' (1989) 23(2) *Modern Asian Studies* 209–231, 222.
9 Ibid 220.
10 See Vasudha Dalmia and Heinrich von Stietencron (eds), *Representing Hinduism: The Construction of Religious Traditions and National Identity* (Sage 1995); Günther D. Sontheimer and Hermann Kulke (eds), *Hinduism Reconsidered* (Manohar 1989); Hawley (n 4); Alfed Hiltebeitel 'Of Camphor and Coconuts' (1991) 15(3) *The Wilson Quarterly* 26–28; Gerald James Larson, *India's Agony Over Religion* (State University of New York Press 1995).

Therefore, many scholars recommend deconstruction of Hinduism to understand its real nature and meaning.[11] Smith by citing Frykenberg, for example pointed out:

> There has never been any such a thing as a single "Hinduism" or any single "Hindu community" for all of India. Nor, for that matter, can one find any such thing as a single "Hinduism" or "Hindu community" even for any one socio-cultural region of the continent. Furthermore, there has never been any one religion – nor even one system of religions-to which the term "Hindu" can accurately be applied. No one so-called religion, moreover, can lay exclusive claim to or be defined by the term "Hinduism." The very notion of the existence of any single religious community by this name has been falsely conceived.[12]

Although the term "Hindu" has a recent origin and has some political and geographical connotations, I am using it as a generic term for the Vedic and *Brahmanic* religion of the Asian subcontinent. Despite the difficulty of defining Hinduism according to a well-constructed Western framework of religion, I am using the term "Hindus" in this chapter to refer to all the communities who believe in the authority of certain core Vedic concepts for the sake of brevity, not the Vedas as a textual source itself. Ferro-Luzzi argues "it is not necessary to abandon the term Hinduism or deny it the status of a religion. What should be abandoned instead is the conviction that all concepts can be defined because they must possess common attributes and clear-cut boundaries".[13] She further argues while quoting Wittgenstein that such concepts are required to be exemplified rather than narrowly defined because they are "held together by a complicated network of similarities overlapping and crisscrossing [and moreover] 'family resemblance' may exist among their members" that follow them.[14] The element that holds all this together very loosely is the perception that there is a vision of Order, which is both seen and unseen, and which connects all together into some kind of giant spider web, in which every component has specific roles to fulfil, ideally. This vision of *Rta* or *Satya*[15] leaves ample room for specifics and is in fact highly dynamic and situation-specific, thus replicating the global nature of law itself as a deeply plural phenomenon.[16]

11 Brian K. Smith, 'Questioning Authority: Constructions and Deconstructions of Hinduism' (1998) 2(3) *International Journal of Hindu Studies* 313–339.
12 Ibid 316.
13 Gabriella Eichinger Ferro-Luzzi, 'The Polythetic-Prototype Approach to Hinduism' in Günther-Dietz Sontheimer and Hermann Kulke (eds) *Hinduism Reconsidered* (2nd edn., Manohar 2001).
14 Wittgenstein as quoted in Ibid 295.
15 Werner Mesnki, *Hindu Law: Beyond Tradition and Modernity* (OUP 2003).
16 Werner Menski, *Comparative Law in a Global Context: The Legal Systems of Asia and Africa* (CUP 2006).

3. Environmental Ethics and Hindu Religion

The Western discourse on ethics is a majorly rationalistic construction that prescribes a consistent set of moral norms of behaviour which are independent of subjective and culture specific connotations. In contrast to this, the Indian ethics are culturally and religiously embedded normative guidelines that do not conform to the principles of meta-ethics. The Indian preoccupation with mysticism and life-denying theologies negate the possibility of having a rationally grounded school of ethics.[17] But do we really need an abstract theory of ethics to deal with the practical problem of environmental crisis? Will the traditional Western notion of ethics as a branch of secular philosophy serve to address the issues arising out of ecological crisis? Ado Leopold through his construct of land ethics popularised the idea that there is a great need of new environmental ethics for the west.[18] Later, Lynn White Jr. argued that the roots of environmental problems lie in the Christian idea of the self that designates the individual as viceroy of God on earth and thus empowers and encourages individuals to think of themselves as limitlessly powerful agents, forgetting the sense of connectedness and responsibility to a larger whole. Therefore, the Western ethics cannot fully embrace the ecological crisis of the present time, as it has defined away, as it were, the sense of responsibility and replaced it with a preference for rights and entitlements. In fact, there is a need to abandon the Western individualistic ethics and look for alternatives that emphasise connectedness to address the ecological crisis.[19] The key ideological problem here appears to be the modern view that this would constitute a return to "religion", and thus to something "medieval" that modernity and its secular foundations sought to overcome. However, it appears to be a fundamental error to presume that traditional religions are purely "religious". In recent times, a good body of literature has emerged that advocates for taking seriously the basic values of Asian religions like Hinduism, Buddhism[20] and Jainism[21] as alternatives to develop a new environmental ethics, a methodological approach which has become quite mature now.

Sarvepalli Radhakrishnan with reference to the Indian ethics argues that both theology and metaphysics can essentially be a source of ethics. He writes,

> Any ethical theory must be grounded in metaphysics, in a philosophical conception of the relation between human conduct and ultimate reality. As we

17 Purushottama Bilimoria, Joseph Prabhu and Renuka Sharma (eds), *Indian Ethics: Classical Traditions and Contemporary Challenges* (Vol. 1, Ashgate Publishing 2007) 30.
18 Ado Leopold, *A Sand County Almanac: And Sketches Here and There* (OUP 1949).
19 White Jr. (n 1).
20 Anand Singh, *Planet, Plants and Animals: Ecological Paradigms in Buddhism* (Primus Books 2019).
21 Aidan Rankin, *Jainism and Environmental Philosophy: Karma and the Web of Life* (Routledge 2018).

> think ultimate reality to be, so we behave. Vision and action go together. If we believe absurdities, we shall commit atrocities.[22]

The Indian ethics are not abstract categories, something that is purely "religious" or ideological; rather, they are embedded in actions which are in turn conditioned by not only secular universal moral principles as is the case with Western ethics, but also include religious norms and rituals. The ethical notion of *Dharma*, for example, is an all-encompassing whole which subscribes to both religious principles and secular law. Bilimoria and others explain the notion of *Dharma* in the following manner:

> Dharma is the fixed position of duty and of right, in the sense of what is proper and normative. It is by no means restricted to the realm of personal ethics, but it also designates religious observance and secular law, prescribing the individual's social and legal standing within the wider domains of community, caste, and station. Expanding its range even further, dharma connotes a general principle or law of nature to which the individual is bound in a two-fold sense, both in terms of supporting the cosmic, social, and personal orders and deriving from them a corresponding obligation. Thus, as universal order, it assigns to each entity, personal or impersonal, its specific place within the wider community.[23]

The ethical notion of *Dharma* is a broad concept, and it permeates the whole cosmic order that sustains everything, whether animate or inanimate. *Dharma* circumscribes duty and obligation not only towards the ultimately unknown higher being but also towards the most miniscule creature of the universe. This is the most ecologically sensitive ethical guide that suggests the mutual connection between rights and duties which are essential to, as Bilimoria and others argue,

> maintaining the cosmic, social, and structural orders of the universe. . . . Dharma with its roots in *dhr* (sustaining) and Vedic *ṛta* (order), can open up a more holistic, organic and ecologically enlightened perspective as a contrast to the more nature-subjugating, individualistic and competitive environment within which we conceptualize ethics.[24]

Building on this Vedic foundation of *Rta*, the classical Indian notion of *Dharma* that establishes the interconnectedness and interdependence between man and nature through the system of rights and obligations towards each other seems quite suitable to answer the moral questions that arise from the ecological crisis of the twentieth and twenty-first century. In this chapter, I shall explore

22 Sarvepalli Radhakrishnan, *Eastern Religions and Western Thought* (Galaxy Books 1959) 80.
23 Bilimoria et al (n 17) 24.
24 Ibid 25.

the Hindu ethical notions like *Dharma* and other related concepts which have shaped and defined the environmental actions and outlook of the Indian state. These ethical notions provide situation-specific guidelines to the individual as well as statecraft to make moral choices to maximise the common good. My reference to the state here means the actions and outlook of the king or ruler in the pre-independence period and government in the post-independence period. The Indian state in the post-independence period declared itself as a secular democracy, and therefore the direct application of any ethical notion which is sourced from Hindu religion becomes untenable. The Indian ethical notion of *Dharma* is a religiously embedded non-secular normative category which is quite distinct from that of the Western understanding of ethics. At the same time, it also has secular dimensions, which cannot be defined away by efforts to "other" traditional Asian religions. It will be interesting to see how the formally secular Indian state in the post-independence era has actually worked in the area of environment protection, and it will be particularly instructive to examine to what extent Hindu ethical notions influence the Indian environmental stewardship.

4. The Idea of Self and Its Relation With Nature in Hinduism

The Hindu idea of self and its interconnectedness with nature can be analysed by evaluating the four-fold purposes of life, which are *Kārma*, *Artha*, *Dharma* and *Moksha*. According to the classical Hindu literature, the fourfold goal of Hindu life can be attained by observing the fourfold *Varṇa* system – *Brāhmin*, *Kṣatriya*, *Vaiśya* and *Śūdra* – and passing through the four stages of life, *Brahmacāri*, *Gribastha*, *Vānaprastha* and *Saññyāsin*.[25] It may look a little awkward to the outside observer of the Hindu religion that as the individual progresses through the life stages, he or she becomes disconnected from the outside world. The goal of *Moksha* is sometime interpreted as liberation from this-worldly things, and when an individual enters into the stage of *saññyāsin*, he or she becomes disinterested towards the outer world.[26] However, on deeper reflection, this process is also designed to result in a reconnection to the whole.

Moksha as a purpose of life, however, is concerned with attaining the virtue of selflessness which is possible when one succeeds to the last stage of the fourfold stages of life and becomes a *saññyāsi* (renouncer). In this stage, man renounces all the attachments with the world. This is, however, not something akin to leaving the physical world but rather renouncing the attachments and physical involvement in the worldly affairs, as this may become a source of illusion. In the process of becoming *saññyāsi*, man gets re-assimilated to everything and merges

25 Radhakrishnan (n 22) 351.

26 Lance E. Nelson, 'The Dualism of Nondualism: AdvaitaVedānta and the Irrelevance of Nature' in Lance E. Nelson (ed), *Purifying the Earthly Body of God: Religion and Ecology in Hindu India* (D.K. Printworld 2000) 61–88.

again with nature, and there remains no difference between man and nature. According to Radhakrishnan, the goal of the Hindu way of life "is to change body into soul, to discover the world's potentiality for virtues, and derive happiness from it".[27] The purpose of the Hindu way of life, which every Hindu has to shape for himself or herself, is to acquire coordination and perfection of body, mind and soul, which in principle is possible by observing all the three disciplines – goals of life, social ordering and stages of life. To achieve the perfect coordination of body, mind and soul and attain final destiny of life, the individual is required to strive for "a progressive training, [and] a gradual enlarging of the natural life accompanied by an uplifting of all its motives".[28] The idea of self, according to the Hindu perspective of life, is, thus, it seems, despite all the focus on individual salvation, to be in perfect harmony with nature. The relationship between man and nature is not of dominance or subjugation but of harmony.

Given this relationship of the self with nature, it will be interesting to analyse how the Indian state has viewed its role and responsibility towards nature, since the state is, in Aristotelian words, an individual writ large. For this purpose, the chapter evaluates and analyses the classical Hindu texts to explore the nature of duties assigned to the head of the state or king with reference to environmental stewardship. Secondly, the chapter analyses the nature of the policies of colonial India on environmental protection. And lastly, it examines the various phases of political development in independent India and its appositeness for the state-environment relationship.

5. The Place of Nature in Classical Hindu Texts

Much historical evidence suggests that in the pre-Vedic age, the people of the Indus valley used to live on the banks of a river amidst dense forests and thus developed special relations with the powers of nature. They adorned and worshipped the various objects of nature like air, water, fire, earth and ether, which were later on classified as the five great elements of existence called *Pancabhutas*. The animals and trees were considered sacrosanct and were treated as an integral part of "higher order of being(s)". The place of divinity during this period was not in the sky, but rather gods and goddesses were very much a part of the natural world. Natural phenomena which could be directly observed, like day and night, sun, moon and stars, etc., and natural forces like rain, wind, fires, etc. were either elevated to the status of divinity or symbolised as expression of divine powers. The natural environment, thus, became an integral part of the spiritual as well as social life of Hindu people.[29]

In the Hindu religion, the whole cosmos is projected as a manifestation that reflects the human body. The various verses of the *Rigveda* on creation describe

27 Radhakrishnan (n 22) 351.
28 Ibid.
29 Bilimoria et al (n 17) 299.

the entire universe in various ways as a body of the Supreme being, and the Supreme being is projected both as the creator and the created. In a way, this is not different from Christian and other religious systems and forms of belief. Similarly, the *Purāṇaic* literature advocates "the unity of all sentient (*cetanā*) and non-sentient (*acetanā*) beings".[30] Hinduism transcends the human/non-human boundaries, however. "The *Viṣṇu Purāṇas* [for example] informs us that gods, men, animals, reptiles and birds are but the various forms of the creator *Brahmā*, since these have emerged from his limbs".[31] Accordingly, there is a close relation between nature and God. Life in Hinduism is, thus, considered sacrosanct, and therefore every living creature is viewed with respect. Only God has a sovereign right over the life of both human and non-human creatures, and therefore there is no scope of dominance and control of man over the life of other creatures without justification.[32]

The *Puranas* have strong ecological underpinnings, and these Hindu texts ask the people to observe high moral values and ecological ethics by leading a life of righteousness and playing a role of ecological stewardship. The *Purānic* texts like *Agni* and *Matsya Purāṇas* plead to the people to look after flora and fauna and consider all the creatures as their family members. The *Brahmavaivarta Purāṇas* and *Bhaviṣya Purāṇa* place higher value on trees than sons, since trees are more useful and helpful in difficult times.[33] The *Matsya Purāṇa*, for example instructs people to nourish trees since one tree has the value of ten sons.[34] The *purāṇic* literature is full of metaphors, narratives and stories that reflect the ecological sensibilities of the people. The *purāṇic* peoples as an act of atonement for anything done against nature undergo specific remorse or perform some rituals according to the nature of the wrong deed. Bilimoria and others argue, "The authors of the *Purāṇas* decried and prohibited the killing of animals either for game or for food as this would upset the eco-balance of nature", although these injunctions also clarify that the killing of animals was prevalent in India in the ancient time.[35] This was how the *purāṇic* peoples exhibited their ecological sensibilities and maintained an ecological balance.

6. Hindu Statecraft and Environmental Management

The role and responsibility of the king in the management of natural resources and protection of the environment has been explained in many classical Hindu

30 Ibid 304.
31 Ibid.
32 O.P. Dwivedi and B.N. Tiwari, *Environmental Crisis and Hindu Religion* (Gitanjali Publishing House 1987) 4–5.
33 Bilimoria et al (n 17) 305.
34 Vasudha Narayanan, '"One Tree is Equal to Ten Sons": Hindu Responses to the Problems of Ecology, Population, and Consumption' (1997) 65(2) *Journal of the American Academy of Religion* 291–332, 300.
35 Bilimoria et al (n 17) 308.

texts. Moreover, Indian history is full of examples that reflect the strong practices of ecological stewardship by rulers and the Indian state. Rulers like Ashoka, Akbar, Shivaji and Vansh Pradip of the Samar estate in Rajasthan were all nature lovers and took great interest in the conservation and protection of trees.

The question now arises, what encouraged these rulers to establish harmony with nature and plant trees, while performing the duties of statecraft? One of the pillar edicts of Ashoka in connection with his plantation and other environmental related works says, "I have done what I have done primarily in order that the people may follow the path of Dharma with faith and devotion".[36] McGee argues that it is difficult to discern the ecological aspect of these acts of kings from the classical Indian textual sources, but it is "clear that the earth was given in trust to a King for his protection and development".[37] Similarly, Romila Thapar as cited by McGee argued that Ashoka's actions were more informed by the sense of *Dharma* understood as social responsibility rather than economic interests.[38] In other words, there is recognition of economic necessities, but also an expectation that any natural resources should be used responsibly.

The underlying vision of this is that humans are not the absolute owners of this earth and its resources, but temporary beneficiaries of usufruct rights. While this is less clear-cut with regard to every single individual, in the classical Hindu texts, kingship has been described as a trust. Land and its resources are given to the king as a trust, and the king is responsible for its protection. If the king fails to protect land from degradation and natural resources from depletion, he has no moral right to retain the throne. McGee argued that the king is obliged and bound through the coronation oath, as it is mentioned in the *Yajurveda Saṃhitā* and *Śanti Parva* of the *Mahabharata*, to protect and preserve the land and its resources.[39]

Arthaśāstra, one of the most significant Indian classical treatises on statecraft (*rājādharma*), prescribes various codes of conduct for the king to deal with the questions of morality while running the affairs of the state. Although the primary focus of *Arthaśāstra* is legal and political administration of the state and acquisition of wealth as well as revenue generation, the text equally pays attention to the management and protection of forests, animals, water resources and other natural objects. There are specific injunctions for the king in the *Arthaśāstra* to ensure protection against over-exploitation of natural resources, pollution of water bodies, deforestation, over-tilling of arable land etc. The *Arthaśāstra* contains numerous provisions of punishments for those who violate the norms of animal welfare and disturb the ecological balance. These injunctions reflect the

36 N.A. Nikam and Richard Mckeon (eds, trs), *The Edicts of Asoka* (University of Chicago Press 1978) 65.

37 Mary McGee, 'State Responsibility for Environmental Management: Perspective from Hindu Texts on Polity' in Christopher Key Chapple and Mary Evelyn Tucker (eds), *Hinduism and Ecology: The Intersection of Earth, Sky, and Water* (OUP 2000) 59–100, 61.

38 Ibid 61.

39 Ibid 62.

strong ecological sensibilities of the author as well as the people of that period. Bilimoria and others argue:

> The *Arthaśāstra* shows a remarkable understanding . . ., [and] deep knowledge of the diversity and fauna, plant varieties, animals life, and naturally occurring minerals etc., as well as the appropriate "sciences"(metallurgy, animal husbandry, game-keeping, irrigation, public works, etc.). In all, the first principle seemed to be a more tolerant attitude towards the "dark" regions and threatening inhabitants of the forest, before any official moves are made to reach out for the beneficial resources. In other words, Kauṭilya underscored respect for the nature.[40]

Kauṭilya's *Arthaśāstra* in the very first verse suggests and prescribes that the accrual and maintenance of the earth and its resources is the prime concern of the king.[41] The protection and maintenance of natural resources in the *Arthaśāstra* is also linked as a source of revenue generation, defence and leisure. *Arthaśāstra*, though it recommends the management and conservation of the earth, clearly suggests a complete government control over land and its natural resources with the purpose of generating revenue for the state. Whether this goes as far as claiming, in a modern context, the privileges of "eminent domain", the absolute ownership of the land of the nation would be a pertinent research question. The ruler certainly has an obligation to secure responsible use of the land and its resources to protect the public interest, not to fulfil his own personal greed. The topics like agricultural administration, forest conservation, disaster management and environmental policies have been dealt with in considerable detail in the *Arthaśāstra*, and all these subjects come under the direct purview of the king. Kautilya suggests that it is the responsibility of the king to formulate and implement specific laws that ensure proper administration of these subjects.[42] The *Arthaśāstra* prescribes fines of varying severity depending on the nature of anti-environmental activities like polluting water with human and animal defecation and urination, disposing of dust on the roads, cutting trees indiscriminately, destroying forests and groves and disposing of the bodies of dead animals in open spaces. It is the responsibility of the king to levy fines to maintain the integrity of the environment.

Gadgil and Guha point out that *Arthaśāstra* served as a good source of environmental management in India during the time of Mauryans, Kushanas, Chalukyas and other empires, and intriguingly, "a new form of territorial control

40 Bilimoria et al (n 17) 310.

41 R.P. Kangle, *The Kauṭiliya Arthaśāstra: An English Translation with Critical and Explanatory Notes* (University of Bombay Press 1972); Patrick Olivelle, *King, Governance, and Law in Ancient India: Kauṭilya's Arthaśāstra* (OUP 2013).

42 George Alfred James, 'Environment and Environmental Philosophy of India' in Baird J. Callicott and James McRae (eds), *Environmental Philosophy in Asian Traditions of Thoughts* (State University of New York Press 2014) 3–24.

over living resources – control by the state" emerged with the carving out of hunting preserves and elephant forests.[43] Although Laurie Patton warns against the over-romanticising of Hindu attitude towards nature, particularly in the reading of classical Hindu texts,[44] Gadgil maintains that the exploitation of land and its resources were based on ecological prudence in the South Asian subcontinent during ancient times. This is quite evident in the *Arthaśāstra*, which issues specific injunctions to the king and his ministers to ensure equilibrium between exploitation and conservation through various conservation methods like protection of elephant forests and maintenance of hunting reserves.[45] McGee argues, "The duties of the King as articulated in the *Arthaśāstra* and other *rājadharma* resources involve the domination and exploitation of natural resources".[46] But at the same time we find injunctions and proclamations for the protection of these resources and the king and his superintendents are entrusted with the duty to protect these resources. She further argues that the provision of fines in the *Arthaśāstra* does provide an insight into the prevailing concerns for public health and environment protection and the responsibility of the state and king towards it. She argues that though Kautilya's *Arthaśāstra* is mainly concerned with the economic value of natural resources rather than religious value, the fine prescribed for injuring trees and other natural objects of religious importance is higher.[47] This implies that the *Arthaśāstra* does concede the religious value of earth and its resources and the king is bound by his *Dharma* to protect the earth and its resources.

The classical Hindu texts such as *Manu Smriti*, *Santi Parva* of *Manābharata* and *Yajnavalkay Smriti* provide more philosophical insights into the Hindu religion and its relation with nature. In the *Manu Smriti*, for example, it is said that the king is under *Dharmic* duty to protect and guard the roadside watering places, sacred tress and wild places.[48] The water bodies were considered highly precious with religious importance, and "if a man destroys a pond he should be physically punished by drowning or by simple killing; but even if (the criminal) repairs it, he should pay the highest level of fine".[49] The king in the *Manu smriti* is also advised to award corporal punishment to a man who destroys seedlings or sells something else in the name of seeds.[50] For the self-penance of various wrong

43 Madhav Gadgil and Ramachandra Guha, *This Fissured Land: An Ecological History of India* (OUP 2012) 75.

44 Laurie Patton, 'Nature Romanticism and Sacrifice in Rgvedic Interpretation' in Christopher Key Chapple and Mary Evelyn Tucker (eds), *Hinduism and Ecology: The Intersection of Earth, Sky, and Water* (OUP 2000), 39–58.

45 Madhav Gadgil, 'Towards an Ecological History of India' (1985) 20(45/47) *Economic and Political Weekly* 1909–1918, 1913.

46 McGee (n 37) 71.

47 Ibid 72.

48 Wendy Doniger and Brian K. Smith (trs), *The Laws of Manu* (Penguin 1991) Ch 9, verses 264–266.

49 Ibid., verse 279.

50 Ibid., verse 277–278.

deeds against nature, *Manu Smriti* advises different kinds of vows to remedy the evil and ritually restore order.

In the *Vishnu Smriti* also, the same kind of injunctions for environment protection can be found. The text prescribes different types of punishments, amercement and penances for those who kill animals, pollute the environment and cut trees. The *Vishnu Smriti* prescribes the highest penalties for those who cut fruit-yielding trees. *The Vishnu Smriti* while enumerating the duties of the king points out that it is the duty of the king to protect flora and fauna and "[h]e must not take delight in hunting".[51]

The question now arises, what binds the king to perform all such duties? The *dharma* of the king is an answer to this question. The notion and concept of *rājadharma* requires a more detailed exploration here to understand how the Hindu king is morally bound to protect the environment.

7. *Dharma* of the King and the Ecological Crisis

The *rājadharma* (Menski, 2009) or the *dharma* of the king is linked with the concept of *dharma*, which has been defined in various situation-specific ways. In fact, the term *dharma* cannot be translated into English language as there is no direct semantic equivalent that conveys the full meaning of the term. The concept of *dharma*, as explained earlier, "has been variously translated as 'duty', 'religion', 'justice', 'law', 'ethics', 'religious merit', 'principle' and 'right' ".[52] It has also been defined as the highest duty and virtue that entails non-injury. Precisely, the concept of *dharma* can be defined as the performance of appropriate rituals and observing high moral principles by any individual.

The *Dharmaśāstras* mandate the individual to lead a life of high moral values according to the four life stages. The Hindu notion of liberation (*moksha*) is a much debated notion in the philosophy of religion. The attitude of non-attachment towards the world is criticised as anti-nature. This notion, however, needs to be explained by juxtaposing it with the notion of *dharma*. The *Dharmaśāstrsas* forbid the use of fire and cooked food for the renouncer since these are symbols of culture while raw food is a symbol of nature. This shows that renouncers are not required to alienate themselves completely from nature; rather they are to renounce the culture, social symbols and other institutions of human society to prepare for themselves becoming part of nature again on death. The idea of renunciation in Hinduism reflects that the ultimate goal of individual life is the merger of the self in the purest possible form with nature by removing any elements of ego from human life. The removal of ego is central to the idea of renunciation, because ego is the source of possessiveness and develops a sense of superiority among human beings over the rest of the species and also over other humans.

51 Julius Jolly, *The Institutes of Vishnu: Sacred Books of East* (Vol. 7, Clarendon Press 1880) 18.
52 Gavin Flood, *An Introduction to Hinduism* (CUP 1996) 52.

Another aspect of *mokhsa* as highlighted by Flood points out that social obligations are more important than liberation, because the *Dharmaśāstras* mandate to fulfil all social responsibilities by the individual before moving on to the final life stage of total renunciation. According to *Dharmaśāstras*, all those who fail to clear their debt which they owe to their teachers, gods and ancestors during their life time go to hell.[53] This shows that social responsibilities and moral obligations are more superior to the goal of individual liberation. In the traditional Hindu political setup, the king was entrusted with the responsibility to maintain social order and establish *Dharma* through deterrent punishment through the means of *danda* (stick). In fact, *danda* is the means through which *Dharma* is established, and "[i]t keeps the whole world in order, governs all created beings, protects them while they sleep and without it there would be no order in society".[54] The *Dharmaśāstra* literature explains that while a *Brahman* is concerned with achieving transcendental goals, the king is responsible for fulfilling the temporal duties with the instrument of *danda*. Since the legitimate use of *danda* lies with the king, it is his duty to protect and govern all that is created within his jurisdiction. In this sense, the king is responsible to protect the environment and manage all the natural resources according to the notion of *Dharma*.

8. British Colonialism and the Changing Value of Nature

With the arrival of British colonialism, the position and power of Hindu kings underwent a drastic change, and their ability to use sovereign power was also compromised. The British Raj introduced a new ethic of public morality which largely conformed to the ideas of rationalism of European enlightenment. These meta-ethics undermined the role of religion in public morality. The notion of *Dharma* which had so far guided the Hindu kings in matters of governance in India since the ancient times did not fit well with the colonial objectives in the changed political milieu. Therefore, the notion of *Dharma* as guiding metaphor for governance remained eluded in all those geographical regions of South Asia which came under the direct control of Britain. The alien administration perceived nature and its resources in those colonised areas only from the utilitarian perspective which was totally devoid of any religiosity that was peculiar to the Asian culture, and was focused on a desire to extract maximum benefits from the colonies.

With the increasing span of British colonialism, the political landscape of South Asia underwent a huge change. The traditional authority of the Indian king was challenged by the colonial forces. During this period, nature and its resources

53 Ibid 64.
54 Ibid 71.

gained high economic value, but considerably lost its religious and ecological connotations even among South Asian rulers. Fisher argues,

> Over this period, European political and economic power increasingly began to affect the Indian environment, altering markets and commodity flows. . . . By the mid-eighteenth century, EIC [East India Company] officers and officials began to intervene more decisively in Indian politics, with increasingly powerful effects on the environment.[55]

Most of the governor-generals of EIC were largely unaware of India's environment, and their posting in India was mostly determined by the politics of competing interests back in the British Parliament. Fisher argues that since these officers were trained in Britain and spent a major part of their life in England, they had considerable impact of the ideology of individualism and private ownership rights. The "Permanent Settlement" of govern-general Cornwallis, for example, "recognized specific Indians as landowners with private property rights over their estates, including the land, riverfronts, enclosed bodies of water, fish, animals, plants, and minerals".[56] This eroded the customary rights of tenancy in India. The benefits of such measures were subjected to debate even by the later British officials, but some argued that it helped the company to ensure fixed revenue generation.

The constructed orientalist image of the Indian king as despot with a sovereign right over everything within his jurisdiction was replicated by the EIC with complete control over the entire flora and fauna unless specific ownership rights of individuals existed which, too, were often denied. This virtually made the EIC a proprietor of everything that was under its jurisdiction. The proprietorship of EIC, nevertheless, should be contrasted with the ownership right of the Indian king. The *Dharmaśāstras* explain that the sovereign right of the king over all the flora and fauna in his jurisdiction is governed by the notion of *Dharma*, whereas the sovereign claim of EIC was purely centred on the materialistic consideration of commercial resource extraction. The EIC and subsequently the direct British Raj created a new culture of total appropriation of all the natural resources by the state, which was resisted by the different stakeholders particularly by the locals and forest-dwellers.

9. Nature as a Resource for Development in the Post-Independence Era

In the post-independence era, the centralised tendencies of the British Raj left a lasting impact on the Constitution makers of India. India emerged as a large

55 Michael H. Fisher, *An Environmental History of India: From Earliest Times to the Twenty-First Century* (CUP2018) 120.
56 Ibid 124.

federation with a very strong central government and declared herself as sovereign, socialist, secular, democratic republic, though the terms "socialist" and "secular" were added in the preamble to the Constitution later by the Forty-Second Amendment of 1976.[57] The central government, being the most powerful organ of the state, assumed the responsibility of environmental stewardship and declared the state as the custodian of nature. This role and position of the central government was akin to the classical role and position of the Hindu king. The fundamental difference in the working of the central government from that of the Hindu king was, however, the usage of religion in deciding matters of public affairs. The Hindu notion of *Dharma*, the primary source of which was religion, did not find a place in the official lexicon of the Indian government; rather, as in colonial times, profit maximisation and developmentalism became the buzz words.

In fact, in the initial years of India's independence, environmental issues were not a subject matter of serious discussion for the Indian government at all. In the initial phase of post-independence, India witnessed a rigorous adoption of the Nehruvian model of development, a pattern that was basically characterised by rapid industrialisation and foreign investment in all those sectors, which could accelerate the economic growth rate of the country. In the near-total absence of any critical voice which could question or challenge the rationale behind such ostensibly developmental endeavours, the developmental agenda was carried out fiercely and relentlessly, without any consideration for its impact on the environment. The Indian policy makers did not take into consideration ecological concerns while they framed policies relating to industry, nuclear energy, hydroelectric energy, forest, agriculture and industry.

The deliberations on the state of India's environment in the post-independence era started only in the aftermath of the Stockholm Conference of 1972 on Human Environment, which greatly influenced Mrs. Indira Gandhi, the then–prime minister of India. She sort of remembered her Indian heritage while listening to the worrying accounts of the global rape of nature. It seems to have left a huge impact on this particular leader, but also her subsequent policies. The post-Stockholm era saw the beginning of the outlining of India's policy on environmental issues at two levels – the constitutional level and pragmatic level.

At the constitutional level, the post-Stockholm era saw the inclusion of various new legislations like Article 48(a) to the Part IV and 51(g) to the newly added Part IV A of the Indian constitution.[58] Two major inferences relating to the state's changed attitude towards the environment can be drawn by the inclusion of these constitutional provisions. One is that all the major components of

57 The Constitution (Forty-Second Amendment Act), Legislative Department, Ministry of Law and Justice, Government of India https://legislative.gov.in/constitution-forty-second-amendment-act-1976.

58 Constitution of India, National Portal of India, Government of India www.india.gov.in/my-government/constitution-india/constitution-india-full-text.

the environment – land, water, air etc. – came under the authority of the central government, which now proceeded to establish specific protective legislations. Two, inclusion of terminologies likes "protect and improve" in the constitutional provision laid the responsibility of protecting and preserving environment both on the government and the citizens alike. Since originally Directive Principles of State Policy were not justiciable in a court of law, it principally means that the safety and management of environment is a moral duty of both the government and the citizens at large. In a way, government knowingly or unknowingly tried to invoke among its citizens the value of social and moral order, or what McGee calls "the fundamental notion of Dharma",[59] most obviously in Article 51-A, the "Fundamental duties of the citizen".

While the post-Stockholm developments in the 1970s did witness a spurt in the number of environmental legislations in India,[60] at the pragmatic level economic development was prioritised before any other issue, including the environment. Such pragmatism has wittingly or unwittingly resulted in reaffirming and entrenching the state monopoly over the use or abuse of nature. Under such a framework, the state has been viewed as a custodian of natural resources, which could be used by its government to accomplish the developmental goals. This firmly established the sovereign right of the state over natural resources, a right which could not be impaired by any internal or external agency under any circumstances. The adoption of such a stance by the Indian government has, however, further alienated many local people from their legitimate claims and natural rights over resources like land and forest use. This imported approach was termed as a "managerial approach".[61] According to this approach, the state can determine its priorities given to the environment over other issues. Indira Gandhi was the most vocal exponent of this approach. It was in her address to the 1972 UN Conference on Human Environment (UNCHE) in Stockholm that she had emphatically articulated India's priorities for development over environmental issues. She held that "development is not the cause of most of these problems but the cure . . . [and that] planned development was an instrument to improve the quality of life".[62]

Although during the 1980s the Supreme Court of India prioritised environment over development in a series of environmental cases,[63] the political development in the late 1980s and early 1990s were not encouraging, and as many as four governments were formed in a very short span of four years. The economic failure and the balance of payment crisis forced India to adopt a set of New Economic Policies (NEP) which were driven by market forces and were least concerned with environmental issues. The Government of India had to adopt a Structural Adjustment Programme (SAP) to improve its fiscal health as advocated

59 McGee (n 37) 83.

60 P. Leelakrishnan, *Environmental Law in India* (2nd edn, LexisNexis Butterworths 2005).

61 Sumi Krishna, *Environmental Politics: People's Lives and Developmental Choices* (Sage 1996).

62 Indira Gandhi, *The Years of Endeavour: Selected Speeches of Indira Gandhi August 1969 – August 1972* (Publication Division Government of India 1975, rpt. 1983).

63 *M. C. Mehta v. Union of India* (1988) AIR 1115, 1988 SCR (2) 530.

by the Bretton Woods institutions. Explaining this state of affair, Sudershan observes, "The environment is now caught in a pincer grip of newly unleashed forces of prosperity, on the one hand and persisting problems of poverty, on the other".[64] The basic thrust of the NEP was to earn foreign exchange by enhancing the export opportunities particularly in the areas of fisheries and aquaculture, floriculture, cash cropping and mining with little concern for environmental conservation or protection. Critiquing the official Indian policy, Kothari retorts, "forex speaks much more powerfully in its current mindset then does environmental sustainability and human rights".[65] The New Economic Policies received a further boost with new expansion plans of integrating the Indian economy with the global market.

10. Ethics and Environment in the Age of Climate Change in India

The post-colonial approach of the Indian state towards the environment was totally devoid of Hindu ethics, as it was a deliberately instrumental and secular set of policies. The post-1990 period further strengthened this approach of the Indian state. It was, however, in the latter half of the first decade of the twenty-first century that the Government of India realised that environmental issues, particularly climate change, are a serious problem that requires immediate attention. The then–Congress prime minister of India, Manmohan Singh, in his address to the Delhi Sustainable Development Summit acknowledged that there is an urgent need to "move away from production and consumption pattern which are carbon intensive and energy-intensive".[66] This underlined the need to make a shift in the lifestyle and to follow a path of low carbon footprints. Lifestyle changes are primarily based on moral choices of the individual, and morality is something which is governed by ethical values of a given community, and not a matter for state regulation.

In the Indian context, these kinds of ethics are not a secular category; rather, they are rooted in the religion. The statement of Manmohan Singh, thus, is more of a moral appeal to the conscience of the individual rather than a plain secular statement, as before. The renewed approach of the Indian state to address environmental problems, particularly climate change, is more pragmatic, since it tacitly acknowledges the importance of Hindu ethics in environmental policy formulations.

A further flip to this line of approach to environmental problems came after 2014 from Prime Minister Narendra Modi, who as leader of the BJP (Bharatiya

64 R. Sudarshan, 'Liberalism and Environment' *The Hindu* (19 April 1996).

65 Ashish Kothari, 'Environment and Economic Policies' (1995) 30(17) *Economic and Political Weekly* 924.

66 Manmohan Singh, 'PM's address at the 11th Delhi Sustainable Development Summit' (2011), https://archivepmo.nic.in/drmanmohansingh/speech-details.php?nodeid=979.

Janata Party), the so-called Hindu nationalist dispensation, began to advocate the need to use Indian cultural ethos to revive and popularise the age-old Indian ideas of harmonious relations with nature.[67] Invocation of Indic cultural norms and religious symbols by the government to address climate change signifies the renewed interests in the ecological role of Hindu religion and eagerness to tap huge market of alternative green technologies which may conform to the values of Hindu religiosity. The government of India which symbolically represents the classical Hindu king in contemporary times is trying to ensure through invocation of Hindu ethics, it seems, what Kautilya's *Arthaśāstra* recommends to the king, namely to protect and preserve the *Artha* which is both earth (land, water, air, natural resources and natural order) and wealth (economic and political order).

11. Conclusions

What transpires out of the foregoing discussion is that Hinduism has strong ecological underpinnings that have now been re-vitalised and need to be made applicable to the ecological problems of twenty-first century. Ethics for the care of nature is grounded in the Hindu religion. The Indian ecological ethic is not a purely secular category, since divinity is perceived as embedded in nature. These ecological ethics had guided the Hindu devotee and Indian statecraft alike through centuries. The colonial and post-colonial Indian state, however, subscribed to the imported Western ethics for economic development, which created a strong impersonal image of the Indian state. The colonial and post-colonial Indian state with strong centralised tendencies and central planning asserted its power and took on new roles as the custodian of nature and all the natural resources within its jurisdiction. These imported ethics were subscribed to by many mainstream modern Hindus who advocated that post-colonial India could progress only through large-scale mega-development projects. This imitated and unmindful development led to the ecological crisis since the parameters to measure the development were just economic growth in terms of GDP. The post-independence development was devoid of basic Hindu ethics, which preaches that the self is not atomised and egoistic, but rather interconnected with the whole and the real development is one that ensures the wellbeing of the whole. In the later part of the first decade of the twenty-first century, the Indian state recalibrated its approach towards the issue of climate change, signifying also the revival of Hindu ecological ethics in the mainstream politics, although largely rhetorically. The revival of Hindu ethics in the Indian discourse of climate change is, nonetheless, informed by the green model of economic development that makes good sense for great business opportunities in green technologies.

67 Rajnish Saryal, 'Climate Change Policy of India: Modifying the Environment' (2018) 38(1) *South Asia Research* 1–19.

Bibliography

Bilimoria P., Prabhu J. and Sharma R. (eds), *Indian Ethics: Classical Traditions and Contemporary Challenges* (Vol. 1, Ashgate Publishing 2007).

Brian K.S., 'Questioning Authority: Constructions and Deconstructions of Hinduism' (1998) 2(3) *International Journal of Hindu Studies* 313–339.

Dalmia V. and Stietencron H. (eds), *Representing Hinduism: The Construction of Religious Traditions and National Identity* (Sage 1995).

Doniger W. and Smith B.K. (trs), *The Laws of Manu* (Penguin 1991).

Duara P., 'The New Politics of Hinduism' (1976) 15(3) *The Wilson Quarterly* 42–50.

Dwivedi O.P. and Tiwari B.N., *Environmental Crisis and Hindu Religion* (Gitanjali Publishing House 1987).

Ferro-Luzzi G.E., 'The Polythetic-Prototype Approach to Hinduism' in Günther-Dietz Sontheimer and Hermann Kulke (eds), *Hinduism Reconsidered* (2nd edn, Manohar 2001) 295–304.

Fisher M.H., *An Environmental History of India: From Earliest Times to the Twenty-First Century* (Cambridge Press 2018).

Flood G., *An Introduction to Hinduism* (CUP 1996).

Gadgil M., 'Towards an Ecological History of India' (1985) 20(45/47) *Economic and Political Weekly* 1909–1918.

Gadgil M. and Guha R., *This Fissured Land: An Ecological History of India* (OUP 2012).

Hawley J.S., 'Naming Hinduism' (1991) 15(3) *The Wilson Quarterly* 20–34.

Hiltebeitel A., 'Of Camphor and Coconuts' (1991) 15(3) *The Wilson quarterly* 26–28.

James G.A., 'Environment and Environmental Philosophy of India' in Baird J. Callicott and James McRae (eds), *Environmental Philosophy in Asian Traditions of Thoughts* (State University of New York Press 2014) 3–24.

Julius Jolly (trs), *The Institutes of Vishnu: Sacred Books of East* (Vol. 7, Clarendon Press 1880).

Kangle R.P., *The Kauṭiliya Arthaśāstra: An English Translation with Critical and Explanatory Notes* (University of Bombay Press 1972).

Kothari A., 'Environment and Economic Policies' (1995) 30(17) *Economic and Political Weekly.*

Krishna S., *Environmental Politics: People's Lives and Developmental Choices* (Sage 1996).

Larson G.J., *India's Agony Over Religion* (State University of New York Press 1995).

Leelakrishnan P., *Environmental Law in India* (2nd edn, LexisNexis Butterworths 2005).

Leopold A., *A Sand County Almanac: And Sketches Here and There* (OUP 1949).

McGee M., 'State Responsibility for Environmental Management: Perspective from Hindu Texts on Polity' in Christopher Key Chapple and Mary Evelyn Tucker (eds), *Hinduism and Ecology: The Intersection of Earth, Sky, and Water* (OUP 2000) 59–100.

Mesnki W., *Hindu Law: Beyond Tradition and Modernity* (OUP 2003).

Mesnki W., *Comparative Law in a Global Context: The Legal Systems of Asia and Africa* (CUP 2006).

Narayanan Vasudha, '"One Tree is Equal to Ten Sons": Hindu Responses to the Problems of Ecology, Population, and Consumption' (1997) 65(2) *Journal of the American Academy of Religion* 291–332.

Nelson L.E., 'The Dualism of Nondualism: Advaita Vedānta and the Irrelevance of Nature' in Lance E. Nelson (ed), *Purifying the Earthly Body of God: Religion and Ecology in Hindu India* (D.K. Printworld 2000) 61–88.
Nikam N.A. and McKeon R. (eds, trs), *The Edicts of Asoka* (University of Chicago Press 1978) 65.
Olivelle P., *King, Governance, and Law in Ancient India: Kauṭilya's Arthaśāstra* (OUP 2013).
Patton L., 'Nature Romanticism and Sacrifice in Rgvedic Interpretation' in Christopher Key Chapple and Mary Evelyn Tucker (eds), *Hinduism and Ecology: The Intersection of Earth, Sky, and Water* (OUP 2000) 39–58.
Radhakrishnan S., *Eastern Religions and Western Thought* (Galaxy Books 1959).
Rankin A., *Jainism and Environmental Philosophy: Karma and the Web of Life* (Routledge 2018).
Saryal R., 'Climate Change Policy of India: Modifying the Environment' (2018) 38(1) *South Asia Research* 1–19.
Singh A., *Planet, Plants and Animals: Ecological Paradigms in Buddhism* (Primus Books 2019).
Singh M., 'PM's Address at the 11th Delhi Sustainable Development Summit' (2011), https://archivepmo.nic.in/drmanmohansingh/speech-details.php?nodeid=979.
Sontheimer G.D. and Kulke H. (eds), *Hinduism Reconsidered* (Manohar 1989).
Sudarshan R., 'Liberalism and Environment' *The Hindu* (19 April 1996).
Thapar R., 'Imagined Religious Communities? Ancient History and the Modern Search for a Hindu Identity' (1989) 23(2) *Modern Asian Studies* 209–231.
Weber M., *The Religion of India: The Sociology of Hinduism and Buddhism* (Hans H. Gerth and Don Martindale trs, The Free Press 1958).
White Jr. L., 'Historical Roots of Ecological Crisis' (1967) 155(3767) *Science* 1203–1207.

3 Ubuntu as a Normative Value in the New Environmental World Order

Kyriaki Topidi

1. Introduction

Ubuntu represents the African concept of *humanness*. It reflects the importance of community, solidarity and sharing. It can be found in a number of African societies such as South Africa, Kenya, Nigeria or Zimbabwe.[1] It embodies an understanding of what it means to 'live well' in an African context, and while it is largely untranslatable, it is founded on a relational perspective whereby individuals ought to value each other. In terms of governance, the concept has begun to be considered more seriously as an approach that privileges community rather than individualism in a variety of sectors, including environment management. Following this trend, it will be argued that it offers a viable approach to contemporary environmental governance.

The proposed chapter will begin with the necessary conceptual overview of the notion of Ubuntu, as a worldview rooted in African societies. This overview will cover the lack of a universally agreed definition of the term and the issue of its difficult transposition in Western epistemological thought. It will also explore the main elements of Ubuntu (i.e. survival, solidarity, compassion, respect and dignity).

The following part of the contribution will attempt to answer two questions: The first one will focus on the conceptual uniqueness of the concept, especially as connected to the broader ethical/moral way (or duty) to be in relation to others. The second one will look at whether Ubuntu is indeed applicable only within the African context. The analysis will then justify why Ubuntu can be relevant when connecting the local with the universal in legal and policy terms. The final section of this part will engage with the criticisms raised against Ubuntu, namely its vagueness, its collectivist dimension and its limited 'exportability' due to its perceived anachronistic essence. The analysis will counter-propose a flexible interpretation of the concept where the connection of identity with solidarity becomes

1 Nimi Hoffmann and Thaddeus Metz, 'What Can the Capabilities Approach Learn from an Ubuntu Ethic? A Relational Approach to Development Theory' (2017) 97 *World Development* 153 (14 on line version) https://core.ac.uk/reader/227453720.

DOI: 10.4324/9781003175308-5

adjustable to contemporary conditions. The analysis will additionally consider the colonial and apartheid historical trajectories of the concept and how these have contributed to the shaping of the political aspects of Ubuntu.

Turning to the relevance of the concept for environmental governance purposes, Ubuntu in its current state is threatened by anthropocentric processes connected to the advent of colonialization and globalization. This process is most evident in connection to environment management. Along a line of emerging scholarship, the last part of the chapter will argue that humans and the environment are an inseparable entity that must co-exist in a respectful and non-exploitative manner. In that sense, Ubuntu will be construed in the light of the pre-colonial (but still relevant) approaches of African indigenous knowledge systems towards environmental conservation as part of African collective identity and morality. Ultimately, it will be concluded that the present environmental crisis can be treated as a religious and cultural problem connected to the neglect of Ubuntu and the horizontal relationships among all members of the universe. As such, sustainable utilization, management and conservation of natural resources become religious, cultural and moral issues to which the eco-wisdom of Ubuntu offers a valuable approach useful beyond the confines of the African continent.

2. A Conceptual Overview of Ubuntu

There is a tradition in Southern Africa called *ukusisa*. It involves the lending of a cow and a bull by a family in a rural village to a newly married couple. The intention is that the newlyweds would keep the offspring but would return the cow and bull to their original owners. In this way, the basis for a mutually beneficial transaction would be laid on the basis of kindness and reciprocity but with an eye to the sharing of wealth towards community building.[2] This tradition is part and parcel of African *cultural commons* that value positive communal co-existence and respect towards nature and its resources.[3] These commons combine cultural patterns with nature and can be defined as

> life sustaining or life enhancing resources and services that have not been divided up and assigned a monetary value in the global economy but instead are shared according to evolving arrangements and agreements among members of a community or group.[4]

2 Description of the practice borrowed from Barbara Nussbaum, 'African Culture and Ubuntu: Reflections of a South African in America' (2003) 17(1) *Perspectives* 1, 3.

3 Overson Shumba, 'Commons Thinking, Ecological Intelligence and the Ethical and Moral Framework of Ubuntu: An imperative for sustainable development' (2011) 3(3) *Journal of Medial and Communication Studies* 84.

4 Definition belonging to J. Kenrick, 'Commons Thinking' in Arran Stibbe (ed), *The Handbook of Sustainability Literacy: Skills for a Changing World* (Green Books Ltd 2009) 51.

In this relatively broad cultural commons' context, *ukusisa* can be construed as an expression of Ubuntu. The latter stands apart as a foundation of moral theory, a public policy principle, a normative value in education or in business activities, as a conflict resolution tool, a constitutional value and ultimately also a religious/cultural conviction with wider resonance. Its ingenuity for Western audiences is to be found in the recognition that healthy and prosperous communities cannot thrive unless all of their members lead a dignified existence.[5]

In more scholarly terms, African values constitute an emerging field of studies in the Western context to (re)-discover ethnical modes of existence in today's world. Central to this trend is the concept of Ubuntu as a social philosophy deeply rooted in African culture. It can be essentially approached as "the capacity . . . to express compassion, reciprocity, dignity, harmony and humanity in the interests of building and maintaining community with justice and mutual caring."[6] The core dimension of Ubuntu focuses on the interdependence of human beings by stating that "a person is a person because of others" (*umuntu ngumuntu ngabantu*). From such a view to the world follows that the concept is normatively designed to cultivate trusting, caring and sustainable communities. Within this framework, harmony and the seeking of consensus become important tools but also aims,[7] especially since they generally form an integral part of African culture.

At the same time, Ubuntu should be placed within a broader values' frame: African culture contains important elements of dialogue between humans and other natural beings (e.g. plants, birds, animals[8]) that must co-exist in harmony and on the basis of mutual understanding. The ontological dimension of Ubuntu therefore promotes an ideal of individual development conceived through contact and interaction with others,[9] but without being necessarily synonymous with oppressive communalism.[10]

Translated as 'humanity' or 'humanness',[11] Ubuntu is not philosophically and religiously entirely disconnected from the Western theological concepts such as the instruction to love one's neighbour or the concept of *imago Dei*.[12] At the same time, it does not overlap with the Christian notion of forgiveness, as it relies

5 Tim Murithi, 'A Local Response to the Global Human Rights Standards: The Ubuntu Perspective on Human Dignity' (2007) 5(3) *Globalization, Societies and Education* 277.

6 Nussbaum (n 2) 2. Another possible definition of ubuntu (among the many) can be 'an African value system that is characterized by caring, sharing, compassion, communocracy and related predispositions' [Cf. Reuel J. Khoza, *Let Africa Lead* (Vezubuntu 2005) 269].

7 Nussbaum (n 2) 4.

8 Ibid 8.

9 Thembisile Molose, Geoff Goldman and Peta Thomas, 'Towards a Collective-Values Framework of Ubuntu: Implications for Workplace Commitment' (2018) 6(3) *Entrepreneurial Business and Economics Review* 193, 196.

10 Ibid 196.

11 John L.B. Eliastam, 'Exploring Ubuntu Discourse in South Africa: Loss, Liminality and Hope' (2015) 36(2) *Verbum et Ecclesia* 1, 2.

12 Ibid 2.

on a dual approach based on reparation and reconciliation to resolve conflicts.[13] More concretely, five values of Ubuntu are deemed central to its expression and practice: survival, compassion, spirit of solidarity, respect and dignity.[14] These values operate in synergy creating a 'whole' that is larger than the sum of its 'parts'.[15] Some of the implications deriving from these five principles, which are particularly relevant for the present discussion, are valuing the worth of others (respect/dignity); a shared will to survive and focus (survival); the understanding that difficult goals are achieved collectively (solidarity); reaching out to others to form relationships (compassion).[16] And yet, Ubuntu should not be confused with Marxist collectivism, insofar as "the good of the individual is not subordinated to that of the group".[17]

Ubuntu, as indigenous knowledge, contains consideration about the physical environment, especially as it relates to the social environment of humans and with regards also to the interaction between the two. This is because Ubuntu is a cosmological notion (among numerous other indigenous cosmologies) that is based on the ways that the spiritual and the material aspects of our existence are connected.

More broadly, the power of Ubuntu lies in conditioning social contexts towards greater social justice and equality. As such, it fosters high ethical standards that operate towards solidarity. It reflects a humanistic orientation that claims "I am, because we are; and since we are, therefore I am."[18] It places its primary source of normativity in the relationship with and between people and not on the individual. Its conception of human freedom is, by consequence, one that frames it as a form of interdependence with others and not necessarily as a negative freedom from the interference of others.[19] For these qualities, it has been elevated to a constitutional value in particular in the case of South Africa,[20] which aims to protect humanity's common goals and is closely associated with human dignity. Accepting that human interests are complementary, diversity escapes its framing as a source of conflict. It becomes rather a form of 'normative mutualism' where individual interests are not by definition mutually exclusive.[21]

13 Hoffmann and Metz (n 1) 19 [online version].

14 Also known as the 'Collective-Fingers Theory' [Cf. Lovemore Mbigi and Jenny Maree, *The Spirit of African Transformation Management* (Sigma 1995)].

15 Mzamo P. Mangaliso, 'Building a Competitive Advantage from Ubuntu: Management Lessons from South Africa' (2001) 15(5) *The Academy of Management Executive* 23.

16 A fuller list of implications can be found in Molose et al. (n 9) 199.

17 David W. Lutz, 'African Ubuntu Philosophy and Philosophy of Global Management' (2009) 84 *J Bus Ethics* 313, https://doi.org/10.1007/s10551-009-0204-z.

18 John S. Mbiti, *African Traditional Religions and Philosophy* (Doubleday 1971).

19 Hoffmann and Metz (n 1) 21 [online version].

20 Yvonne Mokgoro, 'Ubuntu and the Law in South Africa' (1998) 1(1) *Potchefstroom Electronic Journal* 15.

21 Leyla Tavernaro-Haidarian, 'Evolving "Discoarse" into Discourse: Ubuntu as a Normative Basis' (2018) 44(1) *Communicatio* 1, 16, DOI: 10.1080/02500167.2017.1415945.

3. Ubuntu and Its Critique

Ubuntu has triggered two streams of opposing arguments, when being considered as a defining African social value: it is either treated as offering significant possibilities for the transformation of society in Africa, or it is considered as a contradicting and largely outdated concept.[22] A critical appraisal of Ubuntu usually includes its vagueness. Metz, in his work, has attempted to add more precision to the concept by narrowing it down to an interpretation whereby "an action is right just insofar as it produces harmony and reduces discord; an act is wrong to the extent that it fails to develop community."[23] In other words, self-realization happens through interpersonal relationships, especially as it focuses on non-material goods.[24] In another well-known critique, Enslin and Horsthemke have questioned the substance and content of Ubuntu: in their view, it has been considerably weakened by inter alia the corruption, autocratic rule, sexism and degradation of the environment within African societies.[25] Its relevance for contemporary African societies is also debated: as a potentially patriarchal and conservative concept, it may have largely lost its appeal, particularly towards younger generations of Africans.[26] It has been reproached for failing to uphold constitutional principles such as equality, as for example it relegates women to a lower status.[27] In that sense, Ubuntu as a collectivist philosophy can be interpreted to contain (and maintain) patriarchy, discrimination and inequality, particularly vis-à-vis women, children, homosexuals/lesbians, in stark contrast to the 1996 South African Constitution fundamental principles for example.[28] The risk of the concept's (political) manipulation along with its purported vagueness has not been presented as conducive to reviving popular appeal towards it.

The question of Ubuntu's universal appeal constitutes a second level of criticism: its lack of homogeneity, according to its critics, makes it weak in its universality.[29] Without a concise framework, it also makes a difficult concept towards theorization, as already mentioned. And yet, Ubuntu's African groundedness

22 Eliastam (n 11) 1.

23 Thaddeus Metz, 'Toward an African Moral Theory' (2007) 15(3) *The Journal of Political Philosophy* 331, 334. This interpretation is interestingly in line with Aristotle's thesis that 'the excellent person is related to his friend in the same way as he is related to himself, since a friend is another himself.' [Cf. Aristotle, *Nicomachean Ethics* (Hackett, 1987) 1170b6–7].

24 Lutz (n 17) 3.

25 Penni Enslin and Kai Horsthemke, 'Can Ubuntu Provide a Model for Citizenship Education in African Democracies?' (2004) 40(4) *Comparative Education* 545.

26 Drucilla Cornell and Karin Van Marle, 'Exploring Ubuntu: Tentative Reflections' (2005) 5(2) *African Human Rights Law Journal* 195, 196.

27 Bernard Matolino and Wenceslaus Kwindingwi, 'The End of Ubuntu' (2013) 32(2) *South African Journal of Philosophy* 197, 204.

28 Ilze Keevy, 'Ubuntu versus the core values of the Southern African Constitution' in Leonhard Praeg and Siphokazi Magadla (eds), *UBUNTU: Curating the Archive* (University of KwaZulu-Natal Press 2014) 78.

29 See for example John Hailey, *Ubuntu: A Literature Review* (Tutu Foundation 2008).

and resonance have functioned well despite the continent's enormous cultural diversity.[30]

The major normative tension regarding Ubuntu arises, however, with regard to the potential conflict between the concept's communitarian ontology and the notion of individual rights (such as human rights) within a liberal frame. This last point leads to a broader discussion on the compatibility of Ubuntu with human rights. The main tension between the two is located in the acceptance that Ubuntu may privilege communal goods over individual ones. By conceiving the individual agent "as necessarily embedded in a network of relationships", one can conclude that individual freedom cannot be compatible with an Ubuntu ethic.[31] It is also liable to perpetuate the patriarchal features within traditional African societies that assign rights in accordance with communal membership, family and status.[32] A challenge to these hierarchies can be, therefore, construed as an affront to the balance and harmony of the community and therefore as contrary to Ubuntu.[33] In simpler words, the choice between following one's community collides with individual rights although "men are largely interdependent that no man is so completely private as never to obstruct the lives of others in any way."[34] If dignity,[35] understood as an integral part of Ubuntu, is self-standing and independent from communal belonging, there is nevertheless potential for conflict. Because this kind of conflict is highly context-dependent, the conclusion of the critiques highlighting this kind of tension have been that

> for more industrialized and globalized societies, in which the liberal ideals of freedom and human rights are of paramount importance in shaping public morality, an ubuntu ethic can only play a much more restricted role than it did in pre-industrialised African societies.[36]

In this sense, the use(s) of Ubuntu can be arguably presented as having contributed to the neglect of the call for redistributive justice, often in the name of public-spiritedness and as an element of a newer form of cultural nationalism.[37]

30 Kwame A. Appiah, 'The Arts of Africa' (1997) 44(7) *The New York Review of Books* 46, 47.

31 Anthony O. Oyowe, 'Strange Bedfellows: Rethinking Ubuntu and Human Rights in South Africa' (2013) 13 *African Human Rights Law Journal* 103, 105.

32 Mfuniselwa J. Bhengu, *Ubuntu: The Global Philosophy for Humankind* (Lotsha Publications 2006) 129.

33 There has been intense feminist critique against Ubuntu as a frame that generates gender inequalities and lesser degrees of dignity for African women. [Cf. Keevy (28) 70]

34 Isaiah Berlin, *Four Essays on Liberty* (OUP 1969) 143.

35 Metz argues on this point that dignity is connected to one's capacity for a freely chosen community and this is how the two normative orderings (i.e. ubuntu and individual human rights) can be potentially reconciled: Taddeus Metz, 'Ubuntu as a Moral Theory and Human Rights in South Africa' (2011) 11(2) *African Human Rights Law Journal* 532, 584.

36 Oyowe (n 31) 124.

37 Christoph Marx, 'Ubu and Ubuntu: On the Dialectics of Apartheid and Nation-Building' (2002) 52 *Politikon*.

When compared with Western legal thought and social organization, which has been largely adversarial, competitive and by extension conflictual,[38] one can explain the resistance to Ubuntu's radically different rationale. But Ubuntu's conception of life within society is not a priori binary and certainly not individualistic. It proposes, instead, a conception of power as "co-created and mutually empowering".[39] With a distinct sub-Saharan origin, its universal dimension remains the subject of intense debate while being often politically abused,[40] largely because it remains in evolution and open to multiple interpretations.

4. Ubuntu in Post-Colonial Terms

Ubuntu, in a post-colonial frame, is defined as a case of 'indigenous knowledge', which, within South Africa in particular, has been the political object of a binary juxtaposition between colonial policies viewed as hegemonic and oppressive, and post-colonial ones emphasizing the inclusion of African indigenous knowledge.[41] It subscribes theoretically to the *Southern Theory* frame which identifies four intellectual sources: indigenous knowledge, alternative universalism, anti-colonial knowledge and Southern critical engagement with the Northern theory.[42]

For the wider populations in Southern Africa, the post-colonial experiences have been rich in violence, brutality and abuses, in opposition to the concept and practice of Ubuntu, but also African humanism more broadly.[43] In terms of its content, Ubuntu's values may have had an adverse impact on societies: for instance, respect to authority has been deemed as a factor encouraging colonization, leading ultimately to submissiveness, dependence and cultural erosion,[44] sealed through the divide-and-rule method by colonialists in Africa. This process has encouraged the birth of neo-colonial states that feature high levels of clientelism and nepotism,[45] ultimately making the state of little or no relevance, particularly to the vast numbers of rural Africans. For instance, the incident of the dumping of toxic waste in Abidjan in 2006 shows in concreto the abstract

38 See on this point Michael Karlberg, *Beyond the Culture of Contest* (George Ronald 2004).

39 Leyla Tavernaro-Haidarian, 'Evolving "Discoarse" into Discourse: Ubuntu as a Normative Basis' (2018) 44 *Communicatio* 1, 6, DOI: 10.1080/02500167.2017.1415945.

40 Keyan G. Tomaselli, 'Our Culture vs Foreign Culture' (2019) 65(6) *Gazette: International Journal for Communication Studies* 427.

41 Aaron T. Sigauke, 'Ubunti/Hunhu in Post-Colonial Education Policies in Southern Africa: A Response to Connell's Southern Theory and the Role of Indigenous African knowledges in the Social Sciences' (2016) 5(1) *Postcolonial Directions in Education* 25, 28.

42 See the seminal Raewyn Connell, *Southern Theory: The Global Dynamics of Knowledge in Social Sciences* (Allen and Unwin 2007).

43 Ama Biney, 'The Historical Discourse on African Humanism: Interrogating the Paradoxes' in Leonhard Praeg and Siphokazi Magadla (eds), *UBUNTU: Curating the Archive* (University of KwaZulu-Natal Press 2014) 40.

44 Jacob Mugumbate and Andrew Nyanguru, 'Exploring African Philosophy: The Value of Ubuntu in Social Work' (2013) 3(1) *African Journal of Social Work* 82, 98.

45 Biney (n 43) 41.

nature of the role of the state (and Ubuntu) within a neo-colonial context. In that case, the government of Côte d'Ivoire waived its right to prosecute the oil-trading company chartering the ship that polluted its waters in exchange for 195 million dollars and only a limited number among the 30,000 victims receiving compensation.[46]

In an opposite vein, Ubuntu has been also translated into a political vision that promotes freedom and respect for all. Nelson Mandela encapsulated the essence of this project by recognizing the inherent propensity of human nature towards generosity, forgiveness, reconciliation. In his words, "[m]an's goodness is a flame that can be hidden but never extinguished."[47]

The message and content of Ubuntu have been nevertheless trapped historically in colonialist terms with implications up to the present era. According to Nyathi:

> Ubuntu is a well-developed system of knowledge that stands in contrast to the dominant Euro-American epistemology. Articulating this alternative epistemology in the white-western world . . . is an extremely challenging task (in the ways it raises 'lost in translation' type issues) but for an African person this challenge is not entirely new. It is an extension of struggles to articulate the identity of Africa and the Africans dating back to the late eighteenth century.[48]

To complicate the transposition of the concept further, Ubuntu has been commonly placed in a historical frame which, according to Gade, involves three distinct phases: a pre-colonial phase, where Ubuntu was placed at the centre of society, leading to harmonious co-existence and prosperity; a second (colonial) phase where Ubuntu inevitably retreated due to the domination of colonialists; and a third phase of its revival and restoration.[49] Such a linear conceptualization of Ubuntu following the cause of history is, however, in itself colonial.[50] This approach has prompted a part of the scholarly body engaged with the concept to treat it exclusively as a "narrative of return",[51] unlikely (and unable) to legitimize

46 See www.africafocus.org/docs12/tox1210.php as quoted in Biney (43) 44.

47 Nelson Mandela, *A Long Walk to Freedom* (Little, Brown and Company 1994) 542.

48 Nceku Nyathi, 'The Organisational Imagination in African Anti-Colonial Thought' (Unpublished Doctoral Dissertation, University of Leicester 2008).

49 Christian B.N. Gade, 'The Historical Development of the Written Discourses of Ubuntu' (2011) 30(3) *South African Journal of Philosophy* 303.

50 Sobantu Sibanda, 'In Search of Social Justice Through Ubuntu: A Critical Analysis of Zimbabwe's Post-Colonial Education for All Policy' (Doctoral Thesis, 2019, Canterbury Christ Church University) [https://repository.canterbury.ac.uk/item/89179/in-search-of-social-justice-through-ubuntu-a-critical-analysis-of-zimbabwe-s-post-colonial-education-for-all-efa-policy].

51 Some of these authors are Bernard Matolino, 'Radicals Versus Moderates: A Critique of Gyekye's Moderate Communitarianism' (2013) 28(2) *South African Journal of Philosophy* 160; Bernard Matolino and Wenceslaus Kwindingwi, 'The End of Ubuntu' (2013) 32(2)

it as a self-standing, authentic and contemporary African value. The concept's revival has been justified, within this stream of scholarship, as being motivated by the desire to return to the pre-colonial era,[52] as a result of the dehumanizing experiences of the colonial era. But while the contemporary understanding of Ubuntu cannot be in fact isolated from the experiences of colonialism, apartheid, individualism and ultimately also globalization, Ubuntu as a "narrative of return" is likely to reinforce the concept's limitations. The historical factors mentioned earlier have indeed contributed to the concept's erosion and/or dilution.[53]

To be more explicit, Ubuntu can be construed as an antithesis to the colonial system in the sense that the latter is based on individualism, a sense of superiority and a lack of understanding of the African conception of "being as belonging".[54] Pre-colonial understandings of Ubuntu echoed a stronger form of communalism, where there was limited space available for rights within an African cosmology.[55] A post-colonial understanding of Ubuntu, on the other hand, due to its encounter with Western concepts of individual entitlements, has shifted to more relative and more moderate understandings[56] of self-identity. The hybridity of the post-colonial African value system is a fact which should not automatically lead, however, to the rejection of Ubuntu per se.

From a different angle, the concept today is commonly addressed through an attempt for a reversal of an understanding of indigenous knowledge as 'inferior' and 'irrelevant' to Western knowledge and policy-framing.[57] The caveat in this process remains of course one where Ubuntu cannot and should not be elevated to the only or exclusive concept of African philosophy.[58] Nor should it be used selectively for one's own private gain.[59] Politically, Ubuntu still stands against violence, greed and individualism, particularly as expressed within colonialism and neo-colonialism.[60]

As a human quality, Ubuntu has been also politically connected with resilience, allowing people to survive and remain still human despite dehumanizing

South African Journal of Philosophy 197; Wim van Binsbergen, 'Ubuntu and the Globalisation of Southern African Thought and Society' (2001) 15(1/2) *Quest: An African Journal of Philosophy* 53.

52 Matolino and Kwindingwi (n 51).

53 Eliastam (n 11) 5.

54 Sibanda (n 50) 52.

55 Ibid 57. It should also be noted that pre-colonial Ubuntu discourse has been mainly captured in oral forms, which has been an additional point of tension for those arguing against the cultural embeddedness of the concept in contemporary African societies.

56 For a similar point, Ibid 58.

57 Sigauke (n 41) 29.

58 Ibid 30.

59 Ibid 38.

60 Munyaradzi Hwami and Dip Kapoor, 'Neo-colonialism, Higher Education and Student Union Activism in Zimbabwe' (2012) 1(1) *Postcolonial Directions in Education* 31.

circumstances, such as apartheid.[61] There is, of course, the counterargument that ubuntu can be a utopian alternative that does not match the African reality where "Africans, who are associated with an ubuntu philosophy . . . are paradigmatic victims of violent regimes of grotesque acts of war that take place between and within states."[62] This does not preclude the aspiration to strive towards more harmonious relationships, where the individual is identified "as special in virtue of her capacity to enter into relationships of identity and solidarity".[63] The active participation of humans on this basis shapes power as relational, consensual and beyond the opposition between individualism and collectivism.[64]

5. Ubuntu as a Constitutional Value

African law constitutes unwritten law, also known as living African customary law.[65] It covers also moral rules and incorporates the relationship with ancestors,[66] through the reflection of social control systems and the cultural orientations of tribal African societies. Its primary aim is the "restoration of the balance upset by an unjust act", in an effort to maintain equilibrium.[67] Ubuntu represents, in this sense, the basis for the authority of law.

Within this frame, it has been elevated to a constitutional value in South Africa, due to its conceptual overlap with human dignity.[68] It delineates a moral space which relies on shared understandings of life in community, of "acting with others, in social practice".[69] As a legal notion, it is characterized by its empirical dimension and its responsiveness to context.[70] It also resonates well within the regional human rights system through the African Charter on Human and

61 Desmond Tutu, *No Future Without Forgiveness: A Personal Overview of South Africa's Truth and Reconciliation Commission* (Rider Random House 2000).

62 Colin Chasi, 'Violent Communication is not Alien to Ubuntu: Nothing Human is Alien to Africans' (2014) 40(4) *Communicatio: South African Journal for Communication Theory and Research* 287, 293.

63 Taddeus Metz, 'African Ethics and Journalism Ethics: News and Opinion in Light of Ubuntu' (2015) 30(2) *Journal of Media Ethics: Exploring Questions of Media Morality* 74, 78.

64 Tavernaro-Haidarian (n 39) 11, in particular the example of the practice of *pungwe* as a method for communities to consult and explore solutions collectively.

65 To be distinguished from codified customary law or official customary law, documented since the period of colonialism. [See Keevy (n 28) 58–59].

66 Mogobe B. Ramose, *African Philosophy through Ubuntu* (Mond Books 2005) 94–95 states: "In African thought, the triad of living, the living dead and the yet-to-be born forms an unspoken and infinite chain of relations which are characteristically a one-ness and a wholeness at the same time."

67 Chukwuemeka Ebo, 'Indigenous Law and Justice' in Gordon R. Woodman and Akintunde O. Obilade (eds), *African Law and Legal Theory* (Dartmouth Publishing 1995) 34.

68 Metz (23) 329.

69 Gessler M. Nkondo, 'Ubuntu as public policy in South Africa: A Conceptual Framework' (2007) 2(1) *International Journal of African Renaissance Studies* 88.

70 Ramose (n 66) 83–84.

Peoples' Rights, in particular the collective rights, and one's duty towards the community (Articles 27–29 of the Charter).

The legal theorization of Ubuntu stems from a distinct starting point, quite different to classical human rights theory, where:

> the self is outside the body, present and open to all. [It] is the result of the expression of all the forces acting upon us. It is not a thing, but the sum total of all the interacting forces. So we must learn to see ourselves as outside, in our appearance, in our acts and relationship, and in the environment around us.[71]

With the individual merging into the group, Ubuntu becomes transformed into an exercise in 'collective survival' guided by cooperation and collective responsibility.[72] From such a conception of Ubuntu have unfolded a number of normative features in the South African context: the value of Ubuntu has been significant in the 1996 Constitution of South Africa although not expressly mentioned in it. It is implicit in the text's recognition of the principles of dignity, non-discrimination and equality, but also the recognition of customary law by courts, subject to the Constitution.[73] The occasion of the *AZAPO* case[74] highlighted the constitutional dimensions of Ubuntu: the case concerned the granting of amnesty to apartheid perpetrators. It was introduced by a black consciousness movement that claimed that amnesty to culprits of the apartheid era was unconstitutional because it prevented the victims from seeking a remedy. It triggered the debate on the notions of responsibility and reparation. The Court found that the aim of the Truth and Reconciliation Committee was to "promote national unity and reconciliation in a spirit of understanding which transcends the conflicts and divisions of the past", rejecting the applicants' claim.[75] For some, the case constitutes an example of the instrumentalization of Ubuntu to avoid taking responsibility for harm done. The case, as decided, also excluded the principle that under African law, there is no concept of prescription as "time cannot delete the truth," at least until the equilibrium is restored.[76] In a more positive light, along with a number of additional cases, it demonstrated how the vagueness of the concept can be turned into an

71 Augustine Shutte, *Ubuntu: An Ethic for a New South Africa* (Cluster Publications 2001) 22–23.

72 Tom Zwart, 'Using Legal Culture to Further the Implementation of International Human Rights: The Receptor Approach' (2012) 34 *Human Rights Quarterly* 555.

73 Section 211(3) of the 1996 Constitution of the Republic of South Africa.

74 *Azanian Peoples Organization (AZAPO) and Others v President of the Republic of South Africa and Others*, 1996 (4) SA 671 (CC).

75 *AZAPO V TRC* at para.677.

76 Jack H. Driberg, 'The African Conception of Law' in Eugene Cotran and Neville N. Rubin (eds), *Readings in African Law* (Frank Cass 1969) 172.

opportunity to adjust it to the customary realities of the legal system, including to advance human rights.[77]

In later cases, Ubuntu was used, albeit in a limited way, to justify the Court's decisions. In *Koyabe*, the Constitutional Court, deciding on a migration case declared that it was illegal to declare foreigners as illegal inhabitants without a reasoned decision and added:

> In the context of a contemporary democratic public service like ours where the principles of *batho pele*, coupled with the values of *ubuntu*, enjoin the public service to treat people with respect and dignity and avoid undue confrontation.[78]

In *Barkhuizen v Napier*, the Court was even more explicit by finding that "[n]otions of fairness, justice and equity, and reasonableness cannot be separated from public policy. Public policy takes into account the necessity to do simple justice between individuals. Public policy is informed by the concept of ubuntu."[79] Sachs J in *Port Elizabeth Municipality* took an additional step by declaring:

> We are not islands unto ourselves. The spirit of ubuntu, part of the deep cultural heritage of the majority of the population, suffuses the whole constitutional order. It combines individual rights with a communitarian philosophy and should be considered when dealing with foreigners.[80]

The use of Ubuntu was also pronounced in the case of *Afri-Forum v Malema*,[81] where the Equality Court had to decide whether the then–Youth leader of the African National Congress (ANC), Julius Malema, was guilty of hate speech. Lamont J in finding against the defendant stated that complying with the issued order was a matter of "both law and ubuntu".[82]

Used as an aide to constitutional interpretation, Ubuntu represents therefore a contextual factor that South African judges have not hesitated to use in a number of cases,[83] covering an extensive remit of legal areas such as criminal law, con-

77 Chuma Himonga, 'The Right to Health in an African Cultural Context: The Role of Ubuntu is the Realisation of the Right to Health with Special Reference to South Africa' (2018) 57 *Journal of African Law* 173.

78 *Koyabe and Others v Minister for Home Affairs and Others* 2010 (4) SA 327, at para.62.

79 *Barkhuizen v Napier* 2007 (5) SA 323, at para. 51.

80 *Port Elizabeth Municipality v Various Occupiers* 2005 (1) SA 517 at para.37.

81 *Afri-Forum v Malema* (20968/2010) [2011] ZAEQC 2; [2011] 4 All SA 293 (EqC).

82 *Afri-Forum v Malema* (2011) at para. 111.

83 See indicatively the widely cited case law of the Constitutional Court such as *S v Makwanyane*; *Port Elizabeth Municipality v Various Occupiers* 2005 (1) SA 517; *Dikoko v Mokhatia* 2006 (6) SA 235; *Masethla v President of the RSA* 2008 (1) SA 566; *Union of Refugee Women v Private Security Industry Regulatory Authority* 2007 (4) SA 395; *Barkhuizen v Napier* 2007 (5) SA 323; *Koyabe and Others v Minister for Home Affairs and Others* 2010 (4) SA 327.

tract law, social security or migrant law.[84] The use of the concept relies, however, considerably on the creative interpretation of the sitting judges to pursue the harmony and compassion inherent within Ubuntu.[85] As lived experience, it has been relevant for law and decision-making, but the struggle remains to become clearer about how it resonates within society and less why it is conceptually unique.[86]

6. Ubuntu and the Environment

The concept of the *Anthropocene*, as developed in academic literature, describes essentially an era dominated by humankind.[87] An anthropocentric reading of the world treats humans as the focal point, the basic social unit of the world. This human domination offers a two-fold analytical frame: as a call towards measurable indicators based on scientific evidence but also as a frame to debate essential political normative questions backed by solid ecological evidence.[88] Within the latter sense, the fundamental questions contained in its paradigm find a response within Ubuntu.

Debates surrounding the global aspects of environmental governance in a normative sense leave room to ask the important question of what can be learned in both theoretical and empirical terms from Global South approaches to the Anthropocene discourse.[89] This room is not, however, as vast as alternative environmental and developmental paradigms sourced from the Global South deserve. This is because non-Western approaches to natural resource management and sustainable development planning have been often underestimated.[90] This may be because the contrast in the two paradigms could not be greater: a Global North approach to sustainable development in general promotes technological advancement and consumption, while a Global South one,

84 See Thomas Bennett, 'Ubuntu: An African Equity' (2011) 14 *Potchefstroom Electronic Law Journal* 30.

85 Serges Djoyou Kamga, 'Cultural Values as a Source of Law: Emerging Trends of Ubuntu Jurisprudence in South Africa' (2018) 18 *African Human Rights Law Journal* 625, 647.

86 Katherine Furman, 'Ubuntu and the Law: Some Lessons for the Practical Application of Ubuntu' in Leonhard Praeg and Siphokazi Magadla (eds), *UBUNTU: Curating the Archive* (University of KwaZulu-Natal Press 2014) 158.

87 See Paul J. Crutzen, 'Geology of Mankind' (2002) 415(23) *Nature* 6867; Philipp Pattberg and Fariborz Zelli, *Environmental Politics and Governance in the Anthropocene: Institutions and Legitimacy in a Complex World* (Routledge 2016; Barry Gill, 'Global Development in the Anthropocene' (2015) 12(5) *Globalization* 824.

88 Jens Marquardt, 'Worlds Apart? The Global South and the Anthropocene' in Thomas Hickmann, Lena Partzsch, Philipp Pattberg, and Sabine Weiland (eds), *The Anthropocene Debate and Political Science* (Routledge 2018) 200.

89 Ibid 201 asks precisely this question among others.

90 See for example Gwen Ottinger et al., 'Environmental Justice: Knowledge, Technology and Expertise' in Ulrike Felt et al. (eds), *The Handbook of Science and Technology Studies* (MIT Press 2017) 716–725.

including Ubuntu, emphasizes the role of community, autarky, harmony and human mutuality.[91]

And yet, Ubuntu is far from a passive approach to environmental problem-solving despite its treatment as a fragile approach in the context of the Anthropocene. By offering its own holistic understanding on nature, it proposes a context where the humans and nature form a coherent whole. Transposed to environmental governance, Ubuntu begins with questioning (and ultimately rejecting) the assumption that all human actions are motivated by selfishness and are based on conflict-driven relations, where humans compete for resources. More than that, it links environmental scientific knowledge with political action, operating against any nature-society "dualism".[92] For Ubuntu, collectivity and collective agency determine the path towards sustainability. This kind of *ecological intelligence*[93] is based on inclusivity, ethicalness and creativity. It is also a collective kind of intelligence,[94] which treats each element within nature (both animate and inanimate) as a source of vital force. A consequence of this approach to nature leads to the rejection of the exploitation of natural resources and translates instead into their mindful use, only to the extent necessary. Waste and environmental destruction are also rejected by extension. Sustainable development becomes thus harmoniously entangled with cultural diversity.[95]

More concretely, Ubuntu in environmental governance signifies that:

- the placing of private interests ahead of collective ones leads to overexploitation of the environmental resources
- although freedom and equality are an inherent part of Ubuntu, this does not automatically signify that privatization and property rights are aligned with it as well. In fact, Africa's colonial past has developed a systemic aversion to indigenous communal property systems due to this confusion.[96]
- the collective responsibility towards the environment should be promoted, due to the regulation of the exploitation and use of natural resources in cooperative and solidary terms.
- linking Ubuntu with Amartya Sen's Capabilities Approach, the survival of all humans and their access to basic necessities is a direct and non-negotiable implication of its application.[97]

91 Marquardt (n 88) 203.
92 Term borrowed from Marquardt (n 88) 214.
93 Term borrowed from Shumba (n 3) 85.
94 Ibid 87.
95 The World Summit on Sustainable Development in 2002 has already recognized how "cultural diversity is as critical for the world's development as is biodiversity." [Cf. Shumba (n 3) 92].
96 Shumba (n 3) 93.
97 See Mashele Rapatsa, 'Ubuntu and the Capabilities Approach: Basic Doctrines for Calibrating Humanitarian Action' (2016) 9(12) *European Review of Applied Sociology* 12.

The impact of colonization on African values/societies has, nevertheless, slowed down a shift in environmental practices in line with Ubuntu. This process has been aptly summarized as follows:

> Informing the very logic of colonialism was the desire to transform African nature (in the dual sense of the word) to reflect the more advanced, Western nature. On the one hand, colonialists transformed physical nature into a reflection of European spaces by recreating the West in African cities, landscapes and nation-states.[98]

It becomes, therefore increasingly hard to disentangle the role of Ubuntu in environmental governance from its post-colonial framing, very similarly to the political dimensions of the use of the principle.

7. Concluding Remarks: Ubuntu as a Counterhegemonic Movement in Southern Africa?

Ubuntu, in its current, post-colonial form, has extended its use/relevance beyond the narrower kinship-based communities despite its conceptual fuzziness. This extension has brought about a transformation in the formal aspects of Ubuntu praxis:[99] today, Ubuntu is addressed to larger (imagined) communities and is no longer limited to tribal communities. For this reason, in its connection to environmental governance, it can be still considered as a relevant, potentially universally valid approach to protect the environment and live sustainably. The 'price' of the extension of the concept is its growingly abstract nature, as already noted, to achieve universal relevance and resonance.

It should not be nevertheless forgotten that contemporary forms of Ubuntu in its *glocal* dimension have to be interpreted as "an interplay between rights and obligations",[100] although it has been practiced in the past as membership entailing primarily duties and obligations. As such, it "must be understood both as a product of and a critical response to Western modernity".[101] Constitutionalizing ubuntu, as has been the case in South Africa, has not solved an essential concern for environmental governance: notions of shared humanity remain separate and are not to be confused with shared resources.[102]

98 Leonhard Praeg, 'From Ubuntu to Ubuntu: Four Historic a Prioris' in Leonhard Praeg and Siphokazi Magadla (eds), *UBUNTU: Curating the Archive* (University of KwaZulu-Natal Press 2014) 103.

99 Ibid 106.

100 Kwasi Wiredu, 'Social Philosophy in Post-colonial Africa: Some Preliminaries concerning Communalism and Communitarianism' (2008) 27(4) *South African Journal of Philosophy* 332, 333.

101 Praeg (n 98) 114.

102 Ibid 116.

Ubuntu is still far from a complete and static conceptualization of being.[103] It should not be labelled exclusively as a "narrative of return", although the risk is real. Similarly, the risk of reducing or limiting the relationality or historicity of Ubuntu, due to Western-centric lenses, is not completely eliminated either.[104] The concept of Ubuntu, however, is no longer threatened as much by valuable and oftentimes conflicting conceptualizations of its content. Its biggest challenge is at present how to become a broader worldview with implications extending beyond the Southern African context.

A viable option to enhance its crucial contribution to ethics, governance and law would be to move beyond the acceptance of interconnectedness between humans to also cover the environment in which the humans find themselves.[105] Based, however, on the notion of a web of intertwined relationships, ubuntu becomes difficult to define for its specific, itemized attributes on environment, in a clearly separable way from for instance relations with ancestors or other spiritual matters.[106] This is because social justice, as a pursuit integral to Ubuntu, is relational and relies on agreement and consensus in an all-encompassing manner. In other words, "to be just means valuing the views and needs of others beyond your own and living in a manner that embraces these values,"[107] in order to honour both the community spirit but also the collective good. In a world of interconnected levels of governance and given the state of environmental challenges humanity is currently facing, the impact of such an approach on environmental protection and resource management deserves serious consideration beyond the stricter Southern African context.

Bibliography

Appiah K.A., 'The Arts of Africa' (1997) 44(7) *The New York Review of Books* 46–51.

Bennett T., 'Ubuntu: An African Equity' (2011) 14 *Potchefstroom Electronic Law Journal* 30.

Berlin I., *Four Essays on Liberty* (OUP 1969).

Bhengu M.J., *Ubuntu: The Global Philosophy for Humankind* (Lotsha Publications 2006).

Chasi C., 'Violent Communication is not Alien to Ubuntu: Nothing Human is Alien to Africans' (2014) 40(4) *Communicatio: South African Journal for Communication Theory and Research* 287–304.

Chilisa B., *Indigenous Research Methodologies* (Sage 2012).

Connell R., *Southern Theory: The Global Dynamics of Knowledge in Social Sciences* (Allen and Unwin 2007).

Cornell D. and Van Marle K., 'Exploring Ubuntu: Tentative Reflections' (2005) 5(2) *African Human Rights Law Journal* 195–220.

103 Sibanda (n 50) 44.
104 Ibid 50.
105 See Bagele Chilisa, *Indigenous Research Methodologies* (Sage 2012).
106 Sibanda (n 50) 80.
107 Ibid 80.

Crutzen P.J., 'Geology of Mankind' (2002) 415(23) *Nature* 6867.
Driberg J.H., 'The African conception of law' in E. Cotran and N.N. Rubin (eds), *Readings in African Law* (Frank Cass 1969).
Ebo C., 'Indigenous Law and Justice' in G.R. Woodman and A.O. Obilade (eds), *African Law and Legal Theory* (Dartmouth Publishing 1995).
Eliastam J.L.B., 'Exploring Ubuntu Discourse in South Africa: Loss, Liminality and Hope' (2015) 36(2) *Verbum et Ecclesia* 1–8.
Enslin P. and Horsthemke K., 'Can Ubuntu Provide a Model for Citizenship Education in African Democracies?' (2004) 40(4) *Comparative Education* 545–558.
Furman K., 'Ubuntu and the Law: Some Lessons for the Practical Application of Ubuntu' in L. Praeg and M. Siphokazi (eds), *UBUNTU: Curating the Archive* (University of KwaZulu-Natal Press 2014).
Gade C.B.N., 'The Historical Development of the Written Discourses of Ubuntu' (2011) 30(3) *South African Journal of Philosophy* 303–329.
Gill B., 'Global Development in the Anthropocene' (2015) 12(5) *Globalization* 824–827.
Hailey J., *Ubuntu: A literature Review* (Tutu Foundation 2008).
Himonga C., 'The Right to Health in an African Cultural Context: The Role of Ubuntu is the Realisation of the Right to Health with Special Reference to South Africa' (2018) 57 *Journal of African Law*.
Hoffmann N. and Metz T., 'What Can the Capabilities Approach Learn from an Ubuntu Ethic? A Relational Approach to Development Theory' (2017) 97 *World Development* 153–164, https://core.ac.uk/reader/227453720
Hwami M. and Kapoor D., 'Neo-colonialism, Higher Education and Student Union Activism in Zimbabwe' (2012) 1(1) *Postcolonial Directions in Education* 31–66.
Kamga S.D., 'Cultural Values as a Source of Law: Emerging Trends of Ubuntu Jurisprudence in South Africa' (2018) 18 *African Human Rights Law Journal* 625–649.
Karlberg M., *Beyond the Culture of Contest* (George Ronald 2004).
Kenrick J., 'Commons Thinking' in A. Stibbe (ed), *The Handbook of Sustainability Literacy: Skills for a Changing World* (Green Books Ltd 2009).
Khoza R.J., *Let Africa Lead* (Vezubuntu 2005).
Lutz D.W., 'African Ubuntu Philosophy and Philosophy of Global Management' (2009) 84 *Journal of Business Ethics* 313, https://doi.org/10.1007/s10551-009-0204-z.
Mandela N., *A Long Walk to Freedom* (Little, Brown and Company 1994).
Mangaliso M.P., 'Building a Competitive Advantage from Ubuntu: Management Lessons from South Africa' (2001) 15(5) *The Academy of Management Executive* 23–33.
Marquardt J., 'Worlds Apart? The Global South and the Anthropocene' in T. Hickmann, L. Partzsch, P. Pattberg and S. Weiland (eds), *The Anthropocene Debate and Political Science* (Routledge 2018).
Marx C., 'Ubu and Ubuntu: On the Dialectics of Apartheid and Nation-Building' (2002) 52 *Politikon*.
Matolino B., 'Radicals versus Moderates: A Critique of Gyekye's Moderate Communitarianism' (2013) 28(2) *South African Journal of Philosophy* 160–170.
Matolino B. and Kwindingwi W., 'The End of Ubuntu' (2013) 32(2) *South African Journal of Philosophy* 197–205.
Mbigi L. and Maree J., *The Spirit of African Transformation Managemen* (Sigma 1995).

Mbiti J.S., *African Traditional Religions and Philosophy* (Doubleday 1971).
Metz T., 'Toward an African Moral Theory' (2007) 15(3) *The Journal of Political Philosophy* 321–341.
Metz T., 'Ubuntu as a Moral Theory and Human Rights in South Africa' (2011) 11(2) *African Human Rights Law Journal* 532–559.
Metz T., 'African Ethics and Journalism Ethics: News and Opinion in Light of Ubuntu' (2015) 30(2) *Journal of Media Ethics: Exploring Questions of Media Morality* 74–90.
Mokgoro Y., 'Ubuntu and the Law in South Africa' (1998) 1(1) *Potchefstroom Electronic Journal* 15–26.
Molose T., Goldman G.A. and Thomas P., 'Towards a Collective-Values Framework of Ubuntu: Implications for Workplace Commitment' (2018) 6(3) *Entrepreneurial Business and Economics Review* 193–206.
Mugumbate J. and Nyanguru A., 'Exploring African Philosophy: The Value of ubuntu in Social Work' (2013) 3(1) *African Journal of Social Work* 82–100.
Murithi T., 'A Local Response to the Global Human Rights Standards: The Ubuntu Perspective on Human Dignity' (2007) 5(3) *Globalization, Societies and Education* 277–286.
Nkondo G.M., 'Ubuntu as Public Policy in South Africa: A Conceptual Framework' (2007) 2(1) *International Journal of African Renaissance Studies* 88–100.
Nussbaum B., 'African Culture and Ubuntu: Reflections of a South African in America' (2003) 17(1) *Perspectives* 1–12.
Nyathi N., 'The Organisational Imagination in African Anti-Colonial Thought' (Unpublished Doctoral Dissertation, University of Leicester 2008).
Ottinger G. et al., 'Environmental Justice: Knowledge, Technology and Expertise' in U. Felt, et al. (eds), *The Handbook of Science and Technology Studies* (MIT Press 2017).
Oyowe A.O., 'Strange Bedfellows: Rethinking Ubuntu and Human Rights in South Africa' (2013) 13 *African Human Rights Law Journal* 103–124.
Pattberg P. and Zelli. F, *Environmental Politics and Governance in the Anthropocene: Institutions and Legitimacy in a Complex World* (Routledge 2016).
Ramose M.B., *African Philosophy through Ubuntu* (Mond Books 2005).
Rapatsa M., 'Ubuntu and the Capabilities Approach: Basic Doctrines for Calibrating Humanitarian Action' (2016) 9(12) *European Review of Applied Sociology* 12–19.
Shumba O., 'Commons Thinking, Ecological Intelligence and the Ethical and Moral Framework of Ubuntu: An Imperative for Sustainable Development' (2011) 3(3) *Journal of Medial and Communication Studies* 84–96.
Shutte A., *Ubuntu: An Ethic for a New South Africa* (Cluster Publications 2001).
Sibanda S., 'In Search of Social Justice Through Ubuntu: A Critical Analysis of Zimbabwe's Post-Colonial Education for All Policy' (Doctoral Thesis, Canterbury Christ Church University 2019), https://repository.canterbury.ac.uk/item/89179/in-search-of-social-justice-through-ubuntu-a-critical-analysis-of-zimbabwe-s-post-colonial-education-for-all-efa-policy
Sigauke A.T., 'Ubunti/Hunhu in Post-Colonial Education Policies in Southern Africa: A Response to Connell's Southern Theory and the Role of Indigenous African Knowledges in the Social Sciences' (2016) 5(1) *Postcolonial Directions in Education* 25–53.

Tavernaro-Haidarian L., 'Evolving "Discoarse" into Discourse: Ubuntu as a Normative Basis' (2018) 44 *Communicatio* 1–15, https://doi.org/10.1080/02500167.2017.1415945.

Tomaselli K.G., 'Our Culture vs Foreign Culture' (2019) 65(6) *Gazette: International Journal for Communication Studies* 427–444.

Tutu D., *No Future Without Forgiveness: A Personal Overview of South Africa's Truth and Reconciliation Commission* (Rider Random House 2000).

van Binsbergen W., 'Ubuntu and the Globalisation of Southern African Thought and Society' (2001) 15(1/2) *Quest: An African Journal of Philosophy* 53–89.

Wiredu K., 'Social Philosophy in Post-colonial Africa: Some Preliminaries concerning Communalism and Communitarianism' (2008) 27(4) *South African Journal of Philosophy* 332–338.

Zwart T., 'Using Legal Culture to Further the Implementation of International Human Rights: The Receptor Approach' (2012) 34 *Human Rights Quarterly*.

4 Rights of Nature vs. Human Rights?

An Urgent Shift of Paradigms

Ramiro Ávila Santamaría

1. Introduction

Since 2008, when the Rights of Nature were recognized in the Ecuadorian Constitution, I have not stopped asking questions about the implications of this innovation in law and in human rights. I have no definitive answers. Nevertheless, I am sure that Rights of Nature offer radical answers to profound problems that are facing humanity in relation to human beings (violence, poverty, exclusion) and between humans, other species, and the Earth (ecological crisis).

In this chapter, I would like to explore the relationship between nature, humans, and law, with some emphasis on human rights. I will begin with what it is being calling 'Andean neo-constitutionalism'. Second, in order to understand some underlying premises that without context might seem wild, it seems wise to affirm the following: humans have a common origin with the stars and with the rest of the species that inhabit the Earth. Third, I attempt to provide an explanation of the radical separation of the human being from nature. Fourth, I delve into a critical discussion on the discourse of human rights. I argue that the discourse can be counterproductive and functional to the separation of human beings from nature, which favors the current system of exploitation of nature. Fifth, I give a brief description of the ecological crisis, which allows us to reflect on the need to change the paradigm that has led us to this catastrophe. Finally, I affirm that the best antidote for all crises, from law's perspective, is to recognize and apply Rights of Nature.

2. From Denial to Andean Neo-Constitutionalism

I still remember the night I found out that in Montecristi – the place where the Constituent Assembly was meeting – they were discussing the Rights of Nature. My head went to my mental archive. At the time, I had been teaching human rights theory and had had some experience in human rights activism since 1993. With my theories and experiences, I asked myself: what would Nino, Jellinek, Kelsen, Alexy, Ferrajoli, Bobbio, Hohfeld, Peces Barba, and Dworkin say about these rights? What would my professors of constitutional law and human rights think? Would the theories of law justify nature as a holder of rights? How could it

DOI: 10.4324/9781003175308-6

be justified? What legal theory would give some answers? According to accepted theories and law, nature can be appropriated, usable, and sold. Immediately, like most jurists, I said that there was no basis to Rights of Nature. It seemed to me 'absurd', 'ridiculous', a 'novelty', 'meaningless'. The theory I had at that time did not allow me to understand what they were discussing in the Constituent Assembly of Montecristi. I simply was a denier.

I have to confess that I read and reread the text, the famous article 71 of the Constitution, which recognized the Rights of Nature, and I did not understand what were 'vital cycles', 'evolutionary processes' or 'genetic patrimony', '*pachamama*', and '*sumak kawsay*'.

Later on, I understood that I was within that dominant epistemology of blindness, as Boaventura de Sousa Santos called it, which prevents us from seeing other knowledge and sensibilities. The Constitution was approved, and within it one of the most important institutions for contemporary law: Rights of Nature. I became interested in nature. My first intuition was to explore animal rights. I started with Peter Singer (2009) and his *Animal Liberation: The Definitive Classic of the Animal Movement*: There are other living beings who feel pain, and there is a form of discrimination against other beings who, while deserving equal respect, are treated as inferior. Singer calls this fact *speciesism*. In Ecuador, Alberto Acosta and Esperanza Martínez began to publish a collection of books called 'Debates Constituyentes' (Editorial Abya Yala). There was something profoundly innovative in some institutions of the Ecuadorian Constitution, such as plurinationality, interculturality, community democracy, *pachamama, sumak kawsay*, food sovereignty, universal citizenship, the rights of the city. In 2011, they led me to pose the idea that there was a transformative neo-constitutionalism (Ávila Santamaría, 2011) and, years later, an Andean neo-constitutionalism (Ávila Santamaría, 2016).

I am now aware that Ecuador, for the first time in its history and of Western law, articulated with its own voice from the global south and in indigenous language, constitutional institutions. We always put adjectives to the institutions that have been implanted to us from the hegemonic modernity: state, citizenship, democracy, nation, division of powers, human rights. . . . These institutions were imposed without considering indigenous culture. Andean neoconstitutionalism is a set of legal practices of indigenous peoples and social movements that aim the transformation of our societies.

To fully understand Andean neconstitutionalism, an interdisciplinarity and interculturality approach is required, which traditional jurists are not used to. It is necessary, also, to learn from physics, chemistry, biology, and oriental philosophy. Books coming from physics, such as the one written by Frank Wilczek (Nobel Prize in Physics in 2004), *The World as a Work of Art: In Search of Nature's Deep Design* (2016), or the enlightening work by Fritjof Capra and Pier Luigi Luisi (2014), *The Systems View of Life: A Unifying Vision*, are basic to understand the famous 'life cycle' of nature.

Another dimension that emerges in this path of research and exploration to fully understand the rights of nature is spiritualism. Books such as Frei Betto, *The Work of the Artist: A Holistic Vision of the Universe* (1999)*;* Thomas Berry, *The Great Work: Our Way into the Future* (1999); and Lao Tse, *Tao Teh Ching*, provide deep insights to understand nature. The central idea of these works is a call for humility, to contemplate the wonder that is nature, to the need to care for it, and to regain a more balanced relationship between humans and nature. We are part of nature's vital cycles: we need water, air, food, and we, with our waste – natural waste, of course, such as sweat or urine, or even a dead body – also give back what nature needs.

From art, poetry, literature, music, as Wilczek says, 'the world, in its deepest structure, embodies beauty. The idea that there is symmetry in the foundations of nature has come to dominate our understanding of physical reality,' or as Kepler stated, 'I am transported and possessed by an unspeakable euphoria at the divine spectacle of celestial harmony.' Unlike most positivist scientists or jurists, some people never ceased to be closely linked to nature, to appreciate it, to understand it, to be inspired by it.

But there is one more element in the search of Rights of Nature meaning: the struggles of social movements for nature, particularly those of indigenous peoples and environmentalists. There, among all those wonderful and also painful struggles of resistance against the indiscriminate and violent exploitation of nature, I highlight two: the Tagaeris and Taromenanis in Waorani territory and the Yasunidos collective. The first defend their territory with their spears against transnational oil companies; and the Yasunidos, a movement that tried to defend the territory of the Waorani peoples with votes through a referendum. Behind every struggle, every step taken by a Tagaerí in their territory, every young person who collected signatures to make a popular consultation to reverse the decision to exploit oil, was the protection of every living being in the Amazon, and the conviction that oil exploitation produces destruction, pollution, violence, which well deserve to be described as an *ecocide.*

The philosophy and practices of indigenous peoples are a great source of inspiration. If one reads the ethnographies, the works of anthropologists, linguists, missionaries – or, better yet, if one listens to the discourses or has experienced indigenous peoples' culture – one can appreciate another way of living nature. Practices such as asking permission to climb a mountain, asking forgiveness for killing an animal, giving thanks for a harvest, stopping cultivation so that the earth can regenerate, are common in many indigenous peoples.

Therein lies the fundamental sources for understanding the content and scope of Andean neo-constitutionalism and Rights of Nature. Now I suggest, in order to understand Pachamama a little better, to remember who we are and where we come from.

3. The Common Origin[1]

Human beings cannot live without nature. Thanks to nature, we can breathe, quench our thirst, feed our bodies, satisfy the needs that allow us to exist. Water,

1 Information for this section is taken from Brian Thomas Swimme and Mary Evely Tucker, *Journey of the Universe* (Yale University Press 2011).

air, earth, fire, elements that we once thought were the essence of the universe, are indispensable to all life.

We are star-dust, and we have a common origin with the rest of the universe. Our history begins some 13.8 billion years ago. In a complex process of attraction and repulsion, galaxies and stars were formed. One of them, the Sun and the Milky Way, formed about 4.6 billion years ago. The first cells, our great-grandmothers, emerged 4 billion years ago. The first sexual reproduction occurred 1 billion years ago. Plants and animals, starting with algae, fish, salamanders, and insects, populated the planet 500 million years ago. Birds, mammals, and dinosaurs followed 200 million years ago. The first hominids, chimpanzees, appeared 5 million years ago. The first hunters, *Homo erectus,* appeared 1.5 million years ago. Two hundred thousand years ago, humans, *Homo sapiens,* built their first tools, performed burial rites, inhabited Africa. . . . We come from the stars, and every living being is our relative.

During these millions of years, we humans have been part of the great universe, and we follow the rhythm of evolution. Humans are a species that lives as animal-like as any other species.

About 10,000 years before Christ, humans began to make their presence felt on Earth when they domesticated some animals and practiced agriculture. Some humans became sedentary and created the first cities 8,000 years ago. Around the same time, they migrated and inhabited almost every place on Earth.

From then on, the human footprint has been remarkable. Great civilizations were created, such as the Egyptian, Inca, Mayan, Chinese, Greek, Roman, Persian, and Hindu. The respect and admiration for nature persists and is reflected in our religious rites and our deities, except perhaps the Judeo-Christian, who dared to imagine that the human being, and only the human being, is the incarnation of God and is the central being in the universe.

In modernity, in a break with cultural tradition by hegemonic Western thought, the human being decides to break with nature.

4. Human Supremacy

The drama of our relationship with nature is related to modernity. This begins with a violent event – the conquest of America – and is characterized by three basic pillars: rationalism, colonialism, and capitalism. With these three ingredients, our relationship with nature is fractured, and we forget – at least in the hegemonic Western world – a whole tradition of links with nature.

4.1. Scientific Rationalism

Rationalism emerged in the 16th century and began with what is known as the 'Scientific Revolution'. One of the most important milestones of this period is the heliocentric theory, formulated by Copernicus in 1543: Earth is not the center of the universe and goes around the Sun. This fact, together with the invention of the printing press, would change the perspective from the theological to the scientific view. Scientists, in the search of truth, replace priests and church. The university became the main source of knowledge.

On the other hand, Descartes, who wrote *The Discourse on Method*, established rules for knowledge and the basis of the scientific method: whatever does not have a method is neither rational nor reliable. Descartes separates the soul from the body, the animal from the human ('it is not that beasts have less reason than men, but that they have none'[2]), nature is like a machine ('nature we see as a clock, composed of wheels and springs'[3]). From now on, both philosophy and science will accentuate these differences.

The result is that the human being will consider nature as an alien and different entity, an object to be known. The human being is not an animal. The human being is not nature. The human being is superior because he is rational.

The greatest development of rationalism has to do with the invention of the machine and its intensive use in the Industrial Revolution. With machines, both space and time – which were closely linked to nature – disappear. Before the existence of the clock, for example, time was judged according to sunrise, sunset, full moons, high or low tides. Before the existence of trains, cars, or planes, distance was sweated out, long distances implied being on an animal, feeling its tiredness, its breathing, its hunger. With the new means of transport, natural context is just a landscape. We can be 10,000 meters above sea level and not feel the intense cold outside; we can be in the middle of a storm in a car and not be wet. Now, with digital technology, separation with nature is much greater and deeper. We have a virtual time and space. We can be in the middle of a forest and at the same time be on an app that connects you to fashion or collective war games. We do not even feel someone next to us because we are in app looking for 'likes'.

4.2. Coloniality

Coloniality is a phenomenon that began with the conquest of America. It is characterized by the exercise of power through classification. For instance, the category 'Indian' means primitive, and it is opposed to European, meaning civilized people. Aníbal Quijano created this category and considered that there were three manifestations: the coloniality of being, coloniality of knowledge, and coloniality of power.[4]

Coloniality of being has to do with identity and with the acceptance of values and perceptions that come from the global north. *Coloniality of knowledge* has to do with the overvaluation of one way of knowing (scientific rationalism) and the invisibilization or denial of other forms of knowledge, related to the spiritual, 'mythical', folkloric, and other manifestations of human experience. *Coloniality of power* is associated with the capacity to classify and label: poor/rich, normal/abnormal, guilty/innocent, developed/underdeveloped, human/animal.

2 Renato Descartes, *Discurso del método* (first published 1637, Orbis 1983) 94.
3 Ibid 95.
4 Aníbal Quijano, 'Bien vivir: Entre el desarrollo y la des/colonialidad del poder' in *Centro Andino de Acción Popular: Acerca del buen vivir* (CAAP 2011).

Thanks to coloniality, there are superior and inferior humans, the world of culture and the world of nature, the human sciences and the natural sciences.

4.3. Capitalism

Capitalism, understood as a form of economic and social organization based on accumulation and reproduction of capital, gives exchange value to the greatest number of human activities. Something that has a cultural value or satisfies a need, such as water or oxygen, has a price under capitalism. Capitalism is also born with the conquest of America and develops throughout modernity. Nature become a natural resource. Nature must be exploited for human consumption. Nature is like a great reservoir of goods that have to be extracted, transformed, commercialized, accumulated.

Much has been written about capitalism, and I do not intend to discuss or summarize its functioning, its criticisms, and its supposed 'virtues'. I would like to draw attention to what David Harvey, one of the most knowledgeable scholars on Marxist theories and on capitalism, calls 'contradictions' of capitalism,[5] which are directly related to nature. According to Harvey, there are three types of contradictions. The first he calls *fundamentals*, which are those that allow capital to exist or function. Abolishing one of those contradictions would seriously affect the others to the point of the extinction of capital. These contradictions are those that generate the crises of capitalism. The second ones, called *changeables*, 'are unstable and remain in permanent evolutionary change'.[6] Capturing these moments of change are opportunities for transformation, but they are not the same in all times and places. Finally, the ones that interest us for the moment are those that Harvey calls *dangerous*, because they seriously affect both capital and humanity, and cause damage such as the degradation of the planet, the impoverishment of millions of people, the increase of inequalities, the dehumanization of the majority, police and military control and repression, and the conformation of totalitarian democracies.

Those dangers are related with the endless exponential and cumulative growth, which contradicts the growth of productive capital and population: capital preys. Private and corporate interest groups benefit from the accumulation of capital and debts. If debts were eliminated, the increase of capital would enter into crisis. Capital grows without limit and without the need to be linked to production. If, for example, one has US$100 earning interest at 5% per annum, in one year it will be US$105; in 100 years, it will produce US$13,150 and would not stop growing if prolonged over time. 'There are no barriers to unlimited growth.'[7] Capital is in the hands of these rentiers rather than in the hands of productive and industrial capitalists. Neither population nor production can grow infinitely.

5 David Harvey, *Diecisiete contradicciones y el fin del capitalismo* (IAEN 2014).
6 Ibid 98.
7 Ibid 237.

Human beings and nature have limits and can even stop growing. If capital does not grow, it enters into crisis.

The second dangerous contradiction is that capital needs nature to survive and exploits it to the limit of its possibilities. That is why capitalism systematically violates the Rights of Nature and has produced climate change.

The third is the one that Harvey announces as the road to a dystopian world. These two will be discussed in the fourth section, which forces us to rethink economic, social, and cultural rights.

5. A Critical View of Human Rights

Norberto Bobbio considered that in modern times, which have produced so much war and suffering, one of the few ethical 'progresses' we have is human rights.[8]

Human rights limit the power of the government, and empower people to fight for dignity. However, human rights could be used to control and to legitimize power.

The discourse of human rights has been used by those who exercise power with the aim of control.[9] To protect and to promote certain rights, such as individual civil rights, has strengthened the capitalist system and the rights of a few privileged people.[10]

The discourse of human rights could have two opposing objectives. On the one hand, some human rights could legitimize ideologies of proprietary individualism, encourage consumption, and reproduce capitalist disorder, such as the right to private property, freedoms of speech, and freedom of enterprise. The exercising of these rights is not universal, and is enjoyed by a minority.[11] That is why Santos states that 'the vast majority of the world's population is not the subject of human rights, but the object of human rights discourses.'[12] If one compares the difficulties to enjoy the right to health with enjoying the rights of foreign investors or holders of foreign debt – something that has been written about in abundance in Latin America – one will be able to appreciate that the previous statement is not far from reality.

Human rights discourse requires critical thinking, which Santos calls 'the hermeneutics of suspicion'.[13] In applying it, Santos looks at five mirages:

1. Oppression is seen as liberation – like to spread democracy in the Middle East, when George W. Bush invaded Iraq in order to rid it of a dictatorship

8 Norberto Bobbio, *El tercero ausente* (Cátedra 1997).
9 Boaventura de Sousa Santos, *Derechos humanos, democracia y desarrollo* (Dejusticia 2014) 28.
10 Alberto Noguera, *Utopía y poder constituyente: Los ciudadanos ante los tres monismos del Estado neoliberal* (Sequitur 2012) 17.
11 Luigi Ferrajoli, *Los fundamentos de los derechos fundamentales* (Trotta 2001) 29.
12 de Sousa (n 9) 23.
13 Ibid 24.

and impose 'free' elections,[14] or when the right to health is considered to be satisfied by the mere existence of hospitals or by allowing big corporations to sell medicines freely.

2. Other utopian discourses of emancipation and liberation, such as *sumak kawsay* and *Pachamama*, are considered inferior to the struggle for dignity. In these discourses, health, security, and education could have another understanding and other content.
3. The discourse is reduced to legal issues, and the struggles of social movements are decontextualized. For example, an indigenous peoples' movement could claim that the forest is their home, which does not fall within the United Nation´s standard for housing.
4. The discourse of rights may deny contradictions, such as the differences between men and women, north and south, indigenous peoples and extractive companies, indigenous capitalists and mestizo environmentalists.
5. In the hegemonic discourse, human rights can be seen as opposites and in inevitable tension with the state or government. The state can be a fundamental ally in the struggle for rights, or it can be an instrument of the market and corporations.

In sum, in human rights, as in other components of modernity, 'the global north reduces the world to the West's understanding of it, ignoring or trivializing the defining cultural and political experiences of the countries of the global south.'[15] On the other hand, the hegemonic vision, by highlighting the universal, the human, the individual, secularism, rights, the reason of state, has prevented considering the particular and local, nature, the collective, spiritualties, duties, popular reason.[16]

A conservative vision of human rights is an 'ideological quilting',[17] which gives an opposite meaning to the emancipatory or liberating one human rights could offer. This form of understanding of human rights tends towards regulation, order, and submission.[18]

One of the sharpest critics of the hegemonic discourse of human rights is Giorgio Agamben. According to this author, the notion of popular sovereignty and the state as guarantor of rights is nothing more than an abandonment to power.[19] In the state that claims to protect rights, deaths go unpunished, freedoms are restricted, the individual is annulled by the responsible citizen. Governments make use of *the state of exception*, use biopolitics to control bodies and administer human groups as a concentration camp, which 'is the space of that absolute

14 Naomi Klein, *The shock doctrine: The rise of disaster capitalism* (Picador 2007) 415.
15 Boaventura de Sousa (n 9) 34.
16 Ibid 37–55.
17 Slavoj Zizek, *El sublime objeto de la ideología* (Siglo XXI 2005) 143.
18 Boaventura de Sousa Santos, *Crítica de la razón indolente: Contra el desperdicio de la experiencia* (Desclée de Brouwer 2003) 52.
19 Giorgio Agamben, *Homo sacer: El poder soberano y la nuda vida* (Pre-Textos 2003) 18.

impossibility of deciding between fact and law, between norm and application, between exception and rule'.[20]

The capitalist system makes us live 'in a permanent state of mercantile exception. Competition has surpassed any limitation and commercial conflicts are settled by shooting.'[21] Moreover, in the same line, he argues that political and economic systems (nation-state and capitalism) required two techniques to achieve having docile bodies that adapt to an oppressive system: political and cultural techniques.[22]

Among the political ones are the discourse of human rights, by which a person becomes a 'subject' (subject to something and not a holder of rights) to governmental power. Among the cultural technologies, called *technologies of the self*, by which the process of subjectivation is carried out, are 'the most precious core of the biopolitics of modern totalitarianism, on the one hand, and consumer society and mass hedonism, on the other'.[23]

Human rights discourse, norms, and practices could be different and help to fight for a better world. First, we must be aware that the hegemonic discourse is a globalized localism, which makes us consider as universal something that is local.[24] In the counter-hegemonic discourse, the self-determination of peoples is more important than neoliberal development.[25] Also the expansion of freedoms is more important than control and repression in the name of human rights. This understanding of human rights aims to emancipate and liberate individuals and peoples.[26] From this perspective, human rights still have the potential to transform reality.[27]

An example of the hegemonic and controlling and liberating discourse in human rights is offered by Martínez de Bringas. The right to culture from the first paradigm can be understood as 'to mere intellectual property rights, expropriating the value of cultures and providing the basis for a new division of labor';[28] or it can be understood, from a critical and liberating theory of human rights, as a right that materializes self-determination and opens 'to a provocative transliberal juridical pluralism'.[29]

Now, what can human rights say about scientific rationalism, coloniality, and capitalism? Each of these elements of hegemonic modernity can be translated

20 Ibid 221.
21 César Rendueles, *Capitalismo canalla: Una historia personal del capitalismo a través de la literatura* (Seix Barral 215) 27.
22 Agamben (n 19) 14.
23 Ibid 21.
24 de Sousa (n 9) 38.
25 Ibid 80.
26 de Sousa (n 18) 52.
27 Mark Goodale, *Surrendering to Utopia: An Anthropology of Human Rights* (Stanford University Press 2009) 126.
28 Asier Martínez de Bringas, *La cultura como derecho en América Latina. Ensayo sobre la realidad postcolonial en la globalización* (Universidad de Deusto 2003) 22.
29 Ibid 74.

into the language of human rights. Thus, scientific rationalism is associated with the right to education; coloniality with political, identity, and cultural rights; and property rights allows capitalism. From this analysis, human rights could protect the interest of governments and companies.

From a critical and liberating perspective, as Santos suggests, human rights could have another understanding and another application. Scientific rationalism, although it cannot be prohibited, could allow for other ways of understanding that the world could be discriminatory. Coloniality of power, being, and knowledge, although they are forms of exercising the rights of some, could not violate other rights. For example, if it were possible to demonstrate that in a democratic process only persons and groups with strong economic backing can access positions of representation, and this practice prevents other persons and groups, with equal rights but without economic means, from opting for the same positions of representation, we would be talking about a questionable and exclusionary system. In the coloniality of being, although hegemonic identities exist, they cannot be unique. Diversity is a reality in our global community. The same can be said of the coloniality of knowledge. Human rights protect those who opt for scientific rationalism, but they cannot prohibit the existence and emergence of other knowledge, feelings, and epistemic practices. Finally, capitalism, as has been explained, is a questionable system from the perspective of those who are in a situation of oppression or submission.

Poverty and the exclusion of broad sectors of the population can be considered a systematic and generalized violation of social rights. The United Nations rapporteur on extreme poverty considers that poverty 'is characterized by continuous or chronic deprivation of civil, cultural, economic, political and social rights'.[30]

Moreover, the wealth of some, when it is intimately linked to the poverty of others, could be considered a crime.[31] Consequently, capitalism, from the critical viewpoint of constitutionalism and human rights, should have serious restrictions. Therefore, human rights cannot completely prohibit the rights that could sustain scientific rationality, coloniality, and capitalism, but they could limit them when they produce some other rights violations.

Human rights are part of any Western constitution. Human rights are utopian projects and could change lives and communities, could help to resist forms of oppression, allow us to imagine other worlds in which people have dignity.[32] Rodríguez Palop argues and demonstrates that there is a fourth generation of rights, related to the environment, development, and peace, which are based on human needs and solidarity, and which comprise an integral, alternative, and

30 Magdalena Sepúlveda Carmona, 'Proyecto final de los principios rectores sobre la extrema pobreza y los derechos humanos' in *Asamblea General* (UN 2012).

31 María Eugenia Rodríguez Palop, 'Vive usted en un mundo civilizado? El desarrollo sostenible desde el discurso de los derechos humanos' (2005) 18 *Revista de Humanidades* 267.

32 María Eugenia Rodríguez Palop, *La nueva generación de Derechos Humanos. Origen justificación* (Dykinson 2010) 463.

revolutionary project.[33] Human rights discourse could reinvent itself and could help current social, political, and environmental struggles. In this sense, human rights must be taken seriously, as they constitute a horizon and deserve intense dedication and effort and to be assumed to their ultimate consequences.

However, the utopia of human rights is one of many others in the history of humanity. Currently the most acceptable and mobilizing for some, but at the same time it could also be conservative and an ideological device. Aínsa argues that modern utopias rhyme with the reason of the nation-state, have produced monsters, have not remedied the problems they tried to solve, but have aggravated them. Contemporary constitutionalism and rights do not necessarily give an alternative to hegemonic modernity and, in fact, as is the case today, have not effectively limited a system that generates pain, exclusion, marginalization, and environmental crisis.[34] That is to say, from the dominant perspective, in human rights there is a crisis of the utopian transformative function. Although human rights were born as the last utopia, any day another utopia may appear.[35] That other emerging utopia could be the Andean utopia, whose existence is justified for the reasons we will analyze later.

Despite all the criticisms and potentialities of human rights, today we are facing an unprecedented crisis in the history of humanity and planet Earth, which we can call 'ecological crisis' or 'Anthropocene'. This situation poses new and complex challenges to our understanding of human beings on Earth and of our current understanding of human rights.

6. Human Beings and Nature: The Ecological Crisis

The tense relationship between nature and human beings has a long history. Since thousands of years ago, when humans were hunters and collectors, we were a vulnerable species. In modern times, many difficulties have been overcome, such as industrialization to solve the problem of food, which seemed fatal to Malthus, or making desert lands productive. Nature, from the point of view of capital, is internalized in the circulation of capital and the accumulation of goods. Nature is an appropriable and profitable good. Undoubtedly, for this very reason, capital contributes to its reproduction: humans plant forests to have paper, clean water for fish farming, purify water for bottling, fertilize the soil to produce mono-agriculture. But capital is interested in its reproduction and accumulation, not in human beings and their needs, and even less in nature and its biological cycles.

Capital is, therefore, also 'ecological'. The problem is that, in the use and abuse of nature, the effects of human intervention are unpredictable. One of the

33 Ibid 316.

34 Fernando Aínsa, 'Bases para una nueva función de la utopía en América Latina' in Horacio Cerutti y Oscar Agüero (eds), *Utopía y nuestra América* (Abya Yala 1996) 13.

35 Samuel Moyn, *The Last Utopia. Human Rights in History* (Harvard University Press 2010) 10.

most important human inventions that allows industrialization is the use of fossil energy. Its intensive use has produced CO_2 emissions, and the problem of climate change. We require for human survival, as a species, to lower the temperature increase from 4°C to 2°C. The conclusions from the latest global summits on climate change, and the efforts of the state and scientists, are still timid.

We are already witnessing heat waves, desertification, villages that have suffered damage with floods, tremendous fires in forests in Brazil, Australia, and the United States. Some inhabited islands are at risk of disappearing. There are more effects of climate change, more decrease in food productions, loss of ecosystems and diversity, and a serious threat to the survival of humanity on Earth.[36] Thus, Klein argues that capitalism is at war with the Earth and with humanity,[37] and capitalism is winning so far. Laval and Dardot consider that neoliberal capitalism has become the enemy of nature and global warming is 'the most important and most urgent problem ever posed to humanity'.[38]

Capitalism takes advantage of any crisis. Climate change is an opportunity to do business as usual. Forest conservation to clean up CO_2, and the carbon market are priced, bought and sold. Capitalism profits from natural and human catastrophes, as Noami Klein pointed out in *Shock Doctrine*. Nature is still considered a mere commodity, a 'natural resource', a something to be used and abused if one could get profit of it. It is, according to Harvey, like a 'huge gas station', which gives in exchange for money and whenever it is needed. To capitalism, the way to solve the problems that have generated climate change is, paradoxically, to pollute more.[39]

Environmentalism, to be effective, has to be anti-capitalist. Capital always endangers nature and also the human being; it is not interested in registering the negative externalities nor the impact on future generations.[40] In the form of capital intervention, the degradation of nature is like a cancer: it generates disasters; it cannot successfully manage nature due to the primacy of economic interest; thousands of species become extinct every day; biodiversity decreases without precedent; famines are generated by the increase in prices; inequalities multiply; and the elements of nature are valued arbitrarily. For example, some leaves cost a lot, such as cocaine, while others are worth very little, such as mint. 'The relationship of capital to nature and to human nature is extremely alienating.'[41]

The capitalist system generates a dystopian, undesirable world, which is maintained by universal alienation. Alienation has several senses: alienating property to another person who is not the owner (legal); transferring loyalty to another person or institution (social); remaining isolated and separated (passive psychological);

36 Naomi Klein, *This Changes Everything. Capitalism vs. Climate* (Penguin 2014) 14.
37 Ibid 21.
38 Christian Laval and Pierre Dardot, *Común: Ensayo sobre la revolución del siglo XXI* (Gedisa 2015) 17.
39 Klein (n 36) 256.
40 Erik Olin Wright, *Envisioning Real Utopías* (Verso 2010) 69.
41 Harvey (n 5) 255.

showing anger and hostility in the face of pressure (active psychological); inverting reality to deceive (negative ideology). All these forms of alienation exist in capitalism. The alienations produced by capital must be identified, confronted, and overcome. Despite there being an awareness and experiencing of the effects of capitalism, something that affects most of the people in the world, capital subsists and reproduces itself. The alternatives are not clear, and it is not known with what capital can be replaced. Solidarity networks are crisscrossed by the quest for personal advantage and profit. Social movements are fragmented and fail to draw a clear and viable alternative to capitalism.

Current reality, according to Oxfam, shows that the capitalist system, despite being the dominant one, despite having practiced the changes suggested by the doctrinaires, simply continues to produce the same inequality as 500 years ago, because the system lives on the contradictions denounced by David Harvey:

> Extreme inequality in the world is reaching unbearable levels. Today, the richest 1% of the world's population owns more wealth than the remaining 99% of people on the planet. Power and privilege are being used to manipulate the economic system to widen the gap, leaving hundreds of millions of poor people without hope. The current system is not the result of chance, but the result of deliberate political choices, of our leaders listening to the 1% and their supporters, rather than acting in the interests of the majority and the needs of the poorest. The time has come to reject this economic model that only works for a minority.[42]

There is not only inequity and systematic re-production of poverty in capitalism, but also ecological devastation, which is also the result of deliberate political and economic decisions – climate change, the agro-industrial model based on monocultures and deforestation, biocide – the extinction of 70% of known species, similar to that which occurred 65 million years ago.[43] One third of the Earth has been affected by humans. We have altered the composition of the atmosphere. We – human beings – have polluted more than half of the existing water. We have produced more nitrogen than all ecosystems combined.[44]

The damages we have made to nature are irreversible, and the growth model posed by capitalism does not solve them. Growth is exponential. The ways of 'solving' the problem aggravate the situation. Technological solutions do not result in a sustainable society.

Elizabeth Kolbert recalls that in the history of the planet there have been – every 100 million years on average – five extinctions, some because glaciers

42 Oxfam, *Una economía al servicio del 1%. Acabar con los privilegios y la concentración de poder para frenar la desigualdad extrema. 2016* (Oxfam International 2016).

43 Omar Felipe Giraldo, *Utopías en la era de la supervivencia: Una interpretación del buen vivir* (Ítaca 2014) 63.

44 Elizabeth Kolbert, *The sixth extinction: An unnatural history* (Henry Holt Company 2015) 108.

melted, others because of an asteroid impact, others because of volcanic eruptions. It is the first time in the history of the planet that we passed from a geological era to the Anthropocene, the most notable catastrophic event in the history of our planet.[45] The human being, in her/his short life, for the first time could be witnessing an extinction.

Since the Industrial Revolution, we have burned 365 billion metric tons of carbon and sent it into the atmosphere, and lost 180 billion tons of carbon from deforestation. Changes are so fast that species cannot resist or adapt. Thousands of species go extinct every day. One can tell the effects just watching our backyard carefully. Kolbert documented the abundance of some animals 200 years ago and their extinction today. Our geological footprint as a species will take millions of years to be absorbed.[46] Among those documented life-histories lost are penguins, Galapagos tortoises, insects – 2 million species have disappeared and 5,000 are lost every year – some species of rhinoceroses, bears, and tigers only inhabit and can be found in zoos. Our world is like an impoverished zoo, simple, extinct by the massacres made by one single species. If human beings had not shown up in Earth's history, it is possible that all those animals would still exist. But the worst thing is that the human being is not only the protagonist of this sixth extinction, but also will be its own victim.

In this context, we must reflect on law and human rights. How to address these new crises and needs not only for humans, but also for other species on the planet? Do these perspectives affect the way we understand human rights?

7. Human Rights and Rights of Nature

The antidote to the evils of hegemonic modernity – rationalism, which hides other forms of knowledge and relationship with nature; coloniality, which separates and hierarchizes culture over nature; capitalism, which treats nature as an object of appropriation and exploitation – is called 'Rights of Nature'.

Rights of Nature requires another modernity – which Dussel (2000) calls 'transmodernity',[47] and Bolívar Echeverría 'baroque modernity'[48] – decoloniality, and a non-capitalist system, which in the Andean world indigenous people have called *sumak kawsay*. In this modernity proposed, there is room for other knowledge and sensibilities, such as that of indigenous peoples; other subjects, such as the non-human beings that inhabit the planet; and other ways of life based on the satisfaction of natural needs, and not on the accumulation of goods to satisfy artificial 'needs'. Needs are not associated with consumerism but with plenitude of living (*sumak kawsay*).

45 Ibid 124.

46 Ibid 110.

47 Enrique Dussel, 'Europa, modernidad y eurocentrismo' in Eduardo Lander (ed.), *La colonialidad del saber: Eurocentrismo y ciencias sociales. Perspectivas latinoamericanas* (Unesco 2000).

48 Bolívar Echeverría, *La modernidad de lo barroco* (Era 2011).

In this alternative modernity, law must also be different. On the one hand, law cannot protect only one species, but all those that coexist with humans and with which we have co-evolved. If law is for all beings on Earth, then the sources, content and purposes of law must be different.

Sources of Law is what Cullinan calls the 'Great Law', which is none other than the set of relationships between all beings and entities that exist, and we have more in common than we imagine.[49] There are relationships that promote coexistence and survival, and other relationships that degrade those relationships. The capitalist way of dealing with relationships are in direct contradiction with the Great Law.

In terms of *content*, the Rights of Nature are already expressed in the 2008 Constitution of Ecuador (articles 71 to 73), and in the 2010 Universal Declaration of the Rights of Mother Earth.

The Rights of Nature are based on three basic principles: differentiation, autopoiesis, and communion.

Differentiation. Each being and species has its own identity. Evolution has defined different characteristics based on adaptation to the environment. Any tendency towards uniformity, such as conceived in industrial agriculture, is contrary to this principle. In this sense, there is a human right, a right of the ant, a right of the mountains, and a right of the Earth.

Autopoiesis. Each being has its self-regenerating and regulatory capacity. There is a life cycle on every system on Earth, like the water cycle, nitrogen cycle, reproductive cycle. When a human activity impedes or hinders this capacity, it violates the Rights of Nature. It happens, for instance, when there is a transgenic seed that cannot reproduce by itself.

Communion. Every single being in nature, every element on Earth, and humans have evolved through processes of collaboration and solidarity, not individualism or competition. When human systems prevent collaboration, it goes against this principle.

In this framework, human rights should have a completely different conception. First, it is important to avoid connivance with the political and economic system of hegemonic modernity. A human rights perspective adapted to capitalism degrades nature and violates its rights. Second, human rights need to be eco/bio or non-centric, in order to abandon this pernicious protagonism (dictatorship) of human beings on the world. Third, human rights' content must be read not only in terms of interdependence with other rights, which is the traditional conception, but also in terms of interrelation with nature. Fourth, in order to place ourselves in this new way of understanding law, we must combat the divorce that traditional legal positivism advocates between law, social sciences, and natural sciences. Law must interact with physics, biology, geology, poetry, and so on. A lawyer should consider nature as artists do. They never have understood nature as a separate entity from human spirit, body, or soul. Nature

49 Cullinan Cormac, *Wild law: A manifesto for Earth justice* (Chelsea Green 2011).

requires a different sensitivity to understand human rights in terms of the rights of nature.

Let us give some examples to contrast the differences in what would be the traditional way of understanding human rights with a Rights of Nature perspective. The right to health can be measured by the number of doctors, beds, hospitals, vaccines, and drugs. The emphasis on the right to health within a capitalist system is on illness and cure. Fulfilling the right to health is reflected in access to medical care and medicines, better if they are industrially produced. Diseases are, in fact, a big business (as usual).

From a Rights of Nature perspective, by the principle of self-regeneration (autopoiesis), the emphasis should be on prevention. The environment surrounding human beings can produce diseases. This is called, by critical epidemiology, 'determinants of health'.[50] A healthy environment is followed by a healthy human being. Health does not go well with extractivism, with industrial production that uses chemicals, with cheap food, with the pollution produced by the dominant forms of energy consumption. From the Rights of Nature, the right to health demands healthy environments. To have healthy environments, the Rights of Nature must be respected.

One more example. The right to education can be satisfied with access to schools and with a ten-year schooling. If a person knows how to read and write texts, then that person has fulfilled its right to be educated. If someone does not have a school diploma, is illiterate, is expelled from school, then her right is violated.

From the Rights of Nature, the important thing is to have access to the knowledge that allows one to live in harmony with nature. An indigenous person, for instance, who knows how to behave with the forest or the river, who shows respect for the land and allows other beings to exist, could be literate without going to school. Our educational systems have made our children (and any one of us) totally illiterate to do the things necessary to exist. A city person – like me – does not know how to sow, cannot discern the stars, cannot distinguish a poisonous plant from one that provides food, does not know how to relate to other living beings (many times not even with humans can we relate, worse with other beings!). From a Rights of Nature perspective, the current content of the right to education violates other rights, because it prevents us from living in harmony with nature, and does not give us the necessary knowledge to live as just another species among others equally important. We depend on nature to fully exist.

We could analyze some other human rights to appreciate the different approaches, such as the right to social security, work, housing. Law needs to switch to a different paradigm. From the Rights of Nature, law requires other foundations, other content, other accountability, and other forms of enforcement.

50 Jaime Breilh, *Epidemiología crítica: Ciencia emancipadora e interculturalidad* (Fiocruz 2006).

This understanding, moreover, requires a human being with a different behavior, humbler, simpler, more sensitive, more supportive.

A change of paradigm, and changes in the content of law and human rights, is not only necessary, but urgent. In Andean neo-constitutionalism, we find a door and a path to travel on.

Bibliography

Agamben G., *Homo sacer: El poder soberano y la nuda vida* (Pre-Textos 2003).

Aínsa F., 'Bases para una nueva función de la utopía en América Latina' in H. Cerutti y O. Agüero (eds), *Utopía y nuestra América* (Abya Yala 1996).

Ávila Santamaría R., *El neoconstitucionalismo transformador: El Estado y el derecho en la Constitución de 2008* (Abya Yala 2011).

Ávila Santamaría R., *El neoconstitucionalismo andino* (Huaponi 2016).

Ávila Santamaría R., *La utopía andina: Los derechos de la naturaleza y el buen vivir desde la literatura, el derecho y las ciencias sociales* (Akal 2018).

Bauman Z., *Modernidad líquida* (Fondo de Cultura Económica 2015).

Berry T., *The Great Work: Our Way into the Future* (Three Rivers 1999).

Betto F., *La obra del artista: Una visión holística del universo* (Trotta 1999).

Bobbio N., *El tercero ausente* (Cátedra 1997).

Breilh J., *Epidemiología crítica: Ciencia emancipadora e interculturalidad* (Fiocruz 2006).

Capra F. y Luisi P.L., *The Systems View of Life: A Unifying Vision* (CUP 2014).

Cullinan C., *Wild Law: A Manifesto for Earth Justice* (Chelsea Green 2011).

Descartes R., *Discurso del método* (Orbis 1983).

de Sousa Santos B., *Crítica de la razón indolente: Contra el desperdicio de la experiencia* (Desclée de Brouwer 2003).

de Sousa Santos B., *Derechos humanos, democracia y desarroll* (Dejusticia 2014).

Dussel E., 'Europa, modernidad y eurocentrismo' in E. Lander (ed), *La colonialidad del saber: Eurocentrismo y ciencias sociales. Perspectivas latinoamericanas* (Unesco-FACES 2000).

Echeverría B., *La modernidad de lo barroco* (Biblioteca Era 2011).

Ferrajoli L., *Los fundamentos de los derechos fundamentales* (Trotta 2001).

Giraldo O.F., *Utopías en la era de la supervivencia: Una interpretación del buen vivir* (Ítaca 2014).

Goodale M., *Surrendering to Utopia: An Anthropology of Human Rights* (Stanford University Press 2009).

Harvey D., *Diecisiete contradicciones y el fin del capitalismo* (IAEN 2014).

Klein N., *The Shock Doctrine: The Rise of Disaster Capitalism* (Picador 2007).

Klein N., *This Changes Everything. Capitalism vs. Climate* (Penguin Books 2014).

Kolbert E., *The Sixth Extintion: An Unnatural History* (Henry Holt Company 2015).

Laval C. y Dardot P., *Común: Ensayo sobre la revolución del siglo XXI* (Gedisa 2015).

Martínez de Bringas A., *Los pueblos indígenas y el discurso de los derechos* (Universidad de Deusto 2003).

Moyn S., *The Last Utopía. Human Rights in History* (Harvard University Press 2010).

Noguera A., *Utopía y poder constituyente: Los ciudadanos ante los tres monismos del Estado neoliberal* (Sequitur 2012).

Oxfam, *Una economía al servicio del 1%. Acabar con los privilegios y la concentración de poder para frenar la desigualdad extrema. 2016* (Oxfam International 2016).
Quijano A., 'Bien vivir: Entre el desarrollo y la des/colonialidad del poder' in *Centro Andino de Acción Popular: Acerca del buen vivir* (CAAP 2011).
Rendueles C., *Capitalismo canalla: Una historia personal del capitalismo a través de la literatura* (Seix Barral 2015).
Rodríguez Palop M.E., 'Vive usted en un mundo civilizado? El desarrollo sostenible desde el discurso de los derechos humanos' (2005) 18 *Revista de Humanidades: Tecnológico de Monterrey* 261–270, https://bit.ly/31Aieiw.
Rodríguez Palop M.E., *La nueva generación de Derechos Humanos. Origen justificación* (Dykinson/Instituto de Derechos Humanos Bartolomé de las Casas-Universidad Carlos III de Madrid 2010).
Singer P., *Animal Liberation: The Definitive Classic of the Animal Movement* (Harper Perennial 2009).
Swimme T. y Tucker M.E., *Journey of the Universe* (Yale University Press 2011).
Tse L., *Tao Teh Ching* (Biblok Book 2017).
Wilczek F., *El mundo como obra de arte: En busca del diseño profundo de la naturaleza* (Crítica 2016).
Wright E.O., *Envisioning Real Utopías* (Verso 2010).
Zizek S., *El sublime objeto de la ideología* (Siglo XXI 2005).

5 Environmental Ethics in Islam and Greener Shifts Away From Fossil Fuel Dependence in the Middle East

Zainab Lokhandwala

1. Introduction

Islam provides a holistic view of nature and the earth as Allah's creations, and the Quran refers to the relationship between humans and nature on several occasions. Islamic environmental values such as human accountability towards natural resources and conservation of all life forms have been used by burgeoning green movements in the Muslim world to create environmental awareness.[1] Yet by and large, Muslim countries do not rely on Islamic environmental ethics while framing their respective environmental laws and policies. Countries that occupy a front-row seat in the drive towards utilising Islamic principles to solve contemporary environmental challenges have not been entirely successful at doing so. A conceptual analysis of Islamic environmental principles reveals a richness of ecological, eco-juridical, and conservationist themes. While pluralists may argue that the daily lives of Muslims are not guided by state law, as much as they are guided by the Quran, the opposite is true for state law itself.

Islamic environmental ethics are the broad moral principles that can be situated in any of the valid sources of Islamic law and jurisprudence. It is not necessary here to take a deep dive into a general exposition of Islamic legal sources; however, a basic understanding of the Islamic legal tradition ought to suffice as a primer for the layers that will follow. The two main sects within Islam are Sunnism and Shi'ism. Sunnis comprise an 85–90% majority among all Muslims. Even though Shias are a minority at a global level, they are a majority in some countries, such as Iran, Iraq, and Lebanon. Owing to this demographic, Islamic legal scholarship relies predominantly on Sunni sources of law, unless stated otherwise.[2] Within Sunnism, there are four major schools of law: Hanafi, Maliki, Shafi', and Hanbali; whereas under Shi'ism, major schools include Ismaili, Ithna-Ashari, Jafari, Zaidy, etc.

1 Najma Mohamed, 'Revitalizing Islamic Ecological Ethics Through Education' in Michael Peters (ed), *Encyclopaedia of Educational Philosophy and Theory* (Springer 2017) i.
2 For Sunni and Shia Islamic legal scholarship: See Ann Black, Hossein Esmaeili and Nadirsyah Hosen, *Modern Perspectives on Islamic Law* (Edward Elgar 2013) 12–15.

DOI: 10.4324/9781003175308-7

A wide range of Islamic schools have co-existed and co-evolved in different temporal and spatial contexts.[3] For instance, the Islamic legal tradition of Morocco, a North African country that predominantly follows the Maliki school, and has inherited French administrative and judicial law owing to its protectorate status until 1956 starkly contrasts with the Islamic legal tradition of say, Pakistan, a South Asian erstwhile–British colonial country. In the quest towards understanding what the Islamic legal tradition *is*, many scholars restrict their focus to only Islamic sources of law, but what *is* Islamic or not depends heavily on not just the specific Islamic school of law one gives credence to, but also the historical and geographic legal culture of the place itself.

A legal system may be defined as the legal rules, and how they operate procedurally in the legal institutions of any country.[4] Contemporary comparatists have moved away from this narrow definition, stating that legal systems are the general "juristic philosophy and techniques shared by a number of nations with broadly similar legal systems."[5] These characteristics range from historical background and development, distinctive institutions, and ideology to preodminant and characteristic mode of thought and its sources of law.[6] A legal tradition is a legal system in its cultural context.[7] Given this, the concept and nature of Islamic law, that is, its extensive body of sources and literature, are considered by most Muslims to be divine and sacred. Legal principles revealed in the Quran and practiced by Prophet Mohammed (SAW) are immune from critical evaluation. The Islamic legal tradition consists of legal practices, juridical institutions, and determinations that span a period of over 1400 years and have operated in a wide array of historical, cultural, and geographic contexts ranging from Tunisia to Indonesia. This creates a complicated reality of Islamic law which has unfortunately fallen victim to oversimplification and stereotyping.

In the search for Islamic environmental law, it is first pertinent to distinguish Islamic law and Muslim law.[8] Such differentiation is not very clear in many jurisdictions; however, it is still necessary to be made. Islamic law refers to the whole body of religious doctrine deduced from Quran, the Sunnah, and other secondary

3 Intinsar A Rabb, 'Islamic Legal Minimalism: When Jurists and Lawmaking when Jurists Disappear' in Michael Cook, Asma Sayeed and Intinsar Rabb (eds), *Law and Tradition in Classical Islamic Thought: Studies in Honor of Professor Hossein Modarressi* (Palgrave McMillian 2012) 145.

4 Joseph Raz, *The Concept of a Legal System: An Introduction to the Theory of a Legal System* (OUP 2012).

5 George Winterton, 'Comparative Law Teaching' (1975) 23 *Am J Comp L* 69, 70.

6 Conrad Zweigert and Hein Kötz, *An Introduction to Comparative Law* (2nd ed, OUP 1992).

7 John Henry Merryman, *The Civil Law Tradition* (Stanford University Press 1985) 2:

> [Legal traditions] are deeply rooted, historically continued attitudes about the nature of law . . . role of law in . . . society and the polity, the proper organisation and operation of a legal system, and about the way law is, or should be made, applied, studied, perfected, and taught. The legal tradition relates the legal system to the culture of which it is a partial expression. It puts the legal system into cultural context.

8 Khaled M Abou El Fadl, 'The Islamic Legal Tradition: A Comparative Law Perspective' in Mauru Bussani and Ugo Mattei (eds), *Cambridge Companion to Comparative Law* (Cambridge Univ Press 2012) 296.

sources. Muslim law on the other hand is a colonial imposition, wherein countries with sizable Muslim populations adopted the British common law system or the French-based civil law system while retaining Islamic law limited to only personal law matters (such as marriage, divorce, or inheritance). In the post-colonial context, some Muslim countries tried to Islamicise other branches of law, such as commercial and criminal law.[9] In its current form, the Islamic legal tradition found in Muslim countries is thus an amalgamation of Islamic laws and Islamicised laws borrowed and transplanted from Western colonisers. Given such degree of diversity, a search for Islamic environmental law runs the risk of essentialising what Islamic law is.[10]

Some scholars have noted that there is no discipline called 'Islamic environmental law.' This is because

> while Islamic law is proclaimed as a source of the legal system in the constitutions of Muslim countries, it is generally not used for the purpose of nature conservation. However, we can find in Islamic law a theoretical and practical foundation for environmental law.[11]

It is for this reason that this chapter uses the term 'Islamic environmental ethics' rather than 'Islamic environmental law.' Islamic environmental ethics are moral principles on nature and environment that every Muslim must adhere to.[12] These can guide the actions of law and policymakers, whether they be dealing with Islamic or Muslim or Islamicised law in their respective jurisdictions.

2. Principles of Environmental Law in Islam

The Islamic environmental principles listed next are presumably accepted by all Muslims globally, owing to their explicit articulation in the Quran. As per the Islamic worldview, humans and nature are creations of Allah, and are governed by a fixed order (*fitrah*). In essence, humans cannot detach themselves from the rest of Allah's creation. Humans are dependent on the natural world for a multitude of reasons. Such interactions between man and nature sustain and reinforce energy cycles, and ergo fulfil the very purpose of creation itself.[13] Islamic environmental ethics can be derived from these set of broad principles and applied in

9 For example: Libya (1972–74), Pakistan (1979), Iran (1991–96), Mauritania (1983), Yemen (1994), Brunei (2014).

10 Mohammed Sulaiman, 'Between text and Discourse: Re-theorizing Islamic Orthodoxy' (2018) 3(2) *ReOrient* 140.

11 Samira Idllalène, *Rediscovery and Revival in Islamic Environmental Law Back to the Future of Nature's Trust* (CUP 2021) 31–53.

12 Wael Hallaq, 'Groundwork of the Moral Law: A New Look at the Qur'an and the Genesis of Shari'a' (2016) 16 *Islamic Law and Society* 239.

13 Kevin Reinhart, 'Islamic Law as Islamic Ethics' (1983) 11(2) *J Rel Ethics* 186, 189–191.

varied contexts. This section throws light on five Islamic principles from which environmental ethics can be derived.

2.1. *Tawheed*

The principle of *tawheed* is a cardinal principle of Islam. *Tawheed* denotes the oneness, monotheism, or singularity of Allah. The utterance of *shahada* (declaration of faith) is to declare that "there is no Allah, but Allah," which is to declare that there are no other gods, but the real God: Allah, who is the creator, provider, and sustainer of the universe.[14] *Tawheed* stands opposed to atheist or agnostic conceptions of the universe, such as the universe coming into creation by chance, and progressing towards an unknown destiny. All of the substantive content of Islam is based on the foundation of *tawheed*; and several of its principles pertaining specifically to the environment, nature, and biodiversity are entrenched in this foundational belief.

Implicit in the concept of *tawheed* is the idea the entire natural world is Allah's creation, and it is He who administers, controls, nurtures, and sustains all life.[15] Muslims are thus expected to forbear from narrow-mindedness, being prejudicial and self-centred in pursuit of their selfish interests, because it is Allah to whom everything in the world belongs, and it is He who looks upon it.[16] Humans are entrusted to live in harmony with nature, such that the world may evince the glory and oneness of Allah.[17]

2.2. *Ubudiyat*

The term *ubudiyat* means a state of enslavement, which connotes extreme humility and extreme love towards Allah. *Ubudiyat* is the essence of worship in Islam, where one surrenders oneself before Allah absolutely. It is only through *ubudiyat* that a person may attain the highest and most praiseworthy condition in this life and the next. The Quran makes many references to this concept and advocates for inculcating humility as character trait.[18] There is hence a moral code every Muslim is expected to follow by doing the acts Allah has instructed to be done,

14 There are several instances in the Quran that argue and expound upon the concept of *tawheed*. For example: Surah-al-Qasas (28: 70–72): "He is Allah. There is no god worthy of worship except Him. All praise belongs to Him in this life and the next. All authority is His. And to Him you will all be returned."

15 *The Holy Quran*, Surah-al-Baqarah (2: 255).

16 Sayed Sikandar Shah Haneef, 'Principles of Environmental Law in Islam' (2002) 17(3) *Arab Law Quarterly* 241, 245.

17 *The Holy Quran*, Surah-al-Isra (17: 44): "The seven heavens declare His glory and the earth too and those who are therein; and there is not a single thing but glorifies Him with His praise but you do not comprehend their glorification."

18 Different words, such as *khashiyyah*, *tadhurru*, *ikhbat*, *inabat*, *khushu*, *khudu* and *qunut*, etc., have been used to denote extreme humility towards Allah and suggest humility to be an important virtue to be striven towards.

and refrain from actions that He has proscribed.[19] On the one hand, good deeds are considered *ibadat* (worship) of Allah, and on the other, a good deed is one that is done only for Allah, and not for any worldly pursuit.

Ubudiyat entails one's submission to the Higher Wisdom of Allah, which also includes an obligation to protect and preserve life in all its forms.[20] Muslims are expected to develop a deeper understanding of Allah's creation, to gain further insight into Allah's Wisdom.[21] In pursuit of protection and preservation of Allah's creation, humans should avoid wastefulness, destruction, and abuse of natural resources.[22] This integration of physical and spiritual essences of nature fosters sensitivity towards its use and protection, wherein over-exploitation and destruction of nature is seen not just as a physical loss, but also a spiritual one.

2.3. Human Stewardship: Nobility and Accountability

The Islamic worldview perceives humans as *ashraf-ul-makhluqat* (noblest of all creatures).[23] Humans have been blessed with *aql* (intellect), the possession of which is not a matter of accident but that of Divine Will from a Higher Source.[24] Humans have been conferred with the power and responsibility to use their intellect for doing good, and for this purpose, nature's bounties are gifts from Allah such that they may be used judiciously as per Allah's Will.[25] Muslims are expected to appreciate these gifts and be grateful.[26] Humans thus are possessed with the power and authority to utilise natural resources as means for righteous ends.

Such mastery over nature is juxtaposed with a simultaneous obligation of trusteeship (*amanat*), which should not be betrayed.[27] An *amanat* is the responsibility to act as a guardian over something with honesty and sincerity. From an environmental perspective, every person is accountable for the benefits bestowed upon them. Human stewardship encompasses a duality of 'use' and 'protection,' one that echoes the principle of 'sustainable development' under international law. Where use ends and protection begins is a question that has attracted several interpretations.[28]

19 Mohammad Hammoud, 'Environment, Ecology and Islam: Insight' (1990) 5(3) *New South Wales Islamic Foundation* 19, 20.
20 *The Holy Quran*, Surah-al-An'am (6: 38).
21 Mawil Izzi Dien, *The Environmental Dimensions of Islam* (CUP 2000) 8–10.
22 Gillian Rice, 'Pro-Environmental Behavior in Egypt: Is There a Role for Islamic Environmental Ethics?' (2000) 65(4) *J Business Ethics* 373, 380.
23 His Holiness Syedna Mufaddal Saifuddin, *'Allamal Insana Ma'a lam Ya'lam' Nazam Sharif* (Jamea Saifiyah Publications 2016).
24 Yusuf Najmuddin, 'Commentary – '*Fuyuz Falsafat al Aql*' – A Philosophical Discourse' by Dr. Syedna Taher Saifuddin (vol I, 1963) 2.
25 *The Holy Quran*, Surah-al-Luqman (31: 20).
26 *The Holy Quran*, Surah-Ibrahim (14: 32–34).
27 *The Holy Quran*, Surah-al-Ahzab (33: 72).
28 See Odeh Rashed Al-Jayyousi, *Islam and Sustainable Development: New Worldviews* (Routledge 2012); Ibrahim Abdul-Matin, *Green Deen: What Islam Teaches about Protecting the Planet* (Berrett-Koehler 2010) 22.

2.4. Natural Resources and Elements

Across different spheres of Islam, be it literature, architecture, philosophy, etc., the use of natural elements and resources has been rife to symbolise a deeper meaning. For instance, the Quran makes references to water, expressing that water is the basis and origin of all life.[29] Allah has called on humans to appreciate and value water as an essential source of life.[30] To use water is a 'common right' without monopoly, usurpation, or wastage.[31] Along with use, protection is vital for the preservation and continuation of life.[32] Air is also referenced in the Quran as a sustainer of life, a carrier of moisture-laden clouds, and an medium of pollination.[33] Similar to water and air, land and soil are essential for perpetuation of life.

The earth finds a recurring mention in the Quran, at times alluding to its purpose as "established for living creatures"[34] and "making land your home and the home for all terrestrial beings";[35] or its role in the cycle of life as "Allah has made you grow as a plant from earth, then to it He returns you";[36] or derivatives from earth that sustain life as "He has made the mountains to catch and store rain"[37] or "the earth, We have spread it out, and made it in mountains standing firm, and grown in it everything in balance. And we have provided in it sustenance for you."[38]

The importance of plants and animals has been spelt out by referring to their uses to humans, such as,

> Then let man consider his nourishment: that We pour down the rain in showers, and We split the earth in fragments, and therein make the grain to grow, and vines and herbs, and olives and palms, gardens of dense foliage, and fruits and fodder – provision for you and your cattle.[39]

In other cases, a harmonisation between humans and animals is fostered through explication of their characteristics, their social interrelationships, and their symbolic importance, as "There is not an animal on the earth, nor any being that wings its flight, but is a people like unto you."[40]

29 *The Holy Quran*, Surah-al-Anbiya' (21: 30).
30 *The Holy Quran*, Surah-al-Waq'iyah (56: 68–70).
31 *The Holy Quran*, Surah-al-Qamar (54: 28).
32 Abubakr Ahmed Bagade, Abdullatif Tawfik El-Chirazi El-Sabbagh and Mawil Yousuf Izzi-Deen Samarrai, 'Environmental Protection in Islam' (1994) 20 *IUCN Env Pol and L Paper* 2–6.
33 *The Holy Quran*, Surah-al-Hijr (15: 22); Surah-al-Baqarah (2: 164); Surah-al-A'raf (7: 57).
34 *The Holy Quran*, Surah-ar-Rahman (55: 10).
35 *The Holy Quran*, Surah-ar-Rum (30: 20).
36 *The Holy Quran*, Surah-an-Nuh (71: 17–18).
37 *The Holy Quran*, Surah-al-Mursalaat (77: 25–27).
38 *The Holy Quran*, Surah-al-Hijr (15: 19–20).
39 *The Holy Quran*, Surah-al-'Abasa (80: 24–32).
40 *The Holy Quran*, Surah-al-An'am (6: 38).

According to Islamic ideology, these natural elements and resources are seen through the lenses of *tawheed* and *ubudiyat*, wherein all things, the earth, mountains, and different creatures exist to proclaim the glory of Allah and worship him.[41] From this perspective, an obligation to preserve such elements and use them sustainably can be churned out, as their destruction would impede Allah's plan and purpose. Conservation of life is a fundamental tenet of Islam, and thus destruction of nature can be understood as an attempt to impair or obstruct Allah's Wisdom towards His creation.[42]

2.5. *Wastes, Pollution, and Natural Catastrophes*

Islam not only promotes the protection of natural elements and resources, but also makes umpteen references to the harmfulness of natural imbalances. First, cleanliness as an overarching concept is a mandatory tenet of Islam. Muslims are expected to stay clean, and keep their neighbourhoods and homes clean. Purity of heart and cleanliness of the body and one's environment relate to another, so much so that one is reflective of the other.[43] Cleanliness is a religious requirement, and "Allah loves those who keep themselves clean and pure."[44] Polluted and squalid places are to be cleaned, and wastes should be disposed of carefully, such that these areas do not become breeding grounds for disease.

According to the Islamic worldview, all catastrophes befall upon humans due to in part the acts of man. Thus, the occurrence of catastrophic events that cause loss of life, property, etc. is a time of *istighfaar* (seeking forgiveness) from Allah and observing piety and keeping faith.[45] From a socio-political perspective, Islamic faith was initiated and spread in a desert region where natural resources were

41 *The Holy Quran*, Surah-al-Hajj (22: 18); Surah-al-Isra' (17: 44); Surah-ar-Ra'd (13: 15).

42 Islamic jurisprudential principle: whatever is indispensable to fulfil an imperative obligation is itself imperative. Abu al-Su'ud al-Husayni, 'Umdat al-Nazir ʿala al-Ashbah wa'l-Naẓaʾir' (1759) [a commentary Ibn Nujaym, 'Al-Ashbah wa'l-Naẓaʾir' (1652)]; Ahmad Cevdet Pasha, *Al-Majalla al-Ahkam al-Adaliyyah* (Civil Code of the Ottoman Empire) (Create Space Independent Publishers 2016).

43 Outward cleanliness induces and/or reflects cleanliness of the heart, and vice versa. Its counter is also, where a filthy environment induces and/or reflects an impure heart.

44 *The Holy Quran*, Surah-al-Taubah (9: 108).

45 Natural disasters may be seen as (1) punishment: "And whatever of misfortune befalls you, it is because of what your hands have earned; and He pardons much." (ash-Shura 42: 30), "Evil has appeared on land and sea because of what the hands of men have earned, that Allah may make them taste a part of that which they have done, in order that they may return." (ar-Rum 30: 41); (2) warnings: "We will certainly make them taste some of the minor torment (in this life) before the major torment (of the Hereafter), so perhaps they will return." (as-Sajdah 32: 21); (3) a test for believers: "And certainly, We shall test you with something of fear, hunger, loss of wealth, lives and fruits, but give glad tidings to the patient ones." (al-Baqarah 2: 155); "Do you think you will enter the paradise without such (trials) as came to those who passed away before you? They were afflicted with severe poverty and ailments and were so shaken that even the Messenger and those who believed along with him said, 'When (will come) the Help of Allah?' Yes! Certainly, the Help of Allah is near!" (al-Baqarah 2: 214).

limited to begin with. While Islam manifests an anthropocentrism typical to all Abrahamic faiths, it entails a high degree of reverence for nature and natural resources for practical reasons too.[46] Non-environmental specific verses of the Quran can be referred to in this context, such as the concept of *meezan* (balance). Muslims are expected to pursue a balanced life, developing both the material and non-material dimensions.[47] Thus, mindless consumerism, wastefulness, and an overly material pursuit that places a pressure on the natural environment is frowned upon.

Islamic principles that comprise a rich source for Islamic environmental ethics deal with a wide range of subject areas. These are values that humans ought to cultivate in order to foster spiritual, societal, and environmental wellbeing. Yet, there are unresolved questions of reconciliation when one tries to reconcile Islamic principles with the international environmental legal discourse.[48] When placed against the 'mainstream' environmental narrative, several questions arise, such as: is climate change 'anthropogenic' or a natural calamity Willed by Allah? Why are humans, 'the noblest of all creations,' headed towards a mass extinction? How can one escape anthropocentrism (especially when environmental justice now includes concepts such as rights of trees and rivers)?[49] Can Islamic law reconcile with environmental law that is primarily science-driven and not value-driven? Is Islamic law well equipped for tackling the North/South dimension of environmental law? The practical application of Islamic principles in the environmental legal context poses difficulties, as will be discussed in the next section.

3. Application of Islamic Principles in Environmental Law: Potentiality for Fostering Greener Shifts

Islamic environmental law as a body of principles has not been enacted as a legal code or statute in any Muslim country. Islamic law is a key – but not the only source of law in any Muslim state. Even constitutions and laws that clearly state that Islam is the principle source of law do not rely exclusively on Islamic law, as legal principles have been borrowed from a wide array of jurisdictions over the past centuries and have resulted in mixed legal systems.[50] Owing to the importa-

46 Saleem Ali, 'Reconciling Environmental Ethics, Fossil Fuel Dependence, and Climate Change in the Middle East' (2015) 50(2) *Review of Middle Eastern Studies* 172, 174.

47 *The Holy Quran*, Surah-as-Shura' (42: 17); Surah-ar-Rahman (55: 7–9); Surah-al-Hadid (57: 25) encouraging a balance of *din* and *duniya* (faith and the world/spiritual and material). In other verses, the concept of *hayat-tayyebiyyah* (good life) has been expounded, which is a balanced life *inter alia*.

48 Robert McKim, 'On Comparing Religions in the Anthropocene' (2013) 34(3) *Am J Theology and Phil* 248.

49 Tim Stephens, 'Carbon Emissions Trading, Compensation for Soil Pollution, Legal Rights for Rivers, Protection of Biodiversity in Forests, Islamic Environmental Law' (2020) 23 *Asia Pac J Envt'l L* 99.

50 For instance, Saudi Arabia's Basic Law (constitution-like document) states that the Quran is as the constitution itself and Shari'a is its basic law; in Egypt Shari'a is the basis and

tion and subsequent mixture of non-Islamic legal principles, most governments do not enforce all Islamic principles as law.[51] Hence, these principles may have a high degree of influence on the citizenry at large; however, for lawmakers, judges, and lawyers in particular, these principles do not bear any special significance.

Islamic environmental principles can be invoked and employed to specific scenarios in several *locations*: one, environmental courts may use Islamic principles; two, Shari'a Courts/Muslim Law Courts may handle disputes with an environmental dimension (for example: land and water-sharing disputes); three higher/appellate judiciary may 'Islamicise' state environmental law, or 'environmentalise' state Muslim law; four, environmental law preached/sermonised by religious leaders may include an environmental reinterpretation of Islamic principles; and five, Islamic principles applied in the daily affairs of Muslims and communities.

This section tries to *find* in the *locations* to what extent Muslim countries have harnessed the potential of Islamic environmental principles in framing their environmental law and policy. By and large, Muslim countries have failed to incorporate Islamic principles within their state legal systems. It is hence no surprise that the push towards a deeper inquiry into Islamic environmental ethics has come from non-statal entities, such as environmental non-governmental organisations (NGOs), international organisations, academics, activists, and civil society groups.[52] Such a trend is evinced by the Middle East's efforts in combating climate change, wherein the integration of Islamic principles in mainstream environmental and climate discourse has only just begun, owing largely to the efforts of non-state actors.

3.1. In Search of Islamic Principles in Environmental Law of the Middle East

Over the centuries, the Muslim world has been ruled by a plethora of kingdoms and governments that have enacted their own laws and legal codes. Environmental law has not featured as a distinct sphere of law among any of these legal systems. The official legal code of the Ottoman Empire, the *Mejelle*, is an exception, in terms of its detailed provisions derived primarily from the Hanafi

source of all legislations; Libya's constitution states that Islam is the state religion and Shari'a is the source of legislations; Afghanistan declares itself as an Islamic republic, and that in the absence of any constitutional or statutory law over any subject, Hanafi jurisprudence would be applied to the matter; the Iraqi constitution that Islam shall be the state religion and encourages governments to enact Shari'a law. Christie Warren, *Constitutions and Islamic Law* (Oxford Research Encyclopaedia of Religion 2017), https://oxfordre.com/religion/view/10.1093/acrefore/9780199340378.001.0001/acrefore-9780199340378-e-96?rskey=jCzLQm&result=1.

51 Othman Abd-ar-Rahman Llewellyn, 'The Basis for a Discipline of Islamic Environmental Law' in Richard Foltz, Frederisk M Denny and Azizan Baharuddin (eds), *Islam and Ecology: A Bestowed Trust* (Harvard University Press 2003) 186.

52 Persons and organisations involved in drafting the Islamic Climate Change Declaration: See http://islamicclimatedeclaration.org/.

school of jurisprudence. Amongst other distinct categories of law, such as law of contracts and property law etc., environmental law does appear via some very interesting provisions.[53] First, there are rules for the use of community resources, such as grass, fire, water, and naturally growing trees which as "free to be used by all."[54] In the case of water, underground streams, naturally occurring springs, wells, lakes, and seas, these are water sources available to all as gifts of Allah.[55]

The construction of roads or diversion of naturally flowing water was permissible for the benefit of society; however, a decision to do so had to weighed against principles of necessity and proportionality.[56] The *Mejelle* is also very specific with ways in which one may legally reduce these community resources to private property. The "act of acquiring a resource with an intent to make it one's own" is a legal means of property acquisition.[57] For instance, if someone fills a vessel of water from a river, then that water is his/her property; or if one has caused for a tree or grass to grow on his/her land, then such grass or tree is private property. The general principle of one's individual property rights over common resources has been stated with a caveat, that it should "not cause damage to another" *and* [emphasis added] "does not prevent another from taking a community resource".[58] For instance, a person owning a piece of land that is adjacent to a water source such as a river/lake cannot block access to the water when the only access point is through the land. Furthermore, with respect to liability for causing destruction, there are clear provisions with respect to damage caused to private property. Such clarity is missing for the nature and extent of liability for causing damage to common resources.[59]

More than a century after the *Mejelle*, 'environmental law' as a distinct branch of law has emerged only a few decades ago, primarily through the efforts of the Global North. This has led to many Muslim countries trying to synthesise Islamic law with Western environmental principles such as 'common heritage,' 'precautionary principle,' and 'intra and inter-generational equity' through a process of reinvention and reinterpretation.[60] Several Muslim consti-

53 Herbert J Liebesny, 'Religious Law and Westernization in the Moslem Near East' (1953) 2 *J Comp L* 492, 479.

54 *Mejelle Ahkame Adiye* [Islamic Civil Code, hereinafter *Mejelle*] Book 10, Chapter IV (CR Tyser et al, transl 1967, 1901).

55 Ibid, *Mejelle*, Book 10, Chapter IV, para 1, article 1234. See: Melanne Andromecca Civic, 'A Comparative Analysis of the Israeli and Arab Water Law Tradition and Insights for Modern Water Sharing Agreements' (2020) 26(3) *Denver J Int'l L & Pol* 437, 450.

56 Principles of necessity and proportionality which are now widely recognised as common law legal principles can be traced back to the Hanafi school of law, which was later adopted in the *Mejelle*. Ibid, *Mejelle*, Book 10, Chapter IV, para 4, article 1267–68 and 1288.

57 Ibid, *Mejelle*, Book 10, Chapter IV, para 2, article 1249–50.

58 Ibid, *Mejelle*, Book 10, Chapter IV, para 3, article 1254.

59 Ibid, *Mejelle*, Book 8, Chapter II, para 1–3; para 1, articles 912–13 and 917.

60 Richard Foltz, 'Islamic Environmentalism: A Matter of Interpretation' in *Islam and Ecology* (supra n 52) 250, 262.

tutions include a duty (justiciable in some cases) to protect the environment.[61] A brief description of some Muslim countries as case studies shall highlight how Islamic principles are absent in respective environmental legal regimes.

For instance, the Saudi Arabian legal system, one with little to no colonial influence and one of the most well-documented legal systems in the region, proclaims that is based on Quranic and Shari'a law (as per the Wahabi interpretation). Its constitution-like charter, called the Basic Law of Saudi Arabia (*Al-Nizam-al-Asasi-lil-Hukm*) states in Article 32, 'Obligations of the state,' to 'preserve, protect and improve' the environment; Saudi statutory environmental law comprises the General Environment Law and Executive Regulations that provide details for implementation of the General Law.[62] Much of Saudi environmental law and administration is modelled after the USA.[63] This is especially true for the Meteorological and Environmental Protection Agency (MEPA), Saudi's implementing agency, which is very similar to the US' Environmental Protection Agency (EPA).

Post-colonial and post-protectorate examples also show a stark degree of Westernisation of environmental law and ethics. Pakistan, although not an Arab state but considered part of the Greater Middle East, is a Muslim country that gained independence in 1947 from the British. It has inherited the common law system, and is a unique amalgamation of South Asian, Islamic, and British colonial influences. Its activist judiciary has a big role to play in developing its environmental law. For instance, it recognized a right to environment under Article 9 Constitution in 1994.[64] Pakistan has also set up special environmental tribunals that are functional in some provinces, but these operate like civil courts with little to no connection with Islamic principles.[65] In some instances, higher appellate courts in Pakistan reference Islamic environmental ethics; however, the logic of these judgments is based on state constitutional, statutory, or regulatory law. In a landmark case, *Sindh Institute of Urology and Transplantation* v. *Nestle Milkpak Ltd*, the Sindh High Court made a passing reference to Islamic water

61 David Boyd, *The Status of Constitutional Protection for the Environment in Other Nations* (David Suzuki Foundation 2014), https://davidsuzuki.org/wp-content/uploads/2013/11/status-constitutional-protection-environment-other-nations.pdf.

62 General Law (Royal Decree No. 34 (24 September 2001) and Regulations (30 September 2003), together referred to as the General Environmental Law and Rules for Implementation (GERRI). New Environmental Laws have recently been passed, replacing some of the older decrees (Royal Decree No.165 (10 July 2020)) entered into force on 13 January 2021. Introduced 9 new laws (mostly on EIA) that increase the scope of EIA over a wider range of sectors and industries. Environmental laws are implemented by the Meteorological and Environmental Protection Agency (MEPA) under Ministry of Defence.

63 Magda Lovei and Charles Weiss, *Environmental Management and Institutions in OECD Countries: Lessons from Experience* (World Bank 1998) 23.

64 *Zia* v *WAPDA PLD* [1994] SC 693 (Pakistan Supreme Court).

65 Tribunals set up under the Pakistan Environmental Protection Act (PEPA), 1997. See: Martin Lau, 'The Role of Environmental Tribunals in Pakistan: Challenges and Prospects' (2018) 20(1) *Yearbook of Islamic and Middle Eastern Law Online* 1.

law principles, but primarily applied human rights law while reasoning through the matter.[66]

Morocco presents a unique mix of legal influences like Pakistan. It is a Muslim country that was a French protectorate state until 1956. It has inherited much of French administrative law and predominantly follows the civil law system. Following the Arab Spring, Morocco adopted a new constitution and made significant changes in its state legal system. Article 31 Constitution 2011 lays down a right to a safe environment and to sustainable development. In terms of statutory law, Law No.11–03 on waste-disposal, air, water, and regulation of dangerous facilities etc. make up the environmental law of Morocco. Similar to the Pakistani experience, it adopts a rights-based language for its environmental law. There are Shari'a courts that deal with personal matters and civil courts of Morocco have jurisdiction over environmental matters. Much like is the case in both Saudi Arabia and Pakistan, there is little evidence to show that Islamic principles guide environmental decision-making in any way. One faint exception is the 2009 Moroccan water policy, called the 'National Water Plan (PNE),' which references Islamic principles of protection and sustainable use;[67] however, the new 2016 Water Act (Law No. 36–15) makes no such references and is centred around a rights-based conception of water.

The examples of Saudi Arabia, Pakistan, and Morocco show that state lawmakers and judicial officers have not yet incorporated Islamic environmental principles in the overall state philosophy and strategy towards the environment. The environmental legal framework reflects Western juridical features more than it does Islamic features.[68] Each of these countries' constitutions swear allegiance to the Quran and Shari'a, yet they do not go so far as to re-conceptualise Islamic law's applicability in spheres other than personal law. The 'modernisation' of environmental laws in these countries does not reflect a commitment towards seeking guidance from Islamic principles.[69]

A more Islamic-oriented environmental regime would comprise stricter EIA norms that apply Islamic ethical parameters; stronger corporate responsibility to promote social welfare; planned development as per location-specific topography and ecology; environmental accounting for more efficient resource utilisation and avoiding wastage, and so on and so forth. With respect to incorporating Islamic

66 2005 CLC 424, 440 (Sindh High Court at Karachi).

67 Syeda Mariya Absar, 'The Future of Water Resource Management in the Muslim World' (2013) 17/(3) *J Futures Studies* 1.

68 Norah bin Hamad, 'Foundations for Sustainable Development: Harmonising Islam, Nature and Law' (SJD Dissertation, Elisabeth Haub School of Law at Pace University, July 2017), https://digitalcommons.pace.edu/cgi/viewcontent.cgi?article=1019&context=lawdissertations.

69 For instance, in the making of 'modern' Moroccan water law: Sandrine Simon, 'From Traditional to Modern Water Management Systems: Reflection on the Evolution of a "Water Ethic" in Semi-Arid Morocco' in Uli Uhlig (ed), *Current Issues of Water Management* (InTech 2011) 229–258.

environmental ethics within the environmental legal frameworks of Muslim countries, the shift from 'concept' to 'concrete' is a long road ahead – one that some countries may have just embarked upon at least with respect to climate change.

3.2. Middle East's Climate Efforts: A Step Towards Seeking Guidance From Islamic Principles

The Middle East is arguably the most significant region that sustains the fossil fuel economy. Over the past few decades, environmental voices of concern have grown louder within these countries, pushing for a necessary greener shift. The heart of the global oil supply is also home to the holiest of Islamic sites, and a concentration of the largest Muslim population on earth. The Middle East's contribution to global greenhouse gas emissions (GHG) is estimated at 4.2%; however, this does not include international carbon emissions from oil combustion sourced from the Middle East.[70] Given the importance of the Middle East in the global oil supply chain, an energy transition towards cleaner energy has to be both practical and profitable at a rate competitive to oil. Climate approaches are thus inseparable from the larger economic and political context within which the Middle East operates.

The advent of the coronavirus in 2020 has further pushed the environmental and climate agenda into the side lines as most countries in the region are utilising emergency sovereign funds or other discretionary resources to recover from the economic blow the pandemic has inflicted. Desperate relief packages, stimulus plans, and varied forms of compensation for loss of jobs and salaries are the priority rather than environmental spending.[71] Some conflict-ridden Middle Eastern countries have become especially fragile due to the pandemic. Countries such as Syria, Yemen, Iraq, Libya, and parts of Palestine have seen an exacerbation of existing structural weaknesses.[72]

The dominance of and dependence on oil and fossil fuel–led growth in the Middle Eastern region has seen a slow shift towards diversifying of economic portfolios and greater shares of renewables in the energy mix.[73] For instance, a leading figure in the UAE, Sheikh Abdul-Aziz-al-Nuaimi, who labels himself as the 'Green

70 For example, 96% of power generation in the Middle East comes from fossil fuels. For a break-up on different countries in the region: Hamid Bahrampour, 'Evaluation of Renewable Energies Production Potential in the Middle East: Confronting the World's Energy Crisis' (2020) 14(1) *Frontiers in Energy* 42, 43.

71 Tariq Yousef, 'Economic Impact of Covid 19 in the Middle East' *Babel Podcast* (7 April 2020); Dalia Dassa Kaye, 'COVID-19 Impacts on Strategic Dynamics in the Middle East' *The Rand Blog* (22 March 2020), www.rand.org/blog/2020/03/covid-19-impacts-on-strategic-dynamics-in-the-middle.html.

72 Jon Alterman, 'Add Coronavirus to Other Crises, and the Middle East Faces a Catastrophe' *The Hill* (22 March 2020).

73 Abdulnasser Alshaali, 'The Middle East Economies Catch the Dutch Disease: Reliance on a Single Export Commodity have Distorted Government Expenditures and Much More' *The Gulf News* (19 October 2018); 'Saudi Prince says Oil Markets are in Decline' *Climate Change News* (29 July 2019), www.climatechangenews.com/2013/07/29/saudi-prince-says-oil-markets-are-in-decline/.

Sheikh,' is highly responsive and motivated by environmental issues.[74] Over the past few decades, the transformation of Dubai from an oil-reliant economy to a service economy can also be seen as a success story for rapid and prudent diversification. Another instance is that of Masdar City in UAE, a low-carbon urban centre developed to spread environmental awareness and act as a model for future projects.

Masdar City is home to the headquarters of the International Renewable Energy Agency (IRENA). In the past decade, several Middle Eastern states have funded and set up projects under IRENA's aegis. Through such projects, the IRENA continues to be empowered by Gulf governments in assisting them towards a green transition. Some have tried to argue that Middle Eastern support to IRENA reflects these countries' Islamic energy philosophy.[75] Yet, this may be a tenuous link of causation that can only be asserted after further inquiry. While there are several positive trends, overall, Middle Eastern energy transition is much slower than is the need of the hour. When measured against the target of limiting dangerous climate change to 2 degrees, Middle Eastern efforts fall short by a fair margin. Climate Action Tracker's (CAT) 'Effort Sharing' study that researches national emissions policies and their effect on the global effort ranks most Middle Eastern countries' actions as 'inadequate.'[76]

While a lot more needs to be done, there is no denying that states in the region have shown more interest in playing a role in the climate movement that even before. The 2015 'Islamic Declaration on Climate Change' is testimony to a new kind of commitment, one where climate targets and goals are grounded in the Islamic theological context. In August 2015, the coming together of Islamic leaders from 20 countries in Istanbul, Turkey marked a unique moment for Islamic environmental law. This first of its kind 'Islamic Climate Change Symposium' focused on synthesising environmental law principles from within Islamic philosophy and jurisprudence; and it culminated with the adoption of the Islamic Declaration on Climate Change.[77] The timing of this event was most opportune, as it was organised just prior to the 21st Conference of Parties of the UNFCCC (Paris) and followed the famous statement of Pope Francis the same year.[78] The event can be seen as an attempt to join other faith-based calls for climate action in the run up to the Paris Conference.[79]

74 Supra (n 47) Ali at 175.

75 Tallal Turfe, *Energy in Islam: A Scientific Approach to Preserving Our Health and the Environment* (Elmhurst 2011).

76 CAT is a coalition of four research organizations – Climate Analytics, Ecofys, New Climate Institute and Potsdam Institute for Climate Impact Research. See: CAT, 'Effort Sharing Assessment' https://climateactiontracker.org/countries/.

77 'Islamic Declaration on Global Climate Change' (Islamic Climate Change Symposium, 17–18 August 2015 Istanbul), www.ifees.org.uk/wp-content/uploads/2020/01/climate_declarationmmwb.pdf.

78 Correspondent, 'Pope Francis joins Climate Fight' *UNFCCC News* (19 June 2015), https://unfccc.int/news/pope-francis-releases-encyclical-on-climate-and-environment.

79 Bill McKibben, 'Climate Change: A Warning from Islam' *New York Review of Books Daily* (2 October 2015), where he describes the Symposium as "an ongoing shift in the zeitgeist." www.nybooks.com/blogs/nyrblog/2015/aug/24/climate-change-warning-islam.

The event was initiated by a coalition of non-profit organisations, civil society groups, and academics working on creating environmental awareness and education in Muslim societies.[80] These were led by Islamic Foundation for Ecology and Environmental Science (IFEES/EcoIslam), which is supported by the Climate Action Network (CAN), the largest global network of organisations and civil society groups working on climate change. The institutions that were involved in the event along with these groups included the Islamic Scientific Education and Cultural Organisation (ISESCO, an organisation working on the likes of UNESCO for the Muslim world), the Organisation of the Islamic Conference (the largest inter-government organisation of Muslim states), and the International Islamic Fiqh Academy (one of the leading authorities for Islamic philosophy based in Saudi Arabia). Such a high degree of institutional involvement legitimised the message that the Symposium delivered. Subsequently the Declaration was endorsed by the United Nations Environment Programme (UNEP) and UNFCCC.[81]

This event saw the coming together of Islamic law and philosophy experts, who were united in challenging the fossil fuel economy of the Middle East. They deliberated on Islamic principles that could guide decision-makers in respective Middle Eastern countries to make a rapid yet smooth transition.[82] Some government delegations also attended the symposium, whose remarks were predictably reflective of their government's standard policy.[83] Yet, this should not be read for cynicism. The attendance of state delegates itself is a huge diplomatic step towards more Islam-centric environmentalism. The Symposium attracted over 20 Islamic NGOs, members of government, academia, environmental activists, and civil society groups, which resulted in the rolling out of the 'Seven Year Plan for Islamic Action on the Environment.'[84] Along with a plan, a project was launched called the 'Alliance of Religions and Conservation' (ARC) under the leadership of the Earth-Mates Dialogue Centre (EMDC).

The 2015 Declaration is primarily a result of efforts of non-state entities, such as NGOs, activist groups, and academics that have been working towards greater integration of Islamic principles in environmental law and governance. The urgency and scale of the climate change problem has forced the Muslim world into introspection, such that it may contribute solutions from the Islamic realm. On a more broader front, structural and historical factors limit the ability of legal systems in Muslim countries to incorporate Islamic principles; however, this may change in the future if governments are motivated by trends in climate change.

80 Supra (n 78).

81 UNEP, 'How Islam can Represent a Model for Environmental Stewardship' *Ecosystems and Biodiversity: UNEP News* (21 June 2018), www.unep.org/news-and-stories/story/how-islam-can-represent-model-environmental-stewardship.

82 Supra (n 80).

83 Supra (n 81).

84 'The Muslim 7-Year Action Plan (M7YAP) To Deal with Global Climate Change', www.arcworld.org/downloads/Muslim-7YP.pdf.

4. Conclusion

Millions of Muslims are guided by Islamic tenets in their daily lives. In the environmental context, Muslims endeavour towards *tawheed*, *ubudiyat*, stewardship, and respect for natural elements and resources as gifts from Allah. Muslim societies and states are organised not only on the basis of Islamic law. As a result, Islamic environmental precepts remain in the realm of 'abstract' as governments do not have the legal tools to implement them. For more Islam-oriented environmental law, Muslim governments could introduce new Islam-inspired laws; or extant laws could be interpreted Islamically.[85]

This chapter began with a description of relevant terms such as Islamic law, Islamic legal tradition, Islamic environmental law, and Islamic environmental ethics. It then highlighted five principles recognised widely by all Muslims, from which Islamic environmental ethics can be derived. In the third section, it is shown that these principles have a little role to play in state environmental law making and implementation. Owing to the complicated histories of legal systems in Muslim states, Islamic principles have been relegated to the side lines in the environmental arena. This is arguably a perpetuation of the colonial idea of Islamic law being relevant only to the confined sphere of personal law, while other spheres comprised 'modern' and 'secular' laws. However recent trends in combating climate change have sparked an increased interest in Islamic environmental principles, which state and non-state entities are willing to adopt while undertaking more ambitious climate targets. This may lead to greater Islamification of environmental law generally in Muslim countries in the future.

Bibliography

Abdul-Matin I., *Green Deen: What Islam Teaches about Protecting the Planet* (Berrett-Koehler 2010).

Abou El Fadl M.K., 'The Islamic Legal Tradition: A Comparative Law Perspective' in M. Bussani and U. Mattei (eds), *Cambridge Companion to Comparative Law* (CUP 2012).

Absar S.M., 'The Future of Water Resource Management in the Muslim World' (2013) 17(3) *Journal of Futures Studies* 1.

Ali S., 'Reconciling Environmental Ethics, Fossil Fuel Dependence, and Climate Change in the Middle East' (2015) 50(2) *Review of Middle Eastern Studies* 172.

Al-Jayyousi O.R., *Islam and Sustainable Development: New Worldviews* (Routledge 2012).

Alshaali A., 'The Middle East Economies Catch the Dutch Disease: Reliance on a Single Export Commodity have Distorted Government Expenditures and Much More' *The Gulf News* (19 October 2018).

Al-Su'ud al-Husayni A., 'Umdat al-Nazir ʿala al-Ashbah wa'l-Naẓaʾir' (1759) [a commentary Ibn Nujaym, 'Al-Ashbah wa'l-Naẓaʾir' (1652)].

85 Geoffrey Roughton, 'The Ancient and the Modern: Environmental Law and Governance in Islam' (2007) 32 *Columbia J Env'tl L* 99, 126–131.

Alterman J., 'Add Coronavirus to Other Crises, and the Middle East Faces a Catastrophe' *The Hill* (22 March 2020).

Bagade A.A., El-Chirazi El-Sabbagh A.T. and Izzi-Deen Samarrai M.Y., 'Environmental Protection in Islam' (1994) 20 *IUCN Env Pol and L Paper*.

Bahrampour H., 'Evaluation of Renewable Energies Production Potential in the Middle East: Confronting the World's Energy Crisis' (2020) 14(1) Frontiers in Energy 42.

Black A., Esmaeili H. and Hosen N., *Modern Perspectives on Islamic Law* (Edward Elgar 2013).

Boyd D., *The Status of Constitutional Protection for the Environment in Other Nations* (David Suzuki Foundation 2014), https://davidsuzuki.org/wp-content/uploads/2013/11/status-constitutional-protection-environment-other-nations.pdf.

Civic M.A., 'A Comparative Analysis of the Israeli and Arab Water Law Tradition and Insights for Modern Water Sharing Agreements' (2020) 26(3) *Denver J Int'l L & Pol* 437.

Climate Action Tracker, 'Effort Sharing Assessment' (2021), https://climateactiontracker.org/countries/.

Dien M.I., *The Environmental Dimensions of Islam* (CUP 2000).

Foltz R., 'Is there an Islamic Environmentalism?' (2000) 22(1) *Environmental Ethics* 63.

Foltz R., 'Islamic Environmentalism: A Matter of Interpretation' in R. Foltz, F.M. Denny and A. Baharuddin (eds), *Islam and Ecology: A Bestowed Trust* (Harvard University Press 2003).

Hallaq W., 'Groundwork of the Moral Law: A New Look at the Qur'an and the Genesis of Shari'a' (2016) 16 *Islamic Law and Society* 239.

Hamad N., 'Foundations for Sustainable Development: Harmonising Islam, Nature and Law' (SJD Dissertation, Elisabeth Haub School of Law at Pace University July 2017), https://digitalcommons.pace.edu/cgi/viewcontent.cgi?article=1019&context=lawdissertations.

Hammoud M., 'Environment, Ecology and Islam: Insight' (1990) 5(3) *New South Wales Islamic Foundation* 19.

Haneef S.S.S., 'Principles of Environmental Law in Islam' (2002) 17(3) *Arab Law Quarterly* 241.

His Holiness, Saifuddin S.M., *'Allamal Insana Ma'a lam Ya'lam' Nazam Sharif* (Jamea Saifiyah Publications 2016).

Idllalène S., *Rediscovery and Revival in Islamic Environmental Law Back to the Future of Nature's Trust* (CUP 2021).

Kaye D.D., 'COVID-19 Impacts on Strategic Dynamics in the Middle East' *The Rand Blog* (22 March 2020), www.rand.org/blog/2020/03/covid-19-impacts-on-strategic-dynamics-in-the-middle.html.

Lau M., 'The Role of Environmental Tribunals in Pakistan: Challenges and Prospects' (2018) 20(1) *Yearbook of Islamic and Middle Eastern Law Online* 1.

Liebesny H.J., 'Religious Law and Westernization in the Moslem Near East' (1953) 2 *J Comp L* 492.

Llewellyn O.A.R., 'The Basis for a Discipline of Islamic Environmental Law' in R. Foltz, F.M. Denny and A. Baharuddin (eds), *Islam and Ecology: A Bestowed Trust* (Harvard University Press 2003).

Lovei M. and Weiss C., *Environmental Management and Institutions in OECD Countries: Lessons from Experience* (World Bank 1998).

McKibben B., 'Climate Change: A Warning from Islam' *New York Review of Books Daily* (24 August 2015), www.nybooks.com/blogs/nyrblog/2015/aug/24/climate-change-warning-islam/.

McKim R., 'On Comparing Religions in the Anthropocene' (2013) 34(3) *Am J Theology and Phil* 248.

Merryman J.H., *The Civil Law Tradition* (Stanford University Press 1985).

Mohamed N., 'Revitalizing Islamic Ecological Ethics Through Education' in M. Peters (ed), *Encyclopaedia of Educational Philosophy and Theory* (Springer 2017).

The Muslim 7-Year Action Plan (M7YAP) To Deal with Global Climate Change, www.arcworld.org/downloads/Muslim-7YP.pdf.

Najmuddin Y., 'Commentary – '*Fuyuz Falsafat al Aql*' – A Philosophical Discourse' by Dr. Syedna Taher Saifuddin (Vol. I, 1963).

Pasha A.C., *Al-Majalla al-Ahkam al-Adaliyyah* [Islamic Civil Code of the Ottoman Empire] (Create Space Independent Publishers 2016).

Rabb I.A., 'Islamic Legal Minimalism: When Jurists and Lawmaking when Jurists Disappear' in M. Cook, A. Sayeed and I. Rabb (eds), *Law and Tradition in Classical Islamic Thought: Studies in Honor of Professor Hossein Modarressi* (Palgrave Macmillian 2012).

Raz J., *The Concept of a Legal System: An Introduction to the Theory of a Legal System* (OUP 2012).

Reinhart K., 'Islamic Law as Islamic Ethics' (1983) 11(2) *J Rel Ethics* 186.

Rice G., 'Pro-Environmental Behavior in Egypt: Is There a Role for Islamic Environmental Ethics?' (2000) 65(4) *J Business Ethics* 373.

Roughton G., 'The Ancient and the Modern: Environmental Law and Governance in Islam' (2007) 32 *Columbia J Env'tl L* 99.

Simon S., 'From Traditional to Modern Water Management Systems: Reflection on the Evolution of a "Water Ethic" in Semi-Arid Morocco' in U. Uhlig (ed), *Current Issues of Water Management* (InTech 2011).

Stephens T., 'Carbon Emissions Trading, Compensation for Soil Pollution, Legal Rights for Rivers, Protection of Biodiversity in Forests, Islamic Environmental Law' (2020) 23 *Asia Pac J Envt'l L* 99.

Sulaiman M., 'Between text and Discourse: Re-theorizing Islamic Orthodoxy' (2018) 3(2) *ReOrient* 140.

Turfe T., *Energy in Islam: A Scientific Approach to Preserving Our Health and the Environment* (Elmhurst 2011).

UNEP, 'How Islam can Represent a Model for Environmental Stewardship' *Ecosystems and Biodiversity: UNEP News* (21 June 2018), www.unep.org/news-and-stories/story/how-islam-can-represent-model-environmental-stewardship.

Warren C., *Constitutions and Islamic Law* (Oxford Research Encyclopaedia of Religion 2017), https://oxfordre.com/religion/view/10.1093/acrefore/9780199340378.001.0001/acrefore-9780199340378-e-96?rskey=jCzLQm&result=1.

Winterton G., 'Comparative Law Teaching' (1975) 23 *Am J Comp L* 69.

Yousef T., 'Economic Impact of Covid 19 in the Middle East' *Babel Podcast* (7 April 2020).

Zweigert C. and Kötz H., *An Introduction to Comparative Law* (2nd edn, OUP 1992).

6 The Noble Eightfold Path in the Anthropocene

Buddhist Perspectives on Environmental Constitutionalism

Enrico Buono

1. *Indra's Jewel Net*: The '*Intercausal*' Relationships Between Buddhism, (Constitutional) Law and the Environment

As a religious system, Buddhism has been historically neglected by mainstream comparative legal scholarship. Such circumstance presents somewhat of a conundrum in law and religion studies: Buddhism is the fourth largest religion in the world, with over half a billion followers worldwide, and yet its impact on Asian legal orders remains largely underexplored.[1] On the other hand, as an environmental philosophy, Buddhism has witnessed a surge in popularity in recent decades, evidenced by the proliferation of literature on the subject.

To the best of our knowledge, the gap between Buddhist Law and Buddhist Environmental Ethics has not been bridged so far. This chapter will try to shed some light on the possible interrelations between Buddhism, law and environmental matters, focusing on South Asian constitutional texts (and contexts) through the lens of comparative analysis. The remainder of this introductory section briefly addresses preliminary questions on the religious nature of Buddhism and the political implications of its – allegedly legal – rules. The following sections try to cross three *Tibetan bridges*: between Monastic and Secular Buddhist Law; between Buddhist Law and Buddhist Environmental Ethics; between Buddhist Constitutionalism and Environmental Constitutionalism. The second section will thus provide a concise overview of Buddhist Monastic Law, to assess its possible influence on the laity and on secular – or even political – matters; it will then explore the concept of Buddhist Constitutionalism by reviewing the existing literature on the subject. The third section presents some fundamental ideas underlying Buddhist Environmentalism and its relationship with Buddhist Law, through their common grounding in the same *virtue* ethics. The fourth and final section will try to establish a basic theoretical framework for further studies of Buddhist Environmental Constitutionalism, presenting a quantitative and

1 Rebecca R. French, 'What is Buddhist Law?' (2015) 63 *Buff. L. Rev* 833, 836.

DOI: 10.4324/9781003175308-8

textual analysis of six South Asian constitutions: the constitutions of Thailand, Sri Lanka, Myanmar, Laos, Cambodia and – in broader detail – Bhutan.

A full discussion of the origins of Buddhism lies beyond the scope of this study, but some general pointers may prove appropriate. The Buddha entrusted his disciples with the essential core of his doctrine – a pragmatic ethic more concerned with worldly problems than the nature of godhood – in the *Four Noble Truths*: the First Truth (*the truth of suffering*) recognizes that the world is filled with pain and every stage of human life entails suffering; the Second Truth (*the truth of the cause of suffering*) identifies attachment, desire and ignorance as the root causes of all suffering; the Third Truth (*the truth of the end of suffering*) suggests that, in order to eliminate pain, one must rid oneself from all desires and achieve Nirvana, a state of bliss in which ignorance and suffering are overcome; the Fourth Truth (the truth of the path that leads to the end of suffering) dictates the way to obtain release from suffering through enlightenment, known as the *Noble Eightfold Path*.

The Buddha describes the Noble Eightfold Path as the *Middle Way* between the extremes of self-indulgence and of self-mortification, illustrating its steps as *Right Understanding*, to recognize suffering; *Right Thought*, to overcome evil desires; *Right Speech*, to speak without lying; *Right Action*, to act without greed and violence; *Right Livelihood*, to not possess more than is strictly necessary; *Right Effort*, to control all sensual thoughts; *Right Mindfulness*, to achieve absolute presence through spiritual exercises; and *Right Concentration*, to develop mastery of desires and feelings. When grouped together, these practices constitute the *Threefold Path of Training*: *Sila* (*good behaviour*: Right Speech, Right Action, Right Livelihood), *Samadhi* (*equanimity*: Right Effort, Right Mindfulness, Right Concentration), and *Prajna* (*wisdom*: Right Understanding and Right Thought).

As is well recognized, the first Buddhist communities were not directly involved in political and social issues. In the third century BCE, the conversion of Emperor Ashoka allowed Buddhism's outflow from organized monasticism to an increasingly institutionalized laity. With Ashoka – who was identified by later Buddhist literature as the embodiment of the *Cakkavatti* or a 'Wheel-turning' Emperor – a Buddhist idea of royalty was implemented. In the following centuries, Buddhism spread throughout the Indian subcontinent, Sri Lanka, South Asia, China, Japan, Korea and Tibet. Quite paradoxically, Buddhism faced a long decline in its homeland with the Hun invasions and the Muslim conquest of India, until the modern revival led by the Dalit Buddhist Movement, started in the 1950s by Bhimrao Ramji Ambedkar.

It has long been debated whether Buddhism is a religion or a philosophy. According to Huxley, answering this question entails a 'conditional clause:' "If Buddhism is a religion, then Buddhist law is religious law."[2] Huxley then proceeds to ask if Buddhism is theistic, reverential, ethical and ritual, summarizing

2 Andrew Huxley, 'Buddhist Law as a Religious System?' in Andrew Huxley (ed), *Religion, Law and Tradition. Comparative Studies in Religious Law* (Routledge 2002) 143.

the distinguishing elements of religion: firstly, Buddhism does not clearly draw the line between deities and other sentient beings. Divinity is seen as a process – rather than a state – of transcendence: "To the extent that Buddhism is theistic, it is an Andy Warhol theism in which *Everyone can be God for 15 minutes.*"[3] Secondly, Buddhists revere the Buddha, but "more as an intellectual authority than as a God."[4] Thirdly, the reverential and ethical significances of the Buddha "do not combine to make him a religious figure."[5] But lastly, as a ritual practice, "Buddhism looks religious":[6] by shifting the perspective on "the way Buddhists act in public" – Huxley argues – the realization that Buddhists behave "in their public acts of ritual as if the Buddha were Jesus of Nazareth"[7] arises.

Those who dared to reconstruct the legal implications of Buddhist sacred literature have found significant hurdles towards any comparative attempt. French eloquently sets out the case for the 'Missing Discipline' represented by Buddhist legal studies: "How, in the midst of the many inter-, multi-, intra- and pluri- disciplinary study programs that now exist did we miss the study of Buddhist legal systems over the last 2,500 years?"[8] Many have traced this gap back to the 'ghost' of Max Weber,[9] who defined Buddhism "a specifically unpolitical and antipolitical status religion":[10] this *otherworldly* view has undermined the potential of Buddhist legal studies to the point of their ostensible irrelevance in comparative legal scholarship. French and Huxley critically referred to Glenn's seminal *Legal Traditions of the World*, where the author reflects these presumptions by stating that "Because of Buddhist teaching there aren't many lawyer Buddhists"[11] and that Buddhism developed "in a non-political, non-institutional way."[12] Reynolds claimed that this gap derives from an 'Orientalist' perspective, an assumption that can be explained along the lines of Ruskola's idea of legal orientalism:[13] "With an orientalist definition of law, the superior party determines which legal systems are of value and which are not, and perhaps even with the best of intentions, which are 'other-worldly' and therefore not legal."[14] This epistemic arrogance was

3 Ibid.
4 Ibid.
5 Ibid 144.
6 Ibid.
7 Ibid 143.
8 Rebecca R. French, 'The Case of the Missing Discipline: Finding Buddhist Legal Studies' (2004) 52 *Buff. L. Rev* 679, 681.
9 Huxley (n 2) 127.
10 Max Weber, *The Religion of India* (Free Press 1958) 206; cf Huxley (n 2) 127.
11 Hugh Patrick Glenn, *Legal Traditions of the World* (OUP 2000) 292.
12 Ibid 331–332; cf Rebecca R. French and Mark A. Nathan, 'Introducing Buddhism and Law' in Rebecca R. French and Mark A. Nathan (eds), *Buddhism and Law. An Introduction* (CUP 2014) 19.
13 Frank E. Reynolds, 'Buddhism and Law – Preface' (1995) 18 *Journal of the International Association of Buddhist Studies* 1; Teemu Ruskola, *Legal Orientalism: China, The United States, and Modern Law* (Harvard University Press 2013).
14 French (n 1) 850.

vividly illustrated by French in her depiction of the seven 'moves' of Legal Imperialism, but she does not spare some criticism on the reductionist approaches of Legal Romanticists, Legal Activists and Legal Tourists.[15]

Even still, as Schonthal remarked, there are 'gaps within the gaps' in the burgeoning field of Buddhist legal studies, the most relevant of which – for our purposes – are the 'socio-legal study of Buddhism in the contemporary period' and the "formations of Buddhist Constitutionalism."[16]

The metaphor of Indra's Jewel Net – describing the theory of multifactored causation or *codependent origination* – aptly depicts the complex interconnected relationships between Chiba's 'postulative values'[17] of Buddhist ethos and the contexts of Buddhist (Constitutional) Law. The following pages attempt to address some of the previously mentioned gaps.

2. From Buddhist (Monastic) Law to Buddhist (Secular) Constitutionalism

Our work moves from Menski's assumption that the notion of 'religious legal system' is but a "dangerously simplifying poisoned bait," implying that "all legal systems have certain religious elements in them which may be invisible, but which are present and should be brought out by comparative legal analysis."[18] The idea of Buddhist Law is therefore still controversial among scholars and its very opportunity remains questionable. We will briefly explore in this section a stipulative definition of Buddhist Law, substantially overlapping with Huxley's 'trichotomising' model of "the Pali Buddhist legal tradition."[19]

Buddhist Law can be "devised as a set of rules and behaviors, both individual and collective, that reduce the possible instances of desire, ignorance, and anger that can cause immoral actions":[20] its analysis is usually conducted following two approaches. A larger body of literature has addressed the Monastic Law of the *vinaya*, the autonomous legal order enforcing the rules of the *sangha*, the community of *bhikkhus* (monks). Fewer authors have discussed the dimensions of

15 French (n 8) 687.

16 Benjamin Schonthal and Tom Ginsburg, 'Setting an Agenda for the Socio-Legal Study of Contemporary Buddhism' (2016) 3 *Asian Journal of Law and Society* 1, 4–6.

17 According to Masaji Chiba, 'Conclusion' in Masaji Chiba (ed), *Asian Indigenous Law in Interaction with Received Law* (KPI 1986) 393, postulative values are "particular values and ideas and their systems specifically connected with a particular law to ideationally found, justify, or else supplement, criticize the existing positive rules."

18 Werner Menski, 'Hindu Law as a 'Religious' System' in Andrew Huxley (ed), *Religion, Law and Tradition. Comparative Studies in Religious Law* (Routledge 2002) 112.

19 Huxley (n 2) 128; we mostly refer to Pali Buddhism throughout the chapter, adhering to French's rejection of "the assumption that Mahayana and Theravada schools of Buddhism, or various regional forms of Buddhism, were so thoroughly different that one could not productively think about Buddhism and law as a coherent subfield of study." See French (n 8) 679; Schonthal and Ginsburg (n 16) 3.

20 French (n 1) 878.

legal pluralism emerging from the intersection of lay communities and monastic fraternities: contemporary Buddhist Constitutionalism occupies a blind spot in this regard.

Regardless of context, the *fons fontium* or *grundnorm* of Buddhist Law is dhamma,[21] a concept which transcends the distinction between ethics, law and religion, roughly translatable as "the natural order of the universe and society" or as "one's duty or ritual obligations within that order."[22] The concept of dhamma poses a substantial intercultural challenge, as it is "neither 'law' nor 'religion', and yet it encompasses parts of both":[23] its "homeomorphic equivalencies"[24] are not easily found within Western cultures.

The *Vinaya Pitaka* (*Basket of Discipline*, "which we must obey"[25]), "a Buddhist *corpus juris canonici*,"[26] represents just a third of the Buddhist canon (*Tipitaka* or 'Triple Basket'). The second basket is constituted by the *Sutta Pitaka* (*Basket of Discourse*, 'which we must learn'), comprising as many as 10,000 *suttas* (discourses) delivered by the Buddha and his closest disciples. The *Abhidhamma Pitaka* (*Basket of Higher Doctrine*, 'at which we must work progressively'), is a full-fledged commentary of the *suttas*, originated as doctrinal interpretations of the Buddha's discourses by his early disciples. With a deliberate simplification, it could be argued that the *Tipitaka* is the prime written source of Buddhist Law or, at the very least, of Buddhist legal culture.

As the closest thing resembling a legal code in the Buddhist legal tradition, the *vinaya* is a complex system of binding rules meant exclusively for monks and nuns: with its accompanying narrative portions depicting the Buddha as an ethical role model akin to a lawgiver, it actually more closely resembles a body of case law than a structured legal code. The *Vinaya Pitaka* encompasses the rules that guide the life of the bhikkhu both as an individual and as a member of a community: "Whether or not you call this law, I would like to persuade you that the *vinaya* specialists think like lawyers."[27]

At the centre of Buddhist communities lies the *sangha*, a term meaning both 'assembly' and 'community': the *vinaya* has set the standards of individual conduct that differentiate monks from laypeople, but also laid down the rules for monastic life in the 227 rules of the *Patimokkha*. Kieffer-Pülz has aptly identified seven "general legal principles underlying early Buddhist Monastic Law":[28] their

21 We use Pali terminology for well-known concepts such as Nirvana, dharma and karma.
22 French (n 12) 4.
23 Menski (n 18) 112.
24 Raimon Panikkar, 'Is the Notion of Human Rights a Western Concept?' (1982) 30 *Diogenes* 75, 76.
25 Huxley (n 2) 130.
26 Preedee Kasemsup, 'Reception of Law in Thailand – A Buddhist Society' in Masaji Chiba (ed), *Asian Indigenous Law in Interaction with Received Law* (KPI 1986) 287.
27 Huxley (n 2) 131.
28 Petra Kieffer-Pülz, 'What the *Vinayas* Can Tell Us about Law' in Rebecca R. French and Mark A. Nathan (eds), *Buddhism and Law. An Introduction* (CUP 2014) 53.

brief overview might be helpful to establish the boundaries of Buddhist legal culture. According to Kieffer-Pülz, the *vinaya* affirms premodern versions of both the *nulla poena sine lege* and of the culpability principles, discriminating intended from accidental behaviours:

> Intention is a central topic in Buddhist monastic law. Consciousness being so important in Buddhism, intention is so significant that the negligent commission of an intentional crime does not result in an offense, whereas the negligent or intentional commission of a negligent crime leads to an offense.[29]

Even more interesting for our purposes, however, are the principles of unanimous consent in every decision and of equality among all *sangha* members: all votes were, in fact, considered of 'equal value,'[30] unconditioned by seniority or status.

Before proceeding to examine the potential constitutional dimensions of Buddhism, it is important to mention how the paradigm of interdependence – derived from the doctrine of codependent origination – translates into a relation of reciprocity between the *sangha* and the lay community surrounding it. In order to thrive, monasteries depend on charity from lay Buddhists, who gain religious merit in the process. Monks, on the other hand, have a dharmic duty to observe the *vinaya* in their quest for spiritual perfection:

> In other words, this was not a concern only for the individual nun or monk and their *sangha* community; it was a serious issue for the vast number of lay Buddhists who were to receive most of their religious merit through these religious actors.[31]

Assumptions of Buddhism's otherworldly disdain for politics and its "gnostic distaste for the worldly order"[32] have to be challenged. This "stereotyped picture"[33] ignores the "fuzzy"[34] relationship between politics and religion that characterized the historical evolution of Buddhism. Buddhists have always lived under the patronage of kings and had to embrace politics early on. Gunawaradana was the first to theorize the existence of an 'antagonistic symbiosis'[35] between kingship and the *sangha*. Schonthal argues: "Kings had a degree of power over

29 Ibid 54.
30 Ibid 55.
31 French (n 1) 844.
32 Ian Harris, 'Buddhism and Politics in Asia: The Textual and Historical Roots' in Ian Harris (ed), *Buddhism and Politics in Twentieth-Century Asia* (Continuum 1999) 1.
33 Ibid.
34 Ibid.
35 R.A.L.H. Gunawardana, *Robe and Plough: Monasticism and Economic Interest in Early Medieval Sri Lanka* (University of Arizona Press 1979) 344.

monks; monks had a degree of power over kings; monks and kings also needed each other."[36] The use of coercive violence by the state meant the violation of dharmic values, such as compassion (*karuna*) and non-violence (*ahimsa*): a violation that required legitimization by the *sangha*, which received the king's protection in return.

In '*Paliland*'[37] (or 'Theravada Asia'[38]), "the boundaries between royal law, the Buddha's law (dhamma) and monastic norms (*Vinaya*) tended to be, like territorial boundaries, hazy, and shifting."[39] In fact, the foundational paradigm of early Buddhist Constitutionalism – as brilliantly suggested by de Silva-Wijeyeratne – is "cosmological sovereignty," a "totalizing logic," assumed to coincide with dharma, that "informs at an ontological level the telos of kingship."[40] This "single interpenetrating totality"[41] was well reflected into the Buddhist "Leviathan,"[42] the legendary primeval king *Mahasammata* (*the Great Elect*), chosen by the people to end an Hobbesian state of nature and to maintain law and order.

Traditionally, it has been argued that a Buddhist theory of kingship emerged with the rise of the Mauryan Empire: the theory of the 'two wheels,' which divided the 'wheel of the law' (*dhammacakka*), practiced by the *sangha*, from the 'wheel of command' (*anacakka*), exemplified by the king. Born of mutual necessity, this theoretical framework would establish both the *Cakkavatti* ideal of a dharma-abiding king and the 'antagonistic symbiosis' mentioned before. The tales from the previous lives of the Buddha (*Jataka* stories) constitute part of the founding myth of Buddhist kingship: according to Huxley, the "field of Buddhist politics is defined by the political lists" and the "three most important political lists all . . . form part of the . . . *Jataka*."[43] These three political lists are the *Four Solidarities*, the *Four Roads Not to Take* and the *Ten Royal Virtues*: "namely

36 Benjamin Schonthal, 'Formations of Buddhist constitutionalism in South and Southeast Asia' (2017) 15 *I•CON* 705, 713. This is also reflected in the three competing legal systems of monks, laypeople and kings, which were bound respectively by *vinaya*, *dhammasat* and *rajadhamma*. For comprehensive references on Burmese and Thai *dhammasat* and *rajadhamma* texts, see Andrew Huxley, 'Studying Theravada Legal Literature' (1997) 20 *Journal of the International Association of Buddhist Studies* 63.

37 Andrew Huxley, 'Pāli Buddhist Law in Southeast Asia' in Rebecca R. French and Mark A. Nathan (eds), *Buddhism and Law. An Introduction* (CUP 2014) 167.

38 Roshan de Silva-Wijeyeratne, 'Managing Religion and Difference: Ancient Constitutionalism in the Theravada Buddhist Tradition and the Transformative Impact of the Modernist and Post-Colonial Turn' in Susanna Mancini (ed), *Constitutions and Religion* (Edward Elgar Publishing 2020) 193.

39 Ibid 199.

40 Ibid 193.

41 Stanley J. Tambiah, 'The galactic polity in Southeast Asia' (2013) 3 *HAU: Journal of Ethnographic Theory* 503, 508.

42 Andrew Huxley, 'Rajadhamma Confronts Leviathan: Burmese Political Theory in the 1870s' in Ian Harris (ed), *Buddhism, Power and Political Order* (Routledge 2007) 26.

43 Huxley (n 2) 137.

alms-giving, morality, charity, justice, penitence, peace, mildness, mercy, meekness and patience."[44]

The 'ancient constitution' of Buddhist *Paliland* enforced the Ashokan model of the 'mandala state,'[45] made up of the 'galactic polities'[46] first described by Tambiah: this model was "by far the most significant one in the premodern period as it was adopted by the Theravāda Buddhist societies of Sri Lanka and mainland Southeast Asia in the period from the thirteenth to nineteenth centuries."[47] The mandala states would 'pulsate' according to the variable territorial configuration of satellite provinces and principalities, while central royal power 'radiated from a center,' ideally identified with Buddhism, which functioned as an unifying form of 'symbolic capital.'[48]

For this study, it suffices to recall Keyes' definition of the positions held by the "Buddhists who had been engaged in challenging the legitimacy of colonial states" and "their postcolonial descendants."[49] Keyes distinguishes between 'enraged' Buddhists – who promote Buddhist nationalism, sometimes through the use of violence – and 'engaged' Buddhists – who favour peace and sustainable development, sometimes through international networks, reminding us of Santos' 'counter-hegemonic globalization.'[50] Both stances share the presupposition that the "modern state could be challenged on Buddhist moral grounds"[51] and both contributed to the affirmation of contemporary Buddhist Constitutionalism.

Schonthal suggested that

> one finds within Southern Asia a particular template of constitutional law, if not a fully elaborated prototype, that might be called Buddhist constitutionalism. In some cases, such as Bhutan and Thailand, this draws on traditional notions of Buddhist kingship; in all cases it tends to focus on the regulation of religious institutions.[52]

Two 'legal imaginaries' emerge from the analysis of these constitutional texts: a layer of liberal constitutionalism appears superimposed over the traditional narrative.

44 Harris (n 32) 4.
45 de Silva-Wijeyeratne (n 38) 185.
46 Tambiah (n 41) 503.
47 Charles F. Keyes, 'Buddhists Confront the State' in John Whalen-Bridge and Pattana Kitiarsa (eds), *Buddhism, Modernity, and the State in Asia. Forms of Engagement* (Palgrave Macmillan 2013) 20.
48 Tambiah (n 41) 509.
49 Keyes (n 47) 24; de Silva-Wijeyeratne (n 38) 195.
50 Boaventura de Sousa Santos and César A. Rodríguez-Garavito, 'Law, Politics, and the Subaltern in Counter-Hegemonic Globalization' in Boaventura de Sousa Santos and César A. Rodríguez-Garavito (eds), *Law and Globalization from Below: Towards a Cosmopolitan Legality* (CUP 2005).
51 Keyes (n 47) 24.
52 Benjamin Schonthal, 'Securing the Sasana through Law: Buddhist Constitutionalism and Buddhist-Interest Litigation in Sri Lanka' (2016) 50 *Modern Asian Studies* 1, 2.

These Constitutions represent "the latest iterations in a centuries-long tradition of royal polities in which Buddhism is (or should be) specially protected."[53]

As a matter of fact, Buddhism has achieved today some sort of constitutional recognition in every Buddhist-majority country of South Asia: the Constitution of the Kingdom of Cambodia (1993) declares that "Buddhism shall be the religion of the State" (Article 43) and requires the state to "promote and develop Pali schools and Buddhist institutes" (Articles 68); the amended Article 9 of the Lao People's Democratic Republic's Constitution (1991) proclaims that

> the State respects and protects all lawful activities of Buddhists . . . and mobilises and encourages Buddhist monks and novices as well as the priests of other religions to participate in activities that are beneficial to the country and people,

which is quite surprising for a socialist state; Myanmar's Constitution (2008) "recognizes special position of Buddhism as the faith professed by the great majority of the citizens of the Union" (Section 361); the Constitution of the Democratic Socialist Republic of Sri Lanka (1978) "give to Buddhism the foremost place," obliging "the State to protect and foster the Buddha Sasana" (Article 9); the Constitution of the Kingdom of Thailand (2017) requires the king to be a Buddhist (Section 7) and obliges the state to "support and protect Buddhism, which is the religion observed by the majority of Thai people for a long period of time," in order to "promote and support education and dissemination of dharmic principles of Theravada Buddhism for the development of mind and wisdom development," along with "measures and mechanisms to prevent Buddhism from being undermined in any form" (Section 67); lastly, the Constitution for the Kingdom of Bhutan (2008) proclaims Buddhism "the spiritual heritage of Bhutan, which promotes the principles and values of peace, non-violence, compassion and tolerance" (Article 3.1), and requires the king to be a Buddhist (Article 2.1). As arguably one of the most advanced environmental Constitutions in the comparative landscape, it further obliges the state "to create conditions that will enable the true and sustainable development of a good and compassionate society rooted in Buddhist ethos and universal human values" (Article 9.20), cementing the bond between Buddhist and Environmental Constitutionalism.

To reinforce this claim, the final section of this chapter further examines the environmental rules and principles contained in these constitutions.

3. The 'Greening' of Buddhism: Virtue Ethical Perspectives

A new interpretation of the core ethical tenets of Buddhism has been proposed in order to meet the challenges of the global environmental crisis. For instance, the

53 Benjamin Schonthal, 'Buddhism and Constitutional Practice' (2018) 13 *Asian Journal of Comparative Law* 245, 251.

first of the five pañcaśīla – the five precepts (rules of training) that constitute the basic code of ethics to be undertaken by Buddhist laymen – relates to the aforementioned concept of ahimsa, or 'do no harm': "I undertake the training-precept to abstain from onslaught on breathing beings." In environmental terms, this concept has been translated into practices of harmonious relationships with nature, through respect of all life forms. The second pañcaśīla – "I undertake the training-precept to abstain from taking what is not given" – has also been interpreted as a mandate to ensure the protection of the environment against its destruction and exploitation.

The range of concepts elaborated in the previous section – such as those of 'Buddhist ethos,' 'cosmological sovereignty,' 'galactic polities' or the 'ten royal virtues' of 'Wheel-turning' kings – resonates way beyond (the possibility of a) Buddhist Constitutionalism. Although briefly, this section intends to demonstrate that Buddhist Environmental Ethics is rooted in the same paradigms of interdependence that justify Buddhist Law: for our present purposes, it seems that the founding myth of both 'enraged' Buddhist nationalism and 'engaged' Buddhist transnational environmental activism can be traced back to the *Tipitaka* and to the parables of the *Jataka*.

Akegarasu Haya wrote: "Something that is made cannot compare with something that is born,"[54] thus summarizing one possible Buddhist perspective on the environment. Albeit acceptable at an intuitive level, the very existence of environmentalism in Buddhism is highly contested. Revising the categorization first proposed by Harris, Sahni identifies four positions emerging from the growing literature on Environmental Buddhism:[55] the 'Sceptics,' who dispute the ability of Buddhism to support an environmental ethics, according to its allegedly 'dysteological'[56] methodology; the 'Sanguines,'[57] who – more optimistically – try to test the environmental potential of Buddhist nonviolent principles; the 'Positivists,'[58] who rely on original Buddhist sources to verify their environmental tendencies; and 'Partisans' – the majority position[59] – who "appear to be deeply positive and inspiring environmentalists but ineffectual theoreticians."[60]

54 Gyoko Saito and Joan Sweany (trs), *Shout of Buddha, Writings of Haya Akegarasu* (Orchid Press 1977).

55 Pragati Sahni, *Environmental Ethics in Buddhism. A Virtues Approach* (Routledge 2008) 12.

56 Ian Harris, 'Causation and "Telos": The Problem of Buddhist Environmental Ethics' (1994) 1 *Journal of Buddhist Ethics* 45, 54; cf Sahni (n 55) 26.

57 Lambert Schmithausen, *The Problem of Sentience of Plants in Earliest Buddhism* (The International Institute for Buddhist Studies 1991); Alan Sponberg, 'Green Buddhism and the Hierarchy of Compassion' in Mary Evelyn Tucker and Duncan R. Williams (eds), *Buddhism and Ecology: The Interconnection of Dharma and Deeds* (Harvard University Press 1997) 351; cf Sahni (n 55) 21.

58 Joanna Macy, *World as Lover, World as Self* (Parallax Press 1991); cf Sahni (n 55) 16.

59 Allan Hunt Badiner (ed), *Dharma Gaia* (Parallax Press 1990); Mary Evelyn Tucker and Duncan R. Williams (eds), *Buddhism and Ecology: The Interconnection of Dharma and Deeds* (Harvard University Press 1997); Stephanie Kaza and Kenneth Kraft (eds), *Dharma Rain* (Shambhala 2000); cf Sahni (n 55) 16. For a more recent *partisan* perspective on the Anthropocene, see David R. Loy, *Ecodharma. Buddhist Teachings for the Ecological Crisis* (Wisdom Publications 2019).

60 Sahni (n 55) 16.

A "mixed dharmic bag"[61] indeed, but one that contains at least two fundamental principles: interdependence and kamma. The repeatedly mentioned principle of causal interdependence (or of dependent origination) refers to the interdependent nature of things, and has been interpreted both as a 'world-evolution theory' and as a 'personal process.'[62] The former view was clearly illustrated by Buddhadasa Bhikkhu:

> the entire cosmos is a cooperative. The sun, the moon and the stars live together as a cooperative. The same is true for humans and animals, trees, and the earth. When we realize that the world is a mutual, interdependent, cooperative enterprise then we can build a noble environment.[63]

This idea was translated into Thich Naht Hanh's concept of 'interbeing,'[64] a *cosmic ecology* derived in part from the Huayan metaphor of Indra's Jewel Net.

The principle according to which like causes lead to like effects is the law of karma, a principle of causality that requires "seeing interdependence as irreducibly meaningful."[65] A karmic cosmology seems to permeate, in fact, Hershock's "liberation ecology,"[66] emerging from the awareness of 'global interdependence' in the public sphere:

> The environment is the most encompassing of the domains associated with public good, as well as the domain in which critical engagement with processes of interdependence has most explicitly been worked into the making of public policy. Perhaps more importantly, it is also the domain in which the broader public first became aware of the complex interrelatedness characterizing the public sphere as a whole and of how even relatively localized patterns of ill-directed or qualitatively degrading interdependence can have globally adverse effects.[67]

This study does not engage with the debates around contemporary Eco-Buddhism, but we share McMahan's pledge to not "dismiss the current environmental and ethical discourse of Buddhist interdependence as an inadequate

61 Christopher Ives, 'Buddhism: A Mixed Dharmic Bag: Debates about Buddhism and Ecology' in Willis J. Jenkins, Mary Evelyn Tucker and John Grim (eds), *Routledge Handbook of Religion and Ecology* (Routledge 2017) 43.

62 Prayudh Payutto, *Dependent Origination. The Buddhist Law of Conditionality* (Buddhadhamma Foundation 1994) 12.

63 As translated by Donald K. Swearer, 'Principles and Poetry, Places and Stories: The Resources of Buddhist Ecology' (2001) 130 *Daedalus* 225, 229.

64 Thich Nhat Hanh, *Interbeing. The 14 Mindfulness Trainings of Engaged Buddhism* (Parallax Press 2020).

65 Peter D. Hershock, *Buddhism in the Public Sphere. Reorienting Global Interdependence* (Routledge 2006) 8.

66 Ibid 13.

67 Ibid.

representation of traditional Buddhism," as this 'originalist' claim would "fail to take seriously the process of modernity as it manifests itself on the ground": "Like virtually all normative religious reflection, this discourse is practitioners' constructive response to an unprecedented situation, not a historiographical endeavor."[68]

A brief review of Buddhist "environmental virtue ethics allows us to trace a common thread between Buddhist Law and Environmental Buddhism,"[69] all the way back to early Buddhist ethical doctrine. According to Sahni, "what truly sustains the presence of an environmental ethics in early Buddhism is its ethical doctrine embodying virtues."[70] The principle of interdependence would be vacuous without karmic causality: likewise, the Buddhist cosmological notion of nature – with its "weak anthropocentrism"[71] – would remain "incomplete" without the "virtue-based moral theory" woven into the Pali canon.[72] We agree with Sahni's definition of the Buddhist ethos as a 'virtue ethics.' Proven by our analysis of Buddhist Law, its understanding of morality is focused on the character of the person carrying out the act, and not on the action itself (deontology) or its consequences (consequentialism). This alone justifies the identification of intentional action with karma, first pronounced by the Buddha himself. A virtue "is an intentional deed or action whose constant practice necessarily has the ability not only to lead to a certain character but also to a higher goal":[73] Sahni identifies humility, self-acceptance and openness as contemporary equivalents of traditional Buddhist virtues with environmental significance.[74] The author argues that environmental value can be attributed to at least five virtues enshrined in the *Tipitaka*: the virtue of respecting all life (*ahimsa*); simple living and contentment; generosity; responsibility, based on the law of karma, and wisdom.[75] These environmental virtues are clearly present in the *vinaya*: by way of example, monastic law argues against the cutting of trees, the harming of plants, waste discharges – even spitting! – into rivers and canals; *vinaya* rules also promote the planting of trees and the recycling of fabric scraps to turn into robes. The discourses of the *Sutta Pitaka* may provide additional examples: both the "Ten Duties of the King" and the "The Lion's Roar on the Turning of the Wheel" – which provide the basic framework of Buddhist ethics of kingship, as discussed in the previous section – highlight the responsibility of the King to protect all organic life, also reflected in Ashoka's edicts.

Further examples can be found in the *Jataka* collection, the rebirth narratives of the Buddha's past lives: these parables are especially significant since

68 David L. McMahan, *The Making of Buddhist Modernism* (OUP 2008) 180; cf Ives (n 61) 49.
69 Sahni (n 55) 5.
70 Ibid.
71 Ibid 82.
72 Ibid 92.
73 Ibid 123.
74 Ibid 124.
75 Ibid 104–106.

they possess "legal or ethical bearing" and reproduce "provisions from the *Vinaya* which the laity should emulate." The *Jataka* tales allowed the "moral dissemination" of virtues transmitted to the laity: "Some of the virtues are non-violence towards all beings, a spirit of sacrifice on one's own part for a greater good, and loyalty to those things that have served one. All these can be seen as supportive of the cause of nature."[76] 'Partisan' and 'positivist' Buddhist environmentalists alike have extensively employed the Jatakas as metaphors of environmental significance: the *Jatakas* contain an "unconventional environmentalism that can be applied to contemporary environmental matters, provided one is attentive to the distinctive nature of problems that ensue."[77] By a fascinating coincidence, the ten royal virtues also form part of the *Jatakas* which, not surprisingly, served "as a synecdoche for the whole field of political science."[78]

Two tales in particular might bridge the gap between environmental values and the virtues of kingship: the *Mahakapi Jataka* and the *Kurudhamma Jataka*. The former tells the story of the Great Monkey King – none other than the Buddha, of course – who saved the lives of 80,000 monkeys from the arrows of the King of Varanasi by turning his body into a bridge over the Ganges. This tale is "environmentally relevant in pointing out the value of animal life," but also suggests "that the political ruler ought to be harbinger of such sacrifice," as the dying monkey king tells the King of Varanasi:

> Great king, I guard the herd. I am their lord and chief. When they were filled with fear of your archers, I leapt a great distance to save them. . . . Because I could save them, I have no fear of death. Like a righteous king, I could guarantee the happiness of those over whom I used to reign. Sire, understand this truth! If you wish to be a righteous ruler, the happiness of your kingdom, your cities, and your people must be dear to you. It must be dearer than life itself.[79]

The latter as well is a story of two kings: the king of the Kurus (the Buddha in his previous life) and the Kalinga King. In the Kingdom of Kalinga, a prolonged drought brought severe famine, while the Kurus thrived. It was revealed that the prosperity of the Kurus was due to the correct practice of dharma, and once the Kalinga King practiced the *Kurudhamma* rain started falling once again upon

76 Ibid 149.

77 Ibid 163.

78 Ryuji Okudaira and Andrew Huxley, 'A Burmese tract on kingship: political theory in the 1782 manuscript of Manugye' (2001) 257(64) *Bulletin of the School of Oriental and African Studies* 248, 257.

79 E.B. Cowell (ed), *The Jataka, or Stories of the Buddha's Former Births* (Motilala Banarsidass, 2001).

his country. In this parable, the unwholesome karma of a king leads to natural calamities:

> This once more indicates that Buddhists possibly believed that internal values have a connection with external factors and the state of the natural world. This reinforces the virtue of responsibility and strengthens the claims of an environmental virtue ethics even more.[80]

Thus far, we tried to establish Buddhist virtue ethics as the common ground between Environmental Buddhism and Buddhist Constitutionalism: the following section will present an exploratory assessment of Environmental Constitutionalism in Buddhist countries.

4. Preliminary Notes Towards a Definition of Buddhist Environmental Constitutionalism

In order to establish a framework for a preliminary inquiry into Buddhist Environmental Constitutionalism, we will refer to the evolutionary and synchronic taxonomy advanced in this volume by Amirante.[81]

Quite coincidentally, Amirante's model reproduces the 'trichotomising' pattern so often encountered in the Buddhist canon: category *EC* (*Environmental Constitutions*) includes genetically environmental Constitutions, which contained environmental articles "since their first approval":[82] category *REC* (*Revised Environmental Constitutions*) comprises revised environmental Constitutions, in which environmental provisions have been implemented "through amendments";[83] category *SEC* (*Silent Environmental Constitutions*) comprehends constitutional texts that lack environmental provisions altogether, depending only on "judicial decisions . . . by Constitutional and Supreme Courts"[84] to enforce environmental rights.

The Constitutions so far under our scrutiny are mostly young texts: therefore, it can be argued that this circumstance is the major reason why they all firmly belong to category A – with the relevant exception of the Constitutions of Laos and Sri Lanka, both revised in 2015 and thus belonging to category B; Japan and Singapore are the only two countries with substantial Buddhist majorities that might be ascribed to category C, but are both outside the scope of this study. While not denying the relevance of this argument, we would like to prove that

80 Sahni (n 55) 154.

81 Domenico Amirante, 'Environmental Constitutionalism Through the Lens of Comparative Law: New Perspectives for the Anthropocene' in Domenico Amirante and Silvia Bagni (eds), *Environmental Constitutionalism in the Anthropocene* (Routledge 2022).

82 Ibid 151.

83 Ibid 152.

84 Ibid.

some – if not many – elements of Buddhist ethos played a significant role in the establishment of a Buddhist template of Environmental Constitutionalism.

Due to practical constraints, the following analysis cannot provide deeper insights into the complex historical, political and sociological workings of so many countries, nor can it afford to consider the ongoing debate on the enforcement of democracy within them. It is instead aimed at providing a provisional textual framework, by means of a transversal comparison of those South Asian Constitutions that endorse both Buddhism and environmental protection. The available dataset takes into account the date of entry into force of the Constitution, the number of environmental provisions, including the ones introduced after an amendment, the context and systematic collocation of the environmental provision (with particular regard to the allocation of powers), the presence of a given definition of environment and how ancillary and indirect the reference to the environment is.

Before discussing the possibility of Buddhist Environmental Constitutionalism, it is necessary to review a few fundamental environmental provisions: we will add italics to emphasize some choice words for later commentary. The Constitution of the Kingdom of Cambodia (1993) declares that "the State shall protect the environment and the *balance* of natural resources" (Article 59). The Lao People's Democratic Republic's Constitution (1991) proclaims that

> the State promotes the protection and restoration of the environment which has been destroyed and degraded to develop it so that it may become abundant and sustainable. All organizations and citizens *must* protect and preserve the bio-diversity and use natural resources in line with the direction of ensuring sustainability,
>
> (Article 19)

while "giving priority to human resource development . . . in conjunction with *cultural development* and sustainable environment" (Article 21); the socio-economic regime established in Article 13 promotes "*local wisdom*" and is directed to "the sustainability of social development and environment, so as to ensure the mental, physical and economic *wellbeing* of the Lao people"; according to Articles 19, 31, 70.3, 87.9, 88.5, 89, the responsibilities of environmental management and protection are allocated to local government: village chiefs "have the responsibility to . . . take the lead' in the 'protection of natural resources and environment, . . . with a view to maintaining *harmony*" (Article 89). According to Myanmar's Constitution (2008), "The Union shall protect and conserve natural environment" (Section 45): the citizen "has the duty" to participate in "*preservation* and safeguarding of *cultural heritage* and environmental conservation" (Section 390). The Constitution of the Democratic Socialist Republic of Sri Lanka (1978) obliges the State to "protect, preserve and improve the environment for the benefit of the *community*" (Article 14) in a system where "the exercise and enjoyment of rights and freedoms are inseparable from the *performance of duties* and obligations and accordingly it is the duty of every person in

Sri Lanka . . . to protect nature and conserve its riches" (Article 28). The most recent Constitution of the Kingdom of Thailand (2017), in more modern terminology, states that "a person and community shall have the right to . . . manage, maintain and utilise natural resources, environment and biodiversity in a *balanced* and sustainable manner" (Section 43), while having a duty to "cooperate and support the *conservation* and protection of the environment, natural resources, *biodiversity*, and *cultural heritage*" (Section 50); it is therefore the duty of the State to "conserve, protect, maintain, restore, manage and use or arrange for utilisation of natural resources, environment and biodiversity in a *balanced* and sustainable manner, provided that the relevant local people and local community shall be allowed to *participate*" (Section 57); Section 58 envisages the right to prior consultation when

> any undertaking by the State or that the State will permit . . . may severely affect the natural resources, environmental quality, . . . *quality of life* or any other essential interests of the people or *community* or environment, the State shall undertake to study and assess the impact on environmental quality and health of the people or community and shall arrange a public hearing of relevant stakeholders, people and communities in advance in order to take them into consideration.

Common threads emerge from this first reading: Theravadin Constitutions always seem to tie environmental duties with environmental rights in a codependent dimension that is reminiscent of the 'antagonistic symbiosis' described in previous sections. One only has to look to Western Environmental Constitutions to realize that there is often a clear-cut dividing line between duties and rights: actually, it can be argued that 'duty' and 'rights' approaches to environmental protection constitute two different models altogether. We also pointed out how these Constitutions associate environmental protection with the conservation of cultural heritage, which encompasses Buddhist spiritual heritage: this interdependent perspective emerges through wordings such as 'balance,' 'wisdom' (one of the five Buddhist environmental virtues), 'wellbeing,' 'harmony' and 'participation'.

More considerations can be made if we further extend the comparison to the Vajrayana Constitution for the Kingdom of Bhutan, which can be assumed as the paradigm of Buddhist Environmental Constitutionalism. As previously noted, according to Bhutan's Constitution 'true and sustainable development' can only be 'rooted in Buddhist ethos' (Article 9.20). Article 5 defines every Bhutanese "a *trustee* of the Kingdom's natural resources and the environment for the benefit of the present and *future* generations," while repeating the patterns for right-duty relations highlighted earlier. In fact, Section 1 proclaims that every Bhutanese has "the fundamental duty . . . to contribute to the protection of the natural environment . . . and prevention of all forms of ecological degradation" through "the adoption and support of environment friendly practices and policies"; Section 2 defines the corresponding duties of the Royal Government to "protect, conserve and improve the pristine environment" and to "secure ecologically balanced sustainable development while promoting *justifiable* economic and social development" and ensuring "a safe and healthy environment." Section 3 establishes the limit of "a minimum of sixty percent of Bhutan's total land" to be maintained "under forest cover for all time": it is well known that Bhutan is a carbon negative country with the highest rate of forest area in Asia. "*Intergenerational equity*" is also mentioned in Section 4.

Jigme Singye Wangchuck, King Father of Bhutan, argued that "Gross National Happiness is more important than Gross National Product":[85] the concept of Gross National Happiness identifies sustainable development with human happiness "understood in a holistic perspective, that is inclusive of material and spiritual aspects" and involves "the growth of the well-being of the society as a whole."[86] Article 9 thus declares that "the State shall strive to promote those conditions that will enable the pursuit of Gross National Happiness" (Section 2). Four key pillars of Gross National Happiness were gradually articulated in economic development, environmental conservation, cultural preservation and good governance.[87] Gross National Happiness represents the expression of "deeply embedded Buddhist beliefs about the transitory nature of the world" that have "become linked with environmental concerns."[88]

Three virtue-based ethical characteristics of Buddhist Environmental Constitutionalism emerge from our preliminary discussion, all referring back to the influence of codependent origination and karmic causality. Firstly, the State has clear duties towards the environment, reflecting the ideology of *Cakkavatti* kingship and Ashokan proto-environmentalism. Secondly, both the State and its citizens commit to mutual environmental responsibility, firmly grounded in principles of trusteeship – rather than ownership – of natural resources. Lastly, principles of trusteeship also inform the 'cosmic law' of intergenerational equity, aptly expressed by the Dalai Lama himself:

> If we develop good and considerate qualities within our own minds, our activities will naturally cease to threaten the continued survival of life on Earth. By protecting the natural environment and working to halt the degradation

85 Michael S. Givel, 'Gross National Happiness in Bhutan: Political Institutions and Implementation' (2015) 1 *Asian Affairs* 102, 108; cf Alessandro Cenerelli, 'The Constitutional System of the Kingdom of Bhutan' in Domenico Amirante (ed), *South Asian Constitutional Systems* (Eleven International Publishing 2020) 195.

86 Cenerelli (n 85) 195.

87 Richard W. Whitecross, 'Buddhism and Constitutions in Bhutan' in Rebecca R. French and Mark A. Nathan (eds), *Buddhism and Law. An Introduction* (CUP 2014) 359; Richard W. Whitecross, 'Separating Religions and Politics? Buddhism and the Bhutanese Constitution' in Sunil Khilnani, Vikram Raghavan and Arun K. Thiruvengadam (eds), *Comparative Constitutionalism in South Asia* (OUP 2013) 116.

88 Ibid 365.

of our planet we will also show respect for Earth's human descendants – our future generations.[89]

The examples presented in the previous pages highlight the potential usefulness of an approach that envisions Buddhist constitutional culture as a prototype of sensitive Environmental Constitutionalism. Although a preliminary framework – deliberately limited in its scope to quantitative and textual data – we hope our work can open up the way to similar comparative inquiries. Such efforts may further help resolve the question of the relationship between Buddhism and Environmentalism in those South Asian countries where both elements are constitutionally enshrined and – as we tried to demonstrate throughout this chapter – refer to a similar cultural heritage and virtue-based ethical background.

It is a daunting task indeed: a challenge not unlike the one faced by Sun Ngokong – the Thai name for the Monkey King from the legendary *Journey to the West* – who believed to have reached the end of the universe, but was instead desperately leaping on the Buddha's hand.

Bibliography

Amirante D., 'Environmental Constitutionalism Through the Lens of Comparative Law: New Perspectives for the Anthropocene' in Domenico Amirante and Silvia Bagni (eds), *Environmental Constitutionalism in the Anthropocene* (Routledge 2022).

Badiner A.H. (ed), *Dharma Gaia* (Parallax Press 1990).

Cenerelli A., 'The Constitutional System of the Kingdom of Bhutan' in Domenico Amirante (ed), *South Asian Constitutional Systems* (Eleven International Publishing 2020).

Chiba M., 'Conclusion' in Masaji Chiba (ed), *Asian Indigenous Law in Interaction with Received Law* (KPI 1986).

Cowell E.B. (ed), *The Jataka, or Stories of the Buddha's Former Births* (Motilala Banarsidass 2001).

Dalai Lama H.H., 'Foreword' in Allan Hunt Badiner (ed), *Dharma Gaia* (Parallax Press 1990).

de Silva-Wijeyeratne R., 'Managing Religion and Difference: Ancient Constitutionalism in the Theravada Buddhist Tradition and the Transformative Impact of the Modernist and Post-Colonial Turn' in Susanna Mancini (ed), *Constitutions and Religion* (Edward Elgar Publishing 2020).

French R.R., 'The Case of the Missing Discipline: Finding Buddhist Legal Studies' (2004) 52 *Buff L Rev* 679.

French R.R., 'What is Buddhist Law?' (2015) 63 *Buff L Rev* 833.

French R.R. and Nathan M.A., 'Introducing Buddhism and Law' in Rebecca R. French and Mark A. Nathan (eds), *Buddhism and Law. An Introduction* (CUP 2014).

89 Dalai Lama HH, 'Foreword' in Allan Hunt Badiner (ed), *Dharma Gaia* (Parallax Press 1990) v.

Givel M.S., 'Gross National Happiness in Bhutan: Political Institutions and Implementation' (2015) 1 *Asian Affairs* 102.

Glenn H.P., *Legal Traditions of the World* (OUP 2000).

Gunawardana R.A.L.H., *Robe and Plough: Monasticism and Economic Interest in Early Medieval Sri Lanka* (University of Arizona Press 1979).

Hanh T.N., *Interbeing. The 14 Mindfulness Trainings of Engaged Buddhism* (Parallax Press 2020).

Harris I., 'Causation and "Telos": The Problem of Buddhist Environmental Ethics' (1994) 1 *Journal of Buddhist Ethics* 45.

Harris I., 'Buddhism and Politics in Asia: The Textual and Historical Roots' in Ian Harris (ed), *Buddhism and Politics in Twentieth-Century Asia* (Continuum 1999).

Hershock P.D., *Buddhism in the Public Sphere. Reorienting Global Interdependence* (Routledge 2006).

Huxley A., 'Studying Theravada Legal Literature' (1997) 20 *Journal of the International Association of Buddhist Studies* 63.

Huxley A., 'Buddhist Law as a Religious System?' in Andrew Huxley (ed), *Religion, Law and Tradition. Comparative Studies in Religious Law* (Routledge 2002).

Huxley A., 'Rajadhamma Confronts Leviathan: Burmese Political Theory in the 1870s' in Ian Harris (ed), *Buddhism, Power and Political Order* (Routledge 2007).

Huxley A., 'Pāli Buddhist Law in Southeast Asia' in Rebecca R. French and Mark A. Nathan (eds), *Buddhism and Law. An Introduction* (CUP 2014).

Ives C., 'Buddhism: A Mixed Dharmic Bag: Debates about Buddhism and Ecology' in Willis J. Jenkins, Mary Evelyn Tucker and John Grim (eds), *Routledge Handbook of Religion and Ecology* (Routledge 2017).

Kasemsup P., 'Reception of Law in Thailand – A Buddhist Society' in Masaji Chiba (ed), *Asian Indigenous Law in Interaction with Received Law* (KPI 1986).

Kaza S. and Kraft K. (eds), *Dharma Rain* (Shambhala 2000).

Keyes C.F., 'Buddhists Confront the State' in John Whalen-Bridge and Pattana Kitiarsa (eds), *Buddhism, Modernity, and the State in Asia. Forms of Engagement* (Palgrave Macmillan 2013).

Kieffer-Pülz P., 'What the *Vinayas* Can Tell Us about Law' in Rebecca R. French and Mark A. Nathan (eds), *Buddhism and Law. An Introduction* (CUP 2014).

Loy D.R., *Ecodharma. Buddhist Teachings for the Ecological Crisis* (Wisdom Publications 2019).

Macy J., *World as Lover, World as Self* (Parallax Press 1991).

McMahan D.L., *The Making of Buddhist Modernism* (OUP 2008).

Menski W., 'Hindu Law as a 'Religious' System' in Andrew Huxley (ed), *Religion, Law and Tradition. Comparative Studies in Religious Law* (Routledge 2002).

Okudaira R. and Huxley A., 'A Burmese Tract on Kingship: Political Theory in the 1782 Manuscript of Manugye' (2001) 64 *Bulletin of the School of Oriental and African Studies* 248–257.

Panikkar R., 'Is the Notion of Human Rights a Western Concept?' (1982) 30 *Diogenes* 75.

Payutto P., *Dependent Origination. The Buddhist Law of Conditionality* (Buddhadhamma Foundation 1994).

Reynolds F.E., 'Buddhism and Law – Preface' (1995) 18 *Journal of the International Association of Buddhist Studies* 1.

Ruskola T., *Legal Orientalism: China, The United States, and Modern Law* (Harvard University Press 2013).

Sahni P., *Environmental Ethics in Buddhism. A Virtues Approach* (Routledge 2008).
Saito Gyoko and Sweany Joan (trs), *Shout of Buddha, Writings of Haya Akegarasu* (Orchid Press 1977).
Santos B.deS. and Rodríguez-Garavito C.A., 'Law, Politics, and the Subaltern in Counter-Hegemonic Globalization' in Boaventura de Sousa Santos and César A. Rodríguez-Garavito (eds), *Law and Globalization from Below: Towards a Cosmopolitan Legality* (CUP 2005).
Schmithausen., *The Problem of Sentience of Plants in Earliest Buddhism* (The International Institute for Buddhist Studies 1991).
Schonthal B., 'Securing the Sasana through Law: Buddhist Constitutionalism and Buddhist-Interest Litigation in Sri Lanka' (2016) 50 *Modern Asian Studies* 1.
Schonthal B., 'Formations of Buddhist Constitutionalism in South and Southeast Asia' (2017) 15 *I•CON* 705.
Schonthal B., 'Buddhism and Constitutional Practice' (2018) 13 *Asian Journal of Comparative Law* 245.
Schonthal B. and Ginsburg T., 'Setting an Agenda for the Socio-Legal Study of Contemporary Buddhism' (2016) 3 *Asian Journal of Law and Society* 1.
Sponberg A., 'Green Buddhism and the Hierarchy of Compassion' in Mary Evelyn Tucker and Duncan R. Williams (eds), *Buddhism and Ecology: The Interconnection of Dharma and Deeds* (Harvard University Press 1997).
Swearer D.K., 'Principles and Poetry, Places and Stories: The Resources of Buddhist Ecology' (2001) 130 *Daedalus* 225.
Tambiah S.J., 'The Galactic Polity in Southeast Asia' (2013) 3 *HAU: Journal of Ethnographic Theory* 503.
Tucker M.E. and Williams D.R. (eds), *Buddhism and Ecology: The Interconnection of Dharma and Deeds* (Harvard University Press 1997).
Weber M., *The Religion of India* (Free Press 1958).
Whitecross R.W., 'Separating Religions and Politics? Buddhism and the Bhutanese Constitution' in Sunil Khilnani, Vikram Raghavan and Arun K. Thiruvengadam (eds), *Comparative Constitutionalism in South Asia* (OUP 2013).
Whitecross R.W., 'Buddhism and Constitutions in Bhutan' in Rebecca R. French and Mark A. Nathan (eds), *Buddhism and Law. An Introduction* (CUP 2014).

Part II

Principles and Rules

7 From the Principles of International Environmental Law to Environmental Constitutionalism

Competitive or Cooperative Influences?

Pasquale Viola

1. Introduction

The cohesive and coherent environmental action of the international community has nurtured the advancement of a legal environmental consciousness, bridging law and governance concerns related to ecosystems. Since the 1970s, both individual states and the United Nations have been committed to evaluate from a scientific perspective the impact of humankind on the environment. The Stockholm Conference of 1972 is undoubtedly recognised as the first political and (quasi)legal step at the international level towards a rational planning of the analysis of environmental issues, with the target to provide and equip states with instruments capable of facing ecosystems' deterioration. The 1972 Conference still remains the key-stone of an epistemological starting point, giving the evidence of the 'symptoms of the crisis of civilisation' that the world still is going through. Within this novel theoretical background, the environment attracted attention because "it corresponds to a new conception of life with new individual and social values."[1] Thus, the international law regime has moved towards recurring legal topics for the emerging of customary or general principles, with the aim of driving domestic legal systems towards coordinated action. Whether recognised principles respond to the scheme of international legal sources that comprise treaties, customs and general principles of international law is not a rhetorical question. Mostly common shared principles are established through treaties and customs, following a 'top-down' approach vis-à-vis national legal systems. Independently of the acceptance or the rejection of a dualistic understanding of international and domestic legal systems, in contrast, the

1 Alexandre C. Kiss and Jean D. Sicault, 'La Conférence des Nations Unies sur l'environnement (Stockholm, 5/16 juin 1972)' [1972] *Annuaire Français de Droit International* 603.

DOI: 10.4324/9781003175308-10

'bottom-up' designed principles "prioritize multilateral consensus rather than state practice and opinio juris".[2]

Over the past decades, the growing interest for constitutional debates shows the prolific season for comparative constitutional law studies, although mainly focused on Western legal tradition methodology. Due to this new wave of constitutional scholarship, academic debates critically deconstructed the classic concepts related to this field of study, reconsidering 'old-fashioned' definitions, as in theories related to the constituent power, separation of powers, unconstitutional constitutional amendments, etc. This dynamic and vibrant doctrinal activity is going beyond a mere re-conceptualisation of previous schemes, due to the need of dealing with new topics and concerns, encouraging the expansion of a 'comparative constitutional thinking' far from the 'comfort zones' of domestic legal systems.

As far as legal efforts in trying to cope with environmental issues are concerned, the basic question is whether constitutions matter and to what extent environmental constitutionalism is a 'different species' or a genetic and physiological variant of constitutionalism, thus deserving an autonomous epistemological space or demanding for a proper role within already existing theoretical patterns. With the aim of critically addressing the previously mentioned topics, this chapter outlines the system of environmental principles developed within the international community, subsequently focusing on the constitutionalisation of the environment in conventional or innovative forms of constitutionalism.

2. The Rise of International Environmentalism: The Stockholm Conference of 1972

The Stockholm Conference was convened according to the United Nations General Assembly Resolution 2398 (XXIII) of 3 December 1968, on a proposal made by Sweden.[3] Despite the attendance of 113 delegates, covering the most of the UN member states, the USSR, Cuba, Albania and other socialist states did not attend the sessions. In contrast, China participated in the Conference, with a large and "well-prepared" delegation.[4]

The main task of the Conference was to "provide a framework for the comprehensive consideration within the United Nations of the problems of the human environment", with the basic aim of attracting "the attention of governments and public opinion on the importance and urgency of this question and also to identify those aspects of it that can only or best be solved through international

2 David Hunter, 'International Environmental Law' in Paul G. Harris (ed), *Routledge Handbook of Global Environmental Politics* (Routledge 2016) 128. Cf David Hunter et al., *International Environmental Law & Policy* (Foundation Press 2010).

3 Office of Public Information, *Yearbook of the United Nations 1968* (UN 1971).

4 Kiss and Sicault (n 1) 609: "La délégation chinoise était nombreuse, comprenait de bons linguistes, des techniciens assidus et, sans doute, quelques «commissaires politiques»".

cooperation and agreement".[5] This approach represented a sort of compromise, as it is emphasised in the draft Declaration of the Preparatory Committee for the Conference (UN Doc. A/CONF.48/PC.17), between the delegations which were most inclined to principally raise public awareness and concern over environmental issues, and those parties whose objectives were to provide a framework of specific guidelines to future governmental and intergovernmental actions.[6] As per the main draft, the Declaration reflects the rationales of the aforementioned positions, seeking a synthesis between them. The approved final text of the Declaration of the United Nations Conference on Human Environment contains seven points and 26 principles. The general framework is anthropocentric, as some parts of the text point out, e.g., the first proclaim "Man is both creature and moulder of his environment" or the fifth principle: "[t]he non-renewable resources of the earth must be employed in such a way as to guard against the danger of their future exhaustion and to ensure that benefits from such employment are shared by all mankind." Despite the human-centred approach view and the "agglomerate"[7] of social and civil rights along with moral values, the Declaration could be interpreted as the first effort towards an *ante-litteram* account of the Anthropocene. Furthermore, the Declaration introduced principles still shaping the international and national levels of legislation in the environmental field. Among them, the principles included state cooperation for a co-ordinated, efficient and dynamic role of international organisations, along with the principles favouring the protection and improvement of the environment, as well as liability and compensation for the victims of pollution and other damages due to cross-boundaries harming activities.[8]

In the four decades post the Stockholm Conference, several international agreements sponsored by the UN and international agencies have been signed and ratified by the states, many of them creating a suitable legal framework for national legislation to limit anthropogenic impact on the environment.[9] In spite of the 'truism', the blatant ineffectiveness and the difficulties in the negotiations to establish a strictly binding legal tool,[10] the Stockholm Conference still symbolises the successful intervention of the international community to cope with environmental issues by virtue of turning the spotlight on such concerns and outlining key principles.

5 UN General Assembly Resolution 2398, *Problems of the Human Environment*, A/RES/2398(XXIII) (3rd of December 1968).

6 *See* also Philippe Sands and Paolo Galizzi (eds), *Documents in International Environmental Law* (CUP 2004).

7 Kiss and Sicault (n 1) 612. According to the authors of this essay, the heterogeneous core of the principles represents an attempt to find an ideological base for the environment.

8 Articles 21, 22 and 25, Stockholm Declaration of the United Nations Conference on the Human Environment, 16th of June 1972.

9 Andronico O. Adede, 'The Treaty System from Stockholm (1972) to Rio de Janeiro (1992)' [1995] *Pace Environmental Law Review* 33.

10 Benoit Meyer, *The International Law on Climate Change* (CUP 2018).

3. The Legacy of International Environmental Law: Principles

The proliferation of non-treaty norms enlarges the list of general principles and declarative law.[11] According to this scholarship, principles may have three main patterns of establishment: 1) from the field of international law to single domestic systems; 2) among states, in which they emerge and then merge at the international level; 3) from one domestic legal system to others through legal migrations or transplants. I may add another form of principles that could be defined as 'suspended', when it comes into existence in the international field, but its effectiveness is questioned because it is not ratified or not enforced by states. This kind of principle follows a fourth pattern of establishment, since it could become a topic within the civil society's domain, which can push national politics to take care of the adoption of such principle through a bottom-up approach.

Following the four patterns for the recognition of a common legal frame, both the international regime and national domains have elaborated a wide body of principles to tackle environmental concerns.[12] Of course, even before the first environmental legal attempts, state sovereignty was one of the key-principles of international law. A more precise provision related to sovereignty and environment was framed in the Stockholm Declaration of 1972 and was proposed in the same terms by the Rio Declaration in 1992, then re-enacted in more recent venues. In a broader sense, the environmental framework gave to the concept of sovereignty a stricter meaning than the one developed in the general theory of law, expressing the right of individual states to exploit national resources according to their environmental and developmental policies, inside their own jurisdiction and without harming any area beyond.[13] The road to the recognition of the duty to avoid transboundary environmental damages as a principle of international law has been developing throughout decades, as witnessed by the Trail Smelter Case.[14] The main steps in bridging this obligation with environmental issues may be traced back in four steps: 1) principles 2 of the Stockholm Declaration and

11 Daniel Bodansky, *The Art and Craft of International Environmental Law* (Harvard University Press 2010). Cf Duncan B. Hollis, *The Oxford Guide to Treaties* (OUP 2020).

12 On the revival of rationality in the post-modernity and environmental principles see Nicolas de Sadeleer, *Environmental Principles: From Political Slogans to Legal Rules* (2nd edn, OUP 2020).

13 Although the clear assessments referring the exercise of sovereignty inside national borders, the extraterritorial application of a state jurisdiction is a more discussed topic. For an introduction to the topic see Harold Maier, 'Extraterritorial Jurisdiction at a Crossroads: An Intersection Between Public and Private International Law' [1982] *American Journal of International Law* 280; Petra Gümplová, 'Sovereignty over natural resources. A normative reinterpretation' [2019] *Global Constitutionalism* 7.

14 Austen L. Parrish, 'Trail Smelter Déjà Vu: Extraterritoriality, International Environmental Law, and the Search for Solutions to Canadian-U.S. Transboundary Water Pollution Disputes' [2005] *Boston University Law Review* 363; Jean-Frédéric Morin et al., *Global Environmental Politics* (OUP 2020).

21 of the Rio Declaration; 2) the General Assembly Resolution n. 2996, that recognises the spirit of co-operation and good-neighbourliness; 3) Art. 20 of the Agreement on the Conservation of Nature and Natural Resources (ASEAN Convention, 1985); 4) the advisory opinion of the International Court of Justice about the Legality of the Threat or Use of Nuclear Weapons.[15]

Another key-principle is the 'common but differentiated responsibilities and respective capabilities', which marks a global and shared obligation for states according to their historical and contemporary profiles. This principle has been elaborated to emphasise the role and the duties of developed countries and the needs of developing and least developed ones. In direct or indirect ways, the principle of cooperation is crucial for international efforts aiming at integration in environmental matters.[16]

Nowadays, within the international law regime and in domestic legal domains, five key principles play a pivotal role in dealing with environmental issues: 1) sustainable development, 2) polluter-pays, 3) preventive action, 4) precautionary principle, and 5) public participation, access to information and justice.

The Brudtland Report proposed a definition of sustainable development, trying to take into account both present and future generations, as well as global needs and limitations. For its own multiple and complex meaning, sustainable development encompasses a corollary of normative principles and descriptive approaches: 1) intergenerational equality; 2) sustainable use; 3) equitable use; 4) integration.[17]

According to the polluter-pays principle, a subject must afford the costs for compensation and losses derived from his own pollutant activities. Despite seeming clearly formulated, this principle's efficacy at the international level is undermined by questions related to the nature of the subject (i.e., state, private or public, etc.), the broader meaning of pollutant activities, and the problematic interpretation of liability according to legal and technical standards. Although

15 Philippe Sands et al., *Principles of International Environmental Law* (3rd edn, CUP 2018) 210.

16 See Oran R. Young, *International Cooperation: Building Regimes for Natural Resources and the Environment* (Cornell University Press 1989). About a theoretical frame of the object of the cooperation's efforts and the suitable way to comply with international obligation, see Scott Barrett, 'A Theory of Full International Cooperation' [1999] *Journal of Theoretical Politics* 519.

17 Sands et al. (n 15) 219. At least see Alan Boyle and David Freestone (eds), *International Law and Sustainable Development: Past Achievements and Future Challenges* (OUP 1999); Marie-Claire Cordonier Segger and Ashfaq Khalfan, *Sustainable Development Law: Principles, Practices, and Prospects* (OUP 2004); Duncan French, *International Law and Policy of Sustainable Development* (Manchester University Press 2005). For a critical approach to this principle: Sam Adelman, 'The Sustainable Development Goals, anthropocentrism and neoliberalism' in Duncan French and Louis J. Kotzé (eds), *Sustainable Development Goals: Law, Theory and Implementation* (Elgar 2018).

it was first elaborated in international legal sources, this key principle becomes more effective when translated into national ones.[18]

Regarding technical and scientific standards, the principle of preventive action demands that states prevent or limit the damages to the environment. It has been implemented in international cases[19] and conveyed under various forms in numerous treaties. For instance, some elements of this principle can be found in the 1933 London Convention on the Preservation of Fauna and Flora in their Natural State,[20] while a precise formulation firstly appeared in the 1985 Vienna Convention for the Protection of the Ozone Layer. This principle does not define any general obligation not to harm the environment, but a duty to undertake action at an early stage, with the aim of reducing pollution's effects, rather than focusing on restorative engagements and programmes.[21]

When there is a lack of scientific certainties, the precautionary principle demands avoidance of activities that may cause environmental damages. Compared to sustainable development and preventive action, during the '80s domestic[22] and international legal systems started to anticipate the protection of the environment, trying to compensate the uncertainties regulating the risk. From a perspective that locates science into political and legal discourse, this principle brings ethics, politics and law into the scientific debate, striking a balance in risk regulation.[23]

The last developments in the international environmental regime highlight the trend towards a more inclusive approach, focusing on the access to information, on justice and on a more suitable recognition of public participation.[24] To this

18 Sands et al. (n 15) 240; Priscilla Schwarz, 'The polluter-pays principle' in Michael Faure (ed), *Elgar Encyclopedia of Environmental Law* (Elgar 2018).

19 Cf, for instance, International Court of Justice, Case Concerning Pulp Mills on The River Uruguay (Argentina v. Uruguay), Judgment of 20th of April 2010. For a doctrinal approach: Oscar Schachter, 'The Emergence of International Environmental Law' [1991] *Journal of International Affairs* 457; Sands et al. (n 17); Emma Lees and Jorge E. Viñuales (eds), *The Oxford Handbook of Comparative Environmental Law* (OUP 2019).

20 See Articles 5, 9, 12 and the Protocol, Convention relative to the Preservation of Fauna and Flora in their Natural State (8th of November 1933).

21 Max V. Soto, 'General Principles of International Environmental Law' [1996] *ILSA Journal of International & Comparative Law* 192. Cf Leslie-Anne Duvic-Paoli, *The Prevention Principle in International Environmental Law* (CUP 2018).

22 See Sands et al. (n 15) 229, where the authors highlight the pivotal role of the West German legislation according to this principle.

23 Joakim Zander, *The Application of the Precautionary Principle in Practice: Comparative Dimensions* (CUP 2010).

24 Cf Michael Mason, *Environmental Democracy* (Earthscan 1999); Sheila Jasanoff, 'The Dilemma of Environmental Democracy' [1996] *Issues in Science and Technology* 63; Jeremy Wates, 'The Aarhus Convention: A Driving Force for Environmental Democracy' [2005] *Journal for European Environmental & Planning Law* 2. In reference to regional cooperation on such matters, the Escazù Agreement (entered into force in April 2021) implements the access to information, public participation and justice in environmental matters in Latin America and the Caribbean (https://treaties.un.org/pages/ViewDetails.aspx?src=TREATY&mtdsg_no=XXVII-18&chapter=27&clang=_en).

end, the Aarhus Convention of 1998 developed some principles also enshrined in the Rio Declaration. These developments are indicative of the increasing efforts to guarantee a bottom-up approach, as well as a more 'public-friendly' regime, conveying some precise necessities: 1) the participation of citizens, especially in the decision-making processes; 2) the access to information related to the environment; 3) the need to facilitate and encourage public awareness; 4) an "effective access to judicial and administrative proceedings, including redress and remedy".[25]

4. Constitutions, Constitutionalism(s) and the Environment

The meaning of the term 'constitution' has changed over time, from a simple implementation or body of rules into a legal norm enacted by a constituent power,[26] in which "the fundamental political choices of an organised community are expressed by a written code—rational, methodical and systematic—that governs the state powers in an organic and functional way".[27] Furthermore, constitutions offer functional instruments as forms of guarantees to limit the political power, i.e., the judicial review of legislation, which may even limit the legislative's amending power. Along with few examples of uncodified fundamental texts, such as those of the United Kingdom and New Zealand, every state adopted a written constitution to define the contours of their political and legal systems. Whether pristine or secondary, internally legitimate or imposed, autochthonous or borrowed, constitutional texts reflect to a certain extent both an endogenous claim and a global trend.

Considering "constitutionalism [a]s the political theory that generally accompanies the technique",[28] constitutional experiences inspired autonomous or context-related forms of constitutionalism. An example of such attitude could be traced back in several theories, and scholars seem to find common features usually summarised in an adjective to be prepended to the noun 'constitutionalism' (e.g., authoritarian, post-authoritarian, global, neo-, etc).

In spite of the 'pluri-generational' aim of constitutions, some of them, through amendments or the entry into force of entirely new texts, seem to follow up-to-date concerns, both transnational and domestic. Environmental degradation is one of these pervasive topics within the current debate, thus nurturing a key-question: is environmental constitutionalism a 'different species' or a genetic and physiological variant of other theories? In trying to find an answer, I will focus

25 Principle 10, Rio Declaration on Environment and Development of 1992.

26 Giovanni Sartori, 'Constitutionalism: A Preliminary Discussion' [1962] *The American Political Science Review* 853.

27 Roberto L. Blanco Valdés, 'Costituzionalismo' in Lucio Pegoraro (ed), *Glossario di Diritto pubblico comparato* (Carocci 2011) 64.

28 Martin Loughlin, 'What is Constitutionalisation?' in Petra Dobner and Martin Loughlin (eds), *The Twilight of Constitutionalism?* (OUP 2010) 55.

on three relevant theories regarding contemporary facets of constitutionalism: 1) transformative; 2) global; 3) *nuevo constitucionalismo latinoamericano.*

4.1. Transformative Constitutionalism

In his influential work on South African legal culture and constitutionalism,[29] Karl E. Klare underlined the country's transition from authoritarianism to a new culture of justification, "in which every exercise of power is expected to be justified".[30] The shift from authoritarianism to an argumentative democracy serves the enhancement of the constitutional provisions devoted to "[h]eal the divisions of the past and establish a society based on democratic values, social justice and fundamental human rights".[31] Thus, the need to find a synthesis between the legal constraints of the rule of law and the political features of a constitutional project to fulfil "transformative hopes".[32]

Critically rethinking the role of constitutional adjudication in South Africa during the 1990s, Karl E. Klare defines transformative constitutionalism as

> a long-term project of constitutional enactment, interpretation, and enforcement committed (not in isolation, of course, but in a historical context of conducive political developments) to transforming a country's political and social institutions and power relationships in a democratic, participatory, and egalitarian direction. Transformative constitutionalism connotes an enterprise of inducing large-scale social change through nonviolent political processes grounded in law. . . . In the background is an idea of a highly egalitarian, caring, multicultural community, governed through participatory, democratic processes in both the polity and large portions of what we now call the 'private sphere.'[33]

In spite of the lack of a single definition, the term 'transformative' implies several features on which scholars agree, as well as uncertain semantic areas. In fact,

29 Karl E. Klare, 'Legal Culture and Transformative Constitutionalism' [1998] *South African Journal on Human Rights* 146.

30 Ibid. See Etienne Mureinik, 'A Bridge to Where? Introducing the Interim Bill of Rights' [1994] *South African Journal on Human Rights* 32. Through a distant debate with Etienne Murienik, Karl E. Klare emphasised the importance of adjudication for justification, due to its means and scopes, which are more inclined to reason, rather than to imposition. Such argumentative and justificatory activity demands for a "conscientious judge" that is determined in order to rectify and revise the legal system, dismissing apartheid laws. About the "cross-over" and the clashes between the modernistic and transformative constitutionalism of contemporary South Africa and the legacy of common law and Roman-Dutch tradition see Dennis M. Davis and Karl E. Klare, 'Transformative constitutionalism and the common and customary law' [2010] *South African Journal on Human Rights* 402.

31 Preamble, Constitution of the Republic of South Africa, 1996.

32 Klare (n 29) 150.

33 Ibid.

Upendra Baxi argues that such form of constitutionalism opens the debate on "what is transformed and what is left intact"[34] inside the contrast between continuity and change, to define the dominant, emergent and residual cultures,[35] and addressing "multiple and intersecting inequalities".[36]

4.2. Global Constitutionalism

The theoretical context of scholars dealing with the concept of global constitutionalism seems to be quite wide, and they are still searching for an ultimate definition. Basically, such a form of constitutionalism refers to the international law field and to a multilevel governance that demands systemic coherence, due to the emergence of a global standard and a post-national governance.[37] To this end, Anne Peters and Klaus Armingeon point out that such global standard shares—or demands for—some features with domestic constitutionalism "in a rudimentary form",[38] although they are very different from state-nations' constitutions:[39]

> [t]hey (roughly) set in place political institutions and define their competences, lay down the terms of membership, establish the relations between the members and the community, and (again roughly) regulate the institution's core functions of lawmaking, conflict resolution, and law enforcement . . . contain rules for their own amendment.[40]

About legal transplants among domestic legal systems and between the domestic and the international legal fields, Mattias Kumm highlights the doubt arising from the constitutionalist narrative connected to the hegemony of Western thought, questioning whether such "universalist pretentions" are different from other supposed civilisational impositions, and to what extent global

34 Upendra Baxi, 'Preliminary Notes on Transformative Constitutionalism' in Oscar Vilhena et al. (eds), *Transformative Constitutionalism: Comparing the Apex Courts of Brazil, India and South Africa* (Pretoria University Law Press 2013) 23.

35 Supra, 23f.

36 Catherine Albertyn, 'Cultural Diversity, "Living Law," and Women's Rights in South Africa' in Daniel Bonilla Maldonado (ed), *Constitutionalism of the Global South: The Activist Tribunals of India, South Africa, and Colombia* (CUP 2013) 164. For a critical assessment on transformative constitutionalism in South Africa: Sanele Sibanda, 'When Do You Call Time on a Compromise? South Africa's Discourse on Transformation and the Future of Transformative Constitutionalism' [2020] 24 *Law, Democracy & Development* 384.

37 On the emergence of a global administrative law cf Benedict Kingsbury et al., 'The Emergence of Global Administrative Law' [2005] *Law and Contemporary Problems* 18, quoted in Anne Peters and Klaus Armingeon, 'Introduction – Global Constitutionalism from an Interdisciplinary Perspective' [2009] *Indiana Journal of Global Legal Studies* 385.

38 Peters and Armingeon (n 37) 388.

39 Ibid 389.

40 Ibid 387f.

constitutionalism is inclusive,[41] especially towards other regions with different cultures and traditions,[42] such as Asia, Africa or Latin America.[43]

However, despite some incertitude, global constitutionalism in its prescriptive and descriptive facets cannot be assumed as a classical form of constitutionalisation, but as "an academic and political agenda which identifies and advocates the application of constitutionalist principles".[44]

Currently, the growing interest towards post-national layered systems and the dedifferentiation trends also serve as limit to unconstitutional drifts, once they foster the implementation of a global constitutional order and a constitutionalisation culture beyond the state-nation paradigm.[45] Moreover,

> "the tradition of constitutionalism remains the best-stocked normative reservoir from which [responsible politics] may draw and the most persuasive medium in which it may be articulated." In effect, global constitutionalism deploys . . . a constructive, not obstructive, critical potential.[46]

In spite of the critical potential and theoretical attitude, global constitutionalism may evolve in empirical and pragmatic ways, fostering issues on whether it is possible to divide the dedifferentiation of constitutional and legal tools from the homologation of legal traditions, nurturing concerns arising from the long-term impact of semantic and cultural diversity.

41 Mattias Kumm, 'On the History and Theory of Global Constitutionalism' in Takao Suami et al (eds), *Global Constitutionalism from European and East Asian Perspectives* (CUP 2018), which affirms, in reference to the statement "[t]he West is no more closely associated with constitutionalism than with competing ideas", that "the link between 'the West' and global constitutionalism is significantly more attenuated than it is often portrayed to be"; to this end, "constitutionalist ideas have been and continue to be, at various times, in various jurisdictions, subject to rejection and contestation in the West, both fundamentally and with regard to specific manifestations" (198). See also Pasquale Viola, *Costituzionalismo autoctono. Pluralismo culturale e trapianti giuridici nel subcontinente indiano* (BUP 2020).

42 Cf Boaventura de Sousa Santos, *Epistemologies of the South: Justice Against Epistemicide* (Routledge 2014); H. Patrick Glenn, *Legal Traditions of the World: Sustainable Diversity in Law* (5th edn, OUP 2014).

43 See Werner Menski, *Comparative Law in a Global Context: The Legal Systems of Asia and Africa* (CUP 2006).

44 Peters and Armingeon (n 37) 389.

45 The term 'dedifferentiation' defines the global trend in "blurring" the boarders between national, transnational and supranational legal orders, as observed in Aydin Atilgan, *Global Constitutionalism: A Socio-legal Perspective* (Springer 2018). See also Anne Peters, 'Compensatory Constitutionalism: The Function and Potential of Fundamental International Norms and Structures' [2006] *Leiden Journal of International Law* 579; Peters and Armingeon (n 37) 390.

46 Anne Peters, 'The Merits of Global Constitutionalism' [2009] *Indiana Journal of Global Legal Studies* 411.

4.3. Nuevo Constitucionalismo Latinoamericano

Despite the lack of scholarly agreement on the definition of recent Latin American constitutional experiences and their magnitude, several authors have proposed the label of *nuevo constitucionalismo latinoamericano* to define a peculiar form of constitutionalism, far from a merely legal debate, predominantly grounded on "popular claims and social movements",[47] as well as on popular participation in the constituent phase, interculturalism, new emerging legal subjects and rights, and the quest for different economic paradigms.[48]

The valuable analysis by Carlos Manuel Villabella Armengol provides a more comprehensive account on the Latin American *nuevo constitucionalismo* through 14 features:[49] 1) historically rooted preambles with programmatic features; 2) specific parts devoted to the constitutional pact; 3) aspirational aspects, as well as teleological and axiological provisions; 4) constitutional supremacy clause; 5) unconventional definition of the state model;[50] 6) social features of the state; 7) plurinationality and interculturalism; 8) enforcement of constitutional rights by specialised courts or tribunals; 9) really avant-garde recognition of constitutional rights and new legal subjectivities; 10) constitutional and value-rooted duties; 11) strong enforcement of constitutional rights; 12) favour for regional cooperation; 13) pivotal role of the welfare state; 14) people's participation in amending procedures.

47 Roberto Viciano Pastor and Rubén Martínez Dalmau, 'El nuevo constitucionalismo latinoamericano' [2011] *Revista general de derecho público comparado* 1; Lucio Pegoraro and Angelo Rinella, *Sistemi costituzionali* (Giappichelli 2020) 96.

48 Silvia Bagni, 'Hitos de democratización de la justicia constitucional en América Latina: una mirada desde afuera' in Rosario Tur Ausina (ed), *Problemas actuales de Derecho constitucional en un contexto de crisis* (Comares 2015); Josefina A. Méndez López and Danelia Cutier Mustelier, 'La participación popular en el nuevo constitucionalismo latinoamericano. Una mirada desde la perspectiva de los derechos' [2010] *Revista del Instituto de Ciencias Jurídicas de Puebla* 94.

49 Carlos M. Villabella Armengol, 'Constitución y democracia en el nuevo constitucionalismo latinoamericano' [2010] *Revista del Instituto de Ciencias Jurídicas de Puebla* 49. For an introductory outline see Aarón A. Castillo Fernández, 'Constitucionalismo Latinoamericano. Definición, características, problemas y perspectivas de futuro' [2015] *Epikeia. Derecho y política* 1.

50 Villabella Armengol (n 49). Art. 1 of the Constitution of Bolivia: "Bolivia is constituted as a Unitary Social State of Pluri-National Communitarian Law (*Estado Unitario Social de Derecho Plurinacional Comunitario*)"; Art. 2 of the Constitution of Venezuela: "Venezuela constitutes itself as a Democratic and Social State of Law and Justice"; Art. 1 of the Constitution of Ecuador: "Ecuador is a constitutional State of rights and justice, a social, democratic, sovereign, independent, unitary, intercultural, multinational and secular State. It is organized as a republic and is governed using a decentralized approach."

The *nuevo constitucionalismo latinoamericano* goes far beyond a mere legalisation, paying specific attention to the democratic legitimation of the legal system,[51] opening to a *democracia multidireccional y republicana*.[52]

As far as the possibility of constitutional borrowings or migrations of the *nuevo constitucionalismo* are concerned, different theoretical perspectives provide diverse considerations. For instance, when the geographical and cultural aspect prevails or these constitutions are considered as an epiphenomenon[53] of other forms of constitutionalism (mainly neoconstitutionalism),[54] as well as in those critical analyses that reduce the innovative and emancipatory features of this phenomenon, the *nuevo constitucionalismo latinoamericano* appears to be a mere context-related experience, with specific roots and aims, as well as a contemporary acknowledgment of conventional constitutionalism.

4.4. *Applying the Concept of 'Environment' to Selected Forms of Constitutionalism*

The concept of environment is not excluded from the aforementioned theoretical debates. For instance, in reference to transformative constitutionalism in South Africa, Melanie Murcott proposes the concept of "transformative environmental constitutionalism", which seeks to incorporate environmentalism and environmental constitutionalism as a key concern of a transformative project based on ecocentrism. In this regard, she argues that "ecocentrism can be pursued by lawyers and applied by courts so as to be more responsive to the challenges and context of the Anthropocene."[55] This position is mainly addressed to the South

51 Roberto Viciano Pastor and Rubén Martínez Dalmau, 'Aspectos generales del nuevo constitucionalismo latinoamericano' in VV.AA., *El nuevo constitucionalismo en América Latina* (Corte Constitucional del Ecuador para el período de transición 2010); Alfredo Ramírez-Nárdiz, 'Nuevo constitucionalismo latinoamericano y democracia participativa: ¿progreso o retroceso democrático?' [2016] *Vniversitas* 349.

52 Multidirectional and republican democracy. Villabella Armengol (n 49).

53 Pegoraro and Rinella (n 47).

54 The constitutional texts corresponding to this scholarly debate highlights some specific features of neoconstitutionalism: 1) the semantic values of the constitutions go beyond the formal legal semantics, finding their source of legitimation in extra-legal values; 2) the enforceability of "direct and material" provisions; 3) the judiciaries and their powers are grounded on a "creative and dialectical, synchronously different and diachronically changing" jurisprudence, fostering judicial activism; 4) argumentative approach to solve clash of principles; 5) constitutionalisation of the legal system; 6) new rights and legal subjects, paying more attention to inequalities, minorities and cultural issues; 7) *drittwirkung*; 8) the state pivotal role and the rejection of a "mundialización neoliberal de una gobernanza sin gobierno o gobernanza global". Villabella Armengol (n 49). Cf Miguel Carbonell (ed), *Teoría del neoconstitucionalismo. Ensayos escogidos* (Trotta 2007).

55 Melanie Murcott, 'Transformative Environmental Constitutionalism's Response to the Setting Aside of South Africa's Moratorium on Rhino Horn Trade' [2017] *Humanities* 3. See also Id., 'Introducing Transformative Environmental Constitutionalism in South Africa' in Erin Daly et al. (eds), *New Frontiers in Environmental Constitutionalism* (UNEP 2017); Id.,

African experience, but can easily migrate into other legal systems dealing with social justice concerns, whether they are within the so-called Global South or the Western legal tradition.

Global constitutionalism seems to nurture "environmental expectations". However, as David Bodanski affirms, there is no international environmental legal regime that we could refer to as a proper constitutional order. Additionally, he argues that the body of principles of international environmental law are "weak and vague", even those that more defined, like the precautionary principle and the principle of sustainable development, due to their "different meanings that they hardly exercise real constraint on the behavior of states or international institutions".[56]

The environment and related concerns represent important aspects of the *nuevo constitucionalismo latinoamericano*. For instance, the Constitution of Ecuador 'celebrates' Nature or Pachamama (Mother Earth), "of which we are a part and which is vital to our existence",[57] while the Constitution of the Plurinational State of Bolivia provides for a quite detailed discipline related to environmental rights, although there is no direct recognition of the Nature's locus standi.[58] The innovative weight of these constitutional trends could be traced back within the transformative claims based on extra-legal domain's issues and on the bottom-up instances of participation, whether they are a *fictio juris* or a proper example of spaces for political participation. However, some scholars have adopted a more dubitative approach in reference to the novelty and uniqueness of this constitutional phenomenon. To this end, Roberto Gargarella emphasises that the constitutions considered as the emblems of the *nuevo constitucionalismo* embraced the traditional characteristics of the organisation of powers already adopted since the 19th century, while the aspects related to constitutional rights just implemented the 20th century's constitutional ideas.[59]

'The Procedural Right of Access to Information as a Means of Implementing Environmental Constitutionalism in South Africa' in James R. May and Erin Daly (eds), *Implementing Environmental Constitutionalism: Current Global Challenges* (CUP 2018).

56 Daniel Bodansky, 'Is There an International Environmental Constitution?' [2009] *Indiana Journal of Global Legal Studies* 580. He also argues that: "Moreover, even to the extent that they do serve a constitutional function by articulating a set of overarching, shared values, this is only one of several constitutional functions" (580).

57 Preamble, Constitution of Ecuador, 2008. See also Art. 71 and 72, Constitution of Ecuador, 2008.

58 See Art. 34, Constitution of the Plurinational State of Bolivia, 2009. On the legal status of the Nature in Bolivia see Ley de derechos de la Madre Tierra, n. 71/2010. For a specific analysis on this topic see Serena Baldin, *Il buen vivir nel costituzionalismo andino. Profili comparativi* (Giappichelli 2019).

59 Roberto Gargarella, 'Sobre el "Nuevo constitucionalismo latinoamericano"' [2018] *Revista Uruguaya de Ciencia Política* 129. See also Ramiro Ávila Santamaria, *En defensa del neoconstitucionalismo transformador: los debates y los argumentos* (Universidad Andina Simón Bolívar 2012). Cf Armin von Bogdandy et al. (eds), *Transformative Constitutionalism in Latin America* (OUP 2017).

5. Environmental Constitutionalism from Different Viewpoints: 'The Good, the Bad and the Ugly'

The chapter authored by Domenico Amirante and published in this book offers a complete insight on the shift from a mere 'constitutionalisation of the environment' to environmental constitutionalism.[60] Thus, I address only some important theoretical yardsticks of environmental constitutionalism to later discuss the different approaches that scholarly debates assume in reference to this new phenomenon of constitutionalism.

Within contemporary societies, humans and the environment are connected as never before. The human domination questions the role of the environment in moral debates and legal—constitutional—discourses. On this issue, I may recall two postulations. Assuming human beings as major driving forces, on the one hand, the Anthropocene "very specifically indicates the loss of resilience and functional integrity of the Earth and its systems";[61] on the other, this new concept—rather than a geological era—"highlights the interconnectedness of natural Earth processes, or put differently, the interconnected nature of the environment, the reciprocity of its processes, and the many linked cause-and-effect relationships that exist on a global scale".[62]

In reference to the need of constitutional transformations, Louis J. Kotzé emphasises the current loss of harmony of the Earth system, which is "erratic, unpredictable, unstable and operating in a 'no-analogue state'".[63] Considering human beings as the major driving forces of such change, the law may at least influence social behaviours that impact on the environment. Thus, while the Anthropocene offers an 'intellectual space' for the current crises deriving from the global-sociological changes, constitutionalism is functional to this new 'mindset', offering a proper regulatory ground for

> a familiar way of thinking about, designing and applying laws that must establish and maintain order; provide long-term societal and political stability and socio-ecological security; and achieve integration and unification as far as a global identity that is based on a specific ethic of care is concerned, including consensus on matters of common public concern that will increasingly arise as a result of the Anthropocene's global socio-ecological crisis.[64]

60 See Domenico Amirante, 'Environmental Constitutionalism through the Lens of Comparative Law: New Perspectives for the Anthropocene', in this book at p. 148–167.

61 George M. Woodwell, 'On Purpose in Science, Conservation and Government: The Functional Integrity of the Earth Is at Issue Not Biodiversity' [2002] *Ambio* 432.

62 Louis J. Kotzé, 'Rethinking Global Environmental Law and Governance in the Anthropocene' [2014] *Journal of Energy & Natural Resources Law* 132.

63 Louis J. Kotzé, *Global Environmental Constitutionalism in the Anthropocene* (Hart Publishing 2016) 178.

64 Ibid 199–200. For further theoretical horizons, see Ibid 247. See also Gregorio Mesa Cuadros, 'Environmental Rights, Responsibility and Care: A New Constitutional Paradigm' in

As David Boyd highlights in his seminal work *The Environmental Rights Revolution: A Global Study of Constitutions, Human Rights, and the Environment*,[65] the awareness of global environmental crises fostered a wave of new or amended constitutions dealing with the environment in different legal forms, i.e. as a state positive obligation, individual rights and duties, procedural environmental rights and several other peculiar environmental provisions.[66] Within this framework, provisions recognising the right to a healthy environment are particularly relevant. The majority of the constitutional tools are enforceable, and the right to a healthy environment is mostly considered a fundamental human right, while only in few cases, along with social, economic and cultural rights, it assumes less predominance than civil and political rights. In contrast, only few constitutional texts expressly qualify environmental provisions as unenforceable. One of the main features of this trend is that the constitutionalisation of the environment proves the environment's rising path as human value.[67]

The 'ascent' of the environment as a constitutional matter, worth to be associated with social values, is demonstrated by different but converging provisions already included within the texts and by the dynamic approach that legal systems and public governance are undertaking to accommodate such a legal 'newcomer'. The main effect of this new approach provides a holistic attitude that impacts on legal systems. To this end, along with a convergence that implements a global momentum, James May and Erin Daly argue that the constitutional law field impacts on the domestic legal system and governance, thus fostering legal responses that "can be structural and systemic or individual and incremental".[68] Furthermore, as one of the key-features, the constitutionalisation of the environment helps to frame an enforceable scheme that allows Apex Courts to deal with such issues and to harmonise legal interpretations within subordinate judiciary's levels.[69]

The critical rethinking of 'old-fashioned' legal schemes under an undebatable global socio-ecological crisis could appear a phenomenon on which everybody agrees. However, theoretical positions differ. In other words, it is quite easy to find scholars ready to just consider the environment as another topic law has to deal with, such as, for instance, artificial intelligence or digital security. If only Jules Verne could have been a constitutional lawyer, most probably we

---

Jordi Jaria-Manzano and Susana Borrás (eds), *Research Handbook on Global Climate Constitutionalism* (Elgar 2019).

65 David R. Boyd, *The Environmental Rights Revolution: A Global Study of Constitutions, Human Rights, and the Environment* (University of British Columbia Press 2012).

66 Ibid.

67 Ibid. Cf Domenico Amirante, 'Del Estado de derecho ambiental al Estado del Antropoceno: una mirada a la historia del constitucionalismo medioambiental' [2020] *Revista General de Derecho Público Comparado* 1.

68 James R. May and Erin Daly, *Global Environmental Constitutionalism* (CUP 2014) 49.

69 James R. May and Erin Daly (eds), *Implementing Environmental Constitutionalism: Current Global Challenges* (CUP 2018).

would have found traces of new technologies within the first constitutional texts, while the environment could have been addressed in those centuries if it would have been worth it according to the intelligentsia's common sense. Although humankind was directed towards the Anthropocene since the 18th century,[70] still environmental legislation included just single-case palliatives and proto-environmental legislations in response to specific conditions and emergencies, without assuming the shape of a proper legal discipline encompassing moral values worth being constitutionalised. Within this theoretical framework, thousands of legal scholars shaped their own knowledge and understanding of law, and some of them are quite 'fond' of classical theoretical frameworks. Consequently, environmental constitutionalism is seen through different lenses: 'the good', 'the bad' and 'the ugly'. Of course, these perspectives contain value judgments; nevertheless, they offer a brief and direct insight on how legal scholars actually perceive environmental constitutionalism.

Under the 'good' lens, environmental constitutionalism represents the current legal response to cope with the present global socio-ecological crisis, addressing the quest for legal frameworks able to foster adaptation and mitigation actions along with the early environmental law's commitments of conservation and restoration, promoting a legal approach to integrated ecologies.

In spite of the aforementioned bright acclamation of environmental constitutionalism, this phenomenon can be seen as well under the 'bad' lens, i.e., as the evidence of an "aging process [that] has unduly ossified the necessary law-making processes—some have dubbed it a 'green arthritis'—preventing environmental law from always evolving as it should".[71]

In some cases, global concerns for anthropogenic environmental degradation still do not force legal scholars to consider the need for assessing environmental constitutionalism as a new form of constitutionalism. Within the legal debate, there is still the tendency to associate environmentalism with studies in environmental legislation, mixing social movements and legal analyses. Furthermore, under this approach, environmental constitutionalism could appear redundant and restricted by an already established body of international environmental principles and effective domestic legislation. This perspective represents the 'ugly' lens through which environmental constitutionalism is addressed: a sort of 'new-age attempt' to rejuvenate old discourses. From this perspective, it seems to be a dialogue among 'advocates' without 'sceptics', characterised by the fact that "both the nature of the debate and the relative isolation of the literature create

70 Paul J. Crutzen, 'The "Anthropocene"' in Eckart Ehlers and Thomas Krafft (eds), *Earth System Science in the Anthropocene* (Springer 2006).

71 Richard J. Lazarus, *The Making of Environmental Law* (2nd edn, University of Chicago Press 2004) 168. About the chronological aspects, according to R.J. Lazarus, the development of environmental law discipline can be divided into three phases related to specific decades: 1) "Building a Road" (1970s); 2) "Expanding the Road" (1980s); 3) "Maintaining the Road" (1990s).

the impression that environmental constitutionalism holds no new insights about the wider project of social values constitutionalism".[72]

6. Conclusion. Beyond Mutual Influences: International Environmental Law and Environmental Constitutionalism

The recognition of international environmental principles does not automatically foster the implementation and the enforcement of environmental provisions. As a response to this lack of effectiveness, national legal systems have initiated the path towards the constitutional recognition of the environment. In spite of the hypothetical existence of a global constitution, and considering the "Babel-like quality of the discourse about international constitutionalism",[73] the key-question remains whether domestic constitutional law could be considered a safe haven, both for theoretical and pragmatic issues. This question could be addressed in the following terms:

> [i]n the same way that a crying child who bumps his toe would instinctively run to his mother, in desperate times, regulators and legislators alike seem to seek refuge in the familiar, the constant, and the trusted. Constitutions and constitutionalism have been around since the 17th Century, thus providing a familiar language and the logical "go to" solution for environmental regulators in times of ecological upheaval and regulatory uncertainty.[74]

Some might dissent from this assumption, since other branches of law are far older than the constitutional one. Nevertheless, if one considers the intrinsic features of constitutions, they are the most reliable legal tool for recognising rights and duties, and ensuring political accountability and legal enforcement, along with their 'counter-simple-majority' role with respect to the democratic legislator's choices—although with different degrees of certainty in reference to the legal tradition of the case.

Legal dialogues among states and the international environmental law regime have played a pivotal role in promoting domestic legal responses, basically offering a proper set of principles that could easily be included within national legal systems. However, this process has favoured a sort of 'legal clamp', lacking of a connective tissue between the two legal domains and between law and politics, thus emphasising the deficiencies in legal enforcement and political accountability. With the aim of solving such issues, during the last decades, environment as

72 Lael K. Weis, 'Environmental Constitutionalism: Aspiration or Transformation?' [2018] *International Journal of Constitutional Law* 838.

73 Bodansky (n 56) 567.

74 Louis J. Kotzé, 'The Conceptual Contours of Environmental Constitutionalism' [2015] *Widener Law Review* 189.

a legal-functional topic has claimed its own constitutionalisation, going beyond a mere assimilation to other phenomena of constitutionalism, acquiring a devoted epistemological space. In other words, the interplay between international and domestic actors in coping with environmental concerns has nurtured the rise of a specific form of constitutional approach, which is not the result of theoretical debates, but the scholarly acknowledgment of the factual existence of environmental constitutionalism.

Bibliography

Adede A.O., 'The Treaty System from Stockholm (1972) to Rio de Janeiro (1992)' [1995] *Pace Environmental Law Review* 33.

Albertyn C., 'Cultural Diversity, "Living Law," and Women's Rights in South Africa' in D. Bonilla Maldonado (ed), *Constitutionalism of the Global South: The Activist Tribunals of India, South Africa, and Colombia* (CUP 2013).

Amirante D., 'Del Estado de derecho ambiental al Estado del Antropoceno: una mirada a la historia del constitucionalismo medioambiental' [2020] *Revista General de Derecho Público Comparado* 1.

Atilgan A., *Global Constitutionalism: A Socio-legal Perspective* (Springer 2018).

Ávila Santamaria R., *En defensa del neoconstitucionalismo transformador: los debates y los argumentos* (Universidad Andina Simón Bolívar 2012).

Bagni S., 'Hitos de democratización de la justicia constitucional en América Latina: una mirada desde afuera' in R. Tur Ausina (ed), *Problemas actuales de Derecho constitucional en un contexto de crisis* (Comares 2015).

Baldin S., *Il buen vivir nel costituzionalismo andino. Profili comparativi* (Giappichelli 2019).

Barrett S., 'A Theory of Full International Cooperation' [1999] *Journal of Theoretical Politics* 519.

Baxi U., 'Preliminary Notes on Transformative Constitutionalism' in O. Vilhena et al. (eds), *Transformative Constitutionalism: Comparing the Apex Courts of Brazil, India and South Africa* (Pretoria University Law Press 2013).

Blanco Valdés R.L., 'Costituzionalismo' in Lucio Pegoraro (ed), *Glossario di Diritto pubblico comparato* (Carocci 2011) 64.

Bodansky D., 'Is There an International Environmental Constitution?' [2009] *Indiana Journal of Global Legal Studies* 567.

Bodansky D., *The Art and Craft of International Environmental Law* (Harvard University Press 2010).

von Bogdandy A. et al. (eds), *Transformative Constitutionalism in Latin America* (OUP 2017).

Boyd D.R., *The Environmental Rights Revolution: A Global Study of Constitutions, Human Rights, and the Environment* (University of British Columbia Press 2012).

Boyle A. and Freestone D. (eds), *International Law and Sustainable Development: Past Achievements and Future Challenges* (OUP 1999).

Carbonell M. (ed), *Teoría del neoconstitucionalismo. Ensayos escogidos* (Trotta 2007).

Castillo Fernández A.A., 'Constitucionalismo Latinoamericano. Definición, características, problemas y perspectivas de futuro' [2015] *Epikeia. Derecho y política* 1.

Cordonier Segger M.-C. and Khalfan A., *Sustainable Development Law: Principles, Practices, and Prospects* (OUP 2004).

Crutzen P.J., 'The "Anthropocene"' in Eckart Ehlers and Thomas Krafft (eds), *Earth System Science in the Anthropocene* (Springer 2006).
Davis D.M. and Klare K.E., 'Transformative Constitutionalism and the Common and Customary Law' [2010] *South African Journal on Human Rights* 402.
Duvic-Paoli L.-A., *The Prevention Principle in International Environmental Law* (CUP 2018).
French D., *International Law and Policy of Sustainable Development* (Manchester University Press 2005).
Gargarella R., 'Sobre el "Nuevo constitucionalismo latinoamericano"' [2018] *Revista Uruguaya de Ciencia Política* 129.
Glenn H.P., *Legal Traditions of the World : Sustainable Diversity in Law* (5th edn, OUP 2014).
Gümplová P., 'Sovereignty Over Natural Resources. A Normative Reinterpretation' [2019] *Global Constitutionalism* 7.
Hollis D.B., *The Oxford Guide to Treaties* (OUP 2020).
Hunter D., 'International Environmental Law' in P.G. Harris (ed), *Routledge Handbook of Global Environmental Politics* (Routledge 2016).
Hunter D. et al., *International Environmental Law & Policy* (Foundation Press 2010).
Jasanoff S., 'The Dilemma of Environmental Democracy' [1996] *Issues in Science and Technology* 63.
Kingsbury B. et al., 'The Emergence of Global Administrative Law' [2005] *Law and Contemporary Problems* 18.
Kiss A.C. and Sicault J.D., 'La Conférence des Nations Unies sur l'environnement (Stockholm, 5/16 juin 1972)' [1972] *Annuaire Français de Droit International* 603.
Klare K.E., 'Legal Culture and Transformative Constitutionalism' [1998] *South African Journal on Human Rights* 146.
Kotzé L.J., 'Rethinking Global Environmental Law and Governance in the Anthropocene' [2014] *Journal of Energy & Natural Resources Law* 132.
Kotzé L.J., 'The Conceptual Contours of Environmental Constitutionalism' [2015] *Widener Law Review* 189.
Kotzé L.J., *Global Environmental Constitutionalism in the Anthropocene* (Hart Publishing 2016) 178.
Kumm M., 'On the History and Theory of Global Constitutionalism' in T. Suami et al. (eds), *Global Constitutionalism from European and East Asian Perspectives* (CUP 2018).
Lazarus R.J., *The Making of Environmental Law* (2nd edn, University of Chicago Press 2004).
Lees E. and Viñuales J.E. (eds), *The Oxford Handbook of Comparative Environmental Law* (OUP 2019).
Loughlin M., 'What is Constitutionalisation?' in Petra Dobner and Martin Loughlin (eds), *The Twilight of Constitutionalism?* (OUP 2010).
Maier H., 'Extraterritorial Jurisdiction at a Crossroads: An Intersection Between Public and Private International Law' [1982] *American Journal of International Law* 280.
Mason M., *Environmental Democracy* (Earthscan 1999).
May J.R. and Daly E., *Global Environmental Constitutionalism* (CUP 2014) 49.
May J.R. and Daly E. (eds), *Implementing Environmental Constitutionalism: Current Global Challenges* (CUP 2018).

Méndez López J.A. and Cutier Mustelier D., 'La participación popular en el nuevo constitucionalismo latinoamericano. Una mirada desde la perspectiva de los derechos' [2010] *Revista del Instituto de Ciencias Jurídicas de Puebla* 94.
Menski W., *Comparative Law in a Global Context: The Legal Systems of Asia and Africa* (CUP 2006).
Mesa Cuadros G., 'Environmental Rights, Responsibility and Care: A New Constitutional Paradigm' in J. Jaria-Manzano and S. Borrás (eds), *Research Handbook on Global Climate Constitutionalism* (Elgar 2019).
Meyer B., *The International Law on Climate change* (CUP 2018).
Morin J.-F. et al., *Global Environmental Politics* (OUP 2020).
Murcott M., 'Introducing Transformative Environmental Constitutionalism in South Africa' in Erin Daly et al. (eds), *New Frontiers in Environmental Constitutionalism* (UNEP 2017).
Murcott M., 'Transformative Environmental Constitutionalism's Response to the Setting Aside of South Africa's Moratorium on Rhino Horn Trade' [2017] *Humanities* 3.
Murcott M., 'The Procedural Right of Access to Information as a Means of Implementing Environmental Constitutionalism in South Africa' in James R. May and Erin Daly (eds), *Implementing Environmental Constitutionalism: Current Global Challenges* (CUP 2018).
Mureinik E., 'A Bridge to Where? Introducing the Interim Bill of Rights' [1994] *South African Journal on Human Rights* 32.
Office of Public Information, *Yearbook of the United Nations 1968* (UN 1971).
Parrish A.L., 'Trail Smelter Déjà Vu: Extraterritoriality, International Environmental Law, and the Search for Solutions to Canadian-U.S. Transboundary Water Pollution Disputes' [2005] *Boston University Law Review* 363.
Pegoraro L. and Rinella A., *Sistemi costituzionali* (Giappichelli 2020).
Peters A., 'Compensatory Constitutionalism: The Function and Potential of Fundamental International Norms and Structures' [2006] *Leiden Journal of International Law* 579.
Peters A., 'The Merits of Global Constitutionalism' [2009] *Indiana Journal of Global Legal Studies* 411.
Peters A. and Armingeon K., 'Introduction – Global Constitutionalism from an Interdisciplinary Perspective' [2009] *Indiana Journal of Global Legal Studies* 385.
Ramírez-Nárdiz A., 'Nuevo constitucionalismo latinoamericano y democracia participativa: ¿progreso o retroceso democrático?' [2016] *Vniversitas* 349.
de Sadeleer N., *Environmental Principles: From Political Slogans to Legal Rules* (2nd edn, OUP 2020).
Sands P. and Galizzi P. (eds), *Documents in International Environmental Law* (CUP 2004).
Sands P. et al., *Principles of International Environmental Law* (3rd edn, CUP 2018) 210.
Sartori G., 'Constitutionalism: A Preliminary Discussion' [1962] *The American Political Science Review* 853.
Schachter O., 'The Emergence of International Environmental Law' [1991] *Journal of International Affairs* 457.
Schwarz P., 'The Polluter-pays Principle' in Michael Faure (ed), *Elgar Encyclopedia of Environmental Law* (Elgar 2018).

Sibanda S., 'When Do You Call Time on a Compromise? South Africa's Discourse on Transformation and the Future of Transformative Constitutionalism' (2020) 24 *Law, Democracy & Development* 384.

Soto M.V., 'General Principles of International Environmental Law' [1996] *ILSA Journal of International & Comparative Law* 192.

de Sousa Santos B., *Epistemologies of the South: Justice Against Epistemicide* (Routledge 2014).

Viciano Pastor R. and Martínez Dalmau R., 'Aspectos generales del nuevo constitucionalismo latinoamericano' in VV.AA. (ed), *El nuevo constitucionalismo en América Latina* (Corte Constitucional del Ecuador para el período de transición 2010).

Viciano Pastor R. and Martínez Dalmau R., 'El nuevo constitucionalismo latinoamericano' [2011] *Revista general de derecho público comparado* 1.

Villabella Armengol C.M., 'Constitución y democracia en el nuevo constitucionalismo latinoamericano' [2010] *Revista del Instituto de Ciencias Jurídicas de Puebla* 49.

Viola P., *Costituzionalismo autoctono. Pluralismo culturale e trapianti giuridici nel subcontinente indiano* (BUP 2020).

Wates J., 'The Aarhus Convention: A Driving Force for Environmental Democracy' [2005] *Journal for European Environmental & Planning Law* 2.

Weis L.K., 'Environmental Constitutionalism: Aspiration or Transformation?' [2018] *International Journal of Constitutional Law* 838.

Woodwell G.M., 'On Purpose in Science, Conservation and Government: The Functional Integrity of the Earth is at Issue Not Biodiversity' [2002] *Ambio* 432.

Young O.R., *International Cooperation: Building Regimes for Natural Resources and the Environment* (Cornell University Press 1989).

Zander J., *The Application of the Precautionary Principle in Practice: Comparative Dimensions* (CUP 2010).

8 Environmental Constitutionalism Through the Lens of Comparative Law

New Perspectives for the Anthropocene

Domenico Amirante

1. The Paradox of Environmental Constitutionalism: A Practice in Search of a Theory

The expansion of environmental constitutionalism over the last decades has produced a substantial increase in the number of democratic Constitutions containing environmental rules and principles. Globally, out of the 193 Constitutions of the current member States to the UN, 156 contain today explicit references to the environment.[1] Most of these Constitutions reflect the growing sensitivity and a public common concern towards the protection of the environment. Especially in recent years, the evolution of environmental constitutionalism has gained momentum, marking an upward trajectory: environmental protection has nowadays reached a central position in the world's constitutional systems, with more stringent and, above all, structural forms of protection.

However, the quantitative increase of the number of Constitutions treating environmental themes is only one part of the picture. In fact, if we consider, with Frankenberg, that Constitutions "bear a close relationship to politics and ethics – closer than most other laws" and that they contain "knots of significations", projecting archetypes, patterns, structures, we can affirm that the constitutional commitment towards environment represents an archetype of our times.[2] Despite this glaring evidence, widespread and rooted at the social level, the 'constitutional dimension' of environmental protection is still largely neglected by the political agendas of many governments, and the theoretical status of environmental constitutionalism is still uncertain and in need of discussion and clarification.

1 For a first quantitative analysis of the expansion of environmental constitutionalism, cf David R. Boyd, *The Environmental Rights Revolution: A Study on of Constitutions, Human Rights and Environment* (University of British Columbia Press 2012). The data reported here represent a re-elaboration and updating of those presented in this volume. See also: Roderic O'Gorman, 'Environmental Constitutionalism: A Comparative Study' [2017] 6 *Transnational Environmental Law* 435.

2 Günter Frankenberg, 'Comparing Constitutions: Ideas, Ideals, and Ideology – Toward a Layered Narrative' [2006] 4 *International Journal of Constitutional Law* 439, 440.

DOI: 10.4324/9781003175308-11

In fact, mainstream constitutional law scholarship is hardly interested in environmental issues, while constitutional law handbooks rarely mention this topic, and even a comprehensive compendium, such as *The Oxford Handbook of Comparative Constitutional Law*, excludes environmental issues from sections dedicated to "ideas", "trends" or "overlapping rights".[3] Consequently, a meaningful debate on the constitutional foundations of environmental protection is still restricted to a few specialists of environmental law.[4] Additionally, even from a comparative law perspective, the debate on environmental constitutionalism seems to linger in an embryonic stage, both in the common law and the civil law arenas. There is thus a need for a discussion and a systematisation of the recent developments in environmental constitutionalism, by integrating them in the 'great constitutional debates', namely in the wider framework of the relations between the State, the Constitution, the social communities (including minorities/indigenous people) and the diverse conception of the person/individual. Comparative law, though rarely used in the context of environmental law,[5] may offer the essential methodological toolbox both to assess the innovations and the challenges related to the development of environmental constitutionalism, and to open up a dialogue among the 'constitutional cultures' that support its recent affirmation.

Before engaging in an introductory analysis of environmental constitutionalism through the lens of comparative law, we need to make a few premises/disclaimers. First, we must recognise that environmental law as a whole is a discipline in constant search of its scientific legitimacy, still feeding the "perception of enduring immaturity",[6] and that this aspect often discourages scholars from traditional disciplines (i.e. constitutional law) to take up such a challenge. This feature also partially explains the lesser development of the doctrinal dimension of environmental law, which is predominately discussed only among 'expert' environmental lawyers. Secondly, we must clarify that highlighting the urgent need to discuss environmental problems in constitutional terms does not automatically

3 Michel Rosenfeld and Andràs Sajò (eds), *The Oxford Handbook of Comparative Constitutional Law* (OUP 2012).

4 To the already mentioned studies by Boyd and O'Gorman (quoted in 1), we must add also, James R. May and Erin Daly, *Global Environmental Constitutionalism* (CUP 2014); Louis J. Kotzé, *Global Environmental Constitutionalism in the Anthropocene* (Hart Publishing 2016). For some civil law approaches see Jochen Sohnle (ed), *Environmental Constitutionaslism: What Impact on Legal Systems?* (Peter Lang 2019); Jordi Jaria-Manzano, *La Constitución del Antropoceno* (Tirant lo Blanch 2020).

5 If we exclude some seminal but isolated contributions by Nicholas A. Robinson, 'Comparative Environmental Law: Evaluating How Legal Systems Address "Sustainable Development"' [1997] 27 *Environmental Policy and earlier Law* 338; Dan Tarlock and Pedro Tarak, 'Overview of Comparative Environmental Law' [1983] 13 *Denver Journal of International Law and Policy* 85, a general account on the methodology of comparative environmental law has been offered as recently as in 2019 by Jorge E. Viñuales, 'Comparative Environmental Law: Structuring a Field' in Emma Lees and Jorge E. Viñuales (eds), *The Oxford Handbook of Comparative Environmental Law* (OUP 2019).

6 Elizabeth Fisher and others, 'Maturity and Methodology: Starting a Debate about Environmental Law Scholarship' [2009] 21 *Journal of Environmental Law* 214.

imply the affirmation of a disciplinary supremacy of the constitutional dimension of environmental law over other dimensions, such as the international, the supranational or the administrative/local. On the contrary, we think that a mature development of environmental constitutional law is a necessary step to complete and implement the role of other disciplines in the context of a 'multi-level environmental law and governance', a label that has been abandoned too fast in favour of 'global' or 'transnational' approaches. In this framework, the constitutional dimension is the 'missing link' of the environmental law chain because it is the only level able to give substance to the principles elaborated at the international level by applying them to the national legal system, without leaving the implementation of environmental law and policies to uncoordinated administrative rules and practices or only to judicial responses.[7] Thirdly, we also think that in systematising environmental constitutionalism, one has to avoid the risk of crystallising it in a fixed set of rules since it has an open and evolutionary character, as theorised, among others, by the studies conducted by "critical environmental law".[8] Fourthly, we think that the comparative law methodologies will add useful insights to the ongoing debate on environmental law and particularly on environmental constitutionalism, highlighting some aspects that are substantially neglected by new approaches such as transnational environmental law[9] or global environmental constitutionalism,[10] namely the use of taxonomies, the historical perspective, the relation between environmental 'visions' and legal traditions.

In this chapter, we attempt to point out some building blocks for the construction of a more conscious and culturally and theoretically based debate on environmental constitutionalism in order to overcome the fragmentation of the present scholarly discussion and the relative parochialism of environmental law. For this purpose, we propose some starting exercises using typical comparative methodologies: i) a basic taxonomy on the 'constitutionalisation' of the environment, and ii) an historical account of the development of the constitutional approach from a mere 'constitutionalisation of the environment' to a proper environmental constitutionalism. These exercises will represent the basis for studying the relations between legal traditions, environmental law and constitutional cultures,

7 On the relations between International Environmental Law and Environmental Constitutional Law see Pasquale Viola, 'From the Principles of International Environmental Law to Environmental Constitutionalism: Competitive or Cooperative Influences?' in this book, p. 127–147.

8 Andreas Philippopoulos-Mihalopoulos, 'Towards a Critical Environmental Law' in Andreas Philippopoulos-Mihalopoulos (ed), *Law and Ecology: New Environmental Foundations* (Routledge 2011).

9 For this approach refer to the review *Transnational Environmental Law*, started in 2012, and its inaugural article by Veerle Heyvaert and Thijs Ett, 'Introducing Transnational Environmental Law' [2012] 1 *Transnational Environmental Law* 1.

10 See Klaus Bosselmann, 'Global Environmental Constitutionalism: Mapping the Terrain' [2012] *Widener Law Review* 171; for a critical approach: Daniel Bodansky, 'Is There an International Environmental Constitution?' [2009] *Indiana Journal of Global Legal Studies* 567.

and for systematising the fragmented scholarly debate on environmental constitutionalism. They will also stimulate a true dialogue between the different forms of environmental constitutionalism experienced over the last decades.

Such a dialogue appears as a fundamental step towards a new constitutionalism for the Anthropocene, the new geological era in which the '*homo oeconomicus*' is turning into '*homo destruens*', which requires a radical renovation in order to implement the methods of political action and the legal norms, from the international and state level, to local communities. This implies an epistemological revolution because, as underlined by Robinson, "old assumptions no longer work, and our innovations are now out of date because of the pervasive change that the Anthropocene represents", and consequently "many of our 'business-as-usual' assumptions no longer are reliable".[11] It is therefore necessary to firmly abandon the categories of modern law that, according to Kotzé, "have historically been reserved for fragmented, issue-specific, and narrow legal enquiries that accommodates less alarmist expressions of urgency and that have tolerated weak commitments to ethical responsibility towards the environment".[12] Dealing with the Anthropocene implies the search for new economic, political and legal paradigms, based on the concepts of responsibility and interdependence between human beings and nature. In this context, constitutional law and comparative law are destined to play a pivotal role, incorporating innovations that come from the international and national contexts and articulating effective and coherent frameworks for the action of political and administrative powers, as well as for civil society.

2. Constitutionalising the Environment: A Basic Comparative Taxonomy

Studying environmental constitutionalism in a global comparative perspective requires a meaningful (if basic) taxonomy of Constitutions, a 'state of the art' taking into account the evolutionary character of environmental law. Using a synchronic approach, we can start by classifying three categories of constitutions, considering the ways in which the environmental dimension and its values assume relevance within the overall constitutional structure.[13]

The first category consists of 'Environmental Constitutions'(EC). It includes Constitutions containing, since their first approval, specific articles dedicated to the environment, considering its protection as a decisive point in its original overall structure. The second includes the 'Revised Environmental Constitutions'(REC), in which one or more 'environmental articles' have been

11 Nicholas A. Robinson, 'Fundamental Principles of Law for the Anthropocene?' [2014] 44 *Environmental Policy and Law* 13, http://digitalcommons.pace.edu/lawfaculty/964/.

12 Kotzé (n 4) 7.

13 We already proposed this classification, long back, in a first attempt at structuring a discourse on environmental constitutionalism; see Domenico Amirante (ed), Diritto ambientale e Costituzione. *Esperienze europee* (Franco Angeli 2000) 24ff.

inserted through amendments, which must therefore be harmonised within a constitutional structure and context. The third category includes the systems in which the constitutional protection of the environment, in the absence of specific textual references, depends only on judicial decisions, mostly taken by Constitutional and Supreme Courts ('Silent Environmental Constitutions', or SEC).

If we look at the current division of the world's Constitutions into these three categories, we can appreciate a well-defined picture: today 62% of the constitutional systems fall in to the first category (EC, or Environmental Constitutions), while 17% have Revised Constitutions (REC), and only 21% do not have written references to environmental values or protection (falling in the Silent Environmental Constitutions, SEC). As a whole, 79% of the world's Constitutions at least mention environmental issues, with variable degrees of environmental commitment, but an ample majority (62%) is represented by original Environmental Constitutions (thus bearing in principle a strong commitment), while only 17% are Revised Constitutions. This confirms the present consolidation of both a quantitative and qualitative environmental constitutionalism.

Of course, while dealing with 'Environmental Constitutions' presenting a specific and organic discipline on the environment since their enactment, we will look at relatively young texts. In fact, the interest in the environment, especially in constitutional law, has only developed starting with in the last decades of the twentieth century, roughly around the Seventies. For historical reasons, therefore, the Constitutions which had been in force before this period do not contain norms regarding the environment. In this sense, we can quote the revealing case of article 9 of the Italian Constitution, introducing in 1948 a concept only indirectly referable to the environment, such as landscape protection, that was hardly approved against a strong opposition blaming it as 'superfluous' because of the existence of ordinary legislation on the subject. This shows how in the post–Second World War era, the legal culture in the Western world was still very distant from the environmental sensitivity unanimously shared today. In fact, the first 'new' European Constitution containing references to the environment were enacted in the Seventies (i.e. Greece in 1975, Portugal in 1976 and Spain in 1978), while in the rest of the world (and especially in Asia and Africa), the bulk of the original EC's would come after the Eighties.

The second category includes 'revised environmental Constitutions' in which one or more 'environmental articles' have been implanted in constitutional texts already in force, so that they had to adapt, with some difficulty, to systems not originally oriented towards environmental protection. Normally such Constitutions show only a weak commitment to environmental values, and predominantly relegate environmental concerns to policy objectives, as demonstrated by the majority of the European constitutional amendments (with the notable exception of France, whose "*Charte de l'environment*" came into force only in 2005). The Revised Constitution represent only 17% of the world's environmental constitutional systems, but many of the classic European Constitutions (i.e. Germany, Italy, France, Belgium, Austria) belong to this category.

The third category, representing today only 21%, includes those Constitutions in which there are no textual references to the environment. Here, environmental values and interests emerge mainly in ordinary legislation and judicial decisions, generally by Supreme and/or Constitutional Courts. That does not mean that environmental rules and policies are absent in such constitutional systems, but they are left to the contingencies of political majorities or of judicial activity (or in certain cases of 'judicial activism'), which may oscillate from strong commitment to weak or ineffective protection. Some important common law legal systems fall within this category, such as the United States, Canada, Australia and Great Britain, while civil law or mixed constitutional systems fall predominantly within the EC or REC groups.

From a geographical point of view, today Africa is the continent with a higher percentage of EC, with 75% of the States, followed by Asia with 64%, Europe with 60%, while both the Americas and Oceania consist of only 43% Environmental Constitutions (with the substantial difference that the Americas have 34% REC and only 23% SEC, while Oceania has 57% Silent Environmental Constitutions). The highest rate of Environmental Constitutions in Africa may be partially explained by the political conditions of the continent, where constitutional regimes change more rapidly than in the other parts of the world, indirectly favouring environmental updates.

3. A Brief History of Environmental Constitutionalism: A Counter-Narrative

In the first part of this chapter, we showed how environmental constitutionalism represents today a major feature of world's constitutionalism, while there is a 'small rearguard' of countries (sometimes not politically and legally insignificant, like the USA, the UK, Canada and Australia) not fine-tuning to it. The initial reticence towards the constitutionalisation of the environment of the Seventies and the Eighties has progressively been reversed until the present phase, in which the Constitutions devoid of references to the environment have become residuary with respect to the Environmental Constitutions (EC) and the 'Revised' ones (REC). From this angle, the history of environmental constitutionalism discloses a 'counter-narrative' based on two substantial changes: a progressive emergence of the constitutional dimension of environmental law from an initially internationally driven normative corpus, on one side, and a proactive role played by the constitutional systems from the South of the world, that have become the vanguard of environmental constitutionalism. In both these changes, we can identify an important 'ontological' evolution of environmental law as a whole. In fact, today constitutional environmental provisions are not just possible 'new entries' in legal systems, simply adding another level of protection, regardless of the basic relation between men, society and the environment. On the contrary, the new environmental Constitutions consider that the relation between man and environment/nature is at the core of the constitutional discourse and influences both the genealogy of rights and the organisation of the State.

Adopting an historical approach, we can thus identify three periods for the development of environmental constitutionalism, notably: i) the nascent phase of environment constitutionalism based on an instrumental conception of the environment, developed mainly in European Constitutions (during the Seventies and the Eighties of the past century); ii) the adolescent phase, producing a worldwide development of environmental constitutionalism in many new East European Constitutions but also in other continents, notably Africa and Latin America (during the Nineties); iii) the adult phase, presently driven by the development of a 'new environmental constitutionalism' from the South of the world, with environmental rules and principles reaching the centre of the constitutional stage.

3.1. The Nascent Phase: The European Instrumental Approach

The post–Second World War European Constitutions (France, Italy, West Germany) did not contain rules concerning the protection of environment, although they displayed some indirect references to the environment in relation to the management of land or of the landscape.[14]

Environmental law, as a normative corpus, was substantially originated during the Sixties and the Seventies of the last century by international documents. Its founding episode of is generally considered the 'milestone' United Nations Conference on the Human Environment taking place in 1972 in Stockholm, which, although not producing a legally binding international document, gave impetus to a series of programs on environmental matters (among which the institution of the UNEP – United Nations Environmental Program). This Conference had a great influence not only on the international and national policies for environmental protection, but on the elaboration of environmental law. At the beginning, environmental law was conceived mainly as soft law, based largely on general principles, and as a 'technical matter', highly depending on scientific data, notably on evidence on the effects of pollution and of the degradation of the environment. Consequently, in the first outline of environmental law there was relatively little space left for constitutional law and principles. At that time, environmental policies were dictated at the international level and then simply executed at the national level, essentially by administrative law. In a way, one could say that an 'original sin' of environmental law was the neglect of its constitutional dimension. A side-effect was also the foundation of the discipline on a North-South divide, as illustrated by Atapattu and Gonzales, according the which North-South conflicts "originating in the economic realm have profoundly shaped the evolution of international environmental law and policy",[15]

14 Some, such as Boyd (n 1) 225 ff., include the Italian Constitution of 1948 (considering Art. 9 on landscape) among the first environmental constituencies. However, until the Seventies we could possibly speak only of a 'prehistory of environmental law'.

15 Sumudu Atapattu and Carmen G. Gonzalez, 'The North – South Divide in International Environmental Law: Framing the Issues' in Shawkat Alam and others (eds), *International Environmental Law and the Global South* (CUP 2015) 9.

since Northern consumption patterns "constrain the development of options, of present and future generations, particularly in the global South".[16]

According to this representation, constitutional cultures did not participate as major driving forces to the creation of environmental law and to its initial implementation. In fact, at a global scale the approach to environmental law was marked essentially by a 'human rights' culture, framing environmental protection essentially through the affirmation of a human right to a safe environment, with the consequence of highlighting the individual, *a posteriori* and judicial dimension of environmental law to the detriment of more structural and preventive forms of protection. Soon after Stockholm, some Constitutions of small States included direct references to environmental protection, such as the Constitutions of Panama (1972) and San Marino (1974), but the first organic European environmental Constitution came from Greece, even though the 1975 text did not fully recognise a true right to the environment and considered the protection of the environment as a mere obligation of the State. More interesting in historical perspective are the new Constitutions from the Iberian Peninsula, where in the Seventies the two long-lasting authoritarian regimes of Spain and Portugal were democratised. The Portuguese Constitution of 1976 deals with environmental problems in detail, establishing in Art. 66 a "right to a human, healthy and ecologically balanced environment" accompanied by "the duty to defend it". However, in its initial phase, the Portuguese model raised many objections, so much that in the following years, and until 2005, it was subject to seven constitutional revisions touching the environmental field.[17]

In this phase, the Spanish model, structured mainly on the relation between environmental rules and the 'economic constitution', played a leading role. Upon a first reading of Art. 45 of the Constitution, emerges the dual nature of the Spanish approach, halfway between the recognition of a subjective right and a state-centred approach to environmental protection. The first paragraph contains a typical rights-based approach as it states that "everyone has the right to enjoy an adequate environment for the development of the person, as well as the duty to maintain it". The right to environment is designed here as closely linked to the development of personal integrity in a broad sense: it also involves social, existential and spiritual aspects, anticipating one of the fundamental elements of the evolution of the environmental constitutionalism of the 2000s. Nevertheless, considering the development of environmental interests and values in contemporary Spanish law, it is certainly possible to maintain that, despite the initial enthusiasm, the rights-based approach to the environment has substantially failed. On the contrary, the objective dimension, identifying the right to the environment as a guiding principle for the action of public authorities, has

16 Ibid 10.

17 For an account on the historical development of the Portuguese Constitution from 1976 on, see Carla Amado Gomes, 'Constituição e ambiente: errância e simbolismo' [2012] 9 *Veredas do Direito* 9.

developed consistently. It is possible to synthetically explain this development. First of all, the location of Art. 45 in the Spanish Constitution is quite explicit: it is placed outside of the fundamental rights catalogue, in Chapter III, concerning the guiding principles of the social and economic policies.[18] We must also mention the contribution of the judgments of the Constitutional tribunal, especially on the relation between environmental protection and the economic constitution. In fact, the interpretation of the Constitutional tribunal in some judgments, trying to reconcile economic interests with environmental necessities, makes it possible to identify some guiding principles of a 'Constitution of the sustainable development'. The Court draws up a notion of 'qualitative development', involving an extensive functionalisation of economic rights for the achievement of an adequate level and uniform quality of life, referred to in paragraph 2 of Art. 45. The social function of the environment, therefore, assumes fundamental relevance in the economic Constitution, but must be adjusted through some general principles according to the objectives of economic and social progress. These principles are provided by the second paragraph of Art. 45, making explicit reference to the "rational use of all natural resources", that shall guide all the actions of the legislature and the executive regarding the regulation of economic activities. In this respect, a famous ruling by the Constitutional tribunal identifies environmental protection as an "indispensable ingredient for seasoning all the other sectorial policies".[19]

Apart from the Spanish Constitution, the other 'Reformed Constitutions' of the time (notably the Netherlands, 1983, and Austria, 1984) contain generic references to the protection of the environment as an obligation of the State, without providing for a substantive right to the environment, or outlining a satisfactory definition of the role of environmental values in the Constitution. Overall, the European constitutional texts of the Seventies and Eighties contain a partial vision of environmental protection, mainly based on State action but often included only in the programmatic section of the Constitution. The initial reticence against the full recognition of environmental protection as a right or as a primary public interest can be explained with the needs of economic development and more generally of 'growth', assumed as a prevailing objective over environmental protection. This approach will be confirmed in the next phase of environmental constitutionalism, that will result in a reinforcement of environmental protection and in several cases in the recognition of a right to environment, but always under the pervasiveness of a weak notion of sustainable development, considering economic growth as a primary interest and perpetuating the anthropocentric antagonism between man and nature.

18 On these aspects, see Maria Jesus Montoro Chiner, 'El estado ambiental de derecho. Bases constitucionales' in Francisco Sosa Wagner (ed) *El derecho administrativo en el umbral del siglo XXI: homenaje al profesor Dr. D. Ramón Martín Mateo* (vol. 3, Tirant lo Blanch 2000).

19 Supremo Tribunal Constitucional, case n. 102/95, of 1995.

3.2. The Adolescent Phase: The Worldwide Development of Environmental Constitutionalism in the Nineties

In 1989, when the Berlin Wall crumbled, environmental constitutionalism was still in its nascent state, but in the Nineties there followed a considerable growth in the number of Constitutions providing for environmental protection. There are three fundamental reasons contributing to the expansion of environmental constitutionalism on a global scale. First of all, the awareness of the centrality of environmental issues is due to tragic episodes of environmental disasters which left devastating emotional impacts. Among them, the disasters at Bhopal in 1984 and at the Chernobyl nuclear power plant in 1986 stand out. Furthermore, at the international level, the Rio de Janeiro Conference of 1992 represents a real turning point identifying the protection of the environment as a priority of international politics through the enunciation of a series of innovative principles contained in Agenda 21. The third element, not directly related to environmental issues, but connected to the modalities of development of environmental constitutionalism, must certainly be identified within the wave of political-institutional renewal that followed the fall of the Berlin Wall, which determined a transformation of the geo-political world order, and the consequent reorganisation of the Constitutions of Eastern Europe. The constitutional renewal also drove many countries from other continents (especially Asia and Africa) that were coming out of the Soviet sphere of influence, thus creating an opportunity for them to introduce principles of environmental protection into the new texts.

Naturally, the configuration of environmental protection in the Eastern European systems varied according to national events and surrounding situations, including the economic situations of the individual countries in the Nineties. In general, however, greater attention to environmental profiles was dedicated by the constitutions of countries within the orbit of the European Union such as Hungary, the Czech Republic, Croatia, Slovakia, Bulgaria Poland, Romania, Albania and also Russia. These Constitutions appear to be very sensitive to environmental issues, but they reproduce substantially the 'instrumental' approach of the nascent phase of environmental constitutionalism, although paying more attention to the procedural and participatory aspects of environmental disciplines.

Despite the quantitatively significant impact of the new Constitutions of Eastern Europe, the most interesting cases of constitutional innovation in environmental matters can be identified in the constitutional reform of the German Constitution, amended in 1994 with the insertion of the new Art. 20a, placed in Title II of the Basic Law, among the programmatic principles of the State. The German constitutional amendment is the result of a long and tormented political and doctrinal debate and can be considered as an important stage in the evolution of the European legal thought on the environment. This amendment originates in a certain way from the experiences of the Constitutions of the Seventies, adopting a moderate but effective approach to the environmental question.[20] In fact, the text of Art. 20a locates environmental protections outside of the list of the fundamental rights, indicating that "it is the duty of the State and an obligation towards the future generations, to protect the natural bases of life, within the framework constitutional law and through executive power and jurisdiction". The absence of references to the environment as a subjective right, as well as the identification of a necessary 'legislative intermediation', clearly indicate the compromising nature of the final text of the 1994 revision, which sought to resolve the heated and ideologically polarised debate between radical eco-centric and anthropocentric conceptions of the environment. Generally speaking, Art. 20a is considered to guarantee only a flexible protection to the environment, since, according to the German doctrine,

> in case of conflict between the protection of the environment for its own sake and on the one hand and legitimate human interests on the other, the principle of human dignity . . . which constitutes the fundament of the entire constitutional system, will often result in precedence being allocated to the latter.[21]

This approach perpetuates a clear separation between man and nature and confirms the anthropocentric and technical character of the European constitutional law produced in the second phase of environmental constitutionalism.

3.3. *The Adult Phase: 'New Environmental Constitutionalism' From the South of the World*

In the first decades of the new millennium, environmental constitutionalism took a decisive acceleration especially in qualitative terms. Constitutions with references to environmental protection, have come to cover more than three quarters of the world and their number continues to grow year after year. Moreover, many of the new environmental Constitutions are based on original visions of the relations between man and the environment, considered as basic elements of the whole constitutional order. We have therefore entered a new phase in which the protection of the environment plays the role of a founding value of constitutional systems. As already mentioned, the major impulsions in this direction come from recent Constitutions of the South of the world. The new Constitutions enacted or the constitutional reforms approved after 2000 are at the confluence of different evolutionary processes of world's constitutionalism, ranging from the *revival* of the rights of the indigenous peoples and of chthonic law,[22] to the reco-

20 On the general aspects of the German constitutional revision of 1994 and on the related political and doctrinal debate cf Alexander Proelß, 'Environmental Constitutional Law in Germany: Legal Nature, Scope and Content of the Principle of Environmental Protection' in Sohnle (n 4) 94.

21 Ibid 98.

22 On the chthonic traditions and their influence on legal systems, especially the South of the world, see H. Patrick Glenn, *Legal Traditions of the World: Sustainable Diversity in Law* (5th edn, OUP 2014).

gnition of multiculturalism (also in the forms of an evolution from the federal state to the multicultural or the 'plurinational' state), to the identification of the 'environmental question' as a central element of a State's structure.[23]

In this perspective, notably, the so-called Andean *nuevo constitucionalismo* has triggered great interest (particularly in relation with the Constitutions of Ecuador and Bolivia, enacted respectively in 2008 and 2009), but apart from the ongoing debates on the 'newness' of the Andean constitutionalism,[24] we can identify a worldwide 'new environmental constitutionalism', arising not only from Latin America, but also from Asia, Africa and Oceania.

As regards the Bolivian Constitution, its Preamble starts with an explicit reference to the Mother-Earth (*Pacha Mama*)[25] and the principle of *suma qamaña* (*vivir bien*) is reckoned among the ethical-moral foundations of the plural society that the State promotes (Art. 8). In this context, encouraging and guaranteeing the preservation of the *medio ambiente* is an essential aim and function of the State for the well-being of present and future generations (Art. 9). Hence, in Title II, concerning social and economic rights, Articles 33 and 34 are expressly dedicated to the environment. Here it is recognised that every person has the right to a healthy, protected and sound environment. This right is supported by the faculty to promote legal actions to protect environment, in defence of the individual or of the communities and according to the intergenerational equity. The right to live in a healthy environment is also explicitly recognised in favour of the "nations and aboriginal indigenous peasant peoples" (Art. 30, point 10).[26] Considering the entire constitutional text, as many as forty articles make reference to environmental issues.

In the Ecuadorian Constitution (enacted in 2008 and partially revised in 2015), the right to a healthy environment is placed in the Second Chapter, entitled the "rights of good living" (*buen vivir*). This section ensures the recognition of a wide range of rights, including water, food, right to habitat and housing, as well as to health. Art. 14 recognises the right to live in a healthy and ecologically sound environment, guaranteeing sustainability and elevating to the status of

23 Roberto Viciano Pastor and Rubén Martínez Dalmau, 'El nuevo constitucionalismo latinoamericano: fundamentos para una construcción doctrinal' [2011] 9 *Revista general de derecho público comparado* 1.

24 For a general overview about this debate (in English language) see Armin von Bogdandy and others (eds), *Transformative Constitutionalism in Latin America: The Emergence of a New Ius Commune* (OUP 2017).

25 The Preamble of the Bolivian Constitution states: "In ancient times mountains arose, rivers moved, and lakes were formed. Our Amazonia, our swamps, our highlands, and our plains and valleys were covered with greenery and flowers. We populated this sacred Mother Earth with different faces, and since that time we have understood the plurality that exists in all things and in our diversity as human beings and cultures".

26 In terms of jurisdictional guarantees, alongside the provision for *acción popular* against any act or omission arising from the violation of collective rights or interests inherent to the environment (Art. 135), we must recall the Agri-Environmental Court, defined as the summit of the agri-environmental jurisdiction (Articles 186–189).

"matters of public interest" the protection of the environment, the conservation of ecosystems, biodiversity and the integrity of the genetic heritage of the country. Moreover, Art. 66, placed among the rights of liberty, affirms "the right to live in a healthy environment, ecologically balanced, free of pollution and in harmony with nature". However, the innovative approach of this constitution can be traced above all in Articles 71 to 74, which contain the status of *Pacha Mama*, defined as an entity "where life is reproduced and occurs", and in which the right to full respect of its existence, maintenance and regeneration of its life cycles, of structure, functions and evolutionary processes, in one with the right to reparation in case of environmental damage. The duties and responsibilities of the Ecuadorian people referred to in Art. 83 include the defence of territorial integrity and natural resources, respect for the rights of nature, the preservation of a healthy environment and the exploitation of natural resources in a rational and sustainable way, as well as the conservation of natural heritage.[27]

These two Constitutions can be considered as evolutionary steps into a cultural-historical perspective that has characterised the development of environmental constitutionalism in Latin America in recent decades. In this context, E. Rozo Acuña points at Latin America as the geo-political area more oriented to the construction of a new "socio-environmental State", defined as "that particular type of state organisation . . . which places the themes of the environment among its aims or fundamental purposes".[28] The antecedents of the Bolivian and Ecuadorian environmental Constitutions may be found in earlier text such as the Constitutions of Argentina,[29] Brazil[30] and Colombia.[31]

27 Environmental matters also concern the division of responsibilities between central and local authorities, to which Articles 261, 263, 264 and 267 are dedicated. See also Title VI concerning *Regimen De Desarrollo* constituting the organized, sustainable and dynamic set of economic, political, sociocultural and environmental systems to guarantee the *sumak kawsay*, and Title VII concerning the *Regimen Del Buen Vivir*.

28 Eduardo Rozo Acuña, 'Lo Stato di diritto ambientale con speciale riferimento al costituzionalismo latino-americano' in Eduardo Rozo Acuña (ed), *Profili di diritto ambientale da Rio De Janeiro a Johannesburg. Saggi di diritto internazionale, pubblico comparato, penale ed amministrativo* (Giappichelli 2004) 151.

29 Art. 41 of the Argentine Constitution recognises the right of individuals to a healthy and balanced environment, which is conducive to both human development and productive activities, so that these can meet the present needs without compromise those of future generations. At the same time, however, the duty to preserve the environment is recognised in a provision that is combined with a set of duties of a public nature.

30 Art. 225 of the Brazilian Constitution guarantees the right to a "*meio ambiente ecologicamente equilibrado*". This Article provides for a duty of defence and preservation of the environment from an intergenerational point of view that sees the community and the government as recipients. The latter is responsible for promotion, protection and control, including that of making requests for prior environmental impact studies in order to ensure the effectiveness of the law.

31 On the Colombian Constitution and its related judicial decisions, see Luis Armando Tolosa Villabona, "Vanguardism and Environmental Justice Developments in Colombia", in this book, p. 240–258.

It should however be noted that if Latin America appears the area in which the development of environmental constitutionalism is more widespread and homogeneous, innovations of great interest are not lacking even in other continents of the so-called Global South. In Africa for example, the principle of *Ubuntu*, which has its roots in the chthonic tradition, has recently been re-evaluated.[32] This principle has become one of the cornerstones of the South African constitutional system and a reference point for the decisions of the Constitutional Court. Introduced by the case, *S v. Makwanyane* in 1995, *Ubuntu* stands as a traditional cosmovision orienting the interpretation of legal issues towards a community and solidarity concept.[33] For example, Art. 24 of the South African Constitution, concerning the right to a healthy environment, was interpreted through the *Ubuntu* principle, applying to it a sympathetic and pluri-generational approach. Among the Constitutions containing an indirect protection of the environment, Tanzania (1977) clearly proclaims the principle of *Ujamaa*, following a doctrine formulated by its first president (J.K. Nyerere) that can be summarised as an African declination of socialism based on communitarianism and self-sufficiency. As a result of the application of the *Ujamaa* principle, environmental protection is carried out indirectly in the form of preservation of collective assets. On the basis of the *Ujamaa* principle and of the *Ubuntu* cosmovision, traditional chthonic elements related to the environment have been constitutionalised. These principles have allowed the participation of traditional tribal assemblies to environmental management and decisions. On this point, we can recall the Constitutions of Madagascar (2010), as regards the local assemblies, and of Zimbabwe (2013), listing among the functions of the traditional leaders the management of common lands and the protection of the environment (Art. 282).

Environmental constitutional law also assumes multiple variations in the Asian continent and in Oceania, beyond some well-renowned models, such as the Indian one.[34] Among the recent and most innovative solutions, the Constitution of Bhutan (2008)[35] states that every citizen is "trustee" of the environment and natural resources of the Kingdom, for the benefit of present and future generations. The Preamble of the Constitution of Fiji (2013) declares its commitment

32 For a constitutional account on Ubuntu, see Kyriaki Topidi, "Ubuntu as a Normative Value in the New Environmental World Order," in this book, p. 49–67.

33 Drucilla Cornell and Nyoko Muvangua, *Ubuntu and the Law. African Ideals and Postapartheid Jurisprudence* (Fordham University Press 2012). For a more in-depth look at the politico-juridical implications of Ubuntu in South Africa, see Drucilla Cornell, *Law and Revolution in South Africa. Ubuntu, Dignity, and the Struggle for Constitutional Transformation* (Fordham University Press 2014).

34 On the Indian model of environmental protection and its constitutional implications see Domenico Amirante, 'The Right to Environment in Emerging Economies. An India-China comparison' in Surya Deva (ed), *Socio-Economic Rights in Emerging Free Markets: Comparative Insights from India and China* (Routledge 2016).

35 Art. 5, Constitution of the Kingdom of Bhutan, 2008 reads: "Every Bhutanese is a trustee of the natural resources and the environment of the Kingdom for the benefit of present and future generations".

to the protection of the environment, while in Art. 1, a "prudent, efficient and sustainable relationship with nature" is clearly indicated among the values founding the state itself.[36]

In comparison with the activism and constitutional creativity characterising the development of environmental constitutionalism in the Global South, Western laws are still anchored to the models of environmental protection described in the first and second phases of our historical *excursus*. Some common law countries such as the Great Britain, the United States, Canada and Australia, while recognising the importance of environmental protection at the legislative and the judicial level, have not introduced any constitutional rule yet. The most remarkable recent reform from the West is probably the comprehensive *Charte de l'environnement* approved by France in 2005. It consists of ten articles establishing rights, duties and principles to protect the environment,[37] to be coordinated with the pre-existing constitutional values and precepts of the French *bloc de constitutionnalité*. Alongside elements with a real legal effect (rights, duties and principles), this charter contains other programmatic elements (Articles 8, 9, 10), giving to this text a complex and far-reaching character. It includes the right to live in "a healthy environment" (Art. 1) affirming a subjective dimension of environmental protection.[38] The French doctrine considers this as an autonomous and individual right, capable of integrating the environment into all human activities, although within a predominantly anthropocentric vision.[39] But the real ground-breaking feature of the Charter is certainly the incorporation of the so-called EU 'environmental management principles' (polluter-pays, preventive and precautionary principles) in the Charter.[40] Overall, the Charter is a complete and well-structured text, representing the first example of a global approach to the constitutionalisation of environmental protection in the Western world, although still characterised by a prevailing anthropocentrism.

From the recent evolution of environmental constitutionalism clearly emerges a counter-narrative indicating that the road towards a constitutionalism for the Anthropocene, based on the ideas of interconnectedness with nature and of responsibility towards the environment, considered as a dimension of the human experience and not as an external entity, is pointed out by several Constitutions from the South of the world. Apart from the technical and contextual differences between the these experiences, the common trait is that they all make reference to some ethical, philosophical or religious visions of 'unity' between man and the environment, visions evidently lacking in the secular mainstream

36 Art. 1, Constitution of the Fiji Islands, 2013.

37 Marie-Anne Cohendet, 'The French Charter on the Environment: A Model for Environmental Constitutionalism?' in Sohnle (n 4) 67.

38 Michel Prieur, 'Les nouveaux droits' [2005] *Actual. jur. dr. adm.* 1159.

39 On this point, see Francois Guy Trebulle, 'Du droit de l'homme à un environnement sain. Commentaire' [2005] *Environnement* 18.

40 Yves Jegouzo, 'De certaines obligations environnementales: prévention, précaution e responsabilité' [2005] *Actualité juridique du droit administratif* 1164.

Western theory and practice of environmental constitutionalism developed in the 'nascent' and adolescent' phases of its history. This evidence shows the urgency to deepen a debate to compare the different strains of environmental constitutionalism.

4. Environmental Constitutionalism for the Anthropocene: Bringing Together Constitutional Cultures

Environmental constitutionalism is not a *panacea* for all environmental problems that are, primarily, civilisational issues. If the reception of the Anthropocene thesis requires the elaboration of new principles and rules, especially at a constitutional level, the solution is not a quest for a new 'holy grail' or for another grand environmental narrative. In other terms it is time to avoid unilateral visions leading to narrative traps, like the 'mantra' of sustainable development or of a 'globalising' uniformity based on monist theories, like in the early times of environmental law. Today we are aware that the unavoidable scientific and technical dimension of environmental law, while guiding many normative and operational choices, cannot replace the social and the ethical centrality of environmental normativity. Thus, in the Anthropocene we will learn from the Earth System metaphor that the key characteristic of this new geologic era are "interconnectedness, unpredictability, instability and complexity, instead of taking Holocene stability for granted".[41] Nonetheless this acknowledgment will not lead to an uniform global law or to a new international Leviathan, but most likely to "a framework for rethinking environmental law for the purpose of the Anthropocene".[42] In constitutional terms, this requires nurturing a common but plural environmental constitutional culture, considering not only the normative evolutions but also the related constitutional doctrines and their social, ethical and religious origins.

Actually, if an account on the emerging trends of environmental constitutionalism 'in action' displays a counter-narrative on the development of this branch of environmental law, what is still missing is a scholarly debate comparing the constitutional doctrines sustaining old and new constitutional trends. It is time to develop such a debate debate, to leave the 'safe harbour' of the restricted environmental law community and to start a dialogue between environmental lawyers and constitutional scholars, possibly involving also legal pluralism experts. However, if we look at the recent literature on environmental constitutionalism, we will find some path-breaking monographs inspiring a possible dialogue between constitutional cultures. Boyd's *Environmental Rights Revolution*[43] paved the way for the environmental constitutionalism revival, furnishing a first

41 Louis J. Kotzé, 'Earth System Law for the Anthropocene: Rethinking' [2020] 11 *Transnational Legal Theory* 89.

42 Ibid 103.

43 Boyd (n 4).

quantitative assessment on its development, and highlighted the emergence of an important (if uncoordinated) *corpus* of environmental rights in constitutional texts and judicial decisions. Nevertheless, this contribution is based on a quite traditional common law rights-based approach not addressing the problem of the compatibility of specific judicial solutions with other constitutional cultures. Differently, May and Daly's *Global Environmental Constitutionalism*, while giving a very comprehensive description of the 'field' of environmental constitutionalism, touches on some theoretical problems underling the "value of environmental constitutionalism"[44] in front of the "limitations of international law".[45] Both texts do not venture into a conceptual or comparative analysis of environmental constitutionalism, unlike Kotze's *Global Environmental Constitutionalism in the Anthropocene*, which consecrates a special chapter of his book to the "fundamentals of environmental constitutionalism".[46] Kotze's work is an attempt at structuring the field for a very much needed comparison between the early European ecologic constitutionalism, based on a theoretical discussion on the basis of the "Environmental State", tributary to a civil law style, and the common law interpretation of environmental constitutional as an essentially rights-based discipline. Nevertheless, this very well-structured methodological proposal strangely does not capture the theoretical potential coming from the "new environmental constitutionalism" from the South of the world and of its contributions, produced in the 'adult phase' of environmental constitutionalism.[47]

On the whole, beyond the technical elements linked to new perspectives like the rights of nature, the Earth-System approach or the "climate constitutionalism", we think there is a common background to the innovations coming from Latin America, Asia, Africa and Oceania, based on integral and unitary visions on 'man and nature', inextricably linked within the web of life. Such approaches are not recent ideological constructs, but are rooted in millenary ethical and cultural/religious traditions, ranging from Hinduism, Buddhism, Islam, to Chthonic cultures and Cosmovisions, to which even Christianity is not extraneous, as demonstrated by the environmental awareness generated by the Encyclical *Laudato Si'* by Pope Francis.[48]

A global dialogue on environmental constitutionalism will necessarily start from a comparison between the mainstream legal traditions, the common law with its adjudicative and right-based approach, and the civil law with its focus on the 'Environmental State', none of which has been able to fully address

44 May and Daly (n 4) 36.

45 Ibid 19.

46 Kotzé (n 4) 132.

47 For a co-authored and quite critical account on some Southern experiences cf Paola Villavicencio and Louis K. Kotzè, 'Environmental constitutionalism and the ecocentric rights paradigm: the rights of nature in Ecuador and Bolivia' in Vv.Aa., *New Frontiers in Environmental Constitutionalism* (UNEP 2017) 175.

48 See Luigi Colella, Integral Ecology and Environmental Law in the Anthropocene: the perspective of the Catholic Church, in this book, p. 14–28.

environmental issues. These visions of the link between man and the environment that we can define as 'classic' or 'prevailing' in the elaboration of environmental law must inevitably consider broader and better balanced visions that contemplate the material and spiritual relationship with nature as a fundamental element of their constitutional systems. This will allow to bring together not only the individual dimension (liberal constitutionalism) and the social one (social democratic constitutionalism), but also the biological and natural dimension (new environmental constitutionalism), three aspects that cannot be separated from each other and that constitutional law will have to jointly consider, unless we want to continue offering a partial and sectoral reading of the human experience on Earth. In this perspective, according to a recent book by Jaria-Manzano, the constitutionalism for the Anthropocene requires "a rediscovery of the sacred, which collides with the secularisation that, in a certain way, liberal constitutionalism proposes".[49] Such an approach is in full harmony with the methodological proposals of legal pluralism by scholars like Menski, urging for a reconsideration of the sources of normative production, including those of customary, social and ethical-religious origins.[50]

In the legal culture of the second postwar democratic constitutionalism, and in particular in the Constitutions based on the valorisation of the 'person' in all its manifestations (from the individual to the social, but also to the ethical and spiritual sphere), there are the premises for an integral conception of the relationship between human beings and the environment, based on the consideration that they share the same 'nature'. Today, a dialogue between the different environmental constitutional cultures is not only necessary but represents the only option before us if we want to reverse the process of destruction of life which began with the advent of the Anthropocene.

Bibliography

Amado Gomes C., 'Constituição e ambiente: errância e simbolismo' (2012) 9 *Veredas do Direito* 9.

Amirante D. (ed), *Diritto ambientale e Costituzione. Esperienze europee* (Franco Angeli 2000).

Amirante D., 'The Right to Environment in Emerging Economies. An India-China comparison' in Surya Deva (ed), *Socio-Economic Rights in Emerging Free Markets: Comparative Insights from India and China* (Routledge 2016).

Atapattu S. and Gonzalez C.G., 'The North – South Divide in International Environmental Law: Framing the Issues' in Shawkat Alam and others (eds), *International Environmental Law and the Global South* (CUP 2015).

Bodansky D., 'Is There an International Environmental Constitution?' [2009] *Indiana Journal of Global Legal Studies* 567.

49 Jaria-Manzano (n 4) 338.

50 Cf Werner Menski, *Comparative Law in a Global Context: The Legal Systems of Asia and Africa* (CUP 2009).

von Bogdandy A. et al. (eds), *Transformative Constitutionalism in Latin America: The Emergence of a New Ius Commune* (OUP 2017).
Bosselmann K., 'Global Environmental Constitutionalism: Mapping the Terrain' [2012] *Widener Law Review* 171.
Boyd D.R., *The Environmental Rights Revolution: A Study on of Constitutions, Human Rights and Environment* (University of British Columbia Press 2012).
Cohendet M.-A., 'The French Charter on the Environment: A Model for Environmental Constitutionalism?' in Jochen Sohnle (ed), *Environmental Constitutionaslism: What Impact on Legal Systems?* (Peter Lang 2019).
Cornell D., *Law and Revolution in South Africa. Ubuntu, Dignity, and the Struggle for Constitutional Transformation* (Fordham University Press 2014).
Cornell D. and Muvangua N., *Ubuntu and the Law. African Ideals and Postapartheid Jurisprudence* (Fordham University Press 2012).
Fisher E. and others, 'Maturity and Methodology: Starting a Debate about Environmental Law Scholarship' (2009) 21 *Journal of Environmental Law* 214.
Frankenberg G., 'Comparing Constitutions: Ideas, Ideals, and Ideology – Toward a Layered Narrative' (2006) 4 *International Journal of Constitutional Law* 439, 440.
Glenn H.P., *Legal Traditions of the World: Sustainable Diversity in Law* (5th edn, OUP 2014).
Heyvaert V. and Ett T., 'Introducing Transnational Environmental Law' (2012) 1 *Transnational Environmental Law* 1.
Jaria-Manzano J., *La Constitución del Antropoceno* (Tirant lo Blanch 2020).
Jegouzo Y., 'De certaines obligations environnementales: prévention, précaution e responsabilité' [2005] *Actualité juridique du droit administratif* 1164.
Kotze L.J., *Global Environmental Constitutionalism in the Anthropocene* (Hart Publishing 2016).
Kotzé L.J., 'Earth System Law for the Anthropocene: Rethinking' (2020) 11 *Transnational Legal Theory* 89.
May J.R. and Daly E., *Global Environmental Constitutionalism* (CUP 2014).
Menski W., *Comparative Law in a Global Context: The Legal Systems of Asia and Africa* (CUP 2009).
Montoro Chiner M.J., 'El estado ambiental de derecho. Bases constitucionales' in Francisco Sosa Wagner (ed), *El derecho administrativo en el umbral del siglo XXI: homenaje al profesor Dr. D. Ramón Martín Mateo* (Vol. 3, Tirant lo Blanch 2000).
O'Gorman R., 'Environmental Constitutionalism: A Comparative Study' (2017) 6 *Transnational Environmental Law* 435.
Philippopoulos-Mihalopoulos A., 'Towards a Critical Environmental Law' in Philippopoulos-Mihalopoulos A. (ed), *Law and Ecology: New Environmental Foundations* (Routledge 2011).
Prieur M., 'Les nouveaux droits' [2005] *Actual jur dr adm* 1159.
Proelß A., 'Environmental Constitutional Law in Germany: Legal Nature, Scope and Content of the Principle of Environmental Protection' in Jochen Sohnle (ed), *Environmental Constitutionaslism: What Impact on Legal Systems?* (Peter Lang 2019).
Robinson N.A., 'Comparative Environmental Law: Evaluating How Legal Systems Address "Sustainable Development"' (1997) 27 *Environmental Policy and Earlier Law* 338.
Robinson N.A., 'Fundamental Principles of Law for the Anthropocene?' (2014) 44 *Environmental Policy and Law* 13.

Rosenfeld M. and Sajò A. (eds), *The Oxford Handbook of Comparative Constitutional Law* (OUP 2012).
Rozo Acuña E., 'Lo Stato di diritto ambientale con speciale riferimento al costituzionalismo latinoamericano' in Rozo Acuña E. (ed), *Profili di diritto ambientale da Rio De Janeiro a Johannesburg. Saggi di diritto internazionale, pubblico comparato, penale ed amministrativo* (Giappichelli 2004).
Sohnle J. (ed), *Environmental Constitutionaslism: What Impact on Legal Systems?* (Peter Lang 2019).
Tarlock D. and Tarak P., 'Overview of Comparative Environmental Law' (1983) 13 *Denver Journal of International Law and Policy* 85.
Trebulle F.G., 'Du droit de l'homme à un environnement sain. Commentaire' [2005] *Environnement* 18.
Viciano Pastor R. and Martínez Dalmau R., 'El nuevo constitucionalismo latinoamericano: fundamentos para una construcción doctrinal' (2011) 9 *Revista general de derecho público comparado* 1.
Villavicencio P. and Kotzè L.J., 'Environmental Constitutionalism and the Ecocentric Rights Paradigm: The Rights of Nature in Ecuador and Bolivia' in Vv.Aa. (ed), *New Frontiers in Environmental Constitutionalism* (UNEP 2017) 175.
Viñuales J.E., 'Comparative Environmental Law: Structuring a Field' in Lees E. and Viñuales J. E. (eds), *The Oxford Handbook of Comparative Environmental Law* (OUP 2019).

9 Ecosystem Rights and the Anthropocene in Australia and Aotearoa New Zealand

Elizabeth Macpherson

1. Introduction

Political and legal activism for the rights of ecosystems appears to be gaining traction in Australasia. In Aotearoa New Zealand,[1] a river and a forest are legal persons, with a mountain likely to soon become the third. The rights of an Australian river are now recognised by legislation, and activism continues for the rights of nature and other ecosystems. These developments are attempts to challenge environmental legal and policy frameworks, which are considered inadequate to respond to the challenges of the Anthropocene, including environmental degradation, biodiversity loss and climate change alongside associated economic and social injustices. They may also reflect alternative values and traditions with respect to nature, including the plural law-making and decision-making capacity of Indigenous peoples and/or local communities.

In this chapter, I explore the nascent ecosystem rights 'cases'[2] in New Zealand and Australia, in which natural resources have been recognised as having legal rights or personhood, and consider their significance for environmental law's response to the Anthropocene. In doing so, I consider whether these emerging cases are evidence of a distinctly Australasian variety of transnational environmental constitutionalism.

In both countries there is a governance trend towards legal models that attempt to reflect Indigenous ideas of ancestral or familial relationships with living and integrated natural resources, which ground the models in particular places and with particular peoples as part of complex and interdependent ecosystems. However, the most significant contribution the Australasian cases make to environmental law's response to the Anthropocene, I argue, lies in their 'relational' function – of supporting connections between peoples and place via local involvement with and control over natural resource decision-making pursuant to agreed fundamental values.

1 I subsequently refer to New Zealand by its name in English, although I recognise the ongoing contestation around the validity of this name and the acquisition of sovereignty.

2 I use the word 'cases' in the non-legal sense, to include legislative, administrative or judicial situations.

DOI: 10.4324/9781003175308-12

2. The Anthropocene, Ecosystem Rights and Relational Legal Pluralism

It is commonly asserted that we have entered a new era of human existence called the 'Anthropocene', in which we face serious threats to life on our planet, including climate change, natural resource depletion and contamination, and associated loss of biological diversity and functioning.[3] Those considering the appropriate response of environmental law to the Anthropocene, sometimes argue for 'transformational change'[4] in the principles and tools of environmental regulation, beyond dominant paradigms like 'sustainable development'.[5] This has produced what is described as an 'ontological turn' in global environmental law – allowing alternative constructions of the role of law and society to emerge.[6] As an illustration, Kotzé argues that: "environmental law is also unable to respond to the regulatory challenges that arise from the Anthropocene's complex Earth system. We need a new legal paradigm that is better fit for purpose in the Anthropocene".[7] Amongst these alternative legal constructions, are approaches that apply the logic and language of 'rights'; variously expressed through 'rights of nature', 'earth jurisprudence', or 'environmental personhood' (for which I use the broad catch-all 'ecosystem rights').

The emergence of ecosystem rights is part of a broader project of transnational comparative environmental constitutionalism, which "recognises that the environment is a proper subject for protection in constitutional texts and for vindication by constitutional courts worldwide".[8] The growing list of situations in which a natural resource or system has been recognised as having its own rights, interests, life or personhood is evidence of this transnational environmental constitutionalism.[9]

3 See Paul J Crutzen, 'Geology of Mankind' (2002) 415 *Nature (London)* 23 for an original positing of the Anthrpocene thesis; See also W Steffen and others, 'Planetary Boundaries: Guiding Human Development on a Changing Planet' (2015) 347 *Science (American Association for the Advancement of Science)* 1259855.

4 See, e.g., Mike Young and Christine Esau, *Transformational Change in Environmental and Natural Resource Management: Guidelines for Policy Excellence* (Taylor & Francis Group 2016).

5 See Jonathan Verschuuren, 'The Role of Sustainable Development' in Louis J Kotzé (ed), *Environmental Law and Governance for the Anthropocene* (Hart Publishing 2017) 16; Melinda Harm Benson and Robin Kundis Craig, 'The End of Sustainability' (2014) 27 *Society & Natural Resources* 777.

6 Saskia Vermeylen, 'Materiality and the Ontological Turn' in Louis J Kotzé (ed), *Environmental Law and Governance for the Anthropocene* (Hart Publishing 2017).

7 Louis J Kotzé, 'Earth System Law for the Anthropocene: Rethinking Environmental Law Alongside the Earth System Metaphor' (2020) 11 *Transnational Legal Theory* 75.

8 James R May and Erin Daly, *Global Environmental Constitutionalism* (CUP 2015) 1.

9 See, eg, Constitución de la República del Ecuador 2008 (Ecuador). Te Awa Tupua (Whanganui River Claims Settlement) Act 2017. *Centro de Estudios para la Justicia Social 'Tierra Digna' y otros v Presidente de la Republica y otros* [2016] Corte Constitucional [Constitutional Court], Sala Sexta de Revision [Sixth Chamber] (Colombia) No T-622 of 2016.

The motivation for ecosystem rights, as typically put forward by their proponents, is the need to shift the balance between humans and nature, and elevate the interests of nature above the rights of people to use it.[10] Nature is positioned as intrinsically worthy of protection, independent of (and even superior to) the rights and interests of humans with respect to natural resources.[11] Yet, the core premise of the 'Anthropocene' is that humans have had an irreversible impact on the function of Earth's systems. At its base, therefore, the idea of Anthropocene binds humans to the Earth, seeing nature through the lens of the *Anthropos*.[12]

Ecosystem rights, too, are as much about the rights of humans as they are about the rights of nature, although the particular humans pushing for recognition of their rights *vis-à-vis* nature may have different motivations for doing so. Some are environmental activists who wish to protect natural resources from development. Others are Indigenous communities who seek jurisdiction to govern their natural resources in culturally appropriate ways.[13] Critics of the Anthropocene thesis point to its homogenising effect on humans as a species, which makes all humans responsible for damage to the Earth,[14] obscuring legal pluralism and the different experiences of groups who may themselves be experiencing place-based development impacts and structural oppression on the basis of class, race or sex, for example.[15] Criticisms of ecosystem rights include that they are too radical, too fringe, too privileged or too symbolic to make a practical response to the Anthropocene.[16] Some argue that ecosystem rights may detract attention or energy from other transformative social and political agendas;[17] including the struggle for

10 See, eg, Michelle Maloney, 'Building an Alternative Jurisprudence for the Earth: The International Rights of Nature Tribunal' [2016] *Vermont Law Review* 129.

11 See Susana Borràs, 'New Transitions from Human Rights to the Environment to the Rights of Nature' (2016) 5 *Transnational Environmental Law* 113; C Clark and others, 'Can You Hear the Rivers Sing? Legal Personhood, Ontology, and the Nitty-Gritty of Governance' (2019) 45 *Ecology Law Quarterly* 787.

12 See Donna Jeanne Haraway, *Staying with the Trouble: Making Kin in the Chthulucene* (Duke University Press 2016).

13 James Morris and Jacinta Ruru, 'Giving Voice to Rivers: Legal Personality as a Vehicle for Recognising Indigenous Peoples' Relationships to Water' (2010) 14 *Australian Indigenous Law Review* 49; G Chapron, Y Epstein and JV López-Bao, 'A Rights Revolution for Nature' (2019) 363 *Science*.

14 Anna Grear, 'Re-Encountering the Environmental Legal "Subject"' in Louis J Kotzé (ed), *Environmental Law and Governance for the Anthropocene* (Hart Publishing 2017) 79.

15 Kathleen Birrell and Julia Dehm, 'International Law & the Humanities in the "Anthropocene"' in Shane Chalmers and Sundhya Pahuja (eds), *Routledge Handbook of International Law and the Humanities* (Routledge 2021) 3.

16 See, eg, Ruth Barcan, 'The Campaign for Legal Personhood for the Great Barrier Reef: Finding Political and Pedagogical Value in a Spectacular Failure of Care' (2020) 3 *Environment and Planning E: Nature and Space* 810, 823; Whitney Richardson and John-Andrew McNeish, 'Granting Rights to Rivers in Colombia: Significance for ExtrACTIVISM and Governance' in Judith Shapiro and John-Andrew McNeish (eds), *Our Extractive Age Expressions of Violence and Resistance* (Routledge 2021).

17 Mihnea Tănăsescu, 'Rights of Nature, Legal Personality, and Indigenous Philosophies' (2020) 9 *Transnational Environmental Law* 429; Brad Coombes, 'Nature's Rights as

Indigenous sovereignty, control and ownership over natural resources and related political authority.[18]

The critical scholarship increasingly focuses not on the technical curiosities of legal personhood and standing, but on the relationality between humans and nature reflected in ecosystems rights cases via connection between people and place.[19] As such, the focus is not to choose nature's rights over human rights (say to property or development) but is the human ethics and responsibility to *care*[20] for natural resources as part of living, dynamic and related ecosystems – something that may well be broadly consistent (at least some of the time) with Indigenous belief systems.[21] Such relational thinking reflects the 'relational turn' in socio-legal theory, which departs from static notions of law to a focus on the relational processes of dialogue and negotiation in plural, multicultural legal settings.[22] In the context of Indigenous rights, relational thinking has been applied to the idea of 'legal pluralism', with the intention "not to arrive at a state of finality in the design of formal arrangements, but to create the conditions for an open, inclusive and on-going dialogue", allowing policy-makers to concentrate their efforts on institutions and processes, which accommodate a plurality of interests and allow for change over time.[23]

Framed thus, ecosystem rights can be thought of as "dynamic, multi-faceted process of interactions between humans and nature; in the context of a network

Indigenous Rights? Mis/Recognition through Personhood for Te Urewera' (2020) 2020 *Espace populations sociétés*.

18 Virginia Marshall, 'Removing the Veil from the "Rights of Nature": The Dichotomy between First Nations Customary Rights and Environmental Legal Personhood' [2020] *Australian Feminist Law Journal* 1. Carwyn Jones, *New Treaty, New Tradition: Reconciling New Zealand and Maori Law* (UBC Press 2016) 176. Erin O'Donnell and others, 'Stop Burying the Lede: The Essential Role of Indigenous Law(s) in Creating Rights of Nature' (2020) 9 *Transnational Environmental Law* 403. Mihnea Tănăsescu, 'Rights of Nature, Legal Personality, and Indigenous Philosophies' (2020) 9 *Transnational Environmental Law* 429, 431–434.

19 See also Simon P James, 'Legal Rights and Nature's Contributions to People: Is There a Connection?' (2020) 241 *Biological Conservation* 108325.

20 See Annie Milgin and others, 'Sustainability Crises Are Crises of Relationship: Learning from Nyikina Ecology and Ethics' (2020) 2 *People and Nature* 1210, 1211.

21 Martuwarra RiverOfLife and others, 'Recognizing the Martuwarra's First Law Right to Life as a Living Ancestral Being' (2020) 9 *Transnational Environmental Law* 541; Linda Te Aho, 'Indigenous Challenges to Enhance Freshwater Governance and Management in Aotearoa New Zealand – The Waikato River Settlement' (2009) 20 *Journal of Water Law* 285; Morris and Ruru (n 13); Vanessa Watts, 'Indigenous Place-Thought & Agency amongst Humans and Non-Humans (First Woman and Sky Woman Go on a European World Tour!)' (2013) 2 *Decolonization: Indigeneity, Education & Society* 20; Milgin and others (n 20) 1211; Anne Salmond, *Tears of Rangi: Experiments Across Worlds* (Auckland University Press 2017) 299.

22 Margaret Davies, *Law Unlimited: Materialism, Pluralism, and Legal Theory* (Routledge 2017).

23 Kirsty Gover, *Legal Pluralism and State-Indigenous Relations in Western Settler Societies* (International Council on Human Rights Policy 2009) 8.

of rights, interests, practices, law, policies and institutional cultures".[24] By understanding ecosystem rights approaches as essentially relational, the focus becomes the processes associated with the models. These are typically collaborative governance regimes involving Indigenous peoples, local communities and users and/or governments, as representatives, guardians, voices or faces of nature, all of whom collaborate, negotiate and agree on fundamental values for the management of ecosystems.

3. Emerging Ecosystem Rights in Australasia

3.1. Aotearoa New Zealand

New Zealand is often considered to be 'trailblazing' the global rights of nature movement. Yet, much of the commentary on New Zealand has been written by international advocacy organisations, and the New Zealand ecosystem rights cases actually have little to do with the rights of nature, and turn little on the adoption of personhood as a legal model. The New Zealand cases are really Indigenous rights cases – manifestations of self-determination and pragmatism, via the adoption of a legal mechanism from western law that is broadly approximate to Māori customary law. Still, there is much to be learnt from the New Zealand experience about the promise and risks involved in attempts to recognise or bestow ecosystem rights.

New Zealand was a settler-colony of the British Crown, and remains part of the Commonwealth. It became part of the British Empire in 1840, with the signing of *Te Tiriti o Waitangi* (the Treaty of Waitangi) between the Crown and Māori chiefs.[25] The Māori version of the Treaty guaranteed to the Māori tribes ongoing sovereignty (known in Māori as *tino rangatiratanga*) over their lands, estates, forests, fisheries and other treasures.[26] However, for much of New Zealand's colonial history, the Treaty was ignored.[27] In the 1970s, with the influence of pan-global Indigenous activism, New Zealand embarked on a process of attempting to repair the damage done by colonisation to Māori and the broader country. The Crown established the Waitangi Tribunal to inquire into and make recommendations about historical breaches of the Treaty,[28] and began to negotiate and settle those grievances.[29]

24 Elizabeth Macpherson and others, '"Hooks" and "Anchors" for Relational Ecosystem-Based Marine Management' (2021) 130 *Marine Policy* 104561, http://dx.doi.org/10.1016/j.marpol.2021.104561.
25 The Treaty was signed in Māori and English, but there were significant differences between the two versions, which has produced ongoing constitutional conflict.
26 Te Tiriti o Waitangi (The Treaty of Waitangi) 1840 art 2.
27 See *Wi Parata v The Bishop of Wellington* [1877] 3 NZLR 72 which referred to the Treaty as 'a simple nullity'.
28 Treaty of Waitangi Act 1975.
29 A framework for negotiation and settlement is provided for in the Crown policy New Zealand and Office of Treaty Settlements, *Ka Tika ā Muri, Ka Tika ā Mua: He Tohutohu Whakamārama i Ngā Whakataunga Kerēme e Pā Ana Ki Te Tiriti o Waitangi Me Ngā*

3.1.1 Te Urewera

The first New Zealand ecosystem rights case is that of Te Urewera, a forested National Park covering approximately 212,000 hectares in the eastern North Island. Te Urewera was recognised as a legal person as part of a 2014 Treaty of Waitangi settlement between the Crown and the Tūhoe *iwi* (tribe).[30] This part of New Zealand is remote and mysterious, and although "prized by all New Zealanders as a place of outstanding national value and intrinsic worth' including its 'vast and rugged primeval forest",[31] Te Urewera is generally understood by New Zealanders to be an area of cultural and spiritual importance to Tūhoe.

Tūhoe control and management of the Urewera forest was largely obstructed as a result of successive colonial actions of the Crown and subsequent settler governments, although Tūhoe maintained their assertion of continued sovereignty in the region. Tūhoe did not sign the Treaty of Waitangi on the basis that they wished to retain control over their lands. In 1896, the Crown passed the Urewera District Native Reserve Act, which provided a special regime for a self-governing reserve, which recognised Tūhoe culture and authority.

Partly because of its remote location and partly due to cultural significance, Te Urewera has been a stronghold of Māori resistance to colonisation and continued assertion of tribal sovereignty.[32] However, the forest and people suffered gravely from the impact of colonisation, including large-scale land acquisitions, war, land confiscations, starvation and disease.[33] Most Tūhoe land was confiscated in punishment for Tūhoe 'disloyalty' during the wars, and their authority to govern their own affairs was not recognised by the Crown.[34] In 1954, Te Urewera was declared a national park as a "jewel in the national conservation estate", without consultation with Tūhoe nor recognition that they had any special interest in the land, which is a source of ongoing grievance for the *iwi*.[35]

Claims of Treaty breaches in Te Urewera came before the Waitangi Tribunal in 2003. The Tribunal found that the Crown had breached the Urewera District Native Reserve Act 1896 by carrying out "a determined Crown assault on Te Urewera reserve lands" and that National Park was established in breach of the

---

Whakaritenga Ki Te Karauna = Healing the Past, Building a Future : A Guide to Treaty of Waitangi Claims and Negotiations with the Crown. (2015).

30 'Ngai Tuhoe Deed of Settlement of Historical Claims' www.govt.nz/assets/Documents/OTS/Ngai-Tuhoe/Ngai-Tuhoe-Deed-of-Settlement-4-Jun-2013.pdf.

31 Te Urewera Act 2014 (NZ) s 3(8).

32 Elsdon Best, *Tuhoe, the Children of the Mist: A Sketch of the Origin, History, Myths, and Beliefs of the Tuhoe Tribe of the Maori of New Zealand, with Some Account of Other Early Tribes of the Bay of Plenty District* (Vol 6, 4th edn, Reed 1996).

33 Tănăsescu (n 18) 440.

34 Catherine Iorns Magallanes, 'Nature as an Ancestor: Two Examples of Legal Personality for Nature in New Zealand' (2015) 22 *VertigO: La revue électronique en sciences de l'environnement* 1, 7.

35 Waitangi Tribunal, 'Te Urewera Report Volume 1' (2017) *Wai* 894, https://forms.justice.govt.nz/search/Documents/WT/wt_DOC_134632524/Te%20Urewera%20Vol1WS.pdf.

Treaty.[36] The Tribunal recommended that title to the land be returned to Tūhoe and neighbouring *iwi* and that the National Park be co-managed by Tūhoe and the Crown.

The Crown signed a deed of settlement with Ngāi Tuhoe in June 2013,[37] given legal effect by the Te Urewera Act 2014. Section 3 of the Act includes the following.

The legislation recognises the particular ancestral relationship of Tūhoe with Te Urewera, as their 'homeland',[38] which "gives meaning to Tūhoe culture, language, customs, and identity" including their role as *kaitiaki* (caregivers).[39] The legislation specifically recognises the identity and agency of Te Urewera itself, in prose rarely seen in the statute books:[40]

> (1) Te Urewera is ancient and enduring, a fortress of nature, alive with history; its scenery is abundant with mystery, adventure, and remote beauty.
> (2) Te Urewera is a place of spiritual value, with its own mana [*power*] and mauri [*lifeforce*].
> (3) Te Urewera has an identity in and of itself, inspiring people to commit to its care.

The legislation declares that Te Urewera is a legal entity, and has all the rights, powers, duties, and liabilities of a legal person,[41] which are exercised and performed on behalf of, and in the name of, Te Urewera by Te Urewera Board.[42] The Act vests ownership of the land in Te Urewera, under the governance of the Board.[43] From 2017, the Board consists of six Tūhoe appointees and three members appointed by the Minister of Conservation.[44] The Board is empowered to speak and act on behalf of Te Urewera and is explicitly required to consider and give expression to Tūhoe law and custom.[45] The Act sets out an extensive list of powers and obligations of the Board,[46] including the power to create bylaws.[47]

The Urewera model is the result of many years of Indigenous agitation for the return of ownership and control of traditional land and resources, and

36 Ibid.
37 'Ngai Tuhoe Deed of Settlement of Historical Claims' (n 30).
38 Te Urewera Act 2014 s 3(5).
39 Ibid 3(6).
40 Ibid 3(3).
41 Te Urewera Act 2014 (NZ) s 11(1).
42 Ibid S 11(2).
43 Ibid S 12(2)(C).
44 Ibid S 21.
45 Ibid S 18(3).
46 Ibid S 18.
47 Ibid S 50.

concomitant sovereignty and law-making power.[48] It is, nevertheless, a 'compromise' to Indigenous demands for the return of those lands and resources,[49] through a legal mechanism which enables ownership of the land to neither be vested in the Crown nor the *iwi*.[50]

Te Urewera is not so much about the rights of nature, but about the rights and obligations of people. This 'anthropocentrism' is reflected in the management plan developed by the Board for the forest,[51] *Te Kawa o Te Urewera*, which in its introduction describes its key purpose as[52]

> one that hopes to draw people closer to Te Urewera, to respecting the role that people play in achieving nature's balance if we have a wish for a secure future, and to encourage progress that inspires sustainable and disciplined prosperity.

The Te Urewera model is best described as a framework to regulate an ongoing relationship between the Crown and *iwi* with respect to the forest's management in accordance with agreed values, which sets the groundrules for ongoing contestation and conflict in the exercise of shared political authority.[53] The contribution made by the Urewera ecosystem rights case to the transnational rights of nature project is that it shows the potential for natural resource governance arrangements to better reflect community priorities and values with respect to a resource, and (only thereby) respect the inherent value of the resource itself.

3.1.2 Te Awa Tupua

The second New Zealand ecosystem rights case is that of the Whanganui River, which the local *iwi* call 'Te Awa Tupua'. Like Te Urewera, Te Awa Tupua was recognised as a legal person as part of a Treaty of Waitangi settlement between the Crown and the Whanganui River *iwi* (variously known as Atihaunui or Ngāti Hau). Again, the *iwi* have a special cultural, spiritual and ancestral connection to the river,[54] and have suffered as a result of the Crown's failure to make good on its Treaty obligations.

The Whanganui *iwi* maintained their claims to ownership and control of the river since the signing of the Treaty.[55] Their grievances include Crown obstruc-

48 Te Urewera Act 2014 s 3(10). See Katherine Sanders, '"Beyond Human Ownership"? Property, Power and Legal Personality for Nature in Aotearoa New Zealand' (2018) 30 *Journal of Environmental Law* 207, 210–211.
49 Coombes (n 17).
50 See also Sanders (n 48) 216; Tănăsescu (n 18) 444.
51 Te Urewera Act 2014 Part 2, Subpart 2.
52 'Te Kawa o Te Urewera' (n 2) 12.
53 See also Sanders (n 48) 209.
54 'The Whanganui River Report (Wai 167)' (GP Publications 1999) xiii.
55 Ibid 55–56. See eg *In re the Bed of the Wanganui River* [1962] NZLR 600.

tion of their access to the river for food gathering, navigation and ceremonial uses, and the impact of settler navigation, resource extraction and hydroelectric development in the catchment. The *iwi* took their claims in relation to the river to the Waitangi Tribunal in the 1990s, which the Tribunal reported on in 1999.[56] Extensive evidence was led before the Tribunal about the river interests of the Whanganui *iwi* under Māori customary law. In its findings, the Tribunal framed the interests of the Whanganui *iwi* in the river in terms of "ownership" of a "single and indivisible entity comprised of water, banks, and bed".[57] The Tribunal recommended the return of ownership of the river to the Whanganui *iwi*, and a prolonged (almost 20-year) period of negotiation commenced with the Crown. The Crown maintained that the river could not be owned by the *iwi* as part of any settlement, as under New Zealand common law no one can 'own' water, which is vested in the Crown on behalf of the New Zealand public.[58] As a compromise, the settlement between the Crown and Whanganui *iwi* provided that the river would be given its own legal personhood, with ownership rights vesting in the river itself.[59]

The Te Awa Tupua (Whanganui River Claims Settlement) Act 2017 was subsequently passed to give legal effect to the settlement, and to establish new governance arrangements for the river. The Act recognises the status of the Whanganui river (and its tributaries) as "an indivisible and living whole, comprising the Whanganui river from the mountains to the sea, incorporating all its physical and meta-physical elements".[60] The Te Awa Tupua Act then declares that Te Awa Tupua is a legal person, which has "all the rights, powers, duties, and liabilities of a legal person",[61] which are exercised by the "human face of the river", another entity called Te Pou Tupua, charged with acting in the river's interests.[62] One representative on Te Pou Tupua is to be nominated by the Crown and the other by the Whanganui *iwi*, who are required to make decisions by consensus.

The Act also establishes a collaborative governance regime for the river involving Māori, municipal and central government and private users. In this regime a range of entities are created, and a range of perspectives covered, not just those of Te Pou Tupua or the Whanganui *iwi*.[63] Te Pou Tupua has broad powers although it must act in the interests of the river and consistently with values prescribed for the river's management (called 'Tupua te Kawa') set out in section 13 of the Act. These are the "intrinsic values that represent the essence of Te Awa Tupua", and

56 Ibid.
57 Ibid 337.
58 This is reflected in the Resource Management Act 1991 (NZ) s 354.
59 'Ruruku Whakatupua Te Mana o Te Awa Tupua – Upholding the Mana of the Whanganui River at Māori Law Review', http://maorilawreview.co.nz/2014/05/ruruku-whakatupua-te-mana-o-te-awa-tupua-upholding-the-mana-of-the-whanganui-river/.
60 Te Awa Tupua (Whanganui River Claims Settlement) Act 2017 s 12.
61 Ibid 14.
62 Ibid ss 18–19.
63 Te Awa Tupua (Whanganui River Claims Settlement) Act 2017 ss 27, 29, 35.

are a significant embodiment of the customary law of the Whanganui *iwi*, reflecting their traditional knowledge as established resource managers. They recognise the direct link between the health of the river and the health of the people, and reiterate that the river is an indivisible and living whole from the mountains to the sea incorporating physical and metaphysical elements.

Decision-makers under a range of legislation must recognise, provide for and have regard to the status of Te Awa Tupua as a legal person and the statutory river values, as a 'relevant consideration' in administrative law terms.[64] However, the Te Awa Tupua Act acknowledges that decisions made under other legislation must be exercised consistent with the purpose of that legislation and neither Te Awa Tupua status nor Tupua te Kawa can be determining factors in an administrative decision.[65] Nor does the legislation establish veto rights over development in the river.[66] The water in the river remains vested in the Crown on behalf of the public and the legislation in no way disturbs the existing distribution of use or ownership rights in the river, including public and private use rights, in a provision that expressly protects the rights of hydro-electric power generators (who continue to benefit commercially).[67] In this way, the Te Awa Tupua Act follows the approach taken in a number of earlier settlements, which vest the beds of rivers and lakes in tribal authorities and focus on bringing Māori, public authorities and stakeholders together as part of co-management arrangements.[68]

There is little indication of how the collaborative governance arrangements for Te Awa Tupua are working in practice, as there has been little or no empirical research or monitoring of policy impact carried out. However, like Te Urewera, the Te Awa Tupua Act provides a framework for collaboration, contestation and conflict in the river's management, pursuant to agreed, custom-based values.

3.1.3 Ngā Maunga

There are regular reports of a third natural resource (this time a dormant volcano) having been recognised as a legal person in New Zealand, although as of 2021 the model is under negotiation, and until a settlement is finalised, the precise terms of the agreement are confidential. Again, this model arises out of the Treaty claims of the local *iwi*, with respect to Taranaki Maunga, within another national park on the west coast of the North Island (Egmont National Park).[69]

64 Ibid 15.
65 Ibid s 15(5).
66 Resource Management Act 1991 (NZ) s 46(3).
67 Te Awa Tupua (Whanganui River Claims Settlement) Act 2017 ss 41, 46.
68 See, eg, Waikato-Tainui Raupatu Claims (Waikato River) Settlement Act 2010 (NZ). For the Waikato River, which was recognised as a 'living ancestor' and 'indivisible whole' in a similar way to Te Awa Tupua, albeit without legal personality.
69 'Taranaki Maunga Te Anga Putakerongo (Record of Understanding) 20 December 2017' 6, www.govt.nz/assets/Documents/OTS/Taranaki-Maunga/Taranaki-Maunga-Te-Anga-Putakerongo-Record-of-Understanding-20-December-2017.pdf.

These include a series of historical grievances dating back to the wars of the 1860s when Crown forces deployed 'scorched earth tactics' against Taranaki *iwi* settlements and cultivations, destroying their foodstores and livelihoods. Following the war, the Crown confiscated 1.2 million acres of Taranaki land, and throughout the 20th century continued to enact legislation which prevented the Taranaki *iwi* from controlling their remaining territories.[70]

In December 2017, Ngā iwi o Taranaki and the Crown signed a Record of Understanding under which they agreed that Ngā Maunga (translated as 'the mountains' and previously referred to as Taranaki Maunga, Mount Taranaki and Mount Egmont) will be declared a legal person with a joint governance entity to act in the name of Ngā Maunga,[71] in a similar approach to the Te Awa Tupua and Te Urewera settlements. The Record provides that Ngā Maunga will be recognised as an "indivisible and living whole" and an ancestor with its own legal personhood, and land vested in the Crown under the Mount Egmont Vesting Act 1978 transferred to Ngā Maunga.[72] New legislation will provide for a set of values that recognise the ancestral connection between the Taranaki *iwi* and the mountain, and recognise their cultural obligation to preserve and protect Ngā Maunga.[73] The Record of Understanding explains:[74]

> [For] Iwi of Taranaki, [Ngā Maunga] have been ever present and remain personified ancestors, a site of shared history, a physical resource, and the citadel of a unique ecosystem. Wider Taranaki society continues to look upon these maunga as key reference points for the region, shaping an immediate sense of place and social association with mutual identity. Their presence pervades our scenery, projecting mystery, adventure and beauty, capturing our attention and our imagination in how humanity can be closely bound to a landscape.

The Record of Understanding further provides that the joint governance entity will consist of an equal number of Crown and *iwi* appointees (up to eight in total), who will act as the representative and in the interests of Ngā Maunga.[75] The entity must act consistently with the Maunga values[76] and strive to achieve consensus in decision-making.[77] Although we still know little about the eventual

70 See 'Taranaki Iwi Deed of Settlement Summary' (New Zealand Government) www.govt.nz/browse/history-culture-and-heritage/treaty-settlements/find-a-treaty-settlement/taranaki-iwi/taranaki-iwi-deed-of-settlement-summary/.

71 'Taranaki Maunga Te Anga Putakerongo (Record of Understanding) 20 December 2017' (n 69) s 5.2.

72 'Taranaki Maunga Te Anga Putakerongo (Record of Understanding) 20 December 2017' (n 69) 5.5.

73 Ibid 5.10.

74 Ibid 1.7.

75 Ibid 5.18–5.19.

76 Ibid 5.19.2.

77 Ibid 5.20.

administrative arrangements for Ngā Maunga, it is clear that (like the other New Zealand models) the core function of this model is to recognise the *iwi*'s political authority and culture, and to provide a collaborative governance model that provides a forum for shared authority, contestation, and conflict resolution, pursuant to agreed values.

While not expressly providing for personhood, there are many other instances in which a natural resource is recognised as an ancestor or living entity, in reflection of Māori custom and worldview, as well as other collaborative guardianship models established for the management of a natural resource outside of a specific Treaty context.[78] The Crown has also recently developed broader policies recognising Māori ontologies and legal pluralism (like *kaitiakitanga* or caretaking) and requiring greater collaboration with Māori, which frame natural resources as integrated, vital and interconnected with communities.[79]

3.2. *Australia*

If New Zealand is leading the way on ecosystem rights, Australia is trailing slowly behind, although a number of developments are now underway. The first of these concerns the Yarra River in the State of Victoria (*Birrarung* to the Wurundjeri Nation), which was recognised not as a legal person, but as a "living and integrated natural entity" under the Yarra River Protection (Wilip-gin Birrarung murron) Act 2017 (Vic). The legislation "recognises the intrinsic connection of the traditional owners to the Yarra River and its Country and further recognises them as the custodians of the land and waterway which they call Birrarung".[80] The Act establishes the Birrarung Council – an advisory body established by the Act to advise the Minister and to advocate for protection and preservation of Birrarung, which must have at least two Traditional Owner representatives on it.[81]

The Act also sets out "protection principles" for decision-makers to take into account in planning for the river,[82] and provides for the development of strategic plans for the river,[83] both of which address a range of environmental, cultural and recreational interests. The draft of the Strategic Plan for the river, which was released for public comment in 2020, includes (as one of its performance

78 See eg Kaikoura Te Tai o Marokura Marine Management Act 2014; Fiordland (Te Moana o Atawhenua) Marine Management Act 2005. Ngāti Rangi Claims Settlement Act 2019 s 107(2).

79 'Essential Freshwater Te Mana o Te Wai Factsheet' 6; 'Te Mana o Te Taiao – Aotearoa New Zealand Biodiversity Strategy 2020 Summary', www.doc.govt.nz/nature/biodiversity/aotearoa-new-zealand-biodiversity-strategy/te-mana-o-te-taiao-summary/.

80 Yarra River Protection (Wilip-gin Birrarung murron) Act 2017 preamble.

81 Ibid S 46.

82 Ibid Part 2.

83 Ibid Part 4.

objectives) the creation of a culturally diverse river corridor which acknowledges, protects and commemorates the rich heritage of the Birrarung and its stories.[84]

The Birrarung 'case' was inspired by the Te Awa Tupua model, and similarly arises out of a process of attempting to respond to and repair relationships between the State and Indigenous peoples, although non-Indigenous interests still dominate river governance,[85] and only two Traditional Owner representatives are required on a body of 12. Moreover, the Council's role is limited to an advisory role, and it does not have any decision-making authority, meaning that Traditional Owners are excluded from direct involvement in river management decisions.[86] Nevertheless, the Wurundejeri people recognise the Act as being "incredibly significant", "marking a major step towards acknowledging the rights of Traditional Owners as well as the importance of Traditional Owner language and culture".[87]

A number of similar proposals are in varying stages of activism,[88] some of which have been led by Indigenous groups, although none directly adopt legal personhood in the same way as in New Zealand. One of these concerns the Martuwarra (Fitzroy) River in northwestern Australia, which the Traditional Owners have declared to be a "living ancestral being" with a "right to life", albeit without any formal recognition by the State of Western Australia.[89] The declaration provides that the river must be protected for current and future generations, and managed jointly with the Traditional Owners of the river.

Other developments have been pursued without the leadership or involvement of Indigenous peoples. These include the stalled 2014 Environmental Defenders Office campaign to recognise the Great Barrier Reef as a legal person,[90] and the 2020 resolution of the Blue Mountain Council in New South Wales, to integrate the rights of nature in its municipal planning and

84 See 'Draft Yarra Strategic Plan', https://engage.vic.gov.au/help-us-shape-final-10-year-strategic-plan-yarra-river.

85 Erin O'Donnell, *Legal Rights for Rivers: Competition, Collaboration and Water Governance* (Routledge 2018).

86 Elliott Leonard Provis, 'The Birrarung Act: Between a Decolonial Nation-State and Settler-Colonialism' (2021) *Global Journal of Research in Engineering* https://engineeringresearch.org/index.php/GJRE/article/view/2097; Professor Lee C. Godden, Professor Sue Jackson and Dr Katie O'Bryan, 'Indigenous Water Rights and Water Law Reforms in Australia' (2020) 37(6) *Environmental and Planning Law Journal* 655–678.

87 'Draft Yarra Strategic Plan' (n 84) 20.

88 See e.g. 'Margaret River, Western Australia' (Australian Centre for the Rights of Nature) https://rightsofnature.org.au/communities/margaret-river/; 'Rivers of the West Draft Proposals' (Environmental Justice Australia) www.envirojustice.org.au/wp-content/uploads/2018/06/EJA-Rivers-of-the-West-Draft-Proposals.pdf.

89 Fitzroy River Council, 'Fitzroy River Declaration' (2016), https://static1.squarespace.com/static/5e86add4e98f7421bace70f1/t/5e9fcc157dedb86cbb06a2e9/1587530798453/fitzroy-river-declaration.pdf. See for context, Milgin and others (n 20).

90 See Barcan (n 16) 812.

operations,[91] in a similar way to the many United States municipal rights of nature declarations.[92]

In October 2019, a Rights of Nature and Future Generations Bill was introduced in the Western Australian Legislative Council.[93] The Bill recognises rights of nature as a whole, rather than specific natural resources,[94] in a model closer to the Ecuadorian constitutional protection of the rights of nature than the New Zealand models. The Bill recognises that nature has the right to "naturally exist, flourish, regenerate and evolve" as well as to "recovery, rehabilitation and restoration",[95] and that both nature and future generations have the right to a healthy environment, climate system and biodiversity.[96] Nature's rights do not include personhood, and the Bill specifically provides that the rights do not confer any liabilities, duties or responsibilities on nature.[97] It requires the State to take action to implement the rights of nature,[98] and any person may enforce them (again like the Ecuadorian model), with particular provision for Indigenous people to be joined to any proceeding.[99] The Bill also states that "any permits, approvals, licenses, privileges or other government authority of an action project, activity or development that would violate the provisions of this Act shall be invalid for all purposes",[100] and establishes significant penalties for activities which violate the rights of nature.[101]

The Bill and the Blue Mountains resolution are different from the other Australasian ecosystem rights cases in that they do not establish any guardianship arrangements to represent nature's interests. Nor do they, in focusing on the rights of 'nature' broadly, reflect the connection between people and place so distinctive of the other Australasian cases. In these respects, the models cannot be properly characterised as 'relational': they do not establish a forum for collaboration and conflict, and they fail to recognise the richness of connection between people and place.

91 'Council Resolves to Integrate Rights of Nature into Operations and Planning' *Blue Mountains City Council* (15 April 2020), www.bmcc.nsw.gov.au/media-centre/council-resolves-to-integrate-rights-of-nature-into-operations-and-planning.
92 See Elizabeth Macpherson, 'The (Human) Rights of Nature: A Comparative Study of Emerging Legal Rights for Rivers and Lakes in the United States of America and Mexico' (2021) 31 *Duke Environmental Law & Policy Forum* 327–377.
93 Western Australia, *Parliamentary Debates*, Legislative Council, 28 November 2019, 9513, Diane Evans.
94 Ibid.
95 'Rights of Nature and Future Generations Bill 2019' ss 6(1)(a)-(b) www.parliament.wa.gov.au/Parliament/Bills.nsf/A83E23DAE4373236482584AB002386A7/$File/Bill151-1.pdf
96 Ibid 6(1)(C)-(D), 7.
97 Ibid 9.
98 Ibid 12.
99 Ibid 13.
100 Ibid 19.
101 Ibid 19(1). Evans (n 93) 1.

4. Australasian Environmental Constitutionalism as Relational Legal Pluralism

Are the Australasian ecosystem rights cases suggestive of a "new legal paradigm that is better fit for purpose in the unstable Anthropocene"?[102] The cases are attempts to reflect Indigenous ideas of ancestral or familial relationships with living and integrated natural resources, which ground the models in particular places and with particular peoples as part of complex and interdependent eco-systems. In this sense, they do suggest a new approach for environmental law, indicative of 'ecosystem-based' or 'earth system' perspectives, which embrace the planet's interconnectedness, dynamism and complexity.

They also have 'constitutional' importance,[103] as attempts to elevate the interests of ecosystems above ordinary environmental regulation and competing agendas, via shared values or objectives (for example, the *Kawa* in the New Zealand cases and the protection principles for Birrarung). Unlike the emblematic constitutional rights of nature provisions in places like Ecuador, both the Urewera and Awa Tupua models are provided for outside of New Zealand's core constitutional documents,[104] which do not recognise the Treaty of Waitangi or its principles, Indigenous or cultural rights, or even environmental rights.[105] Yet as Sanders has argued, these models are themselves effectively 'constitutions' which address the structure of power in New Zealand, as they provide frameworks for interactions between the Crown and *iwi*, with particular emphasis on processes and principles which affirm the values of Māori customary law.[106]

The ecosystem rights cases are driven by the concerns of communities for authority and control over natural resources in accordance with their own social, political and environmental values. The cases that are enshrined in legislation (Te Urewera, Te Awa Tupua and Birrarung) have occurred, not in reflection of any inherent rights or agency of nature, but because of the fundamental interests of humans in conjunction with nature. As such, the most significant contribution the Australasian cases make in terms of environmental law's response to the Anthropocene lies in their relational function – not as a discrete recognition event but as an ongoing process of interaction between people and place via local involvement with and control over resource decision-making, in accordance with agreed, fundamental values, that reflect legal pluralism.

When framed as relational, ecosystem rights are not essential to, but enable new legal approaches to regulate the interaction of human societies and nature

102 Kotzé (n 7) 77–78.

103 Louis J Kotzé, 'Global Environmental Constitutionalism in the Anthropocene' in Louis J Kotzé (ed), *Environmental Law and Governance for the Anthropocene* (Hart Publishing 2017) 191.

104 New Zealand Bill of Rights Act 1990 (NZ).

105 Elizabeth Macpherson, *Indigenous Rights to Water in Law and Regulation: Lessons from Comparative Experience* (CUP 2019).

106 Sanders (n 48) 231.

in the Anthropocene, including those underpinned by Indigenous ontologies. Yet while the Australasian cases do, to an extent, recognise and enable this relational legal pluralism, the relevant settler governments still determine the conditions and consequences of that recognition, placing limits as they go. According to Jones, this does not amount to the kind of recognition that is necessary to establish a just relationship between Māori and the Crown.[107] Legal personality is an imposed western legal construct, as distinct from the Māori worldview that natural landscape features have their own *mauri* (or life force), which only serves to reinforce the colonial relationship.[108]

Can these disparate cases in which natural resources have been recognised as having rights, personhood or agency be considered to be an emerging Australasian species of transnational environmental constitutionalism? Although there has been a certain amount of 'borrowing' of models from New Zealand to Australia, there is such variance in the cases and context between the countries that it is difficult, and probably inappropriate, to generalise them as being part of an Australasian approach. However, these may well be examples of an emerging Australasian environmental constitutionalism – an early, tentative, advance towards more fundamental and transformative change.

5. Conclusion

Ecosystem rights are no panacea; their success depends on the effectiveness of surrounding legal, policy and institutional frameworks. Valid questions remain about their coverage, scope and consistency given the *ad hoc* way in which they are developing, and uncertainty surrounding their (mis)match with the logical boundaries of ecosystems. Important criticisms around the impact of ecosystem rights on Indigenous political strategies require further exploration, which should be led by Indigenous scholars and peoples. However, when we understand ecosystem rights approaches as essentially relational, rather than being a substantive end in and of themselves, we can focus better on the processes they may enable, in a way that need not undermine, and may even accompany, more transformative social and ecological agendas.

Bibliography

Barcan R., 'The Campaign for Legal Personhood for the Great Barrier Reef: Finding Political and Pedagogical Value in a Spectacular Failure of Care' (2020) 3 *Environment and Planning E: Nature and Space* 810.

Benson M.H. and Craig R.K., 'The End of Sustainability' (2014) 27 *Society & Natural Resources* 777.

107 Carwyn Jones, *New Treaty, New Tradition: Reconciling New Zealand and Māori Law* (UBC Press 2016) 98.

108 Ibid.

Best E., *Tuhoe, the Children of the Mist: A Sketch of the Origin, History, Myths, and Beliefs of the Tuhoe Tribe of the Maori of New Zealand, with Some Account of Other Early Tribes of the Bay of Plenty District* (Vol. 6, 4th edn, Reed 1996).

Birrell K. and Dehm J., 'International Law & The Humanities in the "Anthropocene"' in Shane Chalmers and Sundhya Pahuja (eds), *Routledge Handbook of International Law and the Humanities* (Routledge 2021).

Borràs S., 'New Transitions from Human Rights to the Environment to the Rights of Nature' (2016) 5 *Transnational Environmental Law* 113.

Centro de Estudios para la Justicia Social 'Tierra Digna' y otros v Presidente de la Republica y otros [2016] Corte Constitucional [Constitutional Court], Sala Sexta de Revision [Sixth Chamber] (Colombia) No T-622 of 2016.

Chapron G., Epstein Y. and López-Bao J.V., 'A Rights Revolution for Nature' (2019) 363 *Science*.

Clark C. and others, 'Can You Hear the Rivers Sing? Legal Personhood, Ontology, and the Nitty-Gritty of Governance' (2019) 45 *Ecology Law Quarterly* 787.

Coombes B., 'Nature's Rights as Indigenous Rights? Mis/Recognition through Personhood for Te Urewera' (2020) 2020 *Espace populations sociétés*.

'Council Resolves to Integrate Rights of Nature into Operations and Planning' *Blue Mountains City Council* (15 April 2020), www.bmcc.nsw.gov.au/media-centre/council-resolves-to-integrate-rights-of-nature-into-operations-and-planning.

Crutzen P.J., 'Geology of Mankind' (2002) 415 *Nature (London)* 23.

Davies M., *Law Unlimited: Materialism, Pluralism, and Legal Theory* (Routledge 2017).

'Draft Yarra Strategic Plan', https://engage.vic.gov.au/help-us-shape-final-10-year-strategic-plan-yarra-river.

'Essential Freshwater Te Mana o Te Wai Factsheet' 6.

Evans D., 'Western Australia' *Legislative Council* (28 November 2019), 9513, 'Rights of Nature and Future Generations Bill Extract from Hansard', www.parliament.wa.gov.au/Hansard/hansard.nsf/0/268DDA295DD2B1C8482584C4001A2EFA/$FILE/C40%20S1%2020191128%20p9513a-9514a.pdf.

Godden P.L., Jackson P.S. and O'Bryan D.K., 'Indigenous Water Rights and Water Law Reforms in Australia' (2020) 37(6) *Environmental and Planning Law Journal* 655–678.

Gover K., *Legal Pluralism and State-Indigenous Relations in Western Settler Societies* (International Council on Human Rights Policy 2009).

Grear A., 'Re-Encountering the Environmental Legal "Subject"' in Louis J. Kotzé (ed), *Environmental Law and Governance for the Anthropocene* (Hart Publishing 2017).

Haraway D.J., *Staying with the Trouble: Making Kin in the Chthulucene* (Duke University Press 2016).

Iorns Magallanes C., 'Nature as an Ancestor: Two Examples of Legal Personality for Nature in New Zealand' (2015) (Special Issue 22) *VertigO: La revue électronique en sciences de l'environnement* 1.

James S.P., 'Legal Rights and Nature's Contributions to People: Is There a Connection?' (2020) 241 *Biological Conservation* 108325.

Jones C., *New Treaty, New Tradition: Reconciling New Zealand and Maori Law* (University of British Columbia Press 2016).

Kotzé L.J., 'Global Environmental Constitutionalism in the Anthropocene' in Louis J. Kotzé (ed), *Environmental Law and Governance for the Anthropocene* (Hart Publishing 2017).

Kotzé L.J., 'Earth System Law for the Anthropocene: Rethinking Environmental Law Alongside the Earth System Metaphor' (2020) 11 *Transnational Legal Theory* 75.

Macpherson E., *Indigenous Rights to Water in Law and Regulation: Lessons from Comparative Experience* (CUP 2019).

Macpherson E., '"Hooks" and "Anchors" for Relational Ecosystem-Based Marine Management' [2021a] 130 *Marine Policy* 104561.

Macpherson E., 'The (Human) Rights of Nature: A Comparative Study of Emerging Legal Rights for Rivers and Lakes in the United States of America and Mexico' [2021b] 31 *Duke Environmental Law & Policy Forum* 327–377.

Maloney M., 'Building an Alternative Jurisprudence for the Earth: The International Rights of Nature Tribunal' [2016] *Vermont Law Review* 129.

'Margaret River, Western Australia' (Australian Centre for the Rights of Nature), https://rightsofnature.org.au/communities/margaret-river/a.

Marshall V., 'Removing the Veil from the "Rights of Nature": The Dichotomy between First Nations Customary Rights and Environmental Legal Personhood' [2020] *Australian Feminist Law Journal* 1.

May J.R. and Daly E., *Global Environmental Constitutionalism* (CUP 2015).

Milgin A. and others, 'Sustainability Crises are Crises of Relationship: Learning from Nyikina Ecology and Ethics' (2020) 2 *People and Nature* 1210.

Morris J. and Ruru J., 'Giving Voice to Rivers: Legal Personality as a Vehicle for Recognising Indigenous Peoples' Relationships to Water' (2010) 14 *Australian Indigenous Law Review* 49.

New Zealand and Office of Treaty Settlements, *Ka Tika ā Muri, Ka Tika ā Mua: He Tohutohu Whakamārama i Ngā Whakataunga Kerēme e Pā Ana Ki Te Tiriti o Waitangi Me Ngā Whakaritenga Ki Te Karauna = Healing the Past, Building a Future: A Guide to Treaty of Waitangi Claims and Negotiations with the Crown* (Office of Treaty Settlements 2015).

'Ngai Tuhoe Deed of Settlement of Historical Claims', www.govt.nz/assets/Documents/OTS/Ngai-Tuhoe/Ngai-Tuhoe-Deed-of-Settlement-4-Jun-2013.pdf

O'Donnell E., *Legal Rights for Rivers: Competition, Collaboration and Water Governance* (Routledge 2018).

O'Donnell E. and others, 'Stop Burying the Lede: The Essential Role of Indigenous Law(s) in Creating Rights of Nature' (2020) 9 *Transnational Environmental Law* 403.

Provis E.L., 'The Birrarung Act: Between a Decolonial Nation-State and Settler-Colonialism' [2021] *Global Journal of Research In Engineering* https://engineeringresearch.org/index.php/GJRE/article/view/2097.

Richardson W. and McNeish J.-A., 'Granting Rights to Rivers in Colombia: Significance for ExtrACTIVISM and Governance' in Judith Shapiro and John-Andrew McNeish (eds), *Our Extractive Age Expressions of Violence and Resistance* (Routledge 2021).

'Rights of Nature and Future Generations Bill 2019', www.parliament.wa.gov.au/Parliament/Bills.nsf/A83E23DAE4373236482584AB002386A7/$File/Bill151-1.pdf

RiverOfLife M. and others, 'Recognizing the Martuwarra's First Law Right to Life as a Living Ancestral Being' (2020) 9 *Transnational Environmental Law* 541.

'Rivers of the West Draft Proposals' (Environmental Justice Australia), www.envirojustice.org.au/wp-content/uploads/2018/06/EJA-Rivers-of-the-West-Draft-Proposals.pdf

'Ruruku Whakatupua Te Mana o Te Awa Tupua – Upholding the Mana of the Whanganui River at Māori Law Review', http://maorilawreview.co.nz/2014/05/ruruku-whakatupua-te-mana-o-te-awa-tupua-upholding-the-mana-of-the-whanganui-river/

Salmond A., *Tears of Rangi: Experiments across Worlds* (Auckland University Press 2017).

Sanders K., '"Beyond Human Ownership"? Property, Power and Legal Personality for Nature in Aotearoa New Zealand' (2018) 30 *Journal of Environmental Law* 207.

Steffen W. and others, 'Planetary Boundaries: Guiding Human Development on a Changing Planet' (2015) 347 *Science (American Association for the Advancement of Science)* 1259855.

Tănăsescu M., 'Rights of Nature, Legal Personality, and Indigenous Philosophies' (2020) 9 *Transnational Environmental Law* 429.

'Taranaki Iwi Deed of Settlement Summary' (New Zealand Government), www.govt.nz/browse/history-culture-and-heritage/treaty-settlements/find-a-treaty-settlement/taranaki-iwi/taranaki-iwi-deed-of-settlement-summary/

'Taranaki Maunga Te Anga Putakerongo' (Record of Understanding 20 December 2017), www.govt.nz/assets/Documents/OTS/Taranaki-Maunga/Taranaki-Maunga-Te-Anga-Putakerongo-Record-of-Understanding-20-December-2017.pdf

Te Aho L., 'Indigenous Challenges to Enhance Freshwater Governance and Management in Aotearoa New Zealand – The Waikato River Settlement' (2009) 20 *Journal of Water Law* 285.

'Te Kawa o Te Urewera', www.ngaituhoe.iwi.nz/te-kawa-o-te-urewera

'Te Mana o Te Taiao – Aotearoa New Zealand Biodiversity Strategy 2020 Summary', www.doc.govt.nz/nature/biodiversity/aotearoa-new-zealand-biodiversity-strategy/te-mana-o-te-taiao-summary/

Vermeylen S., 'Materiality and the Ontological Turn' in Louis J. Kotzé (ed), *Environmental Law and Governance for the Anthropocene* (Hart Publishing 2017).

Verschuuren J., 'The Role of Sustainable Development' in Louis J. Kotzé (ed), *Environmental Law and Governance for the Anthropocene* (Hart Publishing 2017).

Waitangi Tribunal, 'Te Urewera Report Volume 1' [2017] *Wai* 894, https://forms.justice.govt.nz/search/Documents/WT/wt_DOC_134632524/Te%20Urewera%20Vol1WS.pdf

Watts V., 'Indigenous Place-Thought & Agency amongst Humans and Non-Humans (First Woman and Sky Woman Go on a European World Tour!)' (2013) 2 *Decolonization: Indigeneity, Education & Society* 20.

'The Whanganui River Report (Wai 167)' (GP Publications 1999).

Young M. and Esau C., *Transformational Change in Environmental and Natural Resource Management: Guidelines for Policy Excellence* (Taylor & Francis Group 2016).

10 The Animal as a Concern for a Renewed Analysis of the Legal Link Between Human and the Environment

Philippe Billet

1. Introduction

Law's understanding of the world is binary – as banal as it may be, but fundamentally binary: on the one hand, the persons; on the other, things. Anything that is not a person is necessarily a thing. Each qualification justifies a different legal status – essentially different because qualification requires a choice, it formalizes a choice. The person cannot be the object of a dereliction, of an act that would reduce him or her to the rank of a thing: such a dereliction is formally prohibited in the name of human "dignity" (e.g., prohibition of human trafficking, which would make them things, as slaves legally admitted in ancient Rome).

The persons are subjects of rights, the things are mere objects of rights, with a domination of the former over the latter, who have the use and disposal of them – free disposal often.

However, this *summa divisio* is not as absolute as we might tend to believe at first: there is no doubt that, in the name of human dignity, the corporality of man excludes any commerciality or disposition as if he were a thing, which also includes the corpse of the person. Similarly, the use of the body as a thing is prohibited for the sake of public order. But, some elements of the body, which are reproducible, are transferable, either free of charge or not (blood, hair), while other non-reproducible elements are transferred in an altruistic and formally regulated manner (organ donation). The aim is to avoid the dismemberment of the body, which is consubstantial with the person, and the reification that could result. This would imply the negation of his dignity, because he would be reduced to something other than human. This shift can be seen most clearly in some of the cases concerning the qualification of human remains exhibited in museums. They are often referred to as goods, i.e. things.

Thus, certain elements detached from the body (or even the body itself) would be things, banally things, although of human essence. The boundary between the person and things thus shifts imperceptibly, just as the boundary between things and the person.

DOI: 10.4324/9781003175308-13

The recurrent debates on the status of animals illustrate the inventiveness of the law in creating new relationships with the environment, new relationships between humans and others, whether they are "animate" or not. This argument opposes the proponents of anthropocentrism and ecocentrism: the former conceives human beings as the only reason for the existence of the legal system and considers natural resources to be mere objects at their service. The latter conceives nature and its components as real subjects of law, with a legal personality. Today, this theory has come true: for example, the Parliament of New Zealand declares Te Awa Tupua[1] as "an indivisible and living whole, incorporating all its physical and meta-physical elements". "Te Awa Tupua is a legal person and has all the rights, powers, duties, and liabilities of a legal person".[2] For its part, the High Court of Uttarakhand at Nainital declares,

> Accordingly, while exercising the *parens patrie* jurisdiction, the Rivers Ganga and Yamuna, all their tributaries, streams, every natural water flowing with flow continuously or intermittently of these rivers, are declared as juristic/legal persons/living entities having the status of a legal person with all corresponding rights, duties and liabilities of a living person in order to preserve and conserve river Ganga and Yamuna.[3]

However, this recognition was short-lived: this decision was overturned on July 7, 2017 by the Indian Supreme Court,[4] which held that

> Since the rivers flow through several states, only the Centre could frame rules for their management. The ruling also raised questions like whether the victim of a flood in the rivers can sue the State for damages and also about whether the state and its officers will be liable in case of pollution in the rivers in another state through which it flows.

Lake Erie, in the United States, suffered the same fate: in February 2019, the residents of the city of Toledo (Ohio) adopted by referendum the "Lake Erie Bill of Rights" (LEBOR) whereby "Lake Erie, and the Lake Erie watershed, possess

1 "Te Awa Tupua is a spiritual and physical entity that supports and sustains both the life and natural resources within the Whanganui River and the health and well-being of the iwi, hapū, and other communities of the River".

2 Te Awa Tupua Act (Whanganui River Claims Settlement), n° 7, 2017 (15 March 2017).

3 High Court of Uttarakhand at Nainital, March 20, 2017, "The State of Uttarakhand & Ors.", Writ Petition (PIL), n° 126/2014.

4 Special Leave to Appeal (C) n° 016879/2017, "The State of Uttarakhand and Ors. v. Mohd. Salim and Ors.". See Stellina Jolly and K.S. Roshan Menon, 'Of Ebbs and Flows: Understanding the Legal Consequences of Granting Personhood to Natural Entities in India' [2021] *Transnational Environmental Law* 1; Erin L. O'Donnell, 'At the Intersection of the Sacred and the Legal: Rights for Nature in Uttarakhand, India' [2018] 30 *Journal of Environmental Law* 135.

the right to exist, flourish, and naturally evolve." However, this decision was overturned by the Ohio Federal Court on February 27, 2020:

> LEBOR's environmental rights are even less clear than the provisions struck down in those cases. What conduct infringes the right of Lake Erie and its watershed to "exist, flourish, and naturally evolve"? . . . How would a prosecutor, judge, or jury decide? LEBOR offers no guidance. Similar uncertainty shrouds the right of Toledoans to a "clean and healthy environment."[5]

The line between clean and unclean, and between healthy and unhealthy, depends on who you ask. Because of this vagueness, Drewes Farms reasonably fears that spreading even small amounts of fertilizer violates LEBOR. Countless other activities might run afoul of LEBOR's amorphous environmental rights: catching fish, dredging a riverbed, removing invasive species, driving a gas-fuelled vehicle, pulling up weeds, planting corn, irrigating a field, and so on. LEBOR's authors failed to make hard choices regarding the appropriate balance between environmental protection and economic activity. Instead, they used a language that sounds powerful but has no practical effect. Under even the most forgiving standard, the environmental rights identified in LEBOR are void for vagueness.[6]
Most recently, two associated resolutions have recognized the legal personality of the Magpie River – Mutehekau Shipu (Province of Quebec): one of January 18, 2021 of the Council of the Innu of Ekuanitshit and the other of February 17, 2021 of the Regional Municipality of the County of Minganie. They recognize the "fundamental rights" of the Magpie River, established in accordance with the beliefs, customs and practices of the Innu of Ekuanitshit, namely:

> 1) The right to live, to exist and to flow; 2) The right to respect for its natural cycles; 3) The right to evolve naturally, to be preserved and to be protected; 4) The right to maintain its natural biodiversity; 5) The right to maintain its integrity; 6) The right to perform essential functions within its ecosystem; 7) The right to be free from pollution; 8) The right to regeneration and restoration; 9) The right to litigation.

And they have appointed "guardians" with the duty "to act on behalf of the rights and interests of the river and to ensure the protection of its fundamental rights."[7]

This recognition of rights to the benefit of certain natural elements (river, mountain, glacier . . .), the personification of inanimate elements, finds a parallel in the recognition of rights to certain animals, showing similar difficulties.

5 Lake Erie Bill of Rights, *"Section 1 – Statements of Law – A Community Bill of Rights"*, b).
6 "Drewes Farms Partenrship and State of Ohio v. City of Toledo", Case n° 3:19 CV 434.
7 Council of the Innu of Ekuanitshit, Resolution on the Magpie River – Mutehekau Shipu (January 18, 2021).

The animal is a thing since it is not a person. But it is not a thing like the other things, and it seems necessary to go beyond this qualification.

If we take this classification of a thing to its logical conclusion, we reach an impasse, a nonsense which shows that this classification is not adapted to animals. Indeed, an animal is materially and legally a movable thing because it can move, and it is a good when it is appropriated by a person. However, in European Union law, if it is abandoned by its owner, it can only be classified as waste, as the regulations do not expressly exclude it from things that cannot be waste. " 'Waste' means any substance or object which the holder discards or intends or is required to discard."[8] This has been translated into French law as "any substance or object, or more generally any movable asset, which the holder discards or intends or is required to discard."[9] "Any movable asset" means "all movable assets", including any animal, alive or dead, because the regulation does not expressly exclude live animals from its scope. In this context, if we consider the animal as a thing and transform the thing into waste, this means that the abandonment of an animal must respect the legal regime of waste and the hierarchy of waste management methods: reuse, recycling, recovery, elimination. Moreover, it is difficult to imagine an animal-waste walking around a landfill. . . . There is therefore necessarily "something else" than a simple thing.

If the animal is a thing, due to the lack of other choices, then the animal is something other than an ordinary thing. It cannot be treated as an inert thing, as a non-living thing. It is not a simple "movable property" or "immovable by destination", conditions in which the civilist tradition has confined it. What can it be then, and in what capacity, if the "animal condition" must be revisited, if an animal dignity must be defended once it has been admitted that it is a sensitive being? A different thing? A person other than a human person?

2. The Animal, as a Sensitive Being

The recognition of animal sentience is a necessary step towards removing it from its status as a thing. Admitting that animals are capable of sensations and reacting to external stimuli fundamentally distinguishes them from things that one might call "common" or "ordinary". The regulations of most States incorporate this evidence of animal sentience, with highly contrasting situations. It provides a basis for the claims of those who, without necessarily defending the personification of the animal, look to formalize the recognition and protection of its welfare.

In France, animal sentience has been enshrined in the Civil Code, in attempting to reconcile its legal qualification and its affective value while avoiding the creation of an intermediate category between persons and goods, while nevertheless

8 Directive 2008/98/EC of the European Parliament and of the Council of 19 November 2008 on waste and repealing certain Directives, art. 3.

9 French Environnemental Code, art. L. 541–1–1.

recognizing the character of the animal as a sentient being, as the Rural Code already does. However, by adopting the principle that "animals are living beings endowed with sentience," the Civil Code does not fundamentally change their status: it specifies that "subject to the laws protecting them, animals are subject to the regime of property." The French Civil Code thus joins the Law of 10 July 1976 on the protection of nature, which established the principle that "any animal being a sentient being must be placed by its owner in conditions compatible with the biological requirements of its species." This principle has been incorporated *in extenso* into Article L. 214–1 of the Rural Code, which devotes an entire chapter to "The protection of animals", distinguishing between "Pet animals" and "Other animals". All animals are therefore not equal before the law: only appropriate animals are protected with regard to their sentience, whereas the law recognizes "any" animal as a "sentient being". The Penal Code has followed the same path: its chapter on "Serious injuries or cruelties to animals" (Art. 521–1 et seq.) concerns only domestic, tame or captive animals and not wild animals, which are *res nullius*, "things without a master", which are not appropriate. The same unease can be perceived in the Swiss legislator: the Civil Code stresses that "Animals are not things", but mitigates this statement by stating that "unless otherwise provided, the provisions applying to things also apply to animals" (Art. 641).

The perspective is similar in Quebec law: the Animal Welfare and Safety Act (12 December 2015) specifies that "animals are sentient beings that have biological needs," but its scope is limited to "domestic" animals, i.e. "a domestic animal, being an animal of a species or a breed that has been chosen by man to meet certain needs, such as cats, dogs, rabbits, cattle, horses, pigs, sheep, goats and chickens, and their hybrids",

> red foxes and American mink kept in captivity for breeding purposes with a view to dealing in fur, as well as any other animals or fish, within the meaning of the Act respecting the conservation and development of wildlife, that are kept in captivity for breeding purposes with a view to dealing in fur or in meat or other food products, and that are designated by regulation,

and "any other animal to which the Act respecting the conservation and development of wildlife does not apply and that is designated by regulation" (these other animals are designated by the Ministry of Agriculture, Fisheries and Food). This new animal condition extends the "Manifesto for an evolution of the legal status of animals in the Civil Code of Quebec" of January 21, 2014, which stressed the need to go beyond the status of movable thing:

> from a legal point of view, a dog or a cow is no different from a toaster or a chair: they are movable property. In 2014, it has become urgent to break free from the categories of the Civil Code and grant animals a status distinct from

> that of movable property, a status that recognises their ability to feel pleasure and pain, in short, a status of sentient being.[10]

This brings us closer to the World Organisation for Animal Health's "Terrestrial Animal Health Code" (1965), which formulated a series of recommendations ("Recommendations for Animal Welfare", art. 7) to ensure.

> The physical and mental state of an animal in relation to the conditions in which it lives and dies; that the internationally recognised 'five freedoms' (freedom from hunger, thirst and malnutrition; freedom from fear and distress; freedom from physical and thermal discomfort; freedom from pain, injury and disease; and freedom to express normal patterns of behaviour) provide valuable guidance in animal welfare.[11]

Strongly inspired by the "Terrestrial Code", the European Convention for the Protection of Animals kept for Farming Purposes of 10 March 1976 will also enshrine the need for recognition of this welfare. But it only uses the term once in connection with remedying the effects of a malfunctioning technical installation: "When a defect cannot be remedied forthwith, all temporary measures necessary to safeguard the welfare of the animals shall be taken immediately" (art. 7, 2). The principles it lays down, without expressly linking them to welfare, nevertheless determine its components:

> Animals shall be housed and provided with food, water and care in a manner which – having regard to their species and to their degree of development, adaptation and domestication – is appropriate to their physiological and ethological needs in accordance with established experience and scientific knowledge.
>
> (Art. 3)

For its part, the "Protocol to the Treaty of the European Union on protection and welfare of animals" (Amsterdam, 2 Oct. 1997) provides, with a view "to ensure improved protection and respect for the welfare of animals as sentient beings", that

> in formulating and implementing the Community's agriculture, transport, internal market and research policies, the Community and the Member States shall pay full regard to the welfare requirements of animals, while respecting the legislative or administrative provisions and customs of the

10 "Manifesto for an evolution of the legal status of animals in the Civil Code of Quebec" (January 21, 2014).

11 World Organisation for Animal Health, Terrestrial Animal Health Code (1965), "Recommendations for Animal Welfare", art. 7.

> Member States relating in particular to religious rites, cultural traditions and regional heritage.

In this perspective, a definite step forward has been made by the Swiss Federal Ordinance on the Protection of Animals (OPAn) of 23 April 2018, which specifies the modalities imposed by the Federal Act on the Protection of Animals (LPA) of 16 December 2005 to ensure respect for the dignity of the animal and to achieve its well-being. This ordinance is based on formal definitions, which deserves to be highlighted here. Animal dignity characterizes

> the intrinsic value of the animal, which must be respected by those who care about it; the dignity of the animal is violated when the constraint imposed on it cannot be justified by major interests; constraint occurs, in particular, when pain, suffering or damage is caused to the animal, when it is placed in a state of anxiety or degraded, when it is subjected to interventions that profoundly alter its phenotype or abilities, or when it is instrumentalised in an excessive manner.
>
> (Art. 3, a)[12]

Here, animal welfare is notably achieved "when they are kept and fed in such a way that their bodily functions and behaviour are not disturbed and their ability to adapt is not excessively strained"; "when they are given the opportunity to behave in accordance with their species within the limits of their biological capacity to adapt"; "when they are clinically healthy"; and "when they are spared pain, suffering, harm and anxiety" (Art. 3, b).

It is the animal-being, therefore, rather than the animal as a sentient thing. An animal cannot be reduced to a thing in this way, in contradiction with the quality that the law recognizes for it, a quality that is usually recognized for the human person. This brings us closer to the possibility of recognizing the animal as a person, beyond the reification in which it has been kept until now.

3. The Animal, as a Whole Person

In 2010, "based on the principle of the equal treatment of all persons", an international "Declaration of Rights for Cetaceans" was formulated, declaring "all cetaceans as persons have the right to life, liberty and wellbeing." In 2013, India's Ministry of Environment and Forests have expressly prohibited the keeping of captive dolphins for public entertainment in the entire country:

> Whereas cetaceans, in general, are highly intelligent and sensitive, and various scientists who have researched dolphin behavior have suggested that the unusually high intelligence; as compared to other animals means that

12 Ordinance on the Protection of Animals (OPAn) of 23 April 2018, art. 3, b).

> dolphins should be seen as 'non-human persons' and as such should have their own specific rights and is morally unacceptable to keep them captive for entertainment purpose.[13]

His comments were very cautious and carefully measured on this issue: "should be seen as 'non-human persons'" and not "are 'non-human persons'".

Many Latin American jurisdictions have punctually recognized the rights of animals, as if they were persons, but this has never been subsequently confirmed. For example, in Argentina, a federal chamber of criminal cassation granted a request for a habeas corpus order for the release of a female Orangutan born in captivity in a zoo and "detained without trial". It ordered her release on the grounds that her detention in a zoo violated

> in a manifestly illegal and arbitrary manner the right to freedom of movement, the right not to be considered as an object or thing liable to property and the right not to suffer any physical or psychological harm to which Orangutan Sandra is entitled as a non-human person and subject of law.[14]

The Argentine Civil Code, revised the following year, did not, however, consolidate this case law, maintaining the status of animals as things. Other national courts, seized of similar questions, did not follow this reasoning and declined to grant such a status. In the same line, the case of Chuco, a spectacled bear designed as a legal person with the fundamental right to liberty protected by the writ of habeas corpus. But the Colombian Supreme Court reversed the ruling, writing that:

> the writ of habeas corpus is inappropriate in the present case, because it was designed for persons, rational animals, not for non-human or irrational animals, and the foundations of such a decision [i.e. granting a writ of habeas corpus to Chucho] are incompatible with the purpose for which the writ was created.[15]

If we follow the reasoning developed by the promoters of this new status, the animal would become a person, but a "non-human" person, to mark the difference

13 Randall S. Abate, *Climate Change and the Voiceless: Protecting Future Generations, Wildlife and Natural Resources* (CUP 2019) 118–119.

14 Cámara Federal de Casación Penal de la Ciudad Autónoma de Buenos Aires, 18 de Diciembre de 2014, Orangutana Sandra s/ recurso de cadación s/habeas corpus. *(free translation)*. On the consequences of this decision and, in particular, the assignment of this "non-human person" to an animal sanctuary, since it has lost all capacity to evolve in the natural environment, see in particular Poder Judicial de la Ciudad Autónoma de Buenos Aires, Ciudad de Buenos Aires, 21 de octubre de 2015, "Asociacion de funcionarios y abogados por los derechos de los animales y otroscontra GCBA sobre Amparo", Expte. A2174–2015/0.

15 See www.nonhumanrights.org/content/uploads/Chucho-decision.pdf

with man and woman, who are "human" persons by nature, with their own and exclusive status. We write: "The animal". We should have written "Some animals" only. Only certain animals are concerned, on the basis of criteria centred on the close relationship with humans: they are cultural, no doubt, but above all based on "unconscious selection", to use Darwin's expression.[16] The Argentinian court recognized a female monkey as a non-human person based on the arguments of her lawyers, who underlined that she should be recognized as a non-human person

> because she is emotionally connected, she thinks, she feels, she gets frustrated with being locked up, she makes decisions, she has consciousness and perception of time, she cries when she loses (a relative), she learns, she communicates, and she is able to pass on her knowledge.[17]

There is here an induced proximity to humans, a similar behaviour that borders on pathocentrism (the dignity of the animal based on suffering, as a human would suffer, with the same feeling). The goodwill prevails over all other considerations: the earthworm is least likely to obtain non-human status compared to the more iconic panda or polar bear. Social priorities and the ability to meet them ultimately remain the main determinants of protection. This difficulty raises some questions about the determinants of this choice, which leads to discrimination between animals, between those which "deserve" to have a special status and those who do not. This marks the limits of the exercise, which would be irrelevant if it were a mere academic exercise, but which is fundamental if it involves conferring rights on living beings.

Sensitivity cannot be the only criterion, nor can the fact that it is a living being. These criteria are both too indeterminate (what is sentience and how can it be determined in an animal that does not manifest it through "human-like" behaviour, such as cries of pain in the face of suffering . . .) and too broad in scope (bio-centrism can be extended to plants and amoebas . . .). In a caricatural way, if a lobster becomes a non-human person, does this qualification prohibit it from being held in a tank house before being killed? And assuming that it can continue to be consumed and farmed for that purpose, since it is a person, even before it is a non-human person? Or does the animal have only the right to be killed in conditions free of pain, distress and other forms of suffering? In fact, the recognition of its sensitivity does not change its status – it remains an animal – but the regime attached to it must be modified to consider this sensitivity. E.g., the Swiss Federal Ordinance on the Protection of Animals of 23 April 2018 now imposes special conditions for killing the creeping

16 Charles Darwin (1859), *On the Origin of Species by Means of Natural Selection* (John Murray 1859), chapter "Variation and Domestication".

17 Cámara Federal de Casación Penal de la Ciudad Autónoma de Buenos Aires, 18 de Diciembre de 2014, Orangutana Sandra s/ recurso de cadación s/habeas corpus.

decapods (lobsters, spider crabs, etc.) before cooking them: it prohibits the use of aids that injure the soft parts of creeping decapods; the transport of live creeping decapods directly on ice or in ice-cold water; and the keeping of out of the water the creeping decapods that live in water. Creeping decapods should be stunned at the time of killing; if stunning is not possible, all reasonable steps should be taken to minimise pain, suffering and anxiety; the slaughtering of the creeping decapods without stunning is permissible if the method of killing itself induces immediately a lack of consciousness and sensibility, without pain or injury. However, the regulation does not make it a person, even a non-human person, and leaves the question of its status unanswered. This avoidance strategy avoids having to answer the ethical question of holding and eating the animal as a "person".

Effective recognition of this status implies an equivalence ratio between human and animal, likely to put humans in their "right" place, i.e. an element like any other in the world, things and living beings, in equivalent situations and with equal rights. This new special relationship would require that the animal is no longer a mere object of law but becomes a subject of law in its own right, in a relationship based on a balance of rights with humans. Promoting the recognition of the rights of the animal as a person is undoubtedly seductive, in that it renews the intellectual field of reflection on human and animal relationships and, more widely, on man and nature relationships. However, the range of options appears too narrow because, although it takes the opposite view to the anthropocentrism, it remains – paradoxically – anthropocentric. The choice of animals to be protected thus raises questions: in what way and why are some more worthy than others of being recognised as persons? The question is the same for natural spaces: which natural spaces and why? The natural spaces that have been recognized as non-human persons have been recognized because of a particular link with humans, both cultural and cultic – a necessary connection with humans. A more classical relationship is therefore preferred, combining the obligations imposed on human person with his rights, in the name of human dignity. The essence of this dignity lies in the environmental conditions in which man is placed. Man has only attained his humanity because of the quality of his environment, a maieutic condition, just as he will only maintain it by preserving the environment in which he evolves.

In his French novel, *Vendredi ou les limbes du Pacifique*, Michel Tournier makes "his" Robinson lose his human condition in a degraded environment.

> Robinson, in the first moments of his arrival on the island, lies down in the mud. . . . He experiences the feeling of automatic life, he regresses, he literally lives like a pig among pigs. This is his second baptism, his return to limbo. . . . What good is sense, tools, work, on the island, life seeps out of every pore. And the misfortune of the castaway is not shame or animal regression, but that these do not appease his impulse. . . . Without a belief in destiny, no impulse can be satisfied.

In a burst of dignity, which leads him to experiment his condition as a human person compared to his situation as an animal, Robinson rises again, regains his dignity as a human person that he had lost in animality, finds another environment to become a man again, and shapes it to his needs instead of being led by it. The emergence of man's humanity. Humanity thus draws its essence from the relationship between human, the environment, and its components. If these are called into question, altered, or affected, humanity wavers on its foundations, collapses and may disappear.

Without respect for his environment or respect for the animal, man loses humanity. He is deprived of his humanity. An alternative approach would be to make respect for animals a real and effective obligation, without distinguishing between appropriate and non-appropriate animals, and to remove them from their status as things and give them an intermediate status between persons and things, but without making them the persons they are not, even if they are qualified as "non-human", if this were to be confused with the "human" person. This suggestion does not resolve all the difficulties, and particularly does not specify whether this intermediate status should benefit all animals or only some of them. Recognizing nature as a person would not resolve the issue either, as it is a global entity.

4. Conclusion

> *If there were no animals*, says M. de Buffon, *the human nature would be even more incomprehensible*. However, we must not imagine that by comparing ourselves with them, we can ever understand the nature of our being: we can only discover their faculties, and the way of comparison can be an artifice to submit them to our observations,

asked Condillac in his *Traité des animaux* (1755).[18] "What place should the animal have in the mind of a jurist?" one might ask in a more contemporary way. A lawyer who is only a human person, simply tries to translate new human-animal relationships into norms. The recognition of the animal as a "sensitive being" is not only the result of a mirror effect, with man, a living being, looking at another living being who is not human person, but also a kind of assimilation. A different dignity, but dignity all the same, without necessarily resorting to the qualification of 'non-human person' that some people claim. Respect for the other in the same way as the self-esteem, in order not to lose ourselves. In order not to lose our humanity.

Bibliography

Abate R.S., *Climate Change and the Voiceless: Protecting Future Generations, Wildlife and Natural Resources* (CUP 2019) 118–119.

Bonnot de Condillac E., *Traité des animaux* (De Bure 1755).

18 Étienne Bonnot de Condillac, *Traité des animaux* (De Bure 1755) 1.

Darwin C., *On the Origin of Species by Means of Natural Selection* (John Murray 1859), chapter "Variation and Domestication".

Jolly S. and Menon K.S.R., 'Of Ebbs and Flows: Understanding the Legal Consequences of Granting Personhood to Natural Entities in India' [2021] *Transnational Environmental Law* 1.

O'Donnell E.L., 'At the Intersection of the Sacred and the Legal: Rights for Nature in Uttarakhand, India' (2018) 30 *Journal of Environmental Law* 135.

Part III

Actions and Enforcement

11 Courting the Environment

Public Interest Actions in the Global South

Maria Sarah Bussi

1. Postmodernity, Environmental Law and Legal Pluralism

In the globalised world, legal scholars are facing manifold challenges, including those deriving from the possibility of reading legal reality from multiple standpoints.[1] If we admit that nowadays globalisation urges legal theory to "a critical re-examination of its agenda, its heritage of ideas, and its conceptual tools",[2] then the comparatist will have to deal with instruments that need to be constantly retuned. As has been observed, "postmodernism suggests that truth, knowledge and even reality are all culturally relative and that human rationality is heterogeneous and diverse",[3] and therefore, "Law is always something particular, not just a generalised phenomenon, and it is culture-specific because its manifestations depend on socio-cultural settings that differ from place to place and through time".[4]

In this scenario, Environmental Law embodies an emblematic post-modern science for being regulated by principles,[5] and, indeed, it represents a fertile ground to explore how elements, only apparently external to the Law, influence and concur to the production of legal norms and, ultimately, might constitute themselves Law. The same metaphorical image of liquidity elaborated by Z. Bauman for describing our modernity, has been used by W. Menski to illustrate the current global panorama of Law. Considering the law "as a liquid entity that takes different shapes and forms depending on its environment, as does water itself", this Author has presented three models suitable for outlining how the

1 See William Twining, *Globalisation & Legal Theory* (Butterworths 2000) 252 ff.
2 Ibid 10.
3 Werner Menski, *Comparative Law in a Global Context. The Legal Systems of Asia and Africa* (2nd edn, CUP 2006) 11.
4 Ibid 179.
5 Cf Nicolas De Sadeleer, *Environmental Principles: from Political Slogans to Legal Rules* (OUP 2002); Domenico Amirante (ed), *La forza normativa dei principi. Il contributo del diritto ambientale alla teoria generale* (Cedam 2006).

DOI: 10.4324/9781003175308-15

legal systems of the world "manage legal diversity and pluri-legality",[6] drawing up a classification based on the well-known model of law as a kite.[7] In this perspective, legal pluralism represents a point of departure to initiate a dutiful research exercise of innovative framing of Environmental Law, which could fit with liquidity. As a conception emerging "when other systems of law were found working in reality together with the 'law', whether in harmony or in conflict", legal pluralism evidently "must be questioned and discussed not limited to non-Western society but extended to Western society as well".[8]

The present work is an attempt to investigate the circulation and the dissemination in the world map of the remedy of public interest litigation, starting from its widely perceived original ideals as elaborated in the United States, and its application to environmental disputes.

Considering that in many countries of Asia, Africa and Latin America one can find legal tools sharing the deeper purpose of this kind of litigation, a comparison between the Indian "social action litigation"[9] and some judicial actions provided for in the Brazilian legal system will be undertaken.

2. The Origin of Public Interest Litigation and the 'Mirror' of Environmental Disputes

The phenomenon of 'environmental constitutionalism', implying "the recognition that the environment is a proper subject for protection in constitutional texts and for vindication by constitutional courts worldwide"[10] and offering "a *new way of thinking* about the relationship among individuals, sovereign governments, and the environment",[11] draws attention to the relevance of adjudication in environmental matters. Indeed, in particular in those areas where the protection of the environment is rooted in social, ethical, philosophical and religious values, permeating the constitutional fabric, the Judiciary appears to play a pro-active role, to the extent of guaranteeing the enforcement of substantive rights, recognising also procedural remedies for this purpose.

6 Werner Menski, 'The Liquidity of Law as a Challenge to Global Theorising' [2014] XI *Jura Gentium* 19, 24.
7 Werner Menski, 'Remembering and Applying Legal Pluralism: Law as Kite Flying' in Seán Patrick Donlan and Lukas Heckendorn Urscheler (eds), *Concepts of Law: Comparative, Jurisprudential, and Social Science Perspectives* (Routledge 2014).
8 Masaji Chiba, *Legal Pluralism: Toward a General Theory through Japanese Legal Culture* (Tokai University Press 1989) 1-4.
9 According to the definition coined by Upendra Baxi, 'Taking Suffering Seriously: Social Action Litigation in the Supreme Court of India' in Rajeev Dhavan, R. Sudarshan and Salman Khurshid (eds), *Judges and the Judicial Power* (Sweet&Maxwell-Tripathi 1985).
10 James R. May and Erin Daly, *Global Environmental Constitutionalism* (CUP 2014) 1.
11 Ibid 49. On the topic see also Louis J. Kotze, *Global Environmental Constitutionalism in the Anthropocene* (Hart Publishing 2016).

If we take account of one of the peculiarities of environmental law, namely that it concerns collective or diffuse interests,[12] environmental cases cannot but "challenge conventional standing practices".[13]

Traditionally the origins of the issues concerning *locus standi* are traced back to "a new model of civil litigation" – defined by A. Chayes as "public law litigation" – recorded in federal courts of the United States at the end of the Seventies.[14] In contrast to the primal idea that "the lawsuit is a vehicle for settling disputes between private parties about private rights",[15] it was characterised by a "sprawling and amorphous" party structure, conjugated with the conception of lawsuit as "a grievance about the operation of public policy", which results in an idea of relief not devised following the rules of substantive liability, but "fashioned ad hoc on flexible and broadly remedial lines, often having important consequences for many persons including absentees".[16] The development in the USA of this new paradigm of adjudication, opposed to that of positive law, has been identified in the transition from a system "in which social and economic arrangements were remitted to autonomous private action" to "a regulatory system where these arrangements are the product of positive enactment".[17] The tension existing between these two archetypes emerges quite clearly from the reading of the decision *Sierra Club v. Morton* taken in 1972 by the Supreme Court,[18] in particular from the dissenting opinion of Justice Blackmun, who suggests an expansion of traditional standing by recognising "the interest of one who has a provable, sincere, dedicated, and established status" as being ultimately a bearer of environmental values.[19]

While in the United States public interest litigation has served as a great tool for the advancement of the enforcement of civil rights – in a context where the battle on the equality clause has found an answer in the Judiciary since the Sixties[20] – in its diffusion on a global scale it has gained new meanings.

Obviously, the perspective of public interest litigation is only one of the several points of view from which one can explore the subject of adjudication in environmental matter, but here it is considered the most expressive of the relationship existing between Environment and Constitutions. As others rightly pointed out, while the mainstream approach to an investigation on this topic in a comparative perspective focuses on the presence or not of a specialised judicial forum in the legal systems, "the degree to which a court is willing/able to build

12 May and Daly (n 10) 87.
13 Ibid 129.
14 Cf Abram Chayes, 'The Role of the Judge in Public Law Litigation' [1976] 89(7) *Harvard Law Review* 1281 ff.
15 Ibid 1282.
16 Ibid 1302.
17 Ibid 1304.
18 *Sierra Club v. Morton, Secretary of the Interior, et al.*, 405 U.S. 727 (1972).
19 Ibid, Justice Blackmun's dissenting opinion, 755 ff.
20 The reference is to the case *Brown v. Board of Education of Topeka*, 347 U.S. 483 (1954).

up a consistent and environmentally proactive jurisprudence is not determined by the existence or otherwise of a specialist environmental court, particularly in a jurisdictional sense".[21] In fact, if "*specialization* does not in itself solve the challenges of environmental adjudication", on the contrary one should agree with the opinion that "*bespoke* adjudicative rules" can represent a better solution for facing the peculiarities of environmental disputes, which involve procedural and technical aspects and also require evaluation and a fair balance between different values.[22]

However, although "*Brown* becomes a model for a long series of major policy changes initiated by the Warren and Burger Courts at the behest of groups conducting conscious litigation campaigns",[23] public interest litigation in the United States seems to have later experienced various twists and turns. Actually, scholars have underlined how this group engagement mechanism was weakened with time and ceased to grow.[24] On the contrary, in other constitutional experiences it found its fortune and its development, showing a "strong normative ethos of social justice".[25]

In the following pages, a brief survey of the worldwide spread of public interest litigation will be presented. In the numerous legal transplants that this model of adjudication has undergone, crossing the world in a multi-directional dialogue between East, West, North and South, the benchmark for evaluating its diffusion in different legal systems is represented by the expansion of *locus standi*. The latter may be deemed as the 'mirror' of this paradigm of litigation, reflecting the ultimate purpose of this legal arrangement.

3. The Southern 'Geoscheme' of Collective Judicial Remedies for the Protection of the Environment

Moving beyond the US model, whose aforementioned setbacks in the development might also have depended on some characteristics of the American legal and political tradition,[26] the aims of public interest litigation have migrated into or evolved in other constitutional experiences, where it found fertile humus for its advance.

21 Emma Lees, 'Adjudication Systems' in Emma Lees and Jorge E. Viñuales (eds), *The Oxford Handbook of Comparative Environmental Law* (OUP 2019) 807.
22 Ibid 792 and 808 respectively.
23 Martin Shapiro, 'The United States' in C. Neal Tate and Torbjörn Vallinder (eds), *The Global Expansion of Judicial Power* (New York University Press 1995) 47.
24 Cf Werner Menski, Ahmad Rafay Alam, Mehreen Kasuri Raza, *Public Interest Litigation in Pakistan* (Platinum-Pakistan Law House 2000) 114–116.
25 May and Daly (n 10) 137.
26 On these features see Herbert Jacob, 'Courts and Politics in the United States' in Herbert Jacob, Erhard Blankenburg, et al. (eds), *Courts, Law, and Politics in Comparative Perspective* (Yale University Press 1996) 28.

This is probably due to two sets of reasons. The first is related to the emergence of a new category of rights in the second post-war period, expression of the development of social democratic constitutionalism, i.e. social rights. Secondly, one must be aware of the much closer attention paid to welfare in the post-colonial constitutional charters in comparison to the Western legal tradition, because of its tight connection with the protection of fundamental rights.

These processes have led to a different consideration of the collective dimension in certain legal systems of the South, in which the element of diversity, as the main feature of these countries, played a fundamental role.

With the term 'diversity', I refer, in a wider sense, both to multiculturality, namely the presence in the territories of the States that have lived a colonial experience of a plurality of ethnic groups, religions and traditions, but also to the differences existing under the economic profile in the respective societies. These factors – with the entry into force of the current Constitutions – have imposed the need to manage this diversity, by attributing to the equal protection clause a different value compared to that given by the 'North' with its monocultural layout and substantial economic homogeneity.

In this framework, the consciousness of the importance of environmental protection has increased worldwide during the Eighties, also thanks to the impetus given by international law.

In 2019, among the member States of the United Nations, 153 Constitutions included – in various ways – provisions aimed at protecting the Environment.[27] Taking the cue from a taxonomy recently proposed for the classification of the constitutions of the world in accordance with the criteria of environmental protection, it is possible to observe that the countries of the South of the world have a greater aptitude towards the safeguard of the Environment.[28] Evidently the Southern scenario has responded differently to the universal (and, probably, universalistic) tendencies, for having in its own cultural fabric all the elements to make its voice heard louder.

However, it is worth asking: among the legal systems that recognise a real right to a healthy environment in their constitutional charter, how many of them qualify this right as really justiciable? Instead, in how many countries is this result achieved even in the absence of an express provision of a real right?

Giving an answer to these interrogatives turns out to be essential.[29] In fact, "environmental rights are similar to other social and economic rights that are routinely vindicated in the world's courts in that remedying their violation often entails expenditure of significant resources", albeit they "are different in that they often pit human rights claims against each other".[30] This finding leads

27 Domenico Amirante, 'L'ambiente preso sul serio. Il percorso accidentato del costituzionalismo ambientale' [2019] *Fascicolo Speciale, Diritto pubblico comparato ed europeo* 1.

28 Ibid 3–4.

29 On this point, May and Daly (n 10) 109 ff distinguish between "independent", "dependent", "derivative" and "dormant" environmental rights.

30 Ibid 90.

to one of the major questions concerning social and economic rights, which has been acutely summed up in the formula of "the justiciability dilemma".[31] The latter brings to mind the doctrinal debates, following one another through the years, about the role of the Judiciary in the contemporary democracies, launched since judicial review was identified as a counter-majoritarian force in legal systems.[32]

Indeed, an effective protection of the environment requires both the recognition at a constitutional level – textually or via the activity of the Courts – of substantive rights for this purpose and a constitutional justice system whose access may be allowed to individuals or at least to social actors *sensu lato* in this matter. This combination, which goes beyond the mere human rights perspective and prescinds from the injury/remedy pair of the classical adjudication, seems to have been the cornerstone of the advancement of environmental constitutionalism worldwide, as the experiences of the countries mentioned below demonstrate.

In Asia, besides India, higher courts of Pakistan and Bangladesh have given new life to public interest environmental litigation through the use of procedural remedies under the writ jurisdiction and their hermeneutical activity, because "the power to do complete justice gave them the opportunity to be relaxed in environmental standing".[33] This occurs, moreover, in spite of the lack in the respective Constitutions of a formal provision recognising a right to a healthy or clean environment, although in the case of Bangladesh environmental protection appears among the "fundamental principles of state policy".[34] On close examination, the jurisprudence elaborated in Pakistan and Bangladesh on environmental concerns has recently been tested in dealing with the issue of climate change[35] and the problem of plastic pollution,[36] respectively.

With regard to the African continent, two important examples of the spreading of public interest litigation come from the legal systems of South Africa and Kenya.

31 Octavio Luiz Motta Ferraz, 'Between Usurpation and Abdication? The Right to Health in the Courts of Brazil and South Africa' in Oscar Vilhena, Upendra Baxi and Frans Viljoen (eds), *Transformative Constitutionalism: Comparing the Apex Courts of Brazil, India and South Africa* (Pretoria University Law Press-National Law University, Delhi Press 2014) 378 ff.

32 Cf Alexander M. Bickel, *The Least Dangerous Branch. The Supreme Court at the Bar of Politics* (2nd edn, Yale University Press 1986).

33 Jona Razzaque, *Public Interest Environmental Litigation in India, Pakistan and Bangladesh* (Kluwer Law International 2004) 198 for the quotation.

34 Cf article 18-A of the current Constitution of Bangladesh. About Pakistan see also Menski, Rafay Alam, Kasuri Raza (n 24).

35 The reference is to the case decided by the Lahore High Court *Asghar Leghari v. Federation of Pakistan, etc.* (2015) W.P. No. 25501/2015.

36 See the order of the 20th of January 2020 taken by the High Court Division of the Supreme Court on the Writ Petition No. 14941 of 2019, available at www.elaw.org/plastic%5CBD_BELA_Plastic_20Jan20.

The former, in the framework of section 24 of the Constitution,[37] according to section 32(1) of the National Environmental Management Act of 1998 has further extended the *locus standi* in environmental litigation compared to section 38 of the same charter, which guarantees the enforcement of the Bill of Rights through an already extensive standing rule.[38] The latter, with the Constitution of 2010, introduced explicit provisions in order to protect the environment, i.e. articles 42 and 69.[39] However, in the context of the wider standing of article 22, article 70 specifies *inter alia* that in case of the enforcement of environmental rights the applicant "does not have to demonstrate that any person has incurred loss or suffered injury".[40]

Finally, reaching the last stage of the journey that from the South comes to 'another' South, the Latin American panorama shows a multifaceted scenario on the remedies for the protection of the environment. Despite the terminological differences depending on the lack of English colonisation and the prevalent presence of the Spanish one, many countries know judicial tools whose purposes are similar to those of public interest litigation.

In this respect, besides Brazil, two legal systems should be mentioned as mere examples. The Argentinian Constitution, dating back to the Nineties, contemplates the *acción de amparo*, which in cases regarding the right to a healthy environment can be introduced not only by the affected party and the *defensor del pueblo*, but also by associations that have environmental protection among their main objectives.[41] The more recent charter of the Plurinational State of Bolivia contemplates the possibility for individuals, acting in a private capacity or as the representatives of a community, to file the *acción popular* for the protection of rights and collective interests concerning the environment.[42] In both legal systems, the issue of standing rules has been addressed in depth by the respective apex courts. Over the years the *Corte Suprema de Justicia de la Nación* has defined the spaces of the *amparo colectivo ambiental*,[43] while the *Tribunal Constitucional*

37 The provision recognises, *inter alia*, everyone's right to "an environment that is not harmful to their health or well-being".

38 See Tumai Murombo, 'Strengthening locus standi in public interest environmental litigation: Has leadership moved from the United States to South Africa?' [2010] 6(2) *Law, Environment and Development Journal* 163, www.lead-journal.org/content/10163.pdf.

39 Article 42 recognises everyone's "right to a clean and healthy environment" of a wide-ranging tenor, besides which a series of State's obligations and a duty of individuals for environmental protection can be found in article 69.

40 The goal of effectiveness in environmental disputes has also been pursued through the institution of a specialised court according to article 162. See the recent judgment of the Environment and Land Court at Machakos, Elc. Petition No. E06 of 2020, in *John Muthui & 19 others v. County Government of Kitui & 7 others* [2020] eKLR.

41 Cf articles 41 and 43 of the current Constitution of Argentina.

42 Cf articles 135 and 136 of the Constitution of Plurinational State of Bolivia, 2009. It should be underlined that bringing a proceeding of *acción popular* is mandatory for the *Ministerio Público* and the *Defensor del Pueblo*.

43 See, among the many, the recent case *Asociación Argentina de Abogados Ambientalistas de la Patagonia c/ Santa Cruz, Provincia de y otros s/ amparo ambiental, 26/04/2016, Fallos 339:515.*

Plurinacional dealt also with the theme of the link between the protection of indigenous people's rights and the safeguard of the Environment.[44]

In conclusion, the possibility to investigate the commingling of legal systems pertaining to Africa, Asia and Latin America as regards adjudication, already covered for some topics,[45] would deserve further consideration in environmental matters. From an initial analysis, a *fil rouge* seems to connect many of the pieces of the Southern hemisphere together in a whole, which is made up of giving adequate value, in the trial, to the shared nature of environmental rights.

4. Toward a Transversal Comparison Between Asia and America Latina in the Context of "Transformative Constitutionalism"

Considering that the idea of an openness towards collective environmental remedies has spread by now, finding formal recognition in various constitutional charters and acknowledgement by the Judiciary, it is possible to try a comparison between two particular legal systems, namely those of India and Brazil.

From an overall picture, in the public law perspective, these countries seem to have nothing in common, in particular if we consider that from their colonial past both have inherited – according to the classical taxonomies founded on the concept of legal family – a bond with different legal traditions.[46] However, observing them, an extraordinary congeries of ethnicities, religions, customs, traditions and economic conditions, which appears in the constitutional fabric, is silhouetted against the historical background and a high rate of diversity lurks inside their vast borders. This data has led to certain social outcomes and has found an answer in their current legal systems.

If it is true that

> constitutional law can similarly tell stories about how conflicts between citizens and their governors and among citizens themselves are removed from where they arise, the public arenas, and transformed into controversies under constitutional law to be settled by constitutional or supreme courts,[47]

44 See Ariel Pérez Castellón, 'Justicia constitucional en Bolivia. Desafíos y oportunidades para la tutela de los derechos de los pueblos indígenas en conflictos socio-ambientales' [2013] IV(2) *Revista Catalana De Dret Ambiental* 1, www.raco.cat/index.php/rcda/article/view/273856.

45 Daniel Bonilla Maldonado, *Constitutionalism of the Global South. The Activist Tribunals of India, South Africa, and Colombia* (CUP 2013). In particular, cf Mia Caielli, *Cittadini e giustizia costituzionale. Contributo allo studio dell'actio popularis* (Giappichelli 2015).

46 Cf Mathias Siems, *Comparative Law* (CUP 2014) 88.

47 Günter Frankenberg, 'Comparing Constitutions: Ideas, Ideals, and Ideology – toward a Layered Narrative' [2006] 4(3) *International Journal of Constitutional Law* 439, 449.

looking at the constitutional charters of India and Brazil there is much to discover. More than fourteen thousand kilometres separate New Delhi from Brasilia, but an unexplored affinity between the Ashoka Chakra of twenty-four spokes and the positivist motto *Ordem e Progresso* crops out. This resemblance, which spans across the globe from the Tropic of Cancer to the Tropic of Capricorn, unites the north of the Equator with its south and connects the East with the West in a place where the ideals meet.

If ideals are those that "capture the programmatic, utopian, or, at any rate, speculative visions believed to be enshrined in a constitutional document",[48] Indian and Brazilian experiences are closer than they appear.

With reference to the already-mentioned classification elaborated by W. Menski and founded on three major types of legal systems, while Type 1 explains the typical approach of Eurozone countries that aspire to a uniform law, on the contrary, legal systems belonging to Type 2 give more space to indigenous or 'original' peoples, recognising their particular subjective positions in terms of rights, and those of Type 3 go as far as granting the coexistence of religious/community oriented personal laws beside the general laws.[49]

In the framework of this taxonomy, the analysis will be conducted from a particular perspective, the one that recently has united the constitutional systems of India and Brazil under the same label of "transformative constitutionalism".[50] By the latter, some scholars have referred to the legal experiences of India, South Africa and Brazil that through the constituent process have broken with their past, going towards the elaboration of audacious constitutional texts finalized to the establishment of "a new political-moral foundation for each society", with a strong commitment to the implementation of rights, to which has contributed the pro-active role of the apex courts giving rise to "a new world-wide wave of constitutional adjudication".[51] This classification has the merit to focus the attention on "the transformative power of constitutions", which requires dealing with "constitutions as culture and as the imaginations of community" and not only with "constitutions as law and order".[52]

Looking at the evolution of the societies from an anthropological perspective, India has experienced over the centuries – with certain exceptions – a "social stratification of races", first because of the overlapping of invading populations with local communities and second due to the caste system.[53] On the other hand, the origins of Brazilian culture have mainly been traced in a Lusitanian core, but with a strong presence of Indios and African elements, insomuch that

48 Ibid 441.
49 Menski (n 7).
50 See Vilhena, Baxi and Viljoen (eds) (n 31).
51 Ibid 3.
52 Frankenberg (n 47) 450–451.
53 Percival Spear, *Storia dell'India* (2nd edn, Rizzoli 1973) 17.

one of its principal features was identified in the tradition of "social and ethnic democracy".[54]

Therefore, not only with respect to the Indian legal system, but also in *terrae Brasilis*, "*embora prevaleça na tradição brasileira uma 'aparente' hegemonia das formas jurídicas estatais*", the perspective of legal pluralism needs to be taken into due consideration,[55] in order to understand the connection existing in their Constitutions between economic order, welfare, environmental protection and social justice.

4.1. The Public Interest Litigation in India

At the beginning of the Eighties, Justice Bhagwati of the Supreme Court of India identified the heart of public interest litigation in the effort "to secure observance of the constitutional or legal rights, benefits and privileges conferred upon the vulnerable sections of the community and to reach social justice to them".[56]

Evidently, the development in India of this particular kind of action intersects with the institutional background that precedes and follows the so-called Emergency era.[57] In fact, since the first steps taken towards the definitive affirmation of the well-known 'basic structure doctrine',[58] a complex mosaic made of constitutional amendments and tensions with the Judiciary led to the overthrow of the traditional rules that governed the trial.

Articles 48-A and 51-A, containing express provisions regarding the protection of the Environment, were introduced in the Indian charter with the *Constitution (Forty-Second Amendment) Act, 1976* and they represent, therefore, the outcome of that historical period. The inclusion of the former in Part IV, relative to *Directive Principles of State Policy*, and of the latter (with its letter *g*) in a new Part IV-A, dedicated instead to *Fundamental Duties*, has contributed to "weaving environmental law buzzwords . . . into Article 21 of the Constitution".[59] Although in the adoption of these two norms a role must be recognized to

54 Gilberto Freyre, *Interpretazione del Brasile* (Fratelli Bocca Editori 1954) 26 and 83.

55 As demonstrated in the work by Antonio Carlos Wolkmer, *Pluralismo Jurídico. Fundamentos de uma nova cultura no Direito* (3rd edn, Editora Alfa Omega 2001) 90 for the quotation.

56 These words are used by Justice Bhagwati in the judgment *People's Union for Democratic Rights v. India*, AIR 1982 SC 1473, as reported by Satyaranjan Purushottam Sathe, *Judicial Activism in India. Transgressing Borders and Enforcing Limits* (2nd edn, OUP 2003) 207. About this topic, see also Gokulesh Sharma, *Human Rights and Social Justice* (Deep & Deep Publications 2007).

57 Among the wide literature about public interest litigation, see Mamta Rao, *Public Interest Litigation in India: A Renaissance in Social Justice* (2nd edn, Eastern Book Company, 2004); Anuj Bhuwania, *Courting the People: Public Interest Litigation in Post-Emergency India* (CUP 2017).

58 See Manoj Mate, 'Two Paths to Judicial Power: The Basic Structure Doctrine and Public Interest Litigation in Comparative Perspective' [2010] 12 *San Diego International Law Journal* 175, https://digital.sandiego.edu/ilj/vol12/iss1/7.

59 Harish Salve, 'Justice Between Generations: Environment and Social Justice' in Bhupinder Nath Kirpal, Ashok H. Desai, et al. (eds), *Supreme but not Infallible. Essays in Honour of the Supreme Court of India* (OUP 2004) 368.

international law, in view of the Stockholm Declaration of 1972, a more careful analysis highlights further and more relevant aspects. In fact, they fall within a broader constitutional revision project, regarding which it is enough to call the attention on the innovations brought in the Preamble and on the new article 39-A. As observed by some scholars, with this reform "India turned more openly towards certain indigenous concepts to restructure its own model of 'good governance' along ancient Indian principles", indeed the model of public interest litigation developed shortly afterwards finding its roots in "the ancient Hindu strategy of opening the door of the court to anyone who has a grievance", which is connected to the concept of *rājadharma*.[60]

However, the new provisions fit into a constitutional context where the ideal of social justice was already present, for being particularly felt by the emerging democracy, because of its connection with the Hindu jurisprudence of the origins.[61] In this respect, suffice it to look at articles 13, 32 and 38, which embody a triad constituted by the protection of fundamental rights, their enforcement and the welfare of the people. As known, the procedural right of article 32 has represented the flywheel to guarantee substantial rights, essentially through three expedients: expanding the jurisdiction of the Supreme Court beyond writs, deformalising the procedural rules and extending *locus standi*.[62]

Firstly, an extensive interpretation of "appropriate proceedings" has allowed every remedy for the enforcement of fundamental rights to be admitted, because "the procedure, being merely a hand-maiden of justice, should not stand in the way to access to justice".[63] About the second aspect, "the courts allowed informality of procedure by entertaining letters written to judges or to the court as petitions or took cognizance of matters on their own (*suo motu*)".[64] Referring to *locus standi*, an environmental case has paved the way to a wider interpretation of traditional rules, which will lead to the elaboration of the two new procedural categories of 'representative standing' and 'citizen standing'.[65] In *Municipal Council Ratlam v. Shri Vardhichand*,[66] Justice Krishna Iyer, premising that "social Justice is due to the

60 Menski (n 3) 265 and 268.

61 See Vikram Singh Jaswal and Shweta Jaswal *Justice V.R. Krishna Iyer's Concept of Social Justice* (Deep & Deep Publications 2011) 37 ff.

62 On the relationship between procedural aspects of public interest litigation and judicial activism, see Nilanjana Jain, *Judicial Activism in India with Special Reference to the Quest for Social Justice* (Kalpaz Publications 2013) 62 ff.

63 Mahendra P. Singh, *V.N. Shukla's Constitution of India* (11th edn, Eastern Book Company 2010) 325, who refers to *M.C. Mehta v. Union of India* (1987) 1 SCC 395, 406. With reference to the environmental matters, see Razzaque (n 33) 183 ff and Shyam Divan and Armin Rosencranz, *Environmental Law and Policy in India: Cases, Material & Statutes* (2nd edn, OUP 2002) 122 ff.

64 Sathe (n 56) 203.

65 See Clark D. Cunningham, 'Public Interest Litigation in Indian Supreme Court: A Study in the Light of American Experience' [1987] 29 *Journal of the Indian Law Institute* 494.

66 Supreme Court of India, *Municipal Council, Ratlam v. Shri Vardhichand and Ors.*, 1980 AIR 1622.

people", emphasised how "the judiciary must be informed by the broader principle of access to justice necessitated by the conditions of the developing countries and obligate by Article 38 of the Constitution".[67] In particular, citizen standing has found its full recognition in the proceeding *S. P. Gupta v. President of India*, also known as *First Judges' Transfer Case*,[68] in which Justice Bhagwati affirmed that "in public interest litigation . . . any citizen who is acting bona fide and who has sufficient interest has to be accorded standing".[69] In the years that followed this judgment, at least four important cases relative to environmental matters were decided by the Supreme Court on the basis of this principle[70] and, in the post-emergency era, "constitutional interpretation almost assumed the dimensions of a new social movement that had as its principal mission the task of taking peoples' suffering seriously as almost the very essence of constitutional adjudication".[71]

However, from the strong commitment of the Judiciary for the affirmation of a right to a healthy environment and its constant implementation in the course of time,[72] which since 2010 has also involved the National Green Tribunal,[73] emerges how in India the road to environmental protection crossed that of social justice. Although also Jaina and Sikh traditions are permeated by ecological philosophies,[74] this appears as the result of a process that slowly has brought to light the ancient Hindu cosmovision synthesised in the Sanskrit concept *Vasudhaiv Kutumbakam*.[75] The respect for Mother Earth, which embodies the idea that each entity – human or otherwise – inhabiting the world is part of one family, implies respect for social justice as the hallmark of the Indian cultural heritage.[76]

4.2. The Ação Popular *and* Ação Civil Pública *in Brazil*

The protection of the Environment in the Brazilian Constitution is primarily entrusted to Chapter VI, titled *Do Meio Ambiente*, which, although constituted by just one article, has a really wide content.

67 The quotation is reported by M.A.A. Baig, *Environment, Law and Justice* (Regency 1996) 19.
68 AIR 1982 SC 149
69 The quotation is reported by Sathe (n 56) 217.
70 See Divan and Rosencranz (n 63) 138–139.
71 Upendra Baxi, 'The Avatars of Indian Judicial Activism: Explorations in the Geographies of [In]justice' in S.K. Verma and Kusum (eds), *Fifty Years of the Supreme Court of India. Its Grasp and Reach* (OUP 2000) 157.
72 For a detailed analysis of the case-law, see Geetanjoy Sahu, *Environmental Jurisprudence and the Supreme Court. Litigation, Interpretation, Implementation* (Orient BlackSwan 2014).
73 Cf Gitanjali Nain Gill, *Environmental Justice in India: The National Green Tribunal* (Routledge 2017).
74 Christopher Key Chapple, 'India' in Willis Jenkins, Mary Evelyn Tucker and John Grim (eds), *Routledge Handbook of Religion and Ecology* (Routledge 2017) 171 ff.
75 Onkar Prasad Dwivedi, 'Hindu Religion and Environmental Well-being' in Roger S. Gottlieb (ed), *The Oxford Handbook of Religion and Ecology* (OUP 2006) 160 ff.
76 See Jaswal and Jaswal (n 61) 5.

The central core of article 225 can be found in the *caput* and in its first paragraph. The former states that

> *todos têm direito ao meio ambiente ecologicamente equilibrado, bem de uso comum do povo e essencial à sadia qualidade de vida, impondo-se ao Poder Público e à coletividade o dever de defendê-lo e preservá-lo para as presentes e futuras gerações,*

while § 1 lists a series of measures and policies that public powers shall adopt *"para assegurar a efetividade desse direito"*.

It guarantees, therefore, a fundamental right[77] that has as its own object the Environment, qualified as a public asset belonging to the community, but from a perspective of *antropocentrismo alargado*, considering the reference to human health and well-being.[78] The right to an ecologically balanced environment, in its subjective and objective dimension connected to its characteristic of 'third-generation right',[79] has as a counterpart a duty of defence and preservation for the individuals and the State, which has led scholars to define it as a *direito circular*.[80]

It is worth underlining that article 225 is placed in Title VIII concerning the *Ordem Social*, where the programmatic norms prevail,[81] for being intimately linked to Chapter II of Title II relative to social rights, but it is very concrete in its content. This part of the charter, in fact, needs to be read jointly with Title VII about the *Ordem Econômica e Financeira*.[82] If article 193 opens Title VIII with a general provision whereby "the social order is . . . aimed at social well-being and justice", article 170, by providing that "the economic order . . . is intended to ensure everyone a life with dignity, in accordance with the dictates of social justice," refers to a series of principles, including environmental protection (VI). Therefore, the idea of sustainable development, featuring also in article 225 with reference to the present and future generations, is set in a composite picture where economic growth must be conjugated with environmental protection, social justice and well-being.[83]

77 See Andreas Joachim Krell, 'Comentario ao artigo 225, caput' in José Joaquim Gomes Canotilho, Gilmar Ferreira Mendes, et al. (eds), *Comentários à Constituição do Brasil* (Saraiva/Almedina 2013) 2078.

78 Ibid 2080.

79 See, on this point, Supremo Tribunal Federal, ADI MC 3540–1/DF, judgment of 1.9.2005, Tribunal Pleno, Judge-Rapporteur Ministro Celso de Mello.

80 Krell (n 77) 2082.

81 Jorge Miranda, 'A Constituição de 1988. Uma Constituição de esperança' [2008] 45(179) *Revista de Informação Legislativa* 155, 160.

82 Marcus Orione Gonçalves Correia, 'Comentario ao artigo 193' in Canotilho, Mendes, et al. (eds) (n 77) 1892. The text of the Brazilian Constitution in English is available at https://www2.camara.leg.br/atividade-legislativa/legislacao/constituicao1988.

83 Cf Celso Antonio Pacheco Fiorillo, 'Comentario ao artigo 170, IV' in Canotilho, Mendes, et al. (eds) (n 77) 1813.

In this perspective, the role of indigenous people but also of non-indigenous traditional populations (among which the best known is that of Quilombolas), whose rights protection comes from articles 231 and 232 in one case and from article 215 in the other,[84] cannot be underestimated. In fact, if *"em cada terra indígena se encontra uma relação mágica entre os conhecimentos do povo e as manifestações da natureza, importando não só o místico como o fático do espaço territorial"*,[85] in Brazil the protection of the Environment passes also through the safeguarding of this cultural heritage. Lastly, besides the environmental values proper to the chthonic traditions, those belonging to religious beliefs – such as Catholicism or the cults of Umbanda or Candomblé – must be considered as well.[86]

On close examination, the term *Constituição cidadã*, used by the President of the National Constituent Assembly Ulysses Guimarães to define the charter in 1988, expressed the willingness to recognise 'new' rights deriving from collective requests and coming from the social substratum, which has paved the way to a pluralist and multicultural constitutionalism.[87]

This appears evident focusing the attention on those principles identified as supreme values of a "fraternal, pluralist and unprejudiced society, founded on social harmony" in the Preamble or in the reference in article 3 to the development of a "free, just and solidary society" (I) and the promotion of "the well-being of all" (IV) as fundamental objectives of the Federative Republic of Brazil. In the end, as underlined by scholars, the *Estado Ambiental* has its theoretical and legal foundation in the principle of solidarity.[88]

The qualification of the *meio ambiente ecologicamente equilibrado* as a diffuse right has brought the Constituent to provide for two judicial remedies that shall be considered as complementary. Article 5-LXXIII of the charter disciplines the *ação popular*, allowing every citizen to file it in order to nullify an act injurious to the environment. Instead, article 129-III includes, among the institutional functions of *Ministério Público*, that of *"promover o inquérito civil e a ação civil pública, para a proteção do patrimônio público e social, do meio ambiente e de outros interesses difusos e coletivos"*. However, the main legal source of these actions dates back to a period antecedent the advent of the Constitution of

84 See, on the topic, Márcia Dieguez Leuzinger, Kylie Lyngard, 'The Land Rights of Indigenous and Traditional Peoples in Brazil and Australia' [2016] 13(1) *Revista de Direito Internacional* 419.

85 Carlos Frederico Marés de Souza Filho 'Comentario aos artigos 231 e 232' in Canotilho, Mendes, et al. (eds) (n 77) 2152. See, in particular, article 231 § 1.

86 Anna Peterson, 'Latin America' in Jenkins, Tucker and Grim (eds) (n 74) 190 ff.

87 See Antonio Carlos Wolkmer, *História Do Direito No Brasil* (6th edn, Editora Forense 2012) 153–154.

88 José Rubens Morato Leite, Germana Parente Neiva Belchior and Carlos E. Peralta, 'Derecho Constitucional Ambiental Brasileño a la Luz de una Posmodernidad' [2014] V(1) *Revista Catalana De Dret Ambiental* 1.

1988, and it can be found respectively in the *Lei n. 4.717/1965* and in the *Lei n. 7.347/85*.

With respect to *ação popular*, although the standing to sue is recognised to individuals, it seems that it has not found a wide diffusion in environmental matters, considering its object and purpose, and not least its procedural requirements, all elements that appear also linked to its historical development.[89] On the contrary, the introduction of *ação civil pública "significou uma verdadeira revolução no sistema jurídico-processual brasileiro"*.[90]

Over the years the legal discipline of 1985 has been integrated by new legislations, e.g. the *Código de Defesa do Consumidor (Lei n. 8.078/90)*, because of the different fields in which it finds application. Among the numerous procedural aspects that need to be studied, three features deserve to be emphasised.

Firstly, its aim that relates to the liability for environmental damages, thus it *"tem como finalidade o cumprimento de obrigação de fazer, não-fazer, e/ou condenação pecuniária"*.[91] In addition, the *locus standi* is recognised by article 5 to institutional subjects or legal entities.[92] The action could be started indeed by the *União*, the *Estados*, the *Distrito Federal*, the *Municípios*, the *autarquias*, the *empresas públicas*, the *fundações*, the *sociedades de economia mista* and *associações*, beside the *Ministério Público*, which plays the most relevant role in this kind of disputes.[93] Lastly, it is worth mentioning the aspect of the effects *erga omnes* of the judgment given at the end of the proceeding, on which the Supremo Tribunal Federal recently spoke out, declaring the part of article 16 of the *Lei n. 7.347/85* regarding the limit of territorial competence unconstitutional.[94]

So, it seems that *"a lei da Ação Civil Pública foi, assim, instrumento tendente a consagrar, na nova conjuntura, o 'espaço' instituinte da cidadania ativa e da resolução de conflictos colectivos emergentes"*, as pointed out by A. C. Wolkmer.[95]

89 See the detailed analysis given by Poliana Círtia Costa Guimarães, 'Ação popular ambiental e efetividade: análise dos principais aspectos processuais' [2009] 13 *De jure: revista jurídica do Ministério Público do Estado de Minas Gerais* 349, who examines all the procedural interpretative challenges of this remedy.

90 Krell (n 77) 2085. On the topic see Marcelo Abelha, *Ação Civil Pública e Meio Ambiente* (3rd edn, Forense Universitária 2009).

91 Cf Roseane Ferrari, 'Análise Doutrinária E Jurisprudencial Sobre A Ação Civil Pública Como Instrumento Processual E Social De Defesa Do Meio Ambiente' [2015] 10(1) *Revista Eletrônica Direito e Política*, https://doi.org/10.14210/rdp.v10n1.p345-371, 387.

92 See Sílvia Cappelli, 'Ação Civil Pública Ambiental: A Experiência Brasileira. Análise de Jurisprudência' [2004] 2(5) *Cadernos do Programa de Pós-Graduação DIREITO/UFRGS* 682, 683 and the relevant case-law there reported.

93 Ibid 684.

94 See Supremo Tribunal Federal, *Recurso Extraordinário* (RE) 1101937, *Tema 1.075 da repercussão geral*.

95 Wolkmer (n 55) 295.

5. Some Concluding Remarks: The Social Dimensions and Traditional Elements as Driving Forces for the Environmental Revolution

The issue of legal standing, by affecting the access to justice, can determine the effectiveness of environmental adjudication.[96] The question therefore arises whether the extension of *locus standi* could be seen – through the different legal traditions and in the kaleidoscope of the various constitutionalisms – as a necessity to face the complexity of environmental dispute.

Public interest litigation in India "has changed the judicial process from adversarial to polycentric and adjudicative to legislative".[97] In Brazil, the *ação popular* and the *ação civil pública*, being both expression of the judicialisation of politics, represent a tool for defending the Constitution and protecting fundamental rights.[98] Basically, what brings these countries closer is not only the social function of *ius dicere* as a narrative of the decision-making process of the Judiciary, but also the weight given to the openness towards the social actors within the trial. This is related to two aspects that have brought to the attention of the Law other possible relationships with the Environment. There is to consider both the value attributed by the respective legal systems to the collective dimension, made of the earlier mentioned diversities and traditional cultures, and the very idea of Justice embraced by them, because it is designed to avoid that access to jurisdiction might be affected by unfavourable economic conditions.

It is therefore clear that the North of the globalised world should rethink the relation between Law and Environment, firstly under the epistemological profile.

In this perspective, some interesting suggestions come from two authors who have proposed an "ecolegal revolution" founded theoretically on an "ecoliteracy" and, in practice, on an "ecological design".[99] The point of departure of this possible change of mindset is represented by the acknowledgement that, in the Western legal tradition, while Law and hard sciences have rested for many centuries on the same mechanistic paradigm, they have recently lost definitively the possibility to meet, because for about thirty years science has experienced a shift in focus, giving way to a new worldview oriented to ecologic approaches, which is lacking instead in the field of law.[100] Moreover, the conceptual underpinning of "a new critical environmental law" – starting from the ascertainment that the traditional dichotomic legal thinking "remains too positivist for the complexity of

96 As emphasised by United Nations Environment Programme, *Environmental Rule of Law: First Global Report* (UNEP 2019), www.unep.org/resources/assessment/environmental-rule-law-first-global-report, 183 ff.

97 Sathe (n 56) 235.

98 See Amandino Teixeira Nunes Júnior, 'A Constituição de 1988 e a judicialização da política no Brasil' [2008] 45(178) *Revista de informação legislativa* 157.

99 Fritjof Capra and Ugo Mattei, *The Ecology of Law. Toward A Legal System in Tune with Nature and Community* (Berrett-Koehler 2015), in particular 169 ff.

100 Ibid 10 ff.

environmental issues" – has found the answer to the question of how to reconcile ecology and law in equipping Environmental Law with a theoretical apparatus as in the other legal disciplines and forcing it at the same time to confront other domains alien to the legal world.[101]

These two proposals seem to share a similar outlook, which in a long-term process calls attention to the ethic dimension. They evoke the idea of Ecosophy, recently understood as a form of 'wisdom of Earth' that reconciles Man, the cosmos and God,[102] or as an approach that sees the relation between the ecology of the environment, the ecology of society and of individuals in the light of an ethical-political stance.[103] This theory has the merit to underline how social and religious elements have a certain degree of influence in facing environmental issues.

Ultimately, the voices of post-colonial judges, with their environment-related jurisprudence, seem to be giving a strong contribution in 'pluralising' the theories of Justice.[104]

Bibliography

Abelha M., *Ação Civil Pública e Meio Ambiente* (3rd edn, Forense Universitária 2009).

Amirante D. (ed), *La forza normativa dei principi. Il contributo del diritto ambientale alla teoria generale* (Cedam 2006).

Amirante D., 'L'ambiente preso sul serio. Il percorso accidentato del costituzionalismo ambientale' [2019] *Fascicolo Speciale, Diritto pubblico comparato ed europeo* 1.

Baig M.A.A., *Environment, Law and Justice* (Regency 1996).

Baxi U., 'Taking Suffering Seriously: Social Action Litigation in the Supreme Court of India' in Rajeev Dhavan, R. Sudarshan and Salman Khurshid (eds), *Judges and the Judicial Power* (Sweet&Maxwell-Tripathi 1985).

Baxi U., 'On being an 'Activist' Judge not just an 'Active' One!', 11th Commonwealth Magistrates' and Judges' Association Triennial Conference, held in Cape Town on the 27th of October 1997, http://upendrabaxi.in/.

Baxi U., 'The Avatars of Indian Judicial Activism: Explorations in the Geographies of [In]justice' in S.K. Verma and Kusum (eds), *Fifty Years of the Supreme Court of India. Its Grasp and Reach* (OUP 2000).

Bhuwania A., *Courting the People: Public Interest Litigation in Post-Emergency India* (CUP 2017).

101 See Andreas Philippopoulos-Mihalopoulos, 'Looking for the Space between Law and Ecology' in Andreas Philippopoulos-Mihalopoulos (ed), *Law and Ecology: New Environmental Foundations* (Routledge 2011).

102 Cf Raimon Panikkar, *Ecosofia: la nuova saggezza per una spiritualità della terra* (Cittadella Editrice 1993), in particular 107 ff.

103 See Félix Guattari and Franco La Cecla, *Le tre ecologie* (Sonda 2019).

104 See Upendra Baxi, 'On being an 'activist' judge not just an 'active' one!', 11th Commonwealth Magistrates' and Judges' Association Triennial Conference, held in Cape Town on the 27th of October 1997, available at http://upendrabaxi.in/.

Bickel A.M., *The Least Dangerous Branch. The Supreme Court at the Bar of Politics* (2nd edn, Yale University Press 1986).

Bonilla Maldonado D., *Constitutionalism of the Global South. The Activist Tribunals of India, South Africa, and Colombia* (CUP 2013).

Caielli M., *Cittadini e giustizia costituzionale. Contributo allo studio dell'actio popularis* (Giappichelli 2015).

Canotilho J.J.G., Mendes G.F., et al. (eds), *Comentários à Constituição do Brasil* (Saraiva/Almedina 2013).

Cappelli S., 'Ação Civil Pública Ambiental: A Experiência Brasileira. Análise de Jurisprudência' (2004) 2(5) *Cadernos do Programa de Pós-Graduação DIREITO/UFRGS* 682.

Capra F. and Mattei U., *The Ecology of Law. Toward A Legal System in Tune with Nature and Community* (Berrett-Koehler 2015).

Chapple C.K., 'India' in Willis Jenkins, Mary Evelyn Tucker and John Grim (eds), *Routledge Handbook of Religion and Ecology* (Routledge 2017).

Chayes A., 'The Role of the Judge in Public Law Litigation' (1976) 89(7) *Harvard Law Review* 1281.

Chiba M., *Legal Pluralism: Toward a General Theory through Japanese Legal Culture* (Tokai University Press 1989).

Cunningham C.D., 'Public Interest Litigation in Indian Supreme Court: A Study in the Light of American Experience' (1987) 29 *Journal of the Indian Law Institute* 494.

De Sadeleer N., *Environmental Principles: from Political Slogans to Legal Rules* (OUP 2002).

Divan S. and Rosencranz A., *Environmental Law and Policy in India: Cases, Material & Statutes* (2nd edn, OUP 2002).

Dwivedi O.P., 'Hindu Religion and Environmental Well-being' in Roger S. Gottlieb (eds), *The Oxford Handbook of Religion and Ecology* (OUP 2006).

Ferrari R., 'Análise Doutrinária e Jurisprudencial Sobre a Ação Civil Pública Como Instrumento Processual e Social de Defesa do Meio Ambiente' (2015) 10(1) *Revista Eletrônica Direito e Política*, https://doi.org/10.14210/rdp.v10n1.p345-371.

Ferraz O.L.M., 'Between Usurpation and Abdication? The Right to Health in the Courts of Brazil and South Africa' in Oscar Vilhena, Upendra Baxi U. and Frans Viljoen (eds), *Transformative Constitutionalism: Comparing the Apex Courts of Brazil, India and South Africa* (Pretoria University Law Press – National Law University, Delhi Press 2014).

Frankenberg G., 'Comparing Constitutions: Ideas, Ideals, and Ideology – Toward a Layered Narrative' (2006) 4(3) *International Journal of Constitutional Law* 439.

Freyre G., *Interpretazione del Brasile* (Fratelli Bocca Editori 1954).

Gill G.N., *Environmental Justice in India: The National Green Tribunal* (Routledge 2017).

Guattari F. and La Cecla F., *Le tre ecologie* (Riccardo d'Este tr, Sonda 2019).

Guimarães P.C.C., 'Ação popular ambiental e efetividade: análise dos principais aspectos processuais' (2009) (13) *De jure: revista jurídica do Ministério Público do Estado de Minas Gerais* 349.

Jacob H., 'Courts and Politics in the United States' in Herbert Jacob, Erhard Blankenburg, et al. (eds), *Courts, Law, and Politics in Comparative Perspective* (Yale University Press 1996).

Jain N., *Judicial Activism in India with Special Reference to the Quest for Social Justice* (Kalpaz Publications 2013).

Kotze L.J., *Global Environmental Constitutionalism in the Anthropocene* (Hart Publishing 2016).

Lees E., 'Adjudication Systems' in Emma Lees and Jorge E. Viñuales (eds), *The Oxford Handbook of Comparative Environmental Law* (OUP 2019).

Leuzinger M.D. and Lyngard K., 'The Land Rights of Indigenous and Traditional Peoples in Brazil and Australia' (2016) 13(1) *Revista de Direito Internacional* 419.

Mate M., 'Two Paths to Judicial Power: The Basic Structure Doctrine and Public Interest Litigation in Comparative Perspective' (2010) 12 *San Diego International Law Journal* 175, https://digital.sandiego.edu/ilj/vol12/iss1/7.

May J.R. and Daly E., *Global Environmental Constitutionalism* (CUP 2014).

Menski W., *Comparative Law in a Global Context. The Legal Systems of Asia and Africa* (2nd edn, CUP 2006).

Menski W., 'Remembering and Applying Legal Pluralism: Law as Kite Flying' in Seán Patrick Donlan and Lukas Heckendorn Urscheler (eds), *Concepts of Law: Comparative, Jurisprudential, and Social Science Perspectives* (Routledge 2014a).

Menski W., 'The Liquidity of Law as a Challange to Global Theorising' (2014b) XI *Jura Gentium* 19.

Menski W., Alam A.R. and Raza M.K., *Public Interest Litigation in Pakistan* (Platinum Publishing and Pakistan Law House 2000).

Miranda J., 'A Constituição de 1988. Uma Constituição de esperança' (2008) 45(179) *Revista de Informação Legislativa* 155, 160.

Morato Leite J.R., Neiva Belchior G.P. and Peralta C.E., 'Derecho Constitucional Ambiental Brasileño a la Luz de una Posmodernidad' (2014) V(1) *Revista Catalana De Dret Ambiental* 1.

Murombo T., 'Strengthening Locus Standi in Public Interest Environmental Litigation: Has Leadership Moved from the United States to South Africa?' (2010) 6(2) *Law, Environment and Development Journal* 163, www.lead-journal.org/content/10163.pdf.

Panikkar R., *Ecosofia: la nuova saggezza per una spiritualità della terra* (Cittadella Editrice 1993).

Pérez Castellón A., 'Justicia constitucional en Bolivia. Desafíos y oportunidades para la tutela de los derechos de los pueblos indígenas en conflictos socio-ambientales' (2013) IV(2) *Revista Catalana De Dret Ambiental* 1, www.raco.cat/index.php/rcda/article/view/273856.

Peterson A., 'Latin America' in Willis Jenkins, Mary Evelyn Tucker and John Grim (eds), *Routledge Handbook of Religion and Ecology* (Routledge 2017).

Philippopoulos-Mihalopoulos A., 'Looking for the Space between Law and Ecology' in Andreas Philippopoulos-Mihalopoulos (ed), *Law and Ecology: New Environmental Foundations* (Routledge 2011).

Rao M., *Public Interest Litigation in India: A Renaissance in Social Justice* (2nd edn, Eastern Book Company 2004).

Razzaque J., *Public Interest Environmental Litigation in India, Pakistan and Bangladesh* (Kluwer Law International 2004).

Sahu G., *Environmental Jurisprudence and the Supreme Court. Litigation, Interpretation, Implementation* (Orient BlackSwan 2014).

Salve H., 'Justice Between Generations: Environment and Social Justice' in Bhupinder Nath Kirpal, Ashok H. Desai, et al. (eds), *Supreme but not Infallible. Essays in Honour of the Supreme Court of India* (OUP 2004).
Sathe S.P., *Judicial Activism in India. Transgressing Borders and Enforcing Limits* (2nd edn, OUP 2003).
Shapiro M., 'The United States' in C. Neal Tate and Torbjörn Vallinder (eds), *The Global Expansion of Judicial Power* (New York University Press 1995).
Sharma G., *Human Rights and Social Justice* (Deep & Deep Publications 2007).
Siems M., *Comparative Law* (CUP 2014).
Singh J.V. and Jaswal S., *Justice V.R. Krishna Iyer's Concept of Social Justice* (Deep & Deep Publications 2011).
Singh M.P., *V.N. Shukla's Constitution of India* (11th edn, Eastern Book Company 2010).
Spear P., *Storia dell'India* (2nd edn, Rizzoli 1973).
Teixeira Nunes Júnior A., 'A Constituição de 1988 e a judicialização da política no Brasil' (2008) 45(178) *Revista de informação legislativa* 157.
Twining W., *Globalisation & Legal Theory* (Butterworths 2000).
Vilhena O., Baxi U. and Viljoen F. (eds), *Transformative Constitutionalism: Comparing the Apex Courts of Brazil, India and South Africa* (Pretoria University Law Press – National Law University, Delhi Press 2014).
Wolkmer A.C., *Pluralismo Jurídico. Fundamentos de uma nova cultura no Direito* (3rd edn, Editora Alfa Omega 2001).
Wolkmer A.C., *História Do Direito No Brasil* (6th edn, Editora Forense 2012).

12 The Enforcement of New Environmental Rights Through the Courts

Problems and Possible Solutions

Silvia Bagni

1. Introduction: The Need for a New Environmental Legal Paradigm, Based on an Ecosystem Approach

The attention paid by Earth and Environmental Science scholars to the limits of human exploitation of natural resources while respecting the cycles of regeneration, is certainly not a new fact. Reconstructing historically the concept of 'sustainability', Ulrich Grober recalls how the term was scientifically used for the first time by Hans Carl von Carlowitz in his treatise *Sylvicultura oeconomica* in 1713.[1]

Looking for traces of an ecosystem approach to the history of law, Michele Carducci went even further back in time, to the Iroquois' Constitution, probably dating from the 11th century, and to the Forest Charter of 1217.[2]

The international community already began to question the sustainability of our model of economic development and lifestyle during the 1972 United Nations Conference on the Human Environment, after a report commissioned by the *Club di Roma* on the limits of growth.[3] However, the legal value protected by those limits is 'development'.[4] In that context, Nature and ecosystems are considered as objects or resources; or rather, they are seen as interests that are opposed to human ones. Not unsurprisingly, both in the definition of sustainable development and in law, the word used for Nature is 'environment', a concept indicating a container, a physical location, and what surrounds an organism in a given time and space.[5]

1 Ulrich Grober, *Sustainability: A Cultural History* (Green Books 2012) 88.

2 Michele Carducci, 'The Premises of "Constitutional Ecology"' (2020) 17(1) *Veredas do Direito* 89, 96.

3 Donella H. Meadows, Dennis L. Meadows, Jørgen Randers and William W. Behrens III, *The Limits to Growth* (Club of Rome 1972).

4 Klaus Bosselman, 'Shifting the Legal Paradigm: Earth-centred Law and Governance' in Paulo Magalhes, Will Steffen, Klaus Bosselmann, Alexandra Arago and Viriato Soromenho Marques (eds), *The Safe Operating Space Treaty: A New Approach to Managing Our Use of the Earth System* (Cambridge Scholars Publishing 2016) 66.

5 Thomas M. Smith and Robert L. Smith, *Elements of Ecology* (9th edn, Pearson 2015).

DOI: 10.4324/9781003175308-16

However, the value that should be protected is another one, namely "the preservation of the integrity of ecological systems".[6] The integrity of the Earth System (ES) is a precondition for our survival as a species. It derives from the interaction of a complex system of factors and processes. The Planetary Boundaries framework (PB)[7] has identified nine of these as essential to maintaining the system in equilibrium, i.e., in the state that defines the Holocene, the geological era characterized by the development of the human species on the planet. The PB framework defines a safe operating space for humanity: through a double system of thresholds, with respect to control variables for each process, a safe area is identified, within which the current conditions of life can be maintained. This framework was updated in 2015, introducing, among other things, a hierarchy among the parameters: climate change and biosphere integrity interact with all the others and are in themselves sufficient to determine a crisis of the system as a whole, so they have been defined the "core planetary boundaries".[8]

The PB framework itself is not without criticisms and limitations.[9] It is one of the possible ways of measuring the health of ES, one of the possible expressions of the ecosystem approach to global environmental governance, which must be adapted according to the spatial and temporal contexts that are appropriate at any specific moment. How to downscaling the PB framework at national and local level and how to allocate shares of responsibilities among States and non-State actors seems to be one of the most urgent topic to tackle.[10]

The inability of the current system of environmental law to offer solutions to the environmental, climate and energy crisis we are facing at a global level[11] is denounced by the doctrine[12] and more or less explicitly recognized at different institutional levels, starting from the UN Harmony with Nature Programme.

From a legal point of view, most policymakers and lawyers believe that it is sufficient to remedy the implementation flaws of current environmental law. On the other hand, those who take up the challenge of the radical transformation of thought and society aim, instead, at a change in the environmental legal paradigm, inspired by the natural rules that govern ecosystems and by old traditions that have remained faithful to those rules.[13] From a constitutional perspective the

6 Bosselman (n 4) 75.
7 Johan Rockström et al, 'A Safe Operating Space for Humanity' (2009) 461 *Nature* 472.
8 Will Steffen et al., 'Planetary Boundaries: Guiding Human Development on a Changing Planet' (2015) 347 *Science* 736, 743.
9 Rakhyun E. Kim and Luis J. Kotzé, 'Planetary Boundaries at the Intersection of Earth System Law, Science and Governance: A State-of-the-Art Review' [2020] *RECIEL* 1.
10 Ibid 9.
11 www.scientistswarning.org.
12 References in Luis J. Kotzé, 'Earth System Law for the Anthropocene' (2019) 11 *Sustainability* 6796.
13 Silvia Bagni, 'Back to the Future: Building Harmony with Nature in the European Union by Learning from Our Ancestors' in Serena Baldin and Sara De Vido (eds), *Environmental Sustainability in the European Union: Socio-Legal Perspectives* (Edizioni Università di Trieste 2020) 77.

transformation of the legal paradigm,[14] based on an ecosystem approach, represents an ecological conversion, aiming to overcome a law originally based on the exploitation of fossil fuels.

Kim and Bosselmann propose considering the protection and restoration of the integrity of Earth's life-support system "as a potential Grundnorm or goal of international environmental law".[15] The 'or', however, is confusing from the perspective of general legal theory. As Schmidt notes,[16] the protection of ES is a goal, from which to extrapolate a new *Grundnorm*, as a criterion of validity of the system's sources of production. The validity of norms no longer coincides with compliance with internationally assumed constraints, but with their conformity to the 'natural' rules that guarantee the stability of the ES.[17] The parameters of validity are contained in the PB framework.

Kotzé proposes the concept of Earth Law:

> The concept of earth law has not fully developed in the literature. We conceptualize earth law as founded on the recognition that, in the Anthropocene, the Earth is a human-dominated, deeply intertwined, social-ecological system. It is Earth-centred, in the sense that it considers neither humanity nor nature as a central reference point, but rather the entire community of life as the central fulcrum around which it revolves.[18]

Earth Law (EL) differs from the current environmental paradigm in two respects. It has a new object: ecosystems; it has a new geographical dimension of jurisdiction: planetary, and not dominated by the sovereignty of states. The main characteristics of EL can be summarized as follows: inclusivity, i.e. the recognition of the multiplicity of subjects interacting in the ES, without a hierarchical organization (and from which, in some legal systems, the recognition of the rights of Nature derives); interdependency, i.e. the recognition of the relationship of interdependence between man and the other natural elements and of the importance of intra-species, inter-species and inter-generational relations, which is manifested in a spatial dimension – being distinct from that assumed by the current Western legal system, which is limited by the sovereignty of its countries; complexity, i.e., an awareness of the complicated systems of feedback loops affecting natural ecosystemic processes, which implies a holistic and non-sectoral legal approach

14 Kotzé (n 12).

15 Rakhyun E. Kim and Klauss Bosselmann, 'International Environmental Law in the Anthropocene: Towards a Purposive System of Multilateral Environmental Agreements' (2013) 2 *Transnational Environmental Law* 285, 305.

16 Jeremy J. Schmidt, 'The Moral Geography of the Earth System' (2019) 44 *Trans Inst Br Geogr* 721, 728.

17 Annex 11, Michele Carducci et al., *Towards an EU Charter of the Fundamental Rights of Nature. Study* (European Economic and Social Committee 2020) 170 ff.

18 Luis J. Kotzé, Rakhyun E. Kim, 'Earth System Law: The Juridical Dimensions of Earth System Governance' [2019] *Earth System Governance* 1, 7.

to environmental and climate problems, so law becomes adaptive, governed by flexibility rather than rigidity.[19]

Carducci introduces the concept of 'constitutional ecology', featuring a

> reconsideration of the structure not only of legal concepts and categories (remodelling them according to ecological 'conversion' and 'transition'), but also, and above all, of the type of rules ('primary' or 'secondary') that govern the organisation of power, the distribution of competences, the recognition of freedoms and the definition of duties, on the basis of an ecosystem approach to existence.[20]

Gudynas, analysing Ecuador's new Constitution of 2008, spoke of an 'ecological mandate', i.e. the reorientation of its values and norms in the light of the recognition of an intrinsic value to Nature.[21]

All the proposals described previously can be perfectly integrated with each other, having, as a common element, the application of an ecosystem approach, both at national and international level. Although this change of legal paradigm has not yet found full expression in any legal system in the world, traces of ecosystem legal thinking can be discerned in the active legal formants of various countries (§ 2). The aim of this chapter is to describe and compare the transposition of the ecosystem approach, especially in case law. At the moment, it is expressed in two ways: the recognition of rights to Nature (§ 3) and the claim of a right to a stable climate (§ 4). In conclusion, we will try to highlight the similarities and differences between the two solutions, especially in the light of the cultural context of reference (§ 5).

2. Introducing the Ecosystem Approach in Legal Formants

At an international level, there is currently no binding document that specifically commits the community of States to ES balance. Instead, there is a binding sectoral approach, focused on the protection of the two core parameters within the PB framework, namely limits to climate change and the safeguarding of biodiversity. From the preamble and some provisions of the UN Framework Convention on Climate Change (UNFCCC) and the Convention on Biological Diversity, it is clear that their aim is to maintain the ES. These documents can therefore be considered the precursors of EL or the ecosystem approach.

19 Kotzé (n 12).

20 Carducci (n 2) 108.

21 Eduardo Gudynas, *El mandato ecológico. Derechos de la Naturaleza y políticas ambientales en la nueva Constitución* (AbyaYala, 2009); Eduardo Gudynas, *Derechos de la Naturaleza. Etica biocéntrica y políticas ambientales* (1st edn, Plural 2014).

In the absence of a guarantee body, however, such as a Green Authority or International Earth Tribunal, the defence of ES is delegated to national jurisdictions through the constitutionalisation of international law. However, this guarantee solution remains difficult to apply. The treaties mentioned oblige States, not citizens. To derive from these treaties a right (whether human or constitutional) directly enforceable by an individual remains a complex and ambitious interpretative operation. Moreover, even in systems where international law is considered as a parameter of normative constitutionality, the scope of actionability is linked to the specific system of judicial review implemented by each country.

Another problem to be addressed for the national implementation of the ES approach is the difficulty of scaling down the PB framework. The proposal adopts a bottoms-up regulatory perspective, but the methodology needed to understand the overall impact of policies and actions implemented by a single country on its territory, or with respect to a single ecosystem, remains totally unexplored. Moreover, even a top-down regulatory framework would struggle to assign shares of responsibility for each boundary to individual countries. The ecosystem approach provides the guiding principles for building ES law at both international and local levels when considered as autonomous systems; however, the scientific methodology for analysing feedback loops, and thus validating local action on a global scale, remains uncertain.

This problem is circumvented by systems that base the application of the ecosystem approach on cultural rather than scientific grounds. In fact, the ecological mandate integrates this gap through the precautionary principle (interpreted, however, in an autonomous way with respect to that commonly applied in environmental law[22]) and the principle *in dubio pro natura et clima*.[23]

At present, there are basically two ways forward at a national level that are consistent with the implementation of an ES Law: the recognition of Nature or of its constituent elements as a subject of rights and the claim of a (human or constitutional) right to a stable climate, capable of ensuring our survival on the planet. Both of these, although in different ways, are based on the concept of 'right', to establish the existence of a 'duty' for the state to act.

It is important to clarify in what terms, and in which cases, Nature, as a subject of rights, is a legal manifestation of the ecosystem approach. It is not simply a matter of expanding the range of subjects of rights. For this reason, the attribution of rights to animals is not necessarily an expression of the ecosystem approach. It comes with the legal recognition of the existence of interaction between humans, other living beings and the abiotic elements of the environment in which we live. This happens when rights are granted to Nature as an ES, or as a particular ecosystem (a *paramo*, a river basin, the Amazon . . .), whose rights aim to guarantee

22 Olivia Woolley, 'What Would Ecological Climate Change Law Look Like? Developing a Method for Analysing the International Climate Change Regime from an Ecological Perspective' (2020) 29 *RECIEL* 76, 81.

23 Carducci et al. (n 17).

regeneration, the permanence of its state of equilibrium and resilience, i.e., the ability to restore the equilibrium in the face of disturbances. The legal protection of an individual animal or species can be a tool in the service of implementing an ecosystem approach, when it aims to guarantee biodiversity, or defends the relationship between an individual member of a species and other species.

The second approach is the judicial affirmation of a human right to a stable climate in climate justice.

Carducci points out that under this label one can "include everything":[24] it is sufficient that the cause has a *de facto* link with anthropogenic climate change in its object, claim or parameter. Instead, only those lawsuits that pursue 'ecological justice' are an expression of the ecosystem approach. These lawsuits look at climate-altering emissions produced by human activity as a global problem, impacting on the stability of the ES, and thus put on trial the responsibilities of countries (and corporations) to keep climate change below the danger threshold established by the PB framework. "The law on the 'climate-altering legal relationship' is therefore a normative system of prevention from the threats of climate change, to the benefit of present and future human security".[25] It is claimed as a human right, but it concerns the species and the biotic community.[26] It is this supra-individual dimension that expresses the ecosystem approach, so that only cases where action is presented in these terms fall within the scope of our study.

3. Comparing the Two Pathways of Case-Law: Nature's Rights Approach

The first line of jurisprudence decisions incorporating arguments based on the ecosystem approach is that in which the Courts recognize natural elements as having legal subjectivity, responding to claims by individual citizens, communities or environmental associations against State authorities, in which they denounce the state of serious vulnerability of particular ecosystems, due to the excessive and unregulated exploitation of natural resources.

The richest jurisprudence in this field is the Colombian one, analysed in Chapter 13 of this book, so I will only mention some of the arguments used by judges, which are useful for comparison. In judgment T-622 of 10 November 2016, the Colombian Constitutional Court acknowledges that there are several possible interpretations of the environmental guarantees in the Constitution: anthropocentric, biocentric and ecocentric (§ 5.6 ff.). The judge recognises that the ecocentric perspective is fully grounded in the Colombian Constitution and goes so far as to link this interpretation to the constitutional recognition of cultural pluralism.

24 Carducci (n 2) 1355.
25 Ibid 1365.
26 This highlights the ambiguity of the concept of 'human right', strategically used, in this case, for the protection of an asset that goes beyond the human.

The judge also analyses the precautionary principle, from which he derives, in an apparently consequential way, the principle *in dubio pro natura*, as representing one of the core interpretative criteria of ES law (§ 7.39). In fact, the two principles operate on different levels, so that, once again, the judge's argumentation goes far beyond the scope of current environmental law.

In STC 4360/2018, 5 April, the Colombian Supreme Court of Justice frames the problem of Amazon deforestation as a global "anthropocentric and egoistical" lifestyle model and denounces the need for a shift from an anthropocentric view of environmental rights to an "anthropocentric ecocentric" one (§§ 4–5).

The core reasoning of the motivation here is the principle of solidarity, which is expanded to encompass all of humanity and Nature. The cornerstones of this view are intra-species solidarity and the recognition of an intrinsic value to Nature.

The conclusions follow from the application of the principles of precaution, intergenerational equality and solidarity: with the first, the danger of damage is accepted; with the second, it is accepted that the rights of future generations may be violated; with the third, the omissive responsibility of the State is established.

After these two fundamental judgments, many Colombian judges at all levels have recognized rivers and ecosystems as subjects of law, recalling the jurisprudence commented above.

A further potential of the ecosystem approach can be appreciated in the recognition of the territory of the Awá people as a '*víctima del conflicto armado*' by the *Jurisdicción especial para la Paz* in case 02, opened on 10 July 2018.[27] This declaration is based on a cross-cultural interpretation of the concept of victim, through the analysis of the Awá cosmovision, according to which these people belong to 'Katsa Su', Mother Earth, who is alive, is the source of *buen vivir* and the home of the Awá people.

In India, two Writ Petitions are relevant: No.126 of 2014, sent. 20 March 2017 and No.140 of 2015, sent. 30 March 2017, decided by the Supreme Court of Uttarakhand, which granted legal status to the Ganges and Yamuna rivers and their respective source glaciers.

In the first judgment, although the starting point is anthropocentric, the justification that the Court puts forward has cultural and ecosystemic elements. The Court recognizes that the Hindu population is deeply connected with the rivers, which have provided half of India's population with physical and spiritual sustenance since time immemorial. They ensure the physical and spiritual well-being of the communities they flow through, from the mountains to the sea. They are defined as living and breathing entities.

In the second judgment, the Court dwells in much greater detail on the ecosystemic relationship between Man and Nature, on which the jurisprudence concerning the rights of Nature is based.

The ecological aspect here is elevated above the cultural one, which is present in the references to the veneration of trees, as symbols of deities, in both Hindu

27 Case 02 del 2018, Auto SRVBIT – 079, 12 November 2019.

religion and Buddhist philosophy. The Court openly declares its adherence to the new philosophy of the Earth: "The Courts are duty bound to protect the environmental ecology under the 'New Environment Justice Jurisprudence' ". The Court's activism is stated: "Besides our constitutional and legal duties, it is our moral duty to protect the environment and ecology". It not only recognises that rivers and lakes have an intrinsic right not to be polluted, but also equates harm to the person and harm to nature. Finally, the statute of rights recognised to natural entities follows, almost to the letter, the Ecuadorian art. 71 const.: "Rivers, Forests, Lakes, Water Bodies, Air, Glaciers and Springs have a right to exist, persist, maintain, sustain and regenerate their own vital ecology system. The rivers are not just water bodies. These are scientifically and biologically living", and shortly afterwards "We must recognise and bestow Constitutional legal rights to the 'Mother Earth' ". After all, the Ganges River is worshipped by Hindus as 'Ganga Mata', or Mother Ganga.

The two previously mentioned judgments have been challenged in the Supreme Court of India, which stayed the High Court orders on 7 July 2017, on grounds that deny the ecosystem approach adopted by the Uttarakhand Supreme Court.

Recently, the High Court of Punjab and Haryana, in case *CWP No.18253 of 2009 & other connected petitions*, delivered on 2 March 2020, declared Sukhna Lake as a legal entity for its survival, preservation and conservation. All the citizens of U.T. Chandigarh have been declared *loco parentis* as the human face to save Sukhna Lake from extinction, on the basis of the powers that the Court can exercise as *parens patriae*. The lake had long been suffering from phenomena of water degradation (aquatic weeds), soil degradation (siltation), riparian fauna and flora extinction, due to the partly illegal constructions carried out in the area surrounding the lake.

The Court recalls the existence of a duty of Government and Court to protect the environment, based on the doctrine of public trust. In the Supreme Court precedents that are recalled, this doctrine is based on scientific and bibliographical reasoning of an ecological nature, as well as on an ecosystemic interpretation of Article 21 of the Indian Constitution on the right to life. The lake is considered an ecosystem, whose untimely extinction must be prevented. The Courts are duty bound to protect the environmental ecology under the 'New Environment Justice Jurisprudence' and also under the principles of *parens patriae*.

The judge, however, also connects the legal duty to *lato sensu* cultural arguments: "Besides our constitutional and legal duties, it is our moral duty to protect the environment and ecology", so much so that the very long pronouncement closes with the phrase "In holy Guru Granth Sahebji, it is written that *'Pavan paani dharati aakas ghar mandar har bani'*, (Air, water, earth and sky are God's home and temple)", showing the pluralistic and inter-legal nature of the Indian legal system, based on precedents, but also on customs and local traditions.

Last but not least, on 30 January 2019 (Writ Petition No. 13989/2016), the High Court of Bangladesh recognised the Turag River as a living entity, with a view to extending this status to all rivers in the country.

4. Comparing the Two Pathways of Case-Law: The Right to a Climate System Capable of Sustaining Human Life

The second pathway that takes an ecosystem approach is promoted by environmental movements, individual citizens or vulnerable groups, who claim in national courts a constitutional or human right to a stable climate. This right should be matched by an obligation on the part of the State to implement adequate plans and programmes to reduce or eliminate greenhouse gas (GHG) emissions, in accordance with the most recent scientific findings available, in order to prevent the so-called *tipping points* from being exceeded[28] within the parameters of ecological homeostasis.

There are now a large number of climate cases being promoted or pending around the world,[29] but rarely do the courts go so far as to use arguments based on an ecosystem approach.

4.1. The 'Explicit' Ecosystem Approach

In a few cases, judges have grasped the revolutionary scope of the recognition of a right to a stable climate, accepting the challenge of discussing its basis and arguing the merits of its implications for the legal system, with different outcomes on a case-by-case basis.

The US *Juliana case* is an example, brought in 2015 in the District Court of Oregon, Eugene division. The applicants filed a "complaint for declaratory and injunctive relief" based on a "Constitutional Rights and Public Trust Action" against the US Government, a number of federal departments and the Environmental Protection Agency (EPA). The applicants denounced the illegality of the government's climate policy, which, through its actions and omissions, has contributed over the years to an increase in concentrations of GHG in the atmosphere and has not taken necessary and sufficient measures to combat climate change, thus violating the Fifth Amendment and their rights to life, liberty and property, which are formulated as a precondition to the existence of a stable climate system. The US Court of Appeals for the 9th Circuit denied them standing to proceed on the merits in an opinion filed on 17 January 2020.

The case is currently pending. The interlocutory rulings of Judge Aiken of the US District Court, denying the motions to dismiss brought by the Government and some private interveners, as well as the Court of Appeal's own opinion, contain fundamental arguments based on the ecosystem approach.

In her opinion and order of 10 November 2016 (Case No. 6:15-cv-01517-TC), Judge Aiken considers both climate change and its anthropogenic origin as a

28 5th IPCC Report (AR5 2013–14).
29 http://climatecasechart.com.

proven fact. She recalls how unenumerated fundamental rights can also be identified and then embraces the ecosystem approach proposed by the applicants:

> Exercising my 'reasoned judgment,' I have no doubt that the right to a climate system capable of sustaining human life is fundamental to a free and ordered society. . . . Echoing Obergefell's reasoning, plaintiffs allege a stable climate system is a necessary condition to exercising other rights to life, liberty, and property.
>
> (p. 32)

Also from a procedural point of view, standing is acknowledged on the basis of the ecosystem approach, since, alongside the direct and immediate harm to the young plaintiffs' lives, Judge Aiken recalls how the preamble of the US Constitution ascribes constitutional rights also to "posterity". The issue of the rights of future generations is connected to the public trust doctrine, which is also used to establish the existence of a state duty to protect its citizens from climate change. This doctrine has enormous ecological potential, as the trustee's fiduciary duty includes the preservation of future generations' rights and allows for a judicial review of the trustee's actions or omissions.

In the appeal opinion of 17 January 2020, the majority of the Court "reluctantly" denied standing to the young plaintiffs, concluding that "the plaintiffs' case must be made to the political branches or the electorate at large". In this opinion, the claim of a right under the Due Process Clause of the Fifth Amendment to a "climate system capable of sustaining human life" becomes even more central. Indeed, although the action is dismissed on procedural grounds, the Court reasons hypothetically, "assuming such a broad constitutional right exists". The Court, therefore, does not close the door on the recognition of the right, but doubts its power to remedy its violation in the present case.

In her dissenting opinion, Justice Staton dwells on the nature of the right invoked. In particular, she frames the right to a habitable United States in the light of the perpetuity principle, i.e., the need to defend the Nation from destruction, "to secure 'the Blessings of Liberty' not just for one generation, but for all future generations – our 'Posterity' ".

In Nepal, the Supreme Court, Division Bench, in the case of *Advocate Padam Bahadur Shrestha*, Decision no. 10210, dated 25 December 2018[30] issued a writ of *mandamus* against the Nepalese Government to take the necessary steps to implement the existing measures for environmental protection and combating climate change.

The Court defines as "imperative" the adoption of a law that effectively applies an ecosystem approach to the problem of climate change, with a view to achieving 'climate justice': "It is necessary to do a moral, balanced, and responsible usage of the ecological resources that sustain humans and the lives of other species" (§ 4).

30 Order 074-WO-0283 published in: NKP, Part 61, Vol. 3.

The obligation to act derives from the *parens patriae* principle, as the threat that climate change poses to humans, other living beings and the planet's ecosystems is of public interest:

> Climate change has not only affected human lives but all plants and animal species, their habitats and created an imbalance in ecology and biodiversity, therefore making it a matter of public concern. Therefore, while carrying out any activity relating to climate change, it should embrace the principle of climate justice. . . . If only we embrace the principles of sustainable development and allied principles of inter-generational and intra-generational equality, and formulate a law to conserve biodiversity and the ecosystem, we can establish an edifice of climate justice for present and future generations.
>
> (§ 2)

In Ireland, in the case *Friends of the Irish Environment Clg v. The Government of Ireland, Ireland and the Attorney General*,[31] the High Court recently refused to sanction the Irish Government for the alleged insufficiency and inadequacy of the strategies and programmes it adopted in the fight against climate change.

However, it left open the question of the constitutionality of the challenged law. In its reasoning it hypothetically admits the existence of an "unenumerated right to an environment consistent with human dignity". This formula recalls the ecosystem approach, while being constructed on the parameter of human dignity. In fact, the Court recognises that this right is a prerequisite for any other human right, therefore, both an individual and global right, belonging to the individual and the species, with a perhaps broader scope: "is it a civil right of humans or does it extend to animals and ecosystems?" (p. 254).

In *Mathur v. Ontario*,[32] the Superior Court of Justice of Ontario must judge an Application brought by a group of Ontario residents between the ages of 12 and 24, to challenge Ontario's cancellation of the *Climate Change Mitigation and Low-carbon Economy Act, 2016, S.O. 2016, c. 7 ('Climate Change Act')*. The Applicants submit that Ontario's target is insufficiently ambitious, and that Ontario's failure to set a more stringent target and a more exacting plan for combating climate change over the coming decade infringes the constitutional rights of youth and future generations (§ 2).

The issue of the existence of a right to climate protection is addressed on the basis of section 7 of the Charter. Although this provision has never been used to establish a duty of the State to positively guarantee a right, it considers that such an interpretative conclusion is by no means precluded.[33] The Court states that "jurisprudence may someday evolve to encompass positive obligations in the

31 [2019] IEHC 747 The High Court Judicial Review [2017 No. 793 JR], Judgment of Mr. Justice MacGrath delivered on the 19th day of September, 2019.

32 *Mathur v. Ontario* 2020 ONSC 6918.

33 https://www.justice.gc.ca/eng/csj-sjc/rfc-dlc/ccrf-ccdl/check/art7.html.

domain of climate rights." Finally, in justifying standing on behalf of future generations, the court states not only that the case is of constitutional significance, but also that it is a case "of public interest, in that it transcends the interests of all Ontario residents, not just the Applicants' generation or the ones that follow", thus using an ecosystemic argument, which recognizes the universal scope of the right claimed.

4.2. The 'Implicit' Ecosystem Approach

In other cases, the judgement does not focus on the existence of a right to a stable climate. However, in their reasoning, judges use arguments more or less directly based on the ecosystem approach: the principle of solidarity; protection of future generations; the public trust doctrine; *parens patriae*; the principle of shared responsibility.

In Norway, case 18-060499ASD-BORG/03, brought before the Borgarting Court of Appeal against the Norwegian Government, is a judgment of unconstitutionality against a measure to grant ten production licences for oil exploration and extraction in the Barents Sea, for a total of 40 blocks or sub-blocks.[34]

While rejecting the appeal, the decision is significant in that it gives for the first time an interpretation of Article 112 Const., according to which the law is considered not only as a source of obligation for the State, but also as a positive right for citizens. The first paragraph defines the environment not only in terms of the individual right to human health, but also in ecosystemic terms, affirming the need to ensure the productivity and diversity of the natural environment through the management of resources, based on long-term considerations, i.e., capable of ensuring rights also for future generations.

It is precisely because of the 'pre-conditional' nature of climate change with respect to the survival of humanity on the planet that the Court considers judicial review of government decisions to be even more necessary. However, according to the Court, guaranteeing that right means identifying a threshold to be set as a limit to the Executive's discretion, rather than applying a set of guiding principles corresponding to the ecological mandate.

The Court notes that, with regard to GHG emissions, a guarantee of the right recognized by Article 112 would imply an integrated assessment of the different sources of damage production in various sectors (oil activity but also other industrial and non-industrial sectors) and at various levels (local, national, global).[35] This approach is also justified by the constitutional reference to future generations, which can only be guaranteed by an ecosystem approach. However, the scope of the reasoning is again narrowed, in light of the wide margin of appreciation that

34 At the time of writing, the case is pending before the Supreme Court.

35 Vito De Lucia, Ingrid Solstad Andreassen, 'Climate Litigation in Norway. A Preliminary Assessment' (2020) 2 *DPCE Online* 1405, 1414.

the *Storting* and the Government enjoy in defining the priorities to be pursued in the competition between different rights and interests.

Finally, the Court assesses the extension of the climatic impact beyond Norwegian territory. It first recalls the "no harm principle" of international law and then states that assessing environmental harm beyond a country's boundaries is an expression of a solidarity principle. "This involves, in the same way as the principle regarding solidarity across generations, a moral principle that can have major significance in the work on reducing climate changes" (p. 22).

The Norwegian Supreme Court confirmed the legitimacy of the licensing measure on 22 December 2020, with a motivation that removed any trace of an ecosystem approach, even downgrading the very nature of Article 112 Const.

The first case, now universally known, in which the courts have recognised a responsibility of the State for the inadequacy of its policies to combat climate change, with reference to GHG emissions into the atmosphere, is the Dutch *Urgenda case.*

The anthropogenic origin of climate change, as well as the risks at a global level related to the inaction of States in taking drastic measures to limit the emission of climate-altering gases into the atmosphere, are extensively described by the appellant through scientific documentary evidence (primarily the IPCC Reports).

In its first instance judgement of 24 June 2015, the District Court states that "Article 21 of the Dutch Constitution imposes a duty of care on the State relating to the liveability of the country and the protection and improvement of the living environment", even though it recognises the wide discretion of the State in the choice of measures to be adopted to realise this obligation.

On appeal and in cassation, however, the violation of the duty of care is traced back to the violation of human rights under Articles 2 and 8 of the European Convention of Human Rights (ECHR).

In the *La Rose case* (*La Rose v. Canada*, 2020 FC 1008, released on 27 October 2020) 15 children and youth from across Canada filed a Statement of Claim on 25 October 2019, alleging that various conduct on the part of the Canadian State continues to cause, contribute to and allow GHG emissions that are incompatible with a 'Stable Climate System'. They define it as a "stable climate capable of sustaining human life and liberties". They allege the infringement of their constitutional rights under ss. 7 and 15 of the Canadian Charter of rights, and they argue a breach of obligations they claim fall under the 'public trust doctrine'.

The Federal Court, deciding a motion to strike submitted by the Government, considers Charter claims not justiciable. However, the Court analyses the arguments in favour of recognising a violation of the rights invoked. With respect to s. 7, it states that case-law has not closed the door to the possibility of interpreting the Charter as a source of positive obligations on the part of the State to guarantee particular rights.

In New Zealand, in *Sarah Thomson v. The Minister for Climate Change Issues [2017] NZHC 733*, the High Court of New Zealand confirms the justiciability of climate change–related measures, based on a comparative analysis of other similar cases around the world, including the *Urgenda case* itself, stating that all Courts, except Canada, ultimately came to the same conclusion, recognising "the significance of the issue for the planet and its inhabitants" (§ 133).

On 3 February 2021, the Paris Administrative Court held the French State partly responsible for the worsening of the ecological damage caused by anthropogenic emissions of GHG, due to the inadequacy of the results obtained in implementing the commitments to reduce GHG emissions made at international, European and national level (the *Notre Affaire à Tous case*). This, the most recent case to be decided in favour of recognizing State liability for climate damage, is perhaps the least significant in terms of recognizing a right to a stable climate. In fact, the plaintiffs' accusation is based on the State's civil liability for 'ecological damage', defined as "une atteinte non négligeable aux éléments ou aux fonctions des écosystèmes ou aux bénéfices collectifs tirés par l'homme de l'environnement". It is therefore the French legislator who has applied an ecosystem approach to the definition of damage: through the disjunctive in the wording of the article, ecosystems are among the goods that are directly damaged; in addition to man, who is impaired in his perception of the services produced in his favour by nature. We are not discussing the rights of Man, much less of nature; the ecosystem approach is upstream, in the definition of damage. Neither the global dimension of the problem, nor the network of feedback loops feeding it, come into question. What matters is formal respect for the availability quota of the asset protected by the law (the ecosystem functions of the environment), which is affected if the threat is "not negligible".

5. Conclusions: An Intercultural Interpretation of the Ecosystem Approach in Legal Science

The comparison between the two development paths of an ES Law leads us to highlight common elements and many different characteristics.

In all the cases examined, the Courts have accepted climate change and its anthropogenic causes as a judicially proven fact, on the basis of the scientific allegations produced by the parties. The climate and environmental crisis is therefore a judicially established fact and represents the precondition for the development of ecosystem thinking.[36] In return, the so-called 'reservation of science', i.e., the judge's use of scientific data (e.g., the PB framework) as an objective limit to the decision-making and interpretative discretion of the authorities and private persons[37] is still an exception, currently only applied in the *Urgenda* and *Notre Affaire à Tous* cases.

36 Recognition of the environmental and climate crisis as a proven fact does not, however, equate to recognition of the state's obligations or duties towards its citizens; nor of a right to a stable climate; nature's own rights; the existence of a causal link between that situation and state environmental and climate policies; ecological damage. All these situations and legal relationships remain to be proven, as attested by the different solutions proposed by the courts in the cases analysed.

37 Cf. Carducci (n 2) 1363 and 'Contenzioso climatico, illecito civile, termodinamica' laCostituzione.info (2021), http://www.lacostituzione.info/index.php/2021/02/08/

Following the *Urgenda* and *Juliana* cases, many other similar cases have been brought before national courts around the world.[38] This atypical form of circulation of the 'precedent' is testified by explicit reference, at least in the *Urgenda case*, within some of the pronouncements we have analysed (the *Sarah Thomson case* in New Zealand; the Irish case *Friends of the Irish Environment Clg*; the Norwegian case 18-060499ASD-BORG/03).

As for the pronouncements that have recognized natural elements as subjects of law, there has been a strong adherence to the two precedents by the lower Colombian courts, and wide intra-continental circulation among Latin American countries. On the other hand, Indian cases do not recall the Colombian ones, and vice versa, probably because the language problem becomes a strongly inhibiting obstacle.

Finally, there is no cross-fertilization between the two different legal reasonings: judges do not seem to consider that the two different solutions adopted derive from the same ecosystem approach to law, although the arguments recalled tend to overlap. In particular, the Courts that have ruled on the legal personality of Nature use arguments such as the rights of future generations, the precautionary principle, the principle of solidarity and, in India, the doctrines of public trust and *parens patriae*, which are also recalled in case law on the right to a stable climate.

This is probably due to the different cultural approach with which the courts involved regard the problem of the environment and climate crisis. The jurisprudential analysis conducted shows how the shift from an anthropocentric to an ecocentric legal paradigm has a different epistemological foundation between the global North and South: the former is scientistic, the latter biocultural.

For the courts of the Western Legal Tradition, "as a Grundnorm, the planetary boundaries framework offers a rational and empirical basis of normative validity without metaphysical or culturally specific appeals to 'nature' ".[39]

For the courts of the Global South, the paradigm shift is primarily cultural, based on respect for a sustainable Man-Nature relationship, rooted in the cosmovision and traditions of indigenous peoples, which have been confirmed by the latest scientific findings.[40]

---

contenzioso-climatico-illecito-civile-termodinamica/?utm_source=feedburner&utm_medium=email&utm_campaign=Feed:+LaCostituzionePuntoInfo+(La+Costituzione.info.

38 Hillary Aidun and Malia Libby, 'Juliana in the World: Comparing the Ninth Circuit's Decision to Foreign Rights-based Climate Litigation' (2020), http://blogs.law.columbia.edu/climatechange/2020/03/13/juliana-in-the-world-comparing-the-ninth-circuits-decision-to-foreign-rights-based-climate-litigation/.

39 Schmidt (n 16) 728.

40 UNEP/CBD/COP/5/23, pp. 103–109: "It recognizes that humans, with their cultural diversity, are an integral component of many ecosystems" (p. 104). "The ecosystem approach should consider all forms of relevant information, including scientific and indigenous and local knowledge, innovations and practices" (Annex B, p. 107).

The risk for the emerging ES law is to repeat the mistakes made in pursuing an essentially monocultural formulation of 'sustainable development'. The ecosystem approach is inherently intercultural and thus requires an ecology of knowledge, i.e., the integration of Western and ancestral scientific knowledge.

Popular environmentalism in the Global South has both an ecological and a cultural dimension, since it identifies with the claims of indigenous and Afro-descendant peoples, and with marginalised rural and urban communities, to defend and maintain their ancestral traditions. The relationship that these communities have with the land and nature is not reduced to a form of mere economic exploitation. It is based on a set of values and principles, such as responsibility and solidarity towards other living beings and ecosystems, based on the recognition of an intimate and personal relationship with these elements.[41] Environmental conflicts in that part of the world "expresan las tensiones subyacentes de visiones, intereses y cosmovisiones diversas".[42] In Colombia, indigenous justice solves them by applying the principles approved by the community through the *Planes de vida*, which encompass the way of thinking, feeling, acting and relating to the earth, sky and mankind,[43] and are an expression of a form of "desarrollo propio" or "desarrollo indígena", distinct from the Western concept of development.

The contrast between North and South appears clear, but European and North American hostility to the rediscovery of their own traditional culture may just be a legacy of centuries of positivism, rationalism and mechanism. For example, the Irish High Court, in the case of *Merriman et al.*,[44] notes that the applicants, in addition to basing the existence of a right to an environment consistent with the human dignity and well-being of citizens at large on scientific consensus, mention an "emerging theological/philosophical consensus", derived from

> the commonality of views that appears to be shared by all of the major religions on matters environmental, as evidenced by the well-known Assisi Declarations of September 1986 in which distinguished leaders and personages from the Buddhist, Christian, Hindu, Islamic and Judaic faiths individually issued a series of declarations which point to humanity's common destiny as the stewards and trustees of our shared natural environment,

as well as a "secular environmental philosophy, which offers a rational and non-religious basis by which one can arrive at a place not so very far removed from that occupied by the major religious faiths" (p. 242). Nevertheless, the Court refuses to base its considerations on these elements, confirming not only

41 Gregorio Mesa Cuadros, *Ambientalismo popular* (Ediciones desde abajo 2018). Martínez Alier calls it "ecologism of the poor". (cited by Gloria Amparo Rodríguez, 'Prevención y Solución de los Conflictos Ambientales en Territorios Indígenas' (2017) 9 *Sortuz. Oñati Journal of Emergent Socio-legal Studies* 1, 10.

42 Mesa Cuadros (n 41).

43 Rodríguez (n 41) 10.

44 [2017] IEHC 695, 2017 No. 201 JR

the exclusively scientistic approach we have indicated, but also its adherence to a monist and positivist conception of law. On the other hand, in the Norwegian judgment analysed earlier, the Court recognizes that the parameter of constitutionality should be interpreted in the light of moral values, going beyond mere scientific data: "This involves, in the same way as the principle regarding solidarity across generations, a moral principle that can have major significance in the work on reducing climate changes."

Another distinctive element between the two ecosystem approaches studied concerns the origin of impetus for change. In the legal systems without constitutional or legislative clauses attributing legal personality to Nature or to specific elements of Nature, innovation occurred through judicial activism, i.e., on the basis of arguments carried out independently by 'enlightened' judges. The claimants, although always motivated by a clear intention to protect the environment, having in some cases to overcome the hurdle of legal standing, base their claims on anthropocentric arguments, based on the violation of individual, constitutional or human rights. They do not foresee, in any way, the final outcome of the case (i.e., the recognition of Nature as a subject of law): they ask the Court to declare the State responsible for the violation of their constitutional rights, and to impose the necessary measures for their reinstatement. This is a perspective that remains anthropocentric. Only when the jurisprudence of the High Courts is consolidated do the claimants move on to directly request recognition of the legal personality of the natural elements that form the subject of the action. An example is the recent *Parque de los Nevados case* in Colombia.[45]

On the other hand, in the climate cases analysed, it is the plaintiffs themselves who base their actions and demands (more or less explicitly, in a principal or subordinate way) on the recognition of a new right, that of a stable climate, suitable for sustaining human life on the planet, which, while being claimed as a constitutional or human right, intrinsically contains an ecosystemic conceptual core.

The road to the establishment of an ES Law still seems long and uncertain. However, the comparative method has proved to be a useful and valid tool for lawyers, as it is able to highlight what is needed to shift from environmental law to ES law, showing the main obstacles and offering some initial shared solutions. The key step is to train national judges in the principles of the ecosystem approach, which has two implications: firstly, the need to analyse each case with a holistic view, capable of embracing the global impact of each local action. Consequently, the interpretation and application of domestic law must be based on appropriate scientific parameters, such as the PB framework. Secondly, the scientific ecosystem approach must be understood interculturally, on the basis of

45 STL10716-2020, Radicación n. 90309, Acta n. 44, of 25 November 2020, magistrada ponente Clara Cecilia Dueñas Quevedo.

an ecology of knowledge[46] which welcomes, like Mother Earth, every sensibility capable of communicating with her in harmony.

Bibliography

Aidun H. and Libby M., 'Juliana In The World: Comparing The Ninth Circuit's Decision To Foreign Rights-based Climate Litigation' (2020), http://blogs.law.columbia.edu/climatechange/2020/03/13/juliana-in-the-world-comparing-the-ninth-circuits-decision-to-foreign-rights-based-climate-litigation/.

Bagni S., 'Back to the Future: Building Harmony with Nature in the European Union by Learning from our Ancestors' in Serena Baldin and Sara De Vido (eds), *Environmental Sustainability in the European Union: Socio-Legal Perspectives* (Edizioni Università di Trieste 2020).

Bosselman K., 'Shifting the Legal Paradigm: Earth-centred Law and Governance' in P. Magalhes, W. Steffen, K. Bosselmann, A. Arago and V. Soromenho Marques (eds), *The Safe Operating Space Treaty: A New Approach to Managing Our Use of the Earth System* (Cambridge Scholars Publishing 2016).

Carducci M., 'The Premises of 'Constitutional Ecology'' (2020) 17(1) *Veredas do Direito* 89.

Carducci M., 'Contenzioso climatico, illecito civile, termodinamica' [2021] *laCostituzione.info*, www.lacostituzione.info/index.php/2021/02/08/contenzioso-climatico-illecito-civile-termodinamica/?utm_source=feedburner&utm_medium=email&utm_campaign=Feed:+LaCostituzionePuntoInfo+(La+Costituzione.info.

Carducci M. et al., *Towards an EU Charter of the Fundamental Rights of Nature. Study* (European Economic and Social Committee 2020).

De Lucia V. and Andreassen I.S., 'Climate Litigation in Norway. A Preliminary Assessment' (2020) 2 *DPCE Online* 1405.

de Sousa Santos B., 'A Non-Occidentalist West?: Learned Ignorance and Ecology of Knowledge' (2009) 26 *Theory Culture Society* 103.

Grober U., *Sustainability. A Cultural History* (Green Books 2012).

Gudynas E., *El mandato ecológico. Derechos de la Naturaleza y políticas ambientales en la nueva Constitución* (AbyaYala 2009).

Gudynas E., *Derechos de la Naturaleza. Etica biocéntrica y políticas ambientales* (1st edn, Plural 2014).

Kim R.E. and Bosselmann K., 'International Environmental Law in the Anthropocene: Towards a Purposive System of Multilateral Environmental Agreements' (2013) 2 *Transnational Environmental Law* 285.

Kim R.E., Bosselmann K. and Kotzé L.J., 'Planetary Boundaries at the Intersection of Earth System Law, Science and Governance: A State-of-the-Art Review' [2020] *RECIEL* 1.

Kotzé L.J., 'Earth System Law for the Anthropocene' (2019) 11 *Sustainability* 6796.

Kotzé L.J. and Kim R.E., 'Earth System Law: The Juridical Dimensions of Earth System Governance' [2019] *Earth System Governance* 1.

46 Boaventura de Sousa Santos, 'A Non-Occidentalist West? Learned Ignorance and Ecology of Knowledge' (2009) 26 *Theory Culture Society* 103.

Meadows D., Meadows D.L., Randers J. and Behrens III W.W., *The Limits to Growth* (Club of Rome 1972).

Mesa Cuadros G., *Ambientalismo popular* (Ediciones desde abajo 2018).

Rockström J. et al., 'A Safe Operating Space for Humanity' (2009) 461 *Nature* 472.

Rodríguez G.A., 'Prevención y Solución de los Conflictos Ambientales en Territorios Indígenas' (2017) 9 *Sortuz. Oñati Journal of Emergent Socio-legal Studies* 1.

Schmidt J.J., 'The Moral Geography of the Earth System' (2019) 44 *Trans Inst Br Geogr* 721.

Smith T.M. and Smith R.L., *Elements of Ecology* (9th edn, Pearson 2015).

Steffen W. et al., 'Planetary Boundaries: Guiding Human Development on a Changing Planet' (2015) 347 *Science* 736.

Woolley O, 'What Would Ecological Climate Change Law Look Like? Developing a Method for Analysing the International Climate Change Regime from an Ecological Perspective' (2020) 29 *RECIEL* 76.

13 Vanguardism and Environmental Justice Developments in Colombia

Luis Armando Tolosa Villabona

1. Introduction

In the present century, Colombian judges, through their judicial decisions, have been playing a leading and avant-garde role in climate justice. With the approval of the Political Constitution of 1991 (the 'Political Constitution'), there has been growing participation of the judiciary in the dynamics of environmental problems with notable national and international impact.

The Political Constitution embodied provisions advocating for a model of the Environmental Rule of Law within the framework of neo-constitutionalism, as it adopted an ecological trend for the protection of nature's rights. Judges have been receptive and have empowered the Constitution by making it a dynamic and living text. As a result, faced with the various conflicts that must be resolved, citizens have seen in their decisions the possibility of redemption or recognition of minimal rights and guarantees.

Numerous judgments have been handed down throughout the country's geography, including remote areas, in order to build a genuine climate justice and an Environmental Rule of Law. What was the way to arrive at those formulations? The process has multiple causes and is the result of a recovery from the past, an analysis of the present and the projection into the future.

2. Pre-Columbian Roots[1]

The legal developments in the 21st century in Colombian jurisprudence date back to the Pre-Columbian era. This era was marked by notable indigenous cultures with advanced agricultural techniques, ecocentric vision and the utmost respect for nature. Let's think about the Mayans in the *Yucatán* Peninsula, the *Petén* of Guatemala, Honduras and El Salvador and the Aztecs in Southern Mexico. Then, there were the Incas, who occupied Western South America, following the Andes mountain range, from Northern Chile, part of Argentina, Bolivia, Peru, Ecuador

1 Adjective that means prior to the so-called discovery of America by Christopher Columbus, in 1492: RAE, *Dictionary of the Royal Spanish Academy* (Espasa Calpe 2006).

DOI: 10.4324/9781003175308-17

and Southern Colombia. The *chibchas* or *muiscas* were set in the central and surrounding areas of Colombia and the highlands and cold areas of the center of the country, whereas the *Taironas* occupied the *Sierra Nevada de Santa Marta*. Finally, the Caribbean culture spread on the coast of the Atlantic Ocean and the *Arwac* can be found in the regions of the Amazon, Putumayo and Caquetá rivers.

These indigenous cultures[2] held a permanent dialogue with the surrounding reality, they practiced a deep appreciation for mother nature or *pachamama*, the water, the forest, and for all fauna and flora, living in symbiosis with the ecosystem. Nature was decisive in their daily life and in their future because it was the reason for their own existence; they recognized their absolute dependence on it, forming authentic ecosystems, whose daily work was gestated in its preservation to coexist.

Since the arrival of the conquering culture in 1492, strange to the Aboriginal, with violence and destruction, it led to the acculturation and extermination of the population, the imposition of a vision opposed to the indigenous one, that expanded the classification of nature as a thing or a legal good. It indoctrinated the ideologies, philosophies and legal orders prevailing in Europe, against the vernacular, generating a rampant practice of destroying the ecosystem.

Recent studies point out:

> The demographic disaster that led to the disappearance of an incalculable number of groups and cultural forms had as its main cause that newly arrived Europeans occupied the space in which the native ethnic groups had shaped their way of living within the group and some neighborhood relations with others.[3]

The crime of extermination of nature and the Aboriginal caused a huge demographic crisis that led to the need to import slaves from Africa to satisfy the greed for gold, and the creation and maintenance of large farms that toppled entire forests.

> This violence was based on and supported by the prevailing ideology of domination and obedience due to the power sacralized by the conquerors. Those who survived were subsequent victims of the working conditions to which they were subjected, . . . various pretexts were developed to justify the trafficking of slave labor obtained from the black ethnic groups of Africa.[4]

2 Human group with identity awareness, also designated: indigenous people, indigenous population, indigenous nationality; indigenous, pre-Columbian, autochthonous; indigenous shelters, tribes, ethnicities, indigenous race, indigenous biases. Convention 169 of 1989 of the International Labour Organization (ILO) also defines this category.

3 Javier Rodríguez, *Etnias y culturas en el medio ambiente en Colombia* (Editor Pablo Leyva, IDEAM 2001) 424.

4 Ibid 424.

The impact was harmful. Persecution and displacement before the occupation of the historical seats of the original cultures. This spawned peoples' extinction, loss of languages and dialects; contagion of new diseases with unknown cures, aggravating the demographic disaster of the indigenous population. At the same time, the progressive mixture arose because of the massive arrival of Iberians and Africans in the face of the gold rush and Aboriginal wealth. As nature deteriorated, the indigenous population diminished due to ruthless treatment, forced displacement and new diseases.

Significant changes were introduced in the ecological order of such cultures. For instance, the ecological landscape, with the insertion of villages, parishes and dioceses founded in coastal areas, highlands, mountain ranges and plains, was the first affected. The voracity for gold and strategic resources of the time to sustain the expeditions and geopolitical plans of the European monarchies subdued the population and affected the plant biomass by the use of inputs to build villages and carry out extractive mining projects.

Building a house, a place of worship, a boat, navigating rivers and swamps, required cutting down forests (deforestation) and expanding borders by deforesting to find suitable materials. There was no electricity, and no fuel-producing resources were exploited; therefore, forests were used to produce fire and coal. However, nowadays, contrary to Pre-Columbian practices, mountains are cut down and are expected to dry up in the Summer; then they are burned to use their soils for agriculture and livestock, as it occurs today, with the unstoppable ecocide of the Amazon and the *Darién* mutating the forest for illicit crops and illegal livestock. The verbs uprooting, fallowing, deforesting are forms that prevent reproduction, regrowth or reforestation, they are procedures that were in no way used by Aboriginal people, but from that time to this day are daily practices, contrary to the proceeding of the original communities. This was aggravated by the introduction of permanent crops.

That impact is captured by the literature of the time. Inspired by the Greek epic and cavalry books, it did not see Pre-Columbians as equals, as people, or with a vision of otherness, of 'face to face'. It did not see them as real monsters, but as inferior beings and moral spawns based on false interpretations; caused by the erroneous news that some expedition members carried, such as the exceptional anthropophagic behavior that certain natives had to adopt to defend their territory from the invader. This illusory perception was a mean to legitimize the colonizing political project that resulted in the devastation of man and nature.

Lope de Vega's comedy 'New World Discovered by Christopher Columbus' symbolizes the conquering and devastating vision of the environment and the motive of the company: greed and imperialist expansion, simulated by the spread of the faith. It is an adventure of ideological imposition like errant and victorious knights, portrayed by the giant of literature. In allusion to the conquerors, he says: "These, coveting the gold of the Indians, become saints, pretend Christian decorum, while many others carry all the treasure. With false religion and false gods, you come to rob us our gold and women."[5]

In another segment, he points out: "Do not allow them, Providence, to do this to me without justice, because greed leads them to do this diligence. Under the pretext of religion, they will look for silver and gold from the undercover treasure."[6] Lope de Vega draws extermination and domination: "If He, by the gold he encloses, wins the souls you see in Heaven, there is interest, there is not much to be on earth."[7] The playwright describes voracity and ambition, greed and material interest, on the pretext of a spiritual objective and a symbolic sacral dream, where exploitation and disruption of the environment are disguised by the habit of faith. It is the harmful ethical-political principle: the end justifies the means. A poem by a recent Afro-Colombian humanist graphed that tragedy.[8]

Against this traumatic form of action, of outrage and horror, between 1492 and 1620, Friars Bartolomé de las Casas,[9] Antonio de Montesinos[10] and Pedro Claver Corberó[11] rose up in defense of the indigenous people and against the exploitation of the slave population of African origin, the common movement and the anti-slavery struggles of African American communities.[12]

Today Montesinos' denunciation still resounds, on the eve of Christmas in 1511 against the indigenous exploitation and destruction of their lands:

> You are all in mortal sin and in it you live and die, because of the cruelty and tyranny that you use with these innocent people. Say, by what right do you have these Indians in such cruel and horrible servitude? With what authority have you made such abhorrent wars to these peoples who were in their meek and peaceful lands, where so infinite of them with their deaths and havoc, you have consumed? . . . These are not men? Don't they have rational souls? Aren't you forced to love them like yourselves? You do not understand this,

5 Verses 2741 and ss. of Act III of the critical edition of Lemartinel and Minguet.

6 Felix Lope de Vega Carpio, *The New World Discovered by Christopher Columbus* (Colombian Institute of Culture 1971) 58. There is also an *Édition annotée avec notices et biographie* by Ed Barry, professeur au lycée de Tarbes (Garnier 1897).

7 Ibid 58.

8 Manuel Zapata Olivella, *Changó el Gran Putas* (Rei Andes Ltda 1992) 86–87.

9 Jean Dumont, *La incomparable Isabel la Católica* (Encuentro Editions 2012) 159–176. Bartolomé de las Casas (1474–1566) was a Spanish Dominican missionary, bishop of Chiapas, a trusting defender of the indigenous people.

10 Antonio de Montesinos (1475–1540) was also a Spanish Dominican missionary who did his work on the Spanish Island and in Venezuela.

11 Pedro Claver (1580–1654), was known as the 'Slave of the Slaves', or the 'slave of the blacks'. He was a Spanish Jesuit priest who advocated the rights of African slaves in Cartagena, Colombia.

12 Indalecio Liévano Aguirre, *Los grandes conflictos sociales y económicos de nuestra historia* (11 ed. Vol. I, Third World 1985) 19–31; Lewis Hanke, *La lucha por la justicia en la conquista de América* (Editorial Sudamericana 1949).

> you do not feel this? . . . Bear in mind that, in the state you are in, you can no longer be saved more than the Moors or Turks who lack and do not want the faith of Jesus Christ.[13]

Since 1492, there has been an ideological hostility between the two visions – European and pre-Columbian – which generated a rupture and erosion of the conception of Aboriginal people, with serious repercussions due to the disappearance of lives, peoples, nations and resources that involve political, cultural and ecological liability. In the struggle, the conqueror and colonizer won as a *homo faber* of tools and machines, who only believes that he exists in his 'sameness', and all that surrounds him is only a commodity at the discretion of the only subject of rational law.

Cosmologies, theogonies, religions, languages and indigenous beliefs revolved around nature and the universe: the sun (*inti*), the moon (*mama quilla*), the land (*pachamama*), the god of agricultural fertility, the ray (*illapa*), the thunder, the lightning, *Huiracocha*, *Chiminigagua*, *Bachué*, *Bochica*, *Chia*, *Xué*, *Quetzalcoatl*, the *Kukulkán* of the Mayans, the *Kon Tiki* of the *Urus* of Lake Titicaca, in Upper Peru. The infinity of deities[14] structure a symbolic system of protection of everything that surrounds the human being and combines divine and cosmic realities, many of them anthropomorphized by the deep tribute professed to Mother Nature.

These conceptions were not understood by the Iberians; nor have they have been glimpsed today by the dominant universal cultures, but they are of particular importance for the future of the planet and man.

Native properties and communities, indigenous shelters, Jaguar, *taita*, *mama*, corn, traditional custodian, shaman, *amawta*, *tlamatini*,[15] sacred species, nature and its phenomena, *minga*, cultural diversity, self-determination, autonomy, indigenous nation, multicultural nation, territory, land, etc., are words with a philosophical value, a representation and a living historical sense. For example, the notion of territory "has a different meaning among indigenous peoples from that of Western civilization".[16] The exploitation and management of soil and resources that flow from nature differ remarkably from today's prevailing vision. The territory has life in the context of all daily culture because 'being' depends on that and it boasts "intangible components of a symbolic nature that must be

13 Ibid 19–20.

14 The *Popol Vuh* is an important story, which mixes the epic and the legend of the *Mayan-Quiché* civilization, alluding to the creation of the world. In Colombia, different indigenous peoples have a strong cultural tradition about the creation of the world and the insertion of man into nature.

15 *Chamán*, *chamo*, *mamos*, *curaca*, *amawta*, *tlamatini* are different carriers of wisdom and ancestral knowledge. The *chamanes* and the *mamos* are known in the Andean area, in the Peruvian Andean (*amawta*) and in the Aztec culture (*tlamatini*).

16 M. Javier Rodríguez, 'Los movimientos indígenas en América Latina' (2008) 24(2) *Gaceta de Antropología* 16, http://hdl.handle.net/10481/6928.

respected and considered. The land and its resources are sentient beings, they must be cared for, since, the subsistence of the community, . . . the reproduction and social, cultural and material continuity of the group depends on them."[17] As Bartolomé[18] points out, it relates to the idea of sacred 'ethnic territory', and it is not a material or geographical concept.

It is an integrating space, it is a biocentric environment, which enables the 'being', the people, the community. It is life, it is a collective identity,[19] that unifies time and space. It is an idiosyncratic, political and metaphysical image because the "territory not only presupposes the economic resources and subsistence of the group, it also entails symbolic and identity elements, its own cultural reproduction and it is a place where collective memory resides."[20]

It is not a geometric, geographical or fragmentary demarcation. It is "a living organism"[21] that assumes a universe, an indivisibility and identity with it. It is an essential nucleus of survival and life, where the material, the divine, the ancestral, the habitation, the use and the human existence converge. It is nature.

It is a political, existential and symbolic category of the indissoluble man-nature relationship. It is a greater right, it is the *pachamama*, the ancestral hemisphere, it is the *weltanschauung*.

Reichel Dolmatoff, in his archaeological and ethnological research in Colombia and Latin America, when analyzing Aboriginal prehistory, points out that lithic transformations[22] reflect the great success of Pre-Columbian cultures because they were able to coexist with the environment, leaving great ecological teachings for our time and creating a culture where "the jungles and savannahs did not suffer in the process, as they suffer today";[23] in such a way that they have left us a great legacy, consisting of

> the way in which they exploited the diverse environments of the coasts and slopes, the jungles and the highlands, how they knew how to extract their livelihood without destroying the fauna; how they conserved the land with their terraces and canals. This is what the Indians have left us, and this is what archaeology should teach us.[24]

17 Ibid.
18 Miguel Alberto Bartolomé, 'Presas y relocalizaciones de indígenas en América Latina' (1992) 2(4) *Alteridades* 17.
19 Ibid.
20 Rodríguez (n 16) 16.
21 Efrén Trapúes, *Decolonización del Estado en América Latina, en compilación de Víctor M. Ávila y otro* (Universidad Libre 2011) 167. He is a *taita* or indigenous leader of the People of the Pastures.
22 '*Pertenecientes o relativos a la piedra*': RAE, *Essential Dictionary of the Spanish Language* (22 ed. Espasa, 2006) 900.
23 Gerardo Reichel-Dolmatoff, *Colombia indígena, periodo prehispánico. Nueva historia de Colombia* (Vol. 1, Planeta 1989) 61.
24 Ibid 61.

This indigenous worldview is revived in recent Colombian jurisprudence and throughout Latin America, and it builds the new environmental courses. The notions of respect and protection for nature, environmental responsibility of each person, concern for the fundamental rights of future generations, the holistic and symbiotic vision between man and nature of Pre-Columbian thinking, without implying a mechanical return to the past, provides elements for the construction of the concept of Constitutional State and Environmental Law in the jurisprudence perspective.

3. The Legal Framework of the 19th and 20th Centuries: Impact of Pre-Columbian Vision on Environmental Vanguardism

In Colombia, the vision of the environment as a fundamental right, and nature as a subject of rights worthy of protection, instead of a legal object, has its roots in the National Civil Code since May 26, 1873. This vision was further strengthened in the Code of Natural Resources and Environmental protection, Decree 2811 of 1974, in the form of the right to enjoy a healthy environment.

3.1. An Ecological Constitution, Environmental Rule of Law

The Political Constitution can be classified as an ecological text, as it sculpts the most provisions to protect the ecosystem among contemporary supralegal texts.[25] In general terms, it seeks to achieve the harmony of man with nature; it establishes that the right to a healthy environment is fundamental, but also that every person has a duty to protect it.[26] It invigorates the jurisprudence with decisions of global repercussions of the Colombian judiciary. Articles such as 8, 58 and 67, 72–82, and 95 serve that purpose.

Precisely, in Article 79, the healthy environment is embodied as an essential, human and supralegal right:

> All people have the right to enjoy a healthy environment. The law will guarantee community participation in decisions that may affect it. It is the duty of the State to protect the diversity and integrity of the environment, to preserve areas of particular ecological importance and to promote education for the achievement of these purposes.

25 The official interpreter of the 1991 Constitution. The Constitutional Court lists 34 provisions part of the Ecological Constitution, in T-411/1992, 17 June 1992, exp. T -785. Mg. Pon. Alejandro Martínez C.

26 Oscar D. Amaya Navas, *Agua y derechos constitucionales en Colombia* (Vol. 1, Universidad Externado de Colombia 2018) 53.

Article 80 imposes that

> the State will plan the management and use of natural resources, to ensure their sustainable development, conservation, restoration or substitution. In addition, it must prevent and control environmental deterioration factors, impose legal sanctions and demand repair of the caused damages. It will also cooperate with other nations in protecting ecosystems located in border areas.

3.2. Some Subsequent Regulatory Statutes

After the expedition of the Political Constitution, there have been numerous laws and judicial decisions further extending the ecological constitution. For instance, due to the danger to biodiversity from the disappearance of *paramos* in the country, Law 1930 of July 27, 2018 was issued to protect such ecosystem.[27] Furthermore, the Constitutional Court under ruling C-369 of 2019 recognized the right of ethnic communities to be priory consulted before the adoption of any plans or programs in their territories. Some of the latest laws issued are: Law 1968 of 2019 that prohibits asbestos due to its carcinogenic effect, and anti-plastics Law 1973 of 2019.

4. Colombian Jurisprudence Vanguardism

Humans are the most active and predatory species in the ecosystem. How can we make them kinder, more ethical, virtuous and supportive to nature, as a subject of rights, so that the earth and humans do not collapse? Some judicial precedents try to answer this question. Some of the most iconic decisions are presented next.

4.1. The Environment as a Fundamental Right

This is an outstanding aspect when conceiving the right to a healthy environment as fundamental, worthy of protection by guardianship, as well as other judicial instruments by the national courts. The Constitutional Court, in judgment T-411 of 1992,[28] by protecting the right of a person seriously affected in his health by the activity of a mill due to "handling raw material waste, specifically the rice shell that was abandoned and then burned. This produced large amounts of ash, giving rise to lung and respiratory problems

27 This law, in Article 3 defines *Paramo* (moor) as: 'High mountain ecosystem, located between the upper limit of the Andean Forest and, if applicable, the lower limit of glaciers, in which plant associations such as grasslands, *frailejones*, scrublands, meadows and *chuscales* dominate, in addition, there may be formations of low forests and shrubs and present wetlands such as rivers, streams, peatlands, swamps, lakes and lagoons.'

28 The prelude of this thesis is located in the judgment T-406 of 1992 – Ciro Angarita.

in the inhabitants of the places surrounding the Mill."[29] To the collective claim it replies:

> The protection of the environment is not a 'platonic love towards Mother Nature', but the answer to a problem that, if further aggravated at the present pace, would end up raising a real question of life and death: the pollution of rivers and seas, the progressive disappearance of fauna and flora, the atmosphere of many large cities becoming unbreathable due to pollution, the disappearance of the ozone layer, the greenhouse effect, noise, deforestation, increased erosion, the use of chemicals, industrial waste, acid rain, nuclear melons, the impoverishment of the planet's genetic banks, etc., are such vital issues that they deserve a firm and unanimous decision of the world's population. After all, the natural heritage of a country, as with the historical – artistic one, belongs to the people who live in it, but also to the generations to come, since we are in the obligation and challenge of delivering the legacy that we have received in optimal conditions to our descendants.[30]

In another decision, it expresses that

> the right to the environment and in general, the rights of the so-called third generation, have been conceived as a set of basic conditions that surround man, that surround his life as a member of the community and that allow him to survive biologically and individually, in addition to their normal performance and integral development in the social environment. . . . The environment [is] an essential right of human beings, [but also] one of the purposes of the State, because not only the integral development of the human species depends on its realization, but also the protection of the most minimal conditions of survival.[31]

On the same path, months later it reiterates "that a healthy and ecologically balanced environment is a fundamental Constitutional right since its violation directly threatens the perpetuation of the human species and, consequently, the most fundamental right of man: life."[32]

In 1997, after accumulating several environmental cases, it delivered the unification judgment SU 442/97 against disputes where the infringement of the fundamental right to life was reported, as victims of irregular wastewater management. The judges of the instances denied protection, with the thesis that

29 Colombia Const. Court. Judgement T-411/1992, 17 June 1992, exp. T -785. Reporting Judge Alejandro Martínez.

30 Ibid.

31 Colombia Const. Court. Judgement T-415/1992, 17 June 1992, exp. T-101, Reporting Judge. Ciro Angarita.

32 Colombia Const. Court. Judgement T-536/1992, 23 September 1992, Reporting Judge Simon Rodriguez.

rights related to the healthy environment were collective and should be claimed through diffuse or popular actions and not by the rapid and expeditious mechanism of guardianship. It states:

> The State must guarantee the right to enjoy a healthy environment, adopt measures to improve the quality of life of the population and ensure the general well-being, in order to prevent irreparable damage to the person, since in such circumstances, that right is eligible to be protected, as has been stated, through the exercise of guardianship action.[33]

This criterion is reiterated in the constitutionality ruling C-671 of 2001, in those of the Supreme Court of Justice of the *Habeas Corpus* of *Chucho*, in the Amazon and in that of *Isla Parque Salamanca*.

5. Overcoming Anthropocentrism: Towards an Ecocentric-Anthropic View, Nature as a Subject of Laws

In the second decade of the 21st century, Colombian jurisprudence takes a qualitative leap, moving from an anthropocentric vision towards a new model that gives nature an essential and central role. It defends an ecocentric-anthropic vision seeking to overcome the unilateral and selfish conception of man as emperor and sovereign over nature.

In the light of this vision, rulings with a category of universality are made, and consistently state that everything that surrounds man is not an object of inconsiderate exploitation. The theses in force until then, that classified man as the only subject of conquering, colonizing and dominating right of nature, are severely criticized, and the judges rebel against them. Man cannot deforest, dry up swamps and wetlands, change river courses, exploit mercilessly, dig mines of open skies to find wealth, and satisfy his selfish appetite by vilifying nature. Those actions are wrong, lack humanity and trample the rights of current and future generations because they give nature the quality of an inert heritage good.

They censor States for not protecting the ecosystem and order its restoration because nature is a legal entity with personality and subject of rights. In this way, they forge a relationship of dialogue, of creative encounter of man with nature, of alterity and equity between the anthropic or human with the ecocentric or biotic. Man, despite his rationality, is not the only subject that exists in the universe; nature is also a subject with legal personality that demands respect.

33 Colombia Const. Court. Judgement SU-442/1997, 16 September 1997, Reporting Judge Hernando Herrera.

5.1. Judgment T-266 of November 10, 2016[34]

The Colombian Constitutional Court selected an 'acción de tutela' promoted by several communities bordering the Atrato River, against the Colombian State and other agencies. The action sought the protection of fundamental rights related to the environment against the destruction of the ecosystem, the logging of trees and illegal mining that poisons the water of the Atrato River, one of the largest rivers in the world. The protection was initially denied, but the Court revoked that decision and arranged for the recognition of the river as a subject of rights. It ordered action against its pollution and poisoning, due to the illegal exploitation of gold mines and other minerals.

The community denounced the intensive use of illegal mining and forestry methods, executed with heavy machinery – dredgers and backhoes, the use of toxics such as mercury, cyanide and other highly poisonous substances in the Atrato River, its basins, swamps, wetlands and tributaries. It warned of the harmful and irreversible consequences for the environment, the ethnic communities and the environmental balance of the region. It is a crime that poisons the water with mercury to obtain gold bars.

This water from the river and its tributaries are used for direct consumption, agriculture, fishing and daily activities of communities. The environmental damage is irreparable.

The Court, defending the best interests of nature, states that the anthropocentric vision

> conceives human beings . . . as the only reason for the legal system and natural resources as mere objects at their service, . . . [the] biocentric claims more global and supportive conceptions of human responsibility, which advocate – in equal measure – for the duties of man with nature and generations to come; . . . [the] ecocentric postures . . . conceive nature as an authentic subject of rights.[35]

It adds: in

> the ecocentric approach . . . the earth does not belong to man and, on the contrary, it assumes that man belongs to the earth, like any other species. According to this interpretation, the human species is just one more event within a long evolutionary chain that has lasted for billions of years and therefore in no way it is the owner of other species, biodiversity or natural resources nor the fate of the planet. Consequently, this theory conceives *nature as an authentic subject of rights* that must be recognized by the States

34 Colombia Const. Court. Judgement. T-266/2016, 10 November 2016, Reporting Judge Jorge I. Palacio.

35 Ibid.

> and exercised under the tutelage of their legal representatives, for example, by the communities that inhabit it or have a special relationship with it.[36]
> (italic by the author)

That thesis had already been set out in judgments C-632 of 2011 and T-080 of 2015.

Nature is a living organism and entity, "composed of multiple other forms of life and cultural representations, they are subject to individualized rights, which makes them a new imperative of comprehensive protection and respect on the part of States and societies"[37]; it is a challenge to judges the illegal exploitations of nature and its predators to overcome the mercantilist prism of material, genetic or productive utility.

The ruling states that the relationship with nature cannot be purely efficient or dominant because with it, man shares the planet, it connects us all. We are part of a global ecosystem within the framework of "cultural and ethnic pluralism".[38]

As the illegal mining activity "has the potential to damage the health and the environment",[39] it requires the application of the precautionary principle due to the high harmful effects, and therefore "the solution that avoids damage should be preferred, and not the one that allows it."[40]

After demonstrating the harmful environmental effects, it

> [Provides] that the Colombian State exercise legal guardianship and representation . . . in conjunction with ethnic communities living in the Atrato River basin . . . represented by a member of the shareholding communities and a delegate of the Colombian State. . . . And in order to ensure the protection, recovery and . . . conservation of the river, both parties must design and form a commission;[41]

but protection is also the responsibility of all civil society.

The decision also provides the categories 'bioculturality' and 'biocultural rights' as "the relationship of deep unity between nature and human species",[42] composed of: 1. The modes of the cultural ecosystem and territorial diversity. 2. The wealth from cultural diversity, practices, beliefs and languages. 3. The relationships of ancestral cultures with the biodiversity of the place. 4. "The spiritual and cultural meanings of indigenous peoples and local communities on nature".[43] Therefore, these rights must also be protected.

36 Ibid.
37 Ibid.
38 Ibid.
39 Ibid.
40 Ibid.
41 Ibid.
42 Ibid.
43 Ibid.

5.2. *The* Habeas Corpus *Decision of the Spectacled Bear* Chucho *of July 26, 2017 of the Civil Cassation Chamber of the Supreme Court of Justice*[44]

The Supreme Court granted a *Habeas Corpus* to an Andean spectacled bear, 'Chucho', *tremarctos ornatus*, emblematic of the Colombian Andes, now on the way to extinction. This *Habeas Corpus* was first denied by the *a quo* court.

Chucho was transferred and confined in a zoo in Barranquilla, a hot city at sea level, after spending 18 years in the natural reserve *Río Blanco* in the city of Manizales, a cold area in the mountain range, on the basis that environmental authorities could not "guarantee its health and well-being".

The Court granted freedom to Chucho, as it considers it to be a subject of rights, with personality, like nature and animals in general, sentient realities with legal personality. Critical sectors promptly censored the decision, formulating a guardianship action, opposing the application of levels of equality with other subjects of law.[45]

In the emblematic providence, although later revoked by another Chamber, the ecocentric-anthropic vision is defended as a relationship of 'alterity' and respect for the other, it advocates for the responsibility of man, the State and humanity not to reify nature, fauna and flora and preserve the lives of future generations. It says:

> Human is an animal that gives birth, is born, breathes and dies as such, it is a natural reality. The new analysis of our rationality and self-awareness and human development must start from not ignoring our status as living beings and animals.[46]

The new realities are subjects with rights but without duties,

> obligations cannot be imposed on them because they are precisely sentient subjects of rights, against whom the main guardian, representative, informal and responsible agent is man individually or collectively. It is not about the modification of a legal position from an exclusively biological or moralistic perspective, or from pain with a criterion of trivial sensitiveness because animals suffer, but from a different and creative legal philosophical texture; from a radical existential commitment to the life of man himself, of future generations, of species, of the conservation of nature as an individual and collective struggle against the predators of our universe; against those who

44 Colombia, CSJ Civil. AHC4806–2017, *Habeas Corpus* of the 'Chucho' Bear of 26 July 2017, Reporting judge Luis A. Tolosa V. Rad. 17001–22–13–000–2017–00468–02.
45 Colombia, CSJ Labor, STL 12651–2017.
46 Colombia, CSJ Civil. AHC4806–2017, *Habeas Corpus* of the 'Chucho' Bear of 26 July 2017, Reporting Judge. Luis A. Tolosa V. Rad. 17001–22–13–000–2017–00468–02.

day by day destroy it without regard, to satisfy their hoarding and technocratic appetites.[47]

The *Habeas Corpus* is a tool for human freedom, a guarantee that

> is not . . . incompatible to ensure animals as 'sentient beings', and therefore, subjects of rights, entitled to demand through any citizen, the protection of their physical integrity, as well as their care, maintenance or reintegration into their natural habitat.[48]

5.3. *The Guardianship Judgment STC 4360–2018 of April 5, 2018 of the Supreme Court of Justice: The Amazon Subject of Rights*[49]

Twenty-five children, adolescents and young adults between 7 and 25 years, residing in Colombian cities at risk for climate change, pleaded for the protection of their rights to "enjoy a healthy environment", life and health, violated by the state due to climate change and the vital harmful consequences generated by the indiscriminate deforestation of the Amazon.

Taking into account that in the Paris Agreement[50] and Law 1753 of 2015,[51] the government made national and international commitments to "reduce deforestation and greenhouse gas emissions in a climate change context", including reducing "by 2020 the net rate of deforestation to zero in the Colombian Amazon"; but, on the contrary, "the country lost 178.597 hectares in 2016 . . . deforestation increased by 44% compared to the figure reported for 2015", and, of that number, 70,074 hectares correspond to the Amazon, affecting its fundamental rights, the action became urgent. It denounced and proved the "land grabbing (60–65%), illicit crops (20–22%), illicit extraction of mineral deposits (7–8%), infrastructure, agro-industrial crops and illegal wood extraction", with the consequences on biodiversity in the region, global ecosystems and on people's fundamental rights.

In the first instance, the pleas were denied. In the appeal, the Supreme Court reversed the decision, stating the protection of the rights of the plaintiffs, of future generations and the unborn under the principle of solidarity. As opposed to anthropocentrism, it defends the ecocentric-anthropic vision, the need for climate justice, the model of the State of Environmental Law. It gives the President of the Republic and the environmental authorities the order to reduce Amazonian deforestation to zero, and as a mechanism for executing the ruling, it

47 Ibid.
48 Ibid.
49 Colombia, CSJ Civil. STC 4360–2018, Ruling. Guardianship of 5 April 2018, Reporting Judge. Luis A. Tolosa V. Radic. 11001–22–03–000–2018–00319–01.
50 Approved in Colombia by Law 1844 of 2017. Official Journal 50294 of July 14, 2017.
51 For which the National Development Plan was issued 2014–2018.

provides for the celebration of a *PIVAC* (Intergenerational Pact for the Life of the Colombian Amazon).

It points out,

> in order to protect this vital ecosystem for the global development . . . the Colombian Amazon is recognized as an entity, 'subject of rights', holder of protection, conservation, maintenance and restoration by the State and the territorial entities that comprise it.[52]

It also ordered the protection of the fundamental rights of future generations because

> without a healthy environment, subjects of law and sentient beings in general will not be able to survive, let alone safeguard those rights, for their children or for generations to come. Nor can the existence of the family, society or the State itself be guaranteed.[53]

The ruling holds humanity accountable for the disaster due to its hegemonic position, having adopted an anthropocentric and selfish model, it advocates the "anthropic ecocentric" trend, which surpasses "the excessive 'homomensura'[54] 'autistic' anthropocentrism"; this trend takes into consideration the environment within the ideal of progress and the effective notion of sustainable development, in order to achieve "a balance between economic growth, social welfare and environmental protection, [because] the present actions must ensure the possibility of using resources in the future".[55]

The human species must be stripped of its own interest. It is bound to

> consider how our daily actions and conduct also impact society and nature. . . . [T]he scope of protection of the fundamental legal precepts is each person, but also the 'other'. The 'neighbor' is otherness; its essence, the other people who inhabit the planet, also encompassing the other animal and plant species. But it also includes the unborn subjects, who deserve to enjoy the same environmental conditions experienced by us.[56]

52 Colombia, CSJ Civil. STC 4360–2018, Ruling. Guardianship of 5 April 2018, Reporting Judge Luis A. Tolosa V. Radic. 11001–22–03–000–2018–00319–01.

53 Ibid.

54 Protagora, 'El hombre es la medida de todas las cosas, de las que existen en cuanto existen y de las que no son en cuanto no son' in T. Calvo (ed), *De los sofistas a Platón: política y pensamiento* (Cincel 1986).

55 Constitutional Court, Ruling C-389 of 2016.

56 Colombia, CSJ Civil. STC 4360–2018, Ruling Guardianship of 5 April 2018, Reporting Judge Luis A. Tolosa V. Radic. 11001–22–03–000–2018–00319–01.

It rightly defends the rights of future generations, following the criterion of intergenerational equity, in the face of the imminent deterioration of their rights due to deforestation:

> The environmental rights of future generations are based on the (i) ethical duty of the solidarity of the species[57] and (ii) on the intrinsic value of nature. . . . The conservation of the Amazon is a national and global obligation, . . . the main environmental area existing on the planet, for this reason . . . the 'lung of the world'.[58]

It demonstrates the irreparable damage to the Amazon and the exponential increase in destruction, the harmful effects on ecosystem connectivity with the Andes and other areas around the planet that, as a result, affect the lives of all people. It orders "a short-, medium- and long-term action plan that counteracts the rate of deforestation . . . [and] tackles the effects of climate change."[59]

The Colombian State Council in a popular action of March 28, 2014 studied the serious pollution of the Bogota river in its transit through the *Bogotá* Savanna and riverside areas until it flowed into the Magdalena river, and took more than 100 orders to seek the decontamination of that river artery.

5.4. *Other Decisions*

Before and after these rulings, there have been numerous decisions that protect the rights of nature, declaring rivers, regions and moors subjects of rights; therefore, today, there is a great internal jurisprudential movement to protect nature.

6. Conclusions

Colombia's novel jurisprudential doctrine leverages a global vision for the protection of nature's rights, characterized because:

1. It forges an ecocentric-anthropic conception that surpasses the totalitarian vision of anthropocentrism. Nature is a living organism and man, its eternal responsible and guardian, in such a way that it engenders a reciprocal relationship of substantive equality and similarity that, while recognizing the new, takes into account the ancestral knowledge, uses and customs inherited by the aboriginal people.

57 Juan Luis Ruiz de la Peña, 'Ecología y teología' in Xabier Pikaza (ed), *El desafío ecológico: Ecología y humanismo* (Pontifical University of Salamanca 1995) 134.

58 Lewis Munford, *El hombre y su responsabilidad natural* (Mensajero 1987) 102.

59 Colombia, CSJ. Civil. Ruling 4360–2018. Guardianship of April 5, 2018, Reporting Judge. Luis A. Tolosa V. Radic. 11001–22–03–000–2018–00319–01.

As one of the rulings expresses, "[t]he man is not the omnipotent master of the universe, with carte blanche to do what he wants or what suits him at a certain time with impunity."[60] He cannot act superbly because he carves out his self-destruction when he destroys 'otherness', nature. Thus, he destroys his own life and that of future generations, given the close and inseparable relationship between man and nature to be and exist.

2. It encourages an Environmental Rule of Law model. The judges are trying to formulate a new model of 'Constitutional State of Environmental Law', in which the ecosystem, natural resources and the environment are supreme values as the superior form of the political institution. A state of social formation or a relationship of any kind makes no sense when it does not advocate the protection of the life of both man and nature given its reciprocal interdependence.
3. It legitimizes citizen participation in environmental processes. The presented jurisprudence shows the urgent need to seek the participation of citizens as a mean to promote actions, report environmental impacts to judges and urge the compliance of the rulings. Decisions shall not be dead letters or theoretical aspirations if citizens are actively involved in environmental litigation. It is a duty and a right to require the State itself and the world authorities to comply with the judgments and regulations that provide the protection of the ecosystem.
4. It seeks a rule of law with strengthened climate and environmental justice. The Judicial doctrine seeks to materialize climate justice. Of course, there are obstacles in Latin America where the resources to the justice sector are meager or because the other powers of the State delegitimate the decisions. But whether a specialized environmental justice scheme has been adopted or attributed to all judges in a diffuse way, all without distinction, it must embody a sense of belonging and awareness of the seriousness of environmental deterioration. Everyone must be able to make decisions in every ruling for the rights of nature and ecosystem protection.

   The absence of constitutional or legal mechanisms is not an excuse for not adopting decisions to protect the ecosystem. In these cases, the judge must resort to *hard* and *soft law*, in order to strengthen environmental democracy or the 'environmental rule of law'. This will forge effective justice to prevent the destruction of our planet.
5. It strengthens the thesis that the environment is a fundamental right. One of the most momentous elements in the decisions discussed earlier is the conceptualization that the environment is a fundamental right because it is inherent to the human person, worthy of protection through different constitutional actions because it concerns all people. This paradigm must be

60 Colombian Const. Court. Ruling T-411/1992, 17 June 1992, exp. T-785, Reporting Judge Alejandro Martínez.

imposed on every judge in the contemporary State as a basis to fight against the destruction of the ecosystem.

6. Nature is not a legal asset; it is a subject of rights. In the arsenal of precedents, shine the unprecedented application of the paradigm for which I have always advocated in the analysis of these crucial issues, defending it in academic and judicial scenarios. Nature, the ecosystem, is not an object, it is a subject of rights, it has its own attributes, which require protection and guarantee, it is a living organism that determines the life of sentient beings, and of course of man, also composed of individualized subjects, such as rivers, moors, and sentient beings. This means incorporating in practice, in everyday life and daily rationality a concept of alterity and respect for 'otherness', transforming our thinking. Ecosystems and nature are not instrumentalized things or objects that can be exploited, they are realities that have legal existence, representation, life and the right to exist, to be resilient, to be protected and restored.

Human beings, therefore, have legal, political and moral duties and obligations to nature; they are their caregivers, guardians and representatives; therefore, governments and authorities must be rigorous, all of which must be reflected in concrete measures in all human activities. For example, a bank cannot grant loans to those who illegally deforest, pollute or destroy habitats; an educational institution cannot obtain authorization from the State to exist if it does not include environmental protection policies in its different training programs; a chain of stores should not sell products that do not have a seal of non-source or origin from deforested, polluted or illicitly occupied zones when they are reserves or natural parks, nor from areas where indigenous people were displaced. It involves incorporating these categories to make it effective in all areas of life and in the production chain in general. To that extent, there will be a transition to a model of ecocentric-anthropic creative coexistence between men and nature.

Finally, despite the avant-garde nature of this jurisprudence, in Colombia, as in the world in general, destructive actions against the ecosystem grow geometrically with harmful effects for all humanity. Nature is vulnerable; it demands the participation of all people and organizations, of rationality and of the academy in general to urge measures, moving on to concrete actions because the future is obscure. The flora and fauna, the entire environment is being devastated due to impunity. International treaties, agreements and government plans seem like a dream in the face of destruction. Our countries, our planet, man itself and future generations are at risk. We need to act effectively.

In the case of Colombia, its mega biodiversity is in danger. There is an inability of authorities, criminality to deforest is increasing, illicit crops and livestock are expanding illegally, rivers are being poisoned – all of these represent a setback for humanity. Hence, support from the international community is required to protest and seek with the governments of the region effective policies that stop the holocaust.

Bibliography

Amaya Navas O., *Agua y Derechos Constitucionales en Colombia* (Vol. 1, U. Externado de Colombia 2018).
Dumont J., *La incomparable Isabel la Católica* (Encuentro Editions 2012).
Hank L., *La lucha por la justicia en la conquista de América* (Editorial Sudamericana 1949).
Livano Aguirre I., *Los grandes conflictos sociales y económicos de nuestra historia* (Vol. I, 11th edn, Third World 1985).
Lope Carpio F., *El Nuevo Mundo descubierto Cristóbal Colón* (Colombian Institute of Culture 1971).
Reichel-Dolmatoff G., *Colombia indígena, periodo prehispánico* (Vol. 1, New History of Colombia 1989).
Rodriguez J., *Etnias y culturas en el medio ambiente de Colombia. En el medio ambiente en Colombia* (Pablo Leyva IDEAM 2001).
Torrejon F., Cisternas M. and Araneda A., 'Efectos ambientales de la colonización española desde el río Maullín al archipiélago de Chiloé, sur de Chile' (2004) 77 *Rev. chil. hist. nat.* 661.
Zapata Olivella M., *Changó el gran Putas* (Rei Andes Ltda 1992).

Afterword

Final Rallying Call on the Brutal Realities of the Anthropocene and the Necessity of Cosmoprudence to Minimise Human Suffering

Werner Menski

1. Introduction

A disparate collection of articles always poses a challenging task of analysis, as we risk drowning in detail. Discussing environmental constitutionalism in the Anthropocene in terms of values, principles and actions generates a sense of urgency, given the actual and lurking brutal realities of climate change on a global scale. In postmodern times, the challenges of finding adequate responses remain arduous, while time is running out. Complex debates are needed, but must be combined with locally focused effective remedies to minimise suffering, wherever possible. The tools of environmental constitutionalism, developed all over the world with an increasing sense of purpose remain impaired by various corruptions, infirmities and lack of commitment, threatening to disable the full growth of effective environmental constitutionalism in the Anthropocene.

Following calls to take the urgency of effective action seriously, and some clarifications about the Anthropocene and its connections with various academic disciplines, ongoing highly contested discussions regarding the use of language, concepts and methods to tackle the law-related challenges of the Anthropocene are raised here, conscious of the fact that 'law' appears to be widely treated as a critical element in this context.[1] Thereafter, building on recent writing about the life work of Professor Upendra Baxi, and in light of the remarkable Indian constitutional blueprint of 'complete justice', as found in Article 142 of the Indian Constitution of 1950, this final rallying call suggests not a holy grail, but a new practice-focused method of tackling the complex challenges of the Anthropocene through holistic, law-related strategies of affirmative action, specifically in favour of any victims of development and climate change.

The proposed concept of 'cosmoprudence' is, therefore, not an attempt to impose some kind of 'stealth theocracy'.[2] It is a hands-on justice-conscious and

1 Nicholas A. Robinson, 'Fundamental Principles of Law for the Anthropocene?' (2014) 44(1–2) *Environmental Policy & Law* 13–27, 13.

2 Yvonne Tew, 'Stealth Theocracy' (2018) 58 *Virginia Journal of International Law* 31–96 raises this issue specifically for Malaysia, Indonesia and some other Muslim majority countries.

DOI: 10.4324/9781003175308-18

quite realistic, activist strategic response, which takes completely seriously that the grave risk of increased human suffering, which humanity has a collective responsibility to reduce as far as possible, can partly be alleviated if some specific changes are introduced by holistic environmental constitutionalism. The concept and methods of cosmoprudence, reflecting law-related pluralities in everything humans do in various culture-specific ways and different situations, acknowledges specifically the well-recognised importance of values, which occupy a prominent position in the present volume. Decades ago, Professor Chiba seminally called these components 'legal postulates',[3] building blocks of what Professor Baxi has equally seminally, more recently, called social action litigation (SAL) and 'demosprudence'.[4]

In light of the articles in this study, I propose more diligent attention to interdisciplinary and holistic approaches, including consideration of the cosmic dimension. Faced with the looming threats posed by the Anthropocene, all law-related decision makers are not merely responsible to a specific democratic set-up, or a partial set of political considerations, but should ideally take an action-focused holistic, altruistic perspective, targeted to assist especially those who face victimisation to protect all of us in the wake of required new processes of adjustment to promote 'green' technologies and other new responses to climate change. Since increased risks of intolerable precarities are rising, environmental constitutionalism must act responsibly and cannot hide any longer behind modernist hubris and secular apprehensions about 'religion' and/or tradition. Above all, our tortured times demand effective implementation of what may be called some form of 'higher public interest', in fact the best interests of the entire interconnected globe and all its human and non-human components.

2. No Time for Idle Talk: The Urgency of the Task

Apart from multiple disagreements about what is meant by 'law', social science and law-related scholarship struggles with 'critical' perspectives that show proclivities to treat any kind of established 'order' as a form of corruption.[5] Indulging in rhetorics of resistance claims the freedom to engage in cleverly worded

3 Masaji Chiba (ed) *Asian Indigenous Law in Interaction with Received Law* (KPI 1986) 6–7. See also Masaji Chiba, *Legal Pluralism: Towards a General Theory through Japanese Legal Culture* (Tokai University Press 1989; Masaji Chiba, *Legal Cultures in Human Society: A Collection of Articles and Essays* (Shinzansha International 2002).

4 A.K. Sikri, 'Foreword' in Salman Khurshid, Sidharth Luthra, Lokendra Malik and Shruti Bedi (eds), *Judicial Review. Process, Powers, and Problems. Essays in Honour of Upendra Baxi* (CUP 2020) viii–xi. See also Upendra Baxi, 'Demosprudence versus Jurisprudence: the Indian Judicial Experience in the Context of Comparative Constitutional Studies' (2014) 14 *Macquarie Law Journal* 3–23.

5 Sudhir Chella Rajan, *A Social Theory of Corruption: Notes from the Indian Subcontinent* (Harvard University Press 2020).

games, while awareness is rising that the world has entered the Anthropocene.[6] Not only in the country of Amartya Sen's 'argumentative Indians', widespread cluelessness about remedies is reflected in typical ivory tower talk, glorifying that the freedom to indulge in endless argumentation 'sets up a form of democratic practice, which can at least give us the reassurance of having tried'.[7] While some challenges are posed by rising demands to combine theory with practice, and to test both against each other, there is also a renewed strong sense that the modernity-driven, Western narrative of mastery of the world must be revisited.[8] Taking seriously the demand to think across traditions,[9] and to contemporanise such debates,[10] when faced with the brutal realities of the Anthropocene, would also suggest a global revisiting of how we tend to waste intellectual energies in academic one-upmanship, while the world around us is turning into hell for many millions of victims.

The realities of human suffering, partly as a result of law, have long motivated leading legal scholars such as Professor Baxi, a celebrated authority,[11] by now 'a laptop-wielding octogenarian'.[12] He is not a prophet of doom and gloom, but for a recent commentator appears as a 'surprisingly optimistic' activist and analyst of the ills of Indian and global violations of basic human rights.[13] There are good reasons for such optimism, but they may not be those that Baxi himself, as a secular scholar, may wish to discuss in detail. The core issue seems to be how we frame 'law' to resemble entities that modern, doctrinal constitutional lawyers would be prepared to recognise at least as law-related, and then apply them to environmental constitutionalism. So far, numerous competing perceptions on 'governance', let alone 'good governance' and how such modalities relate to social, cultural and religious normativities, in all their ubiquitous pluralities, still populate multiple battlegrounds of epistemology, power and conflict. Large groups of stakeholders in all these fields will tend to cultivate specific partial interests that they would like to see privileged, often out of pure greed.

In such unequal contests, in some kind of feeding frenzy before disaster fully strikes, many victims of development are denied equal rights and fair treatment.[14] Most probably, the already-dominant players will profit more, while the

6 Sudhir Chella Rajan, 'Practising Theory in the Anthropocene. A Postcolonial Quest for Reliable Knowledge' (2017) 52(14) *Economic & Political Weekly* 72–74.

7 Ibid 74.

8 Prathama Banerjee, Aditya Nigam and Rakesh Pandey, 'The Work of Theory. Thinking Across Traditions' (2016) 51(37) *Economic & Political Weekly* 42–50, 43.

9 Ibid 46.

10 Ibid 47.

11 Khurshid et al. (eds) (n 4).

12 Amita Dhanda, 'The Baxian Bioscope on Indian Judicial Process' in Khurshid et al. (eds) (n 4) 145–162, 146.

13 John McEldowney, 'Judicial Review. Perspectives and Reflections for the Twenty-First Century' in Khurshid et al. (eds) (n 4) 60–78, 69.

14 For example, see Felix Padel and Samarendra Das, 'Cultural Genocide and the Rhetoric of Sustainable Mining in East India' (2010) 18(3) *Contemporary South Asia* 333–341; Felix

disadvantaged will lose out further. It is equally likely that the major victims of climate change will never read the kind of book offered here. What they really need, however, is the 'complete justice' that is, on paper, promised by Article 142 of the Indian Constitution and in neighbouring Bangladesh and Nepal.[15]

The so-called 'subaltern' can and do, increasingly, speak up, but most of them suffer in silence and their grievances are not effectively addressed. A sensible exit route from this global negative spiral for the victims of various conflict scenarios over shortages of fairness and justice with regard to environmental constitutionalism cannot simply be to climb on rhetoric or actual barricades of resistance or protest, often in blind rage about perceived and frequently real injustices and deprivations. Far too often this results in further precarities for those who are already victimised. Reduction of conflict, and amelioration of precarious conditions, as several members of the current team of authors found a few years ago,[16] requires often arduous patient negotiation and constructive engagement, ideally on all sides, not merely protest, more conflicts and even wars over environmental resources. I fully agree with Domenico Amirante that constructive dialogue is the only option, but the urgency of global climate predicaments means that we can no longer afford endless discussions, while more millions of people continue to be denied even the most basic rights, given that existing legal orders tend to favour the haves over the have-nots.

In efforts to contribute to ongoing discussions about law-related conflict resolutions, focused this time explicitly on environmental constitutionalism in the Anthropocene, most contributors to the present volume find themselves in a privileged position. Many of us have participated in extended discussions in a series of international Doctoral Training Seminars since 2016, starting in Switzerland, then moving to Southern Italy, and finally meeting amidst the smog and pollutions of Northern India. It has been highly instructive to observe how this particular international academic co-operation turned from an initially more 'academic' pursuit of legal pluralism and socio-legal comparative law towards comparative constitutional law. Almost inevitably, our multiple cross-cultural, transnational exchanges now focus more specifically on practice-related, action-focused concerns to strengthen environmental protection in related efforts to increase human well-being and avoid suffering.

Along the way, we engaged collectively in cultivating deeper knowledge about globally present evidence of legal pluralism in different contexts,[17] examining the-

Padel and Samarendra Das, *Out of This Earth: East India Adivasis and the Aluminium Cartel* (Orient BlackSwan 2010).

15 Shailendra Kumar, 'Sketching the Limits of Article 142 of the Constitution of India. A Constitutional Necessity' in Salman Khurshid et al. (eds) (n 4) 365–383, 365.

16 See Kyriaki Topidi (ed) *Normative Pluralism and Human Rights. Social Normativities in Conflict* (Routledge 2018).

17 In a study dedicated to Masaji Chiba, see earlier Werner Menski, *Comparative Law in a Global Context: The Legal Systems of Asia and Africa* (2nd edn CUP 2006). The increasingly strong link with Italian scholarship and its growing India-focused dimensions is evident in

oretically as well as practically how diverse social normativities and the resulting conflicts may be managed,[18] with spin-offs indicating that whether one navigates with the help of kites or ships, there are always specific mixities of law involved.[19] These often relate to non-state forms of dispute processing, leading to further, exciting new studies, in which local conflicts over environmental protection matters also featured.[20]

From an originally Eurocentric base of co-operation, which always actively sought out and included numerous voices from the global South, this led to further collections of comparative legal studies produced by the Indian partners who in due course joined this international academic enterprise.[21] These writings, too, increasingly recognised the contested forms of human interaction with nature. This, it seems, partly inspired other project partners to explore how various languages and legal systems have coined specific concepts and symbolic phrases to circumscribe various forms of ecosophy and 'the good life'.[22] As a team, we are not alone in this endeavour, as numerous examples of similar concerns and debates are presented in other recent publications.[23]

In this context, we learn that manipulations of the criteria of 'sustainability' have themselves become unsustainable and ineffective.[24] Since the tensions between development and environment are unlikely to subside, assiduous implementation of the principles of 'complete justice', indeed a surprisingly hopeful term that is already part of Indian and some other constitutional frameworks, offers fresh hopes, ensuring that the victims of various adaptation strategies are not left without proper compensation for the significant, often terrible losses they suffer on behalf of others. While scientific support structures can help law-related decision makers to manage adaptation and mitigation processes,[25] the inevitable suffering that such revised development strategies will inflict must be addressed, too. Failure to account for this, while simply viewing the management

---

Domenico Amirante, *Lo Stato Multiculturale* (Bononia University Press 2014); Domenico Amirante, *La Democrazia Dei Superlativi. Il Sistema Constituzionale dell'India Contemporanea* (Edizioni Scientifiche Italiane 2019).

18 See especially W. Menski, 'Introduction: Conflicts over Justice and Hybrid Social Actors as Legal Agents' in K. Topidi (n 16) 1–36.

19 W. Menski, 'On Kites and Ships: Climate Changes in Comparative Law and Judicial Navigation' in Séan Patrick Donlan and Jane Mair (eds), *Comparative Law. Mixes, Movements, and Metaphors*. Felicitation Volume for Prof. Esin Örücü (Routledge 2020) 67–86.

20 Kalindi Kokal, *State Law, Dispute Processing, and Legal Pluralism. Unspoken Dialogues from Rural India* (Routledge 2020).

21 Mahendra Pal Singh and Niraj Kumar (eds), *The Indian Yearbook of Comparative Law 2018* (Springer Nature Singapore 2019).

22 See the Special Issue of Silvia Bagni, M.A. Brightman and A. Furia (eds), 'Searching for Models of Intercultural Management of Social Conflict' (2020) 28(2) *Revista General de Derecho Publico Comparado*.

23 For several examples, see Robinson (n 1) 16–17.

24 Ibid 15 and 17.

25 See Gitanjali Nain Gill, *Environmental Justice in India. The National Green Tribunal* (Routledge 2017).

problems of the Anthropocene as a matter of finding the right balances between international law and national legal orders, will increase human suffering, rather than improve local levels of well-being, ultimately also for those who are privileged. The aim, as this book suggests, is not only to think about how to make Planet Earth as safe as possible. The main ambition, urgently now, should be to include new forms of affirmative action to provide 'complete justice', as effectively as possible, for the victims of development.

The present volume, presenting rich insights into the intricate interactions of cultural and religious values, principles and rules, as well as activist enforcement processes in the context of environmental constitutionalism, thus makes, I suggest, a significant consolidated contribution to understanding what it means to practise cosmoprudence. As Domenico Amirante concludes, a dialogue between the different environmental constitutional cultures is not only necessary for environmental constitutionalism 'in action', but this form of intercultural communication represents the only option for a viable way forward. However, as time is running out, the process of nurturing a common but plural environmental constitutional culture needs to be short-circuited and combined with case-based compensatory activism. The aim is not a quest for a new 'holy grail' or another grand environmental narrative. Rather, the need is for justice, now, and as complete as possible.

3. The Wider Context of the Anthropocene

The Anthropocene has become a scientific reality of major proportions, already felt worldwide. Apparently, 'human ingenuity unintentionally has altered the Earth's carbon and hydrological cycles, and changed the planet so greatly that the International Commission on Stratigraphy is studying whether the Holocene Epoch has ended and the Anthropocene Epoch has begun'.[26] Robinson also comments that 'this finding is a scientific one, not a socio-economic or cultural determination, yet its greatest implications may lie in the realm of the social sciences'.[27] Considered almost ten years later, this clearly identifies the major challenge for socio-legal and comparative law scholarship. It directs our work as responsible law-related academics, much as Professor Baxi has been arguing for decades,[28] towards alleviation of human suffering, recognising also that law itself tends to

26 Robinson (n 1) 13. In fact, the recently deceased Dutch meteorologist and atmospheric chemist Paul J. Crutzen, a Nobel Laureate of 1995, suggested that the Anthropocene started about two centuries ago. See P.J. Crutzen, 'The Anthropocene' in E. Ehlers and T. Krafft (eds) *Earth System Science in the Anthropocene* (Springer 2006) 13–18.

27 Robinson (n 1) 13.

28 Upendra Baxi, '"The Little Done, the Vast Undone". Some Reflections on Reading Granville Austin's *The Indian Constitution*' (1967) 9(3) *Journal of the Indian Law Institute* 323–430; Upendra Baxi, 'Taking Suffering Seriously: Social Action Litigation in the Supreme Court of India' (1985) 4 *Third World Legal Studies*, 107, also in N. Tiruchelvam and R. Coomaraswamy (eds) *The Role of the Judiciary in Plural Societies* (Pinter 1987) 32–49.

create its own victims. Robinson advises speedy engagement to help minimise the inevitable suffering because of various climate change impacts. For, as Robinson has put it, '[i]n the Anthropocene, events will overtake us, and there will be little time for traditional, gradual research methods. New models for research will be forced upon us'.[29]

Most directly evident for the team producing the present volume, we could simply not continue our insightful series of annual conferences in Switzerland, Southern Italy or Northern India, as Covid-19 prevented international travel and direct personal interaction. Yet, motivated by the synergies generated in previous rounds of conferences, including several days at the National Law University in Delhi in the inspiring presence of Professor Baxi in 2018, our collective efforts laid solid foundations especially among younger participants in those seminars.

Above all, the renewed urgency to respond to the challenges of the Anthropocene vindicates our gradually nurtured, pre-existing sensibilities and consciousness about the crucial role of continued global agency of all humans, in terms of either mitigating the already-ongoing processes, adapting to them more or less skilfully, or simply being reduced to suffering the inevitable impending and already visible consequences.[30] It is basically as simple as that, providing a new scenario for the well-known ancient Indian truth that non-action is a form of action, too, and will in this case have numerous terrible consequences.

There is no comprehensive insurance against what we already know is bound to happen, as progression into the Anthropocene is an ongoing measurable, science-based process. For activist environmental constitutionalism, this implies now urgent necessity to make effective use of scientific expertise in law-related decision-making processes. For example, the National Green Tribunal in India has pioneered that '[i]ts decision-makers include both judicial and expert members, reflecting the multidisciplinary scientific nature of environmental cases'.[31]

While everywhere on the globe, '[b]alancing environmental protection with economic development is a supremely challenging task',[32] responsible actions on the part of ecologically conscious humans, and even individual nation states,[33] are clearly no longer sufficient and effective enough. While Robinson raises among seven possible principles for a debate about firmer foundations for environmental rights the concept of 'biophilia',[34] which also has multiple religious and value-based dimensions, other authors have pointed to integrated notions of 'ecosophy' as motivators for individual and community action.[35] Rankin discusses also

29 Robinson (n 1) 15.

30 Ibid., with reference to John P. Holdren, who later became science advisor to US President Obama.

31 George Pring and Catherine Pring, 'Foreword' in Gitanjali Nain Gill (n 25) xix.

32 Ibid xx.

33 Gill (n 25) 30.

34 Robinson (n 1) 19.

35 Aidan Rankin, *Jainism and Environmental Philosophy. Karma and the Web of Life* (Routledge 2018) 25 raises this for Jain communities, who are traditionally reticent about discussing

the concept of Deep Ecology,[36] which in a secular way 'questions the philosophical assumptions behind industrialisation and unrestrained economic expansion, labelling them *anthropocentric*, or human-centred, and advocating in contrast a *bio-centric* or nature-centred approach'.[37]

However, since the environment 'has taken on the widely accepted status of an international and global responsibility albeit with regional partners and individual states acting as local caretakers',[38] there is a definite risk that discussions about environmental constitutionalism focus only on state practice and international norms and concerns, while ignoring the ever-present dimensions of individual values and social normativities, which simply cannot be overlooked.[39]

I am not raising this here to criticise Gill's highly informative specialist study of India's National Green Tribunal, but highlight that Robinson's wider discussion about the major principle of cooperation,[40] and thus of connectedness of everything, is more comprehensive. It connects not just state law and international laws, but explicitly indicates that values and related social normativities must not be missed by the radar of wider discourses about problem-solving and conflict management also in relation to environmental constitutionalism. The subtitle of the present volume clearly indicates our consciousness of these various intersecting scales and the necessary interdisciplinary efforts, as well as the pitfalls that such pluralities undoubtedly generate.

Meanwhile, the clock is ticking, and at all levels, there is simply no place to hide, no mythological Noah's Ark in which members of humanity and all the surviving species can seek shelter till the storms have subsided, the waters have receded and precarity gives way to a new era of harmony with nature. But there is also no reason to sink into despondent despair, simply because the consequences of the irrevocable damage caused by humans are so enormous. Yet much remains to be done, and equally much has to change. As indicated, simply creating a new global human right to a safe environment as foundation for a re-conceived universal right to life is certainly not a sufficient response to the challenges of the Anthropocene.

Reconfiguring the already complicated relations between various forms of theory and practice, what is also needed, worldwide, is a significant change in individual perceptions regarding the need to consume more and more, despite increasing knowledge that such growth is overall damaging, rather than beneficial. A spirit of renunciation, a form of resistance to thoughtless consumerism, needs to be cultivated, in the global North, but also in the global South. This

---

such matters theoretically, but practise various forms of non-violence that reflect environmental concerns as a 'total-field-image'.

36 Ibid 25–26, connected to work by the Norwegian philosopher and environmental activist Arne Naess, *Ecology, Community and Lifestyle: Outline of an Ecosophy* (CUP 1989).

37 Rankin (n 35) 26, italics in the original.

38 Gill (n 25) 30–31.

39 Menski (n 17).

40 Robinson (n 1) 18.

should be accompanied everywhere by state practices of giving up attractive-looking bribing strategies on the part of leaders who often blatantly seek public endorsement of unsustainable growth strategies at the cost of severe environmental damage.

At the same time, it must also be acknowledged that especially governments in 'developing countries' are under immense pressures to bolster basic economic growth and well-being, as not to do so would rapidly be portrayed as failures of governance. Thus, India Global Business of 24 March 2021, an online news service, reported record sales of diesel fuel to the extent of 2.84 million tonnes in the first two weeks of March 2021 and 1.05 million tonnes of petrol in the same period. The same report also emphasised that a newly energised post-Covid India (they thought then!) is seeking to speed up transfer to renewable energies. Such examples show the enormous pressures of satisfying instant demands by 'the people', not just business magnates and states. Such scenarios also illustrate the highly precarious time-lag for introducing greener technologies, confirming Robinson's arguments about the unsustainability of talking about 'sustainable development'.[41] These contradictions and tensions, a tough challenge indeed, are among the reasons why appeals to biophilia and sustainability are still causing leakages in the provision of 'complete justice', necessitating further activist engagement and scrutiny. Switching to a strategy of cosmoprudence, as fast and as radically as possible, appears to recommend itself in light of such grave discrepancies between ideals, necessities and competing stakeholder groups. In short, the focus on Baxian demosprudence risks overlooking that the *demos* itself is inevitably split into competing stakeholder groups.

4. Moving Closer Towards Effective Environmental Constitutionalism

Within a significant literature on the Anthropocene,[42] some work is specifically directed at the global South.[43] Such writing clearly reflects multiple implications for various academic disciplines. Critical discourses provide some indications that

41 Robinson (n 1) 15 and 17.

42 See, for example generally E. Horn and H. Bergtaller, *The Anthropocene. Key Issues for the Humanities* (Routledge 2020). More focused on constitutionalism, see D.R. Boyd, *The Environmental Rights Revolution. A Study of Constitutions, Human Rights and Environment* (UBC Press 2012); L.J. Kotzè, *Global Environmental Constitutionalism in the Anthropocene* (Hart Publishing 2016); L.J. Kotzè (ed), *Environmental Law and Governance for the Anthropocene* (Hart Publishing 2017).

43 For some particularly pertinent titles, see S. Alam, S. Atapattu, C.G. González and J. Razzaque (eds) *International Environmental Law and the Global South* (CUP 2015); D. Schlosberg, *Defining Environmental Justice: Theories, Movements, and Nature* (OUP 2007); L. Westra, *Environmental Justice and the Rights of Indigenous Peoples. International and Domestic Legal Perspectives* (Routledge, 2008). On indigenous dimensions with specific reference to Aboriginal Australia and drawing of images on the ground, see Tyson Yunkaporta, *Sand Talk. How Indigenous Thinking Can Save the World* (Text Publishing 2019).

while the mutual dependency between planet Earth and humans is actually well recognised in principle, modern human manipulations, seeking to satisfy the rapacious hunger and greed for the planet's resources, continue to have completely imbalanced, arbitrary and exploitative implications for many millions of already disadvantaged people. We should also not imagine that growing awareness of environmental disasters has led to consistent ameliorative action. Gill's study on the National Green Tribunal in India, while painting a fairly positive picture, leaves repeatedly no doubt that the problems faced in India are truly gigantic,[44] while the lived reality remains 'disturbing',[45] for example with Delhi's water being undrinkable,[46] and the much-promised good days (*achhe din* in Hindi) kept unfulfilled for most Indians.[47]

Much worse, as already noted, a long history of a significant 'reality gap', specifically between various rhetorics of development and the brutal experiences of displaced local, mainly tribal people cannot be overlooked,[48] all over the world. For India, this means that

> [t]he challenge of the current government is whether or not to perpetuate historic injustices, inequities and discrimination against the weaker sections of society, particularly the tribal. Are the poor to be left experiencing impoverishment, displacement, dispossession and unaccountable environmental degradation?[49]

This rhetorical question, sadly, despite the significant achievements of the National Green Tribunal in India, indicates that the 'frontier mentality' of rapacious business development in India (and elsewhere) today still largely replicates patterns established during the industrial revolution.[50]

As a specialist on South Asia, I have been no stranger to such precarious contradictions, watching many South Asians navigating personally between tendencies towards radical abandonment of the world and rapacious consumption. After studying geography, including geology, a long time ago, later activities included teaching classes and supervising dissertations on environmental jurisprudence and various forms of public interest activism.[51] Much of this related to pollution control in South Asia, even if not specifically identified as such.[52] Along the

44 Gill (n 25) 1.
45 Ibid 2.
46 Ibid 3.
47 Ibid 4.
48 See Padel and Das (n 14).
49 Gill (n 25) 4.
50 Padel and Das (n 14) 334.
51 Relevant resulting studies include Sangeeta Ahuja, *People, Law and Justice. Casebook on Public Interest Litigation* (Vols. 1 & 2, Sangam Books and Orient Longman 1997); Gurjeet Singh, *The Law of Consumer Protection in India. Justice within Reach* (Deep & Deep 1996).
52 See particularly Werner Menski, Rafay A. Alam and Mehreen K. Raza, *Public Interest Litigation in Pakistan* (Platinium and Pakistan Law House 2000).

way, inevitably, I encountered the writings and activism of Upendra Baxi,[53] connecting them to the more subtly philosophical interventions of Masaji Chiba from Japan.[54] Both, in their own ways, partly working together during the 1980s, expressed urgent concerns about how this interconnected world, constantly filling with more and more people,[55] would struggle at some point with the increasing evidence of epistemic violence between global North and global South.

Identifying distinctions between 'the West' and 'the rest', the work of these two important thinkers indicated that there is manifestly no complete agreement regarding the nature of the basic building blocks that one might use to construct culture-specific legal consciousness. Much of modern state-centric law, which Chiba critiqued as 'Western model jurisprudence',[56] is dominated by strong notions of freedom of contract and rights, rather than duties. The writings of Chiba and Baxi, read together, strongly challenged the lack of connectivity in legal scholarship with respective local and often indigenous values, yet with one highly pertinent difference. While Chiba Sensei emphasised the seminal concept of 'legal postulates' as sets of culture-specific values,[57] Professor Baxi's more secular public law theorisation of the socio-political domain led ultimately to the equally seminal notion of 'demosprudence'.[58]

The recently published Baxi Felicitation Volume contains a specific section about socially responsible climate change litigation, highly pertinent here. It is noted that 'Baxi's vision about a more widespread adoption of socially responsible litigation is finding favour in the context of climate change'.[59] This feeds on Baxi's characterisation of India's activist public interest litigation (PIL) as 'social action litigation' (SAL). The matter is, however, more complex than the interaction of state and people within the context of constitutional jurisprudence. McEldowney rightly emphasises Baxi's point 'that the Bhopal case was a missed opportunity to develop a jurisprudence of human solidarity'.[60] When the Bhopal gas leak occurred during the night of 2–3 December 1984, this became one of the biggest industrial disasters of the world. The handling of the ensuing litigation has been described by Baxi as 'the second Bhopal catastrophe',[61] failing to

53 Upendra Baxi, 'Taking Suffering Seriously: Social Action Litigation in the Supreme Court of India' (1985) 4 *Third World Legal Studies* 107; Upendra Baxi and Thomas Paul, *Mass Disasters and Multinational Liability. The Bhopal Case* (The Indian Law Institute 1986); Upendra Baxi and Amita Dhanda, *Valiant Victims and Lethal Litigation. The Bhopal Case* (The Indian Law Institute 1990. Later, see importantly Upendra Baxi, *The Future of Human Rights* (1st ed. 2002, 2nd ed. 2006, 3rd ed. 2008, OUP).

54 Chiba (n 3).

55 Robinson (n 1) speaks of 2 more billion people.

56 Chiba (ed 1986) (n 3) 1–2.

57 Ibid 6–7.

58 See Baxi (n 4).

59 John McEldowney, 'Judicial Review. Perspectives and Reflections for the Twenty-First Century' in Salman Khurshid et al. (n 4) 60–78, 69.

60 Ibid 68.

61 Baxi and Dhanda (n 53) i.

produce, 'for full five years, any entitlement in victims to financial interim relief, medical care and vocational rehabilitation in these halcyon days of judicial activism which has earned the Supreme Court of India a high esteem globally'.[62]

McEldowney's reading of Baxi's reactions reflects a postmodern form of environmental constitutionalism that simply elides or avoids mentioning anything primordial, like 'Nature' or 'religion'. It confirms familiar predominantly secular rationales when we read:

> Throughout Baxi's critical discourse on the inadequacies of the Bhopal litigation, he is surprisingly optimistic that improvements in the legal system and in liability litigation will lead to a better response for victims. This may partly be attributable to his belief in human rights but it is also a belief in litigation and the process under which procedures and substance are examined by courts. The inclusion of pain and suffering is also recognizable in tort compensation systems. This finds convergence with Baxi's attempt to draw inspiration from different aspects of law, philosophy, and social science. . . . Baxi moves the agenda into a means of taking forward steps that will suit a global economy, multinational corporations, and avoid the pitfalls of colonization and imperialism. He fears that this project will not always accomplish what is intended, and there are real fears that human rights will be misaligned into a form of state capture that will dilute its main features and potential for good. . . . Despite such reservations, Baxi is more optimistic when he considers the potential for social [sic] responsible litigation, and this is precisely why he sees the future as being shaped by judicial adjudication.[63]

This noted optimism of Professor Baxi is linked by McEldowney to

> an emerging conceptual framework of public trust applied to climate change that should act as a catalyst for improvements in the environment. This suggests that the good of the community may become a basis for the litigation of the state when the latter is said to be in breach of its duties.[64]

However, faced with issues of climate change in the Anthropocene, it is not feasible to draw national boundaries and think of specific societies or communities, or for that matter, any particular local or national *demos*. The impacts of violations and infringements add to the precarities faced by the entire cosmos. McEldowney suggests next that '[i]t is relatively early days in the use of litigation to influence policy-making',[65] points to evidence problems and issues about *locus standi*, yet also takes an optimistic stance, particularly that scientific evidence

62 Ibid.
63 McEldowney (n 59) 68–69.
64 Ibid 69–70.
65 Ibid 70.

relating to climate change will begin to make a difference.[66] He also cites growing evidence, including a case from Pakistan, where one may begin to see 'possibilities that there is a new era whereby environmental liability will follow the path of climate change'.[67] Other pertinent points are the observation that while climate change litigation may usefully engage human rights, maybe specifically for indigenous communities, here, too, success is not always ensured.[68]

Overall, McEldowney finds that '[t]he strength of Baxi's analysis is that litigation is only one feature of developing social movements and momentum'.[69] He also concludes that Baxi's main message is 'that more attention should be paid to what matters most',[70] which raises the question what that most important entity may be. In the Anthropocene, this could well be the safety of the entire globe. Looking back, however, McEldowney expresses

> a sense that much of Baxi's writings was caught up in an idealized world that few outside a small group of supporters believed was possible. It is almost as if Baxi's time has come after many years when the possibilities in his writings seemed too idealistic than real.[71]

Thus,

> Baxi identifies many of the structural and procedural changes that are necessary to make his vision for effective social litigation a reality. One of the most fundamental changes is to bring academic and intellectual writing into alignment with mapping the social context of problems and their ultimate solution. Setting the constitutional framework is often not an option; setting the cultural analysis is and this is possible even within the confines of a narrowly defined constitutional settlement. Baxi warns against judicial despotism and overly forceful judicial activism that may prove counter-productive.[72]

Far from critiquing these conclusions as inadequate, I highlight later how very useful these comments have been to produce the realisation that in the complex business of comparative constitutional law and global scholarship, too, we sometimes simply do not realise that an important point is being made. When McEldowney suggests in the previous quote that tweaking the constitutional framework is often not an option, he evidently overlooks one important provision of Indian constitutional law, namely the lofty principle of 'complete justice',

66 Ibid 70–71.
67 Ibid 71.
68 Ibid 72–73.
69 Ibid 73.
70 Ibid.
71 Ibid.
72 Ibid 74.

found in Article 142 of the Indian Constitution. Baxi, however, knows this provision very well, which may help to explain his strong optimism.

5. 'Complete Justice' and Its Relevance for the Anthropocene

The discussion so far, I hope, has brought out that globally, the existing super-bricolage of law-related concepts, rules, processes and values, all in maddening competition with each other, have made the study of legal pluralism, the wide field of comparative law, and any attempts to construct a viable transnational comparative constitutional law framework an immensely challenging endeavour. Taking hints from both Chiba and Baxi, I suggest therefore that it makes sense to go one step further by promoting a more radically activist plural form of legal consciousness, which would also constitute a more effective strategy to achieve meaningful 'complete justice' in the age of the Anthropocene.

To reiterate, this concept or strategy may be called cosmoprudence, rather than something social like the Baxian demosprudence. This all-encompassing cosmic terminology signifies awareness, hence a particular kind of legal consciousness, that the undeniable fact of human connectedness at all levels of existence requires a completely all-encompassing approach that cannot leave any specific uncomfortable or unwanted component out of the reckoning. Baxi himself is certainly not unaware of the term 'holistic', for he praised Gill's study precisely as 'a stunning volume on green jurisprudence in India', which provides a ' "holistic" theory of adjudication and social movement for environmental justice'.[73]

The term 'holistic' of course still ticks secular boxes, and provides modernist comfort, whereas anything 'cosmic' seems for many progressive scholars, including Baxi, too polluted by risks of reviving 'religion'. This illustrates the pitfalls of comparing different legal cultures in practice, as highlighted in an important recent study.[74] This specific status of the 'polluted other' arises through association with visions of a superhuman force to which mankind is simply subjected, whether we like this or not. That force may be imagined as an old man with a white beard, or may be prohibited from imagining, as in Islam, but is always a cosmic entity, Nature, or some kind of 'Truth'. The resulting epistemological and ideological tensions about worldviews and belief systems are captured by Glenn's important observation that there are a number of globalisations going on.[75] This also implies that any global uniformisation of regulatory environmental frameworks will continue to suffer from leakages, for which culture and 'religion' will be blamed, while the actual culprit tends to be some kind of corrupted, greedy

73 Gill (n 25) ii.

74 Kirk W. Junker (ed) *Environmental Law across Cultures. Comparisons for Legal Practice* (Routledge 2020), xv–xvii.

75 H.P. Glenn, *Legal Traditions of the World* (2nd edn. OUP 2004) 51.

individual, corporate entity or state, hiding behind asymmetric power structures and different sets of values.

That there can be no absolutely firm litmus test of what will be found universally acceptable arises also from the pithily worded conclusion in an extended conversation that Professor Twining had more than a decade ago with four leading southern voices concerned about the protection of human rights. Twining summed up his findings, writing: 'All four reject strong cultural relativism. They respect cultural diversity and value tolerance, but this involves no commitment to "tolerating the intolerable" '.[76] This offers a glimpse of the limits of law in terms of creating any absolute agreement among all humans about what is ultimately right or wrong.

Regarding values connected to the environment, it is difficult to disagree with Robinson that much remains to be debated about the precise ambits and implications of biophilia, bio-happiness, and related concepts.[77] Since he, too, urges that there is no time left for extended global debate, there is pressure to act responsibly, now, without causing intolerable harm. Yet the dual challenge for practice-focused cosmoprudence remains in place. The continued need for economic and infrastructural development, including the re-vamping of energy production, focused now on renewables rather than continued mass consumption of toxic energy sources, remains a fact. This restructuring process itself will continue to displace many more millions of local people. Since, indeed, this makes any ambitions of complete sustainability unrealistic, the focus must turn to protecting 'complete justice' for the victims of this ongoing process.

There are clear limits, however, for globally focused efforts to promote the avoidance of human suffering and protection of basic rights. These are not effectively guaranteed by more sophisticated global regulatory instruments and tricks of various kinds, which will also take time to be implemented. Meanwhile, disaster management will often be the need of the hour. This reinforces the conclusion that it is preferable to work out appropriate solutions on a case-by-case basis, right now, and wherever needed. Arguments for global recognition of cosmoprudence as a matter of urgent practical need reflect realistic recognition of imponderables in ecological management. For environmental constitutionalism, this implies a straightforward, harsh message: The inherently unrealistic expectation of 'complete justice' must be assiduously ameliorated for any victims of development processes, addressing and redressing their suffering, exactly in the Baxian sense. No ifs and buts, no hiding behind corrupted smokescreens. It is time to act honourably and with full responsibility for all living entities. Whether we call this Swaminathan's 'bio-happiness',[78] the right to whatever Asian, African, Latin American or other form or concept of happiness, or turn it into a human right

76 William Twining (ed), *Human Rights, Southern Voices. Francis Deng, Abdullahi An-Na'im, Yash Ghai and Upendra Baxi* (CUP 2009) 218.

77 Robinson (n 1) 15–17.

78 Ibid 15.

to live in a sound environment as a formally recognised legal right,[79] does not matter. The principle is crystal clear and has little to do with 'religion', however constructed, but with people's need for dignified survival. A key principle in this context has to be fair compensation for losses incurred by victims of ongoing development processes. There is nothing in the relevant law itself to prevent such new form of affirmative action. Article 142(1) of the Constitution of India basically provides:

> The Supreme Court in the exercise of its jurisdiction may pass such decree or may make such order as is necessary for doing complete justice in any cause or matter pending before it, and any decree so passed shall be enforceable throughout the territory of India in such manner as may be prescribed by or under any law made by Parliament and, until provision in that behalf is so made, in such manner as the President may by order prescribe.

I had seen this concept mentioned in various litigation contexts earlier, but it is striking to read now the recent claim that '[i]n fact, the entire environmental jurisprudence in India evolved through the invocation of article 142 of the Constitution of India by the Supreme Court of India'.[80]

There is nothing stopping the Indian legal system to activate this constitutional promise, and many future victims will require this support. The gigantic scale of energy demands in India takes unimaginable proportions in comparison to other countries, for transport, cooling rather than heating in most Indian conditions, communications and much else. Simply stopping the supply of the very substances that magnify and speed up the self-destruction of the globe is therefore not a quick-fix option. The race is on for 'clean' energies, renewables rather than continued mass consumption of carbon, but while such progress is being achieved, much further displacement will occur. This scenario is not restricted to India, so these arguments apply, in principle, across the globe.

There are of course tempting diversions. Emboldened by continued abuse of Nature, human pompousness might even go as far as to claim triumphantly that coining the term 'Anthropocene' is, by itself, convincing proof that humans have finally subjugated Nature. This position nicely suits climate change deniers, and allows many lawyers to think they can carry on as before. However, the cruel reality is different now. If as soon as possible we do not respect the rights of most seriously affected victims, disaster will strike ever more people, all over the world.

6. Conclusions

Perhaps the current Covid pandemic has already taught more people to re-examine our wasteful lifestyles and use of resources. The initial chapters in this book

79 Ibid 15–16.
80 Kumar (n 15) 370.

each provide important insights into how specific cultural or religious traditions have over time generated specific perceptions of the cosmos, the environment, and any entities that are perceived to influence these various domains. Being most familiar with ancient Vedic and later Hindu concepts, I take the example of the ancient concept of macrocosmic Order or Truth, called *rita* in Sanskrit in its more 'religious' sense, and *satya* from a more secular perspective.[81] The sun, for example, is both a manifestation of secular Truth as we can feel its energy, but also manifests *rita*, because humans do not know how it came to be there and why it follows particular patterns of activities.

The fact that ancient Vedic people were afraid of Nature and thus devised many prayers and rituals to pacify it and protect themselves is not unique to ancient India. Robinson mentions 'fear of nature – a legitimate worry about contracting diseases, an ancestral instinctive fear of snakes or a prudent fear of hurricanes',[82] to which one can add well-documented ancient Vedic fears of flash floods, terrible droughts and much more. This indicates that pre-modern humans found it wise to make conscious efforts to live in harmony with nature, rather than seeking to subjugate it. They attempted mitigation, and certainly practised adaptation. The Anthropocene, confirming that modern inventions, whether intentionally or unintentionally, have now left impacts of dangerous imbalances on such holistic forms of order, may help to remind more people in various contemporary cultural contexts of their cultural and religious values and their cosmic connectedness, however tenuous. Respect for this stance does not mean surrender to theocracy, but signifies realism and common sense.

The current volume, presented in parts clustered around cultural and religious values, principles and rules, and specific actions or processes of enforcement of environmental justice, has sought to account for the internal pluralities of the globally present phenomenon of law in different cultural and legal contexts. This makes no claims to comprehensiveness, but by illustrating the pluralities of bricolages that may be debated in relation to environmental constitutionalism in different context we ultimately ask, I think, whether it is actually possible to imagine and work towards a scenario of seeking what in Indian law is known as 'complete justice', in different jurisdictions and under widely divergent regulatory frameworks.

Framing the core message of the present volume in this way is not an attempt on my part to glorify Indian law – an accusation that has often been raised by people who do not trust India to be as innovative and forward-looking as it can be, at times. As Professor Amirante's recent work unambiguously presents, too, for several not so unreasonable reasons, the Indian Supreme Court and the Indian legal order generally, have been facing one complex question after the other about how to manage a massive system of deficits and deficiencies.[83] India

81 Jeanine Miller, *The Vision of Cosmic Order in the Vedas* (Routledge and Kegan Paul 1985).
82 Robinson (n 1) 20.
83 Amirante (n 17).

has been faced since Independence in 1947 with a Malthusian demographic dilemma, a virtual time bomb in a country that is already home to 1.3 billion people. But in India, or the world as a whole, no religion or philosophical system has a monopoly on Nature. All share, of necessity, the realisation that human action in relation to the environment is an ambivalent force that transcends national and communal boundaries.

In a critical re-examination of the foundations of environmental theorising and jurisprudence, it is important to go back to the basics of the world's various languages and cultures, re-examining and reflecting on specific values not only regarding 'law', 'environment' and 'governance', but also concerning specific grammars of culture and politics and their intricate interplay of tradition and modernity. This illustrates, as Professor Amirante also suggests, the continued value of comparative study.

Ultimately, all major 'religious' and cultural traditions appear to share a broad agreement that humans are interconnected entities, while particularly notions of stewardship rather than absolute ownership, and also responsibility and duties, rather than entitlements and rights, seem to be particularly strong all over the global South. Maybe this explains why environmental constitutionalism in the global South seems to be more advanced. The future of climate change in the Anthropocene suggests a scenario of increasing precariousness, more impending disasters and continued victimisation of millions of people. Mindful of the need for further extended debate regarding environmental constitutionalism, but to avoid 'generating only a negative dialectics of despair',[84] also in light of hopes I share with Professor Baxi, the suggestion for strengthening 'complete justice' through cosmoprudence, applied at the local level where specific needs arise, may not be completely misguided.

Bibliography

Ahuja S., *People, Law and Justice. Casebook on Public Interest Litigation* (Vols. 1 & 2, Sangam Books and Orient Longman 1997).

Alam S., Atapattu S., González C.G. and Razzaque J. (eds), *International Environmental Law and the Global South* (CUP 2015).

Amirante D., *Lo Stato Multiculturale* (Bononia University Press 2014).

Amirante D., *La Democrazia Dei Superlativi. Il Sistema Constituzionale dell'India Contemporanea* (Edizioni Scientifiche Italiane 2019).

Bagni S., Brightman M.A. and Furia A. (eds), 'Searching for Models of Intercultural Management of Social Conflict' (2020) 28(2) *Revista General de Derecho Publico Comparado.*

Banerjee P., Nigam A. and Pandey R., 'The Work of Theory. Thinking across Traditions' (2016) 51(37) *Economic & Political Weekly* 42.

Baxi U., '"The Little Done, the Vast Undone". Some Reflections on Reading Granville Austin's *The Indian Constitution*' (1967) 9(3) *Journal of the Indian Law Institute* 323.

84 Rajan (n 6) 72.

Baxi U., 'Taking Suffering Seriously: Social Action Litigation in the Supreme Court of India' (1985) 4 *Third World Legal Studies* 107.

Baxi U., 'Taking Suffering Seriously: Social Action Litigation in the Supreme Court of India' in N. Tiruchelvam and R. Coomaraswamy (eds), *The Role of the Judiciary in Plural Societies* (Pinter 1987).

Baxi U., *The Future of Human Rights* (1st edn 2002, 2nd edn 2006, 3rd edn 2008, OUP).

Baxi U., 'Demosprudence versus Jurisprudence: The Indian Judicial Experience in the Context of Comparative Constitutional Studies' (2014) 14 *Macquarie Law Journal* 3.

Baxi U. and Dhanda A., *Valiant Victims and Lethal Litigation. The Bhopal Case* (The Indian Law Institute 1990).

Baxi U. and Paul T., *Mass Disasters and Multinational Liability. The Bhopal Case* (The Indian Law Institute 1986).

Boyd D.R., *The Environmental Rights Revolution. A Study of Constitutions, Human Rights and Environment* (UBC Press 2012).

Chiba M. (ed), *Asian Indigenous Law in Interaction with Received Law* (KPI 1986).

Chiba M., *Legal Pluralism: Towards a General Theory through Japanese Legal Culture* (Tokai University Press 1989).

Chiba M., *Legal Cultures in Human Society: A Collection of Articles and Essays* (Shinzansha International 2002).

Crutzen P.J., 'The Anthropocene' in E. Ehlers and T. Krafft (eds), *Earth System Science in the Anthropocene* (Springer 2006).

Dhanda A., 'The Baxian Bioscope on Indian Judicial Process' in S. Khurshid, S. Luthra, L. Malik and S. Bedi (eds), *Judicial Review. Process, Powers, and Problems. Essays in Honour of Upendra Baxi* (CUP 2020).

Gill G.N., *Environmental Justice in India. The National Green Tribunal* (Routledge 2017).

Glenn H.P., *Legal Traditions of the World* (2nd edn, OUP 2004).

Horn E. and Bergtaller H., *The Anthropocene. Key Issues for the Humanities* (Routledge 2020).

Junker K.W. (ed), *Environmental Law across Cultures. Comparisons for Legal Practice* (Routledge 2020).

Kokal K., *State Law, Dispute Processing, and Legal Pluralism. Unspoken Dialogues from Rural India* (Routledge 2020).

Kotzè L.J., *Global Environmental Constitutionalism in the Anthropocene* (Hart Publishing 2016).

Kotzè L.J. (ed), *Environmental Law and Governance for the Anthropocene* (Hart Publishing 2017).

Kumar S., 'Sketching the Limits of Article 142 of the Constitution of India. A Constitutional Necessity' in S. Khurshid, S. Luthra, L. Malik and S. Bedi (eds), *Judicial Review. Process, Powers, and Problems. Essays in Honour of Upendra Baxi* (CUP 2020).

McEldowney J., 'Judicial Review. Perspectives and Reflections for the Twenty-First Century' in S. Khurshid, S. Luthra, L. Malik and S. Bedi (eds), *Judicial Review. Process, Powers, and Problems. Essays in Honour of Upendra Baxi* (CUP 2020).

Menski W., *Comparative Law in a Global Context: The Legal Systems of Asia and Africa* (2nd edn, CUP 2006).

Menski W., 'Introduction: Conflicts Over Justice and Hybrid Social Actors as Legal Agents' in K. Topidi (ed), *Normative Pluralism and Human Rights. Social Normativities in Conflict* (Routledge 2018).
Menski W., 'On Kites and Ships: Climate Changes in Comparative Law and Judicial Navigation' in S.P. Donlan and J. Mair (eds), *Comparative Law. Mixes, Movements, and Metaphors. Felicitation Volume for Prof. Esin Örücü* (Routledge 2020).
Menski W., Alam R.A. and Raza M.K., *Public Interest Litigation in Pakistan* (Platinium and Pakistan Law House 2000).
Miller J., *The Vision of Cosmic Order in the Vedas* (Routledge and Kegan Paul 1985).
Naess A., *Ecology, Community and Lifestyle: Outline of an Ecosophy* (CUP 1989).
Padel F. and Das S., 'Cultural Genocide and the Rhetoric of Sustainable Mining in East India' (2010a) 18(3) *Contemporary South Asia* 333.
Padel F. and Das S., *Out of This Earth: East India Adivasis and the Aluminium Cartel* (Orient BlackSwan 2010b).
Pring G. and Pring C., 'Foreword' in G.N. Gill (ed), *Environmental Justice in India. The National Green Tribunal* (Routledge 2017).
Rajan S.C., 'Practising Theory in the Anthropocene. A Postcolonial Quest for Reliable Knowledge' (2017) 52(14) *Economic & Political Weekly* 72.
Rajan S.C., *A Social Theory of Corruption: Notes from the Indian Subcontinent* (Harvard University Press 2020).
Rankin A., *Jainism and Environmental Philosophy. Karma and the Web of Life* (Routledge 2018).
Robinson N.A., 'Fundamental Principles of Law for the Anthropocene?' (2014) 44(1–2) *Environmental Policy &* Law 13.
Schlosberg D., *Defining Environmental Justice: Theories, Movements, and Nature* (OUP 2007).
Sikri A.K., 'Foreword' in S. Khurshid, S. Luthra, L. Malik and S. Bedi (eds), *Judicial Review. Process, Powers, and Problems. Essays in Honour of Upendra Baxi* (CUP 2020).
Singh G., *The Law of Consumer Protection in India. Justice within Reach* (Deep & Deep 1996).
Singh M.P. and Kumar N. (eds), *The Indian Yearbook of Comparative Law 2018* (Springer Nature Singapore 2019).
Tew Y., 'Stealth Theocracy' (2018) 58 *Virginia Journal of International Law* 31.
Topidi K. (ed), *Normative Pluralism and Human Rights. Social Normativities in Conflict* (Routledge 2018).
Twining W. (ed), *Human Rights, Southern Voices. Francis Deng, Abdullahi An-Na'im, Yash Ghai and Upendra Baxi* (CUP 2009).
Westra L., *Environmental Justice and the Rights of Indigenous Peoples. International and Domestic Legal Perspectives* (Routledge 2008).
Yunkaporta Y., *Sand Talk. How Indigenous Thinking Can Save the World* (Text Publishing 2019).

Index

Page numbers followed by "n" indicate a note on the corresponding page.

For Product Safety Concerns and Information please contact our EU
representative GPSR@taylorandfrancis.com
Taylor & Francis Verlag GmbH, Kaufingerstraße 24, 80331 München, Germany

www.ingramcontent.com/pod-product-compliance
Ingram Content Group UK Ltd.
Pitfield, Milton Keynes, MK11 3LW, UK
UKHW020016200926
475702UK00014B/1918
* 9 7 8 1 0 3 2 0 0 7 2 3 6 *